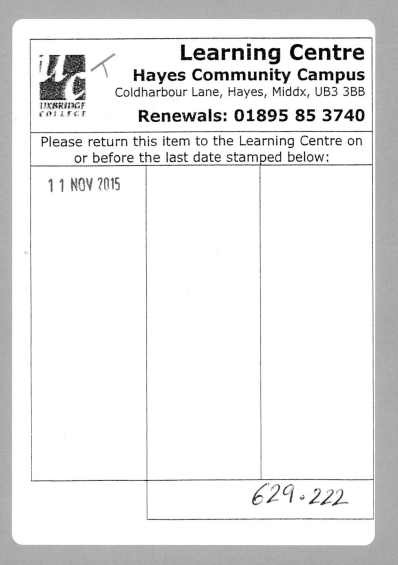

1001 dream cars

Dream Drives and Ultimate Autos

Richard Dredge

Bath · New York · Singapore · Hong Kong · Cologne · Delhi · Melbourne

First published by Parragon in 2008
Parragon
Queen Street House
4 Queen Street
Bath BA1 1HE, UK

Copyright © Parragon Books Ltd 2007

Editorial and design by
Amber Books Ltd
Bradley's Close
74–77 White Lion Street
London N1 9PF
www.amberbooks.co.uk

Project Editor: Sarah Uttridge
Design: Anthony Cohen
Picture Research: Kate Green and Terry Forshaw

Printed in Indonesia

ISBN 978-1-4075-2440-5

Picture Credits:

All images are courtesy of LAT Photographic except for the following:

Art-Tech/IMP: 12(m), 16(br), 66(b), 68(m), 68(tr), 71(t), 78(br), 83(tl), 86(b), 87(br), 88(m), 94(b), 95(tl), 107(b), 109(tr), 114(tl), 114(tr), 116(tr), 117(m), 123(br), 152(b), 190(br), 221(tr), 244(b), 245(t), 245(m), 245(br), 246(tl), 247(t), 248(t), 249(m), 254(t), 257(tl), 257(tr), 257(b), 258(tl), 258(m), 258(b), 259(t), 260(m), 261(tl), 261(m), 261(b), 262(t), 262(b), 263(bl), 264(m), 264(b), 265(m), 268(b), 269(m), 270(bl), 271(t), 271(m), 271(b), 272(tl), 272(tr), 273(b), 291(br), 292(bl), 298(tl), 300(m); **Giles Chapman:** 28(bl), 46(t), 59(tr), 76(tr), 89(b), 93(bl), 102(bl), 103(tl), 103(m), 106(m), 111(t), 112(br), 126(t), 140(m), 147(br), 150(m), 159(bl), 171(t), 230(m), 235(b), 244(m), 256(t), 263(m), 268(m), 270(m), 273(t), 274(m), 308(m), 310(bl), 314(bl), 315(tr), 316(tr); **conceptcarz.com:** 77(t), 98(br), 102(m), 270(t), 280(b); **Richard Dredge:** 6, 9(tr), 12(b), 26(bl), 27(m), 30(bl), 31(m), 32(t), 34(m), 35(b), 37(m), 39(tr), 44(t), 47(b), 48(tl), 48(b), 49(t), 50(br), 51(tl), 52(tl), 52(tr), 53(tl), 53(bl), 53(br), 54/5, 56(tl), 56(br), 57(t), 57(m), 57(br), 58(t), 58(m), 60(bl), 61(all 3), 64(br), 74(m), 74(bl), 75(tl), 75(m), 76(b), 78(m), 79(tl), 80(b), 81(m), 81(br), 84/5, 88(bl), 89/90, 98(m), 102(t), 104(br), 105(m), 106(tr), 107(t), 107(m), 108(bl), 108(br), 109(b), 110(tr), 112(t), 113(b), 115(t), 115(m), 126(m), 128(m), 129(t), 130(bl), 137(m), 138/9, 141(bl), 142(t), 143(tr), 143(m), 143(b), 144(tr), 145(tr), 145(b), 146(tr), 147(m), 147(bl), 152(t), 156/7, 165(t), 165(b), 166/7, 168(bl), 169(b), 170(tr), 170(b), 171(m), 171(b), 180/1, 190(bl), 194(br), 197(m), 200(tl), 201(bl), 202/3, 206(br), 209(t), 212/3, 214(br), 222/3, 229(b), 231(m), 236(tr), 239(m), 240(tl), 240(m), 241(t), 241(bl), 241(br), 244(tr), 245(bl), 247(m), 253(m), 255(b), 260(b), 261(tr), 275(t), 275(b), 287(m), 295(t), 298(tr), 301(tr), 303(m), 313(t), 317(bl), 317(br), 318(tr), 318(m), 318(b); **EMAP Automotive:** 99(m), 119(t), 155(b), 247(b), 286(tl); **Motoring Picture Library:** 71(br), 76(tl), 92(b), 104(t), 104(m), 114(m), 120/1, 249(tr), 254(br), 263(br), 280(tl), 297(m); **Webshots:** 46(tl) (Benoit Dalla Gasperina), 70(m) (Jack Snell), 75(b) (carshowusa), 92(tl) (Jack Snell), 98(bl) (oldiesfan100), 110(m) (vauxnut2), 246(m) (Jack Snell), 249(b) (zodiack101), 258(tr) (Jack Snell), 262(m) (Jack Snell), 281(t) (hasilu), 296(bl) (Norm deCarteret)

CONTENTS

Introduction

When somebody wins the lottery, the first thing they usually do is go out and buy a car that's luxurious and expensive. If there's one thing that allows somebody to show off their status, it's a car. Ever since the first cars trickled off production lines in the late nineteenth century, one-upmanship on the road has been rife. However, as with music, food or any other commodity, tastes vary widely between people and countries, with everybody aspiring to something different. It's that variety which has enabled this book to be compiled; just when you thought it was easy to define a dream car, along comes a list of 1001 of them.

There are so many types of dream car that this book contains no fewer than seven different categories. There's at least one category more of course; those cars that remain dreams, never seeing the light of day in production form. Otherwise known as concepts, prototypes or design studies, dozens appear every year and usually sink without trace. While the genre encompasses some fascinating machinery, the cars in this book have been restricted to solely those you could go out and buy at some time or another – given enough money of course!

From the unveiling of the first horseless carriages in the 1880s, people have aspired to something better than they already have, in terms of personal transport. Throughout the twentieth century, as car design progressed, standards rose inexorably to the point where now that we're at the start of the twenty-first century, for many of us it's hard to imagine aspiring to basic personal transport. However, read on and you'll see that for many people throughout the twentieth century, dream cars weren't necessarily blessed with powerful engines or luxuriously appointed cabins.

Toyota's MR2 breathed new life into the affordable mid-engined sportscar market; its only rival was Fiat's aged X1/9.

Over budget and late, the Veyron was an incredible feat of engineering. It also put Bugatti back on the supercar map.

Dreams on wheels

Over the following pages you'll discover a whole cornucopia of dreams on wheels, from the weird and wonderful to the more familiar. Each chapter is arranged in chronological order as well as alphabetical, encompassing everything from sportscars and muscle cars to strange machines that you may never have heard of. However, obscurity is no barrier to desirability; no matter how weird the car, there will always be somebody out there who wants one!

As you can imagine, with 1001 cars covered between these pages, there are many types of dream car. All the obvious ones are in there, from the supercars to the incredibly luxurious, ultra-low volume models. Ask a schoolboy what his dream car is and there will invariably be talk of modern Ferraris, Lamborghinis, Porsches and the like. However, ask an adult what would be in their dream garage and it's more likely that even if the same marques are mentioned, it will be the classic models that are hankered after.

Step back in time though and the dream car was often a very different beast. In the post-war era, many people were dreaming simply of having their own transport; not fast or luxurious, just something that would offer independence.

The 4CV was very important to Renault in the post-war era – and also to the French, who needed cheap transport.

In the post-war era, many people were dreaming simply of having their own transport; not fast or luxurious, just something that would offer independence.

Jaguar's beautiful XJ Coupé first went on sale in 1975, with a choice of six or 12-cylinder engines.

BMW's Isetta is now very collectable, but when it was new it was too costly and not very practical.

The dream cars of the 1940s were often nothing more than humdrum saloons like the Renault 4CV, Morris Minor or the Crosley.

As the 1940s turned into the 1950s, more and more people aspired to car ownership, and a huge increase in worldwide mass production allowed more and more people to buy their own car. This is the point at which all those dreams started to come true; in the US, families were becoming mobile in ever greater numbers, thanks to the efforts of a whole raft of independent car builders, and the big three, which were churning out full-sized cars in huge numbers. In Europe it was another matter; the microcar was the only way that many could afford their own personal transport, which is why a mass of weird contraptions suddenly sprang from nowhere. It's hard to imagine now, but there were plenty of people who dreamt of buying their own Messerschmitt, Trojan or Isetta. Now things have come full circle, because while those were dream cars when new, they're once again hunted down by collectors, keen to have their own piece of motoring history.

It's a similar story where all the oddballs are concerned; some were dream cars when new and some became dream cars on account of their rarity and lack of conventionality. Ask that schoolboy once again what his dream cars are and it's unlikely he'll have even heard of a Burney Streamline or a Panhard PL17. But his father (or even grandfather) will know all about them, coveting them for the way they didn't try to follow the crowd. On one level they dreamt of their own Hudson, Triumph or Jaguar, because that was an attainable dream – but some dreams should never be realised, which is where the really weird or exotic stuff comes in.

Collectable cars

It's that exotica that fills most of the less comprehensive dream cars books; the ones that merely skim over the surface.

The 911 brand has endured nearly half a century of continuous refinement; this is a 993-generation edition.

Just 2650 examples of Daimler's SP250 were built. They are now collectors' items thanks to their rarity.

They take a very rigid view of what constitutes a dream car, assuming that well-known creators of fast, luxurious and exclusive cars have a stranglehold on the genre. As already demonstrated, nothing could be further from the truth – but the Bugatti Veyron, McLaren F1 and Ferrari 575 Superamerica have easily earned their places here. So have their ancestors; cars such as the Bugatti Type 57 and Ferrari 250GT SWB are as desirable now as when they were new – if not more so.

As time passes by, it's likely that only the more glamorous, exclusive cars of today will become truly collectable, along with the niche products that are not necessarily fast or

expensive, merely unusual. Modern mass-market cars have largely lost the charm and character of their predecessors, and they're much more frequently treated as disposable white goods. As we've all become conditioned to expecting affordable personal transport of our own, we dream only of cars that are likely to remain unattainable. But then it does no harm to dream, because sometimes those dreams can come true.

This Superamerica version Ferrari 575 is ultra-desirable, with its unique pivoting roof.

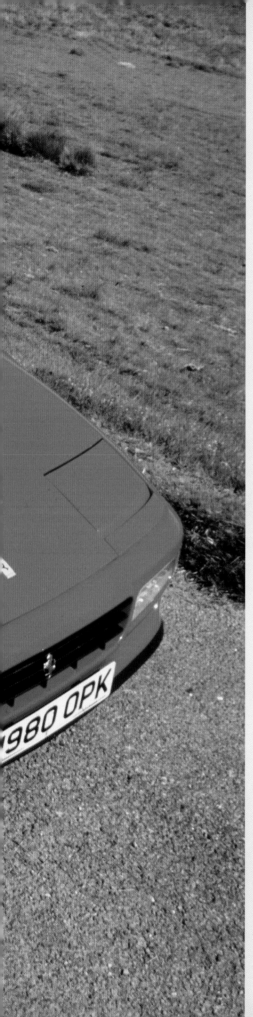

Supercars

While some dream about ultimate luxury, others are more focused on ultimate speed. These are the cars that delivered that; the fastest cars of their time, from the 60HP Mercedes to the unfeasibly fast Bugatti Veyron. At the start of the twentieth century, when the fastest car was barely able to crack 112km/h (70mph), it was suggested that the human body wouldn't be able to cope with speeds of 160km/h (100mph) or more. By the start of the twenty-first century the land speed record was 1227km/h (763mph) and there were already several road cars that could comfortably travel in excess of 321km/h (200mph). As this book went to press, the Bugatti Veyron was the world's fastest production car, but even with its top speed of 405km/h (252mph) there were many who reckoned they could topple it.

When Mercedes launched its 60HP in 1903, its designers and engineers would never have believed that a car could be built that would be able to safely cruise at more than 402km/h (250mph) – even if there isn't anywhere such speeds could realistically be attained for any length of time. In the early nineteenth century, even if an engine could have been coaxed into providing enough power to give such a massive top speed, the braking and suspension systems of the time would never have been able to cope. It's the same with the transmission, for it's in these areas that some astonishingly impressive advances have been made in an amazingly short space of time. The idea of carbon fibre bodywork would have been unthinkable in the 1970s – yet many cars use the technology nowadays. Ceramic braking systems and electro-hydraulically controlled suspension were just a pipe dream

when vehicles such as the Miura arrived in 1966 – but several generations on and Lamborghini is able to offer such refinements on the Murcielago.

In the early days, supercars were little more than thinly disguised racing cars – in many cases there wasn't even any attempt at a disguise. Bugatti's Type 35 was just such a car, but Jaguar did the same thing with its C-Type and D-Type while Sunbeam's 3-Litre was obviously a competition car for the road. To those fortunate enough to be able to buy such cars, a lack of usability didn't matter – more practicality meant less ability where it really mattered.

Not all road racers had to be raw and impractical though; the Mercedes 300SL Gullwing was swift yet able to cross continents in one run. The same was true of Aston Martin's DB6 as well as Maserati's Ghibli and many more of the period; cars that were fabulously fast in their day and luxurious too. However, they were all flawed in one way or another, and that's where the really impressive engineering has taken place in recent years. Supercar drivers no longer have to tolerate overheating, a heavy clutch or zero visibility just to have a car that looks sensational. While even the most prestigious models were often thrown together with little or no attempt at maintaining quality, the supercars of the twentieth century are more beautifully made than ever, while also being faster and more usable.

Crucially though, supercars no longer have to be mid-engined or mere two-seaters. There are now plenty of estate cars and saloons too that offer space for five (and their luggage too) while also packing 367kW (500bhp) and a top speed nudging 321km/h (200mph). Now that would have been fantastic at the turn of the twentieth century.

Successor to the Testarossa, Ferrari's F512M was aggressive rather than lithe.

MERCEDES 60

The Mercedes 60, with its low chassis and cast-alloy engine, used technology from which the majority of modern cars have evolved. With a pressed-steel chassis frame and two- or four-seater bodywork, the car featured semi-elliptic leaf-spring suspension and wooden wheels. One of these cars won the 1903 Gordon Bennett race.

COUNTRY OF ORIGIN	GERMANY
YEARS OF PRODUCTION	1903–04
DISPLACEMENT	9293CC (567CI)
CONFIGURATION	FRONT-MOUNTED 4-CYL
TRANSMISSION	4-SPEED MANUAL, REAR-WHEEL DRIVE
POWER	44KW (60BHP)
TORQUE	N/A
TOP SPEED	106KM/H (66MPH)
0–96KM/H (0–60MPH)	N/A

STUTZ BEARCAT

The first car to come from the Stutz Car Company, the Bearcat promised nothing in the way of creature comforts, as it was a thinly disguised racer for the road. There were no brakes at the front; there were rear drum brakes, though, to haul the car down from its potential 129km/h (80mph) top speed.

COUNTRY OF ORIGIN	USA
YEARS OF PRODUCTION	1914–17
DISPLACEMENT	6388CC (390CI)
CONFIGURATION	FRONT-MOUNTED 4-CYL
TRANSMISSION	3-SPEED MANUAL, REAR-WHEEL DRIVE
POWER	44KW (60BHP)
TORQUE	N/A
TOP SPEED	129KM/H (80MPH)
0–96KM/H (0–60MPH)	N/A

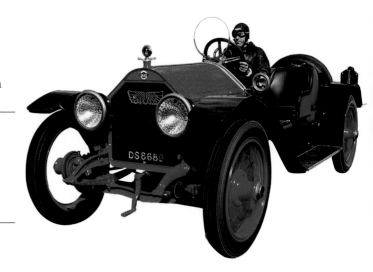

BUGATTI TYPE 35

Until the Type 35, little attention was paid to race car design. This car turned that corner, with its polished alloy spoked wheels and lithe bodywork. Initially, there was a 1990cc (121ci) engine fitted; this was supercharged for the 35C, while the 35T received a 2262cc (138ci) unit. The Type 35B combined these features with a supercharged 2.3-litre engine.

COUNTRY OF ORIGIN	FRANCE
YEARS OF PRODUCTION	1924–31
DISPLACEMENT	2262CC (138CI)
CONFIGURATION	FRONT-MOUNTED 8-CYL
TRANSMISSION	4-SPEED MANUAL, REAR-WHEEL DRIVE
POWER	96KW (130BHP)
TORQUE	N/A
TOP SPEED	201KM/H (125MPH)
0–96KM/H (0–60MPH)	7.0SEC

SUNBEAM 3-LITRE

With a seven-bearing crankshaft, dry-sump lubrication and a pair of overhead camshaft, the 3-Litre's powerplant was groundbreaking. This was the first car to be sold in the UK with a twin-cam engine, but the chassis couldn't handle the power thanks to primitive suspension and an engine that was mounted too far forward.

COUNTRY OF ORIGIN	UK
YEARS OF PRODUCTION	1925–30
DISPLACEMENT	2916CC (178CI)
CONFIGURATION	FRONT-MOUNTED 6-CYL
TRANSMISSION	4-SPEED MANUAL, REAR-WHEEL DRIVE
POWER	68KW (93BHP)
TORQUE	N/A
TOP SPEED	145KM/H (90MPH)
0–96KM/H (0–60MPH)	24SEC

BENTLEY 4.5-LITRE

The last of the four-cylinder Bentleys, the 4.5-Litre was a heavy car and as a result it didn't feel as sporting as other cars from the company. Consequently, Bentley racing driver Henry Birkin created a supercharged version of the 4.5-Litre. This went against the orders of W.O. Bentley, but the cars became legendary racers.

COUNTRY OF ORIGIN	UK
YEARS OF PRODUCTION	1927–31
DISPLACEMENT	4398CC (268CI)
CONFIGURATION	FRONT-MOUNTED 4-CYL
TRANSMISSION	4-SPEED MANUAL, REAR-WHEEL DRIVE
POWER	76KW (104BHP)
TORQUE	N/A
TOP SPEED	177KM/H (110MPH)
0–96KM/H (0–60MPH)	N/A

MERCEDES SSK/SSKL

Based on the supercharged Model K, there were four stages in the evolution of this model. At first, there was the S, for Sport. This was followed by the SS (Super Sport) and the SSK (K for Kurz, or short-wheelbase). The final stage was the ultra-rare SSKL, the L denoting 'Lightweight' thanks to the car's drilled chassis.

COUNTRY OF ORIGIN	GERMANY
YEARS OF PRODUCTION	1928–32
DISPLACEMENT	6789CC (414CI)
CONFIGURATION	FRONT-MOUNTED 6-CYL
TRANSMISSION	4-SPEED MANUAL, REAR-WHEEL DRIVE
POWER	165KW (225BHP)
TORQUE	569NM (420LB FT)
TOP SPEED	201KM/H (125MPH)
0–96KM/H (0–60MPH)	9.5SEC

ALFA ROMEO 6C 1750

With great handling and superb design, the Alfa Romeo 6C is one of the most sought-after prewar classic vehicles – especially because it was fast, capable of a genuine 153km/h (95mph). The 1752cc (107ci) twin-cam six-cylinder engine was optionally available with a supercharger; such cars were badged Gran Sports.

COUNTRY OF ORIGIN	ITALY
YEARS OF PRODUCTION	1929–33
DISPLACEMENT	1752CC (107CI)
CONFIGURATION	FRONT-MOUNTED 6-CYL
TRANSMISSION	4-SPEED MANUAL, REAR-WHEEL DRIVE
POWER	63KW (85BHP)
TORQUE	N/A
TOP SPEED	153KM/H (95MPH)
0–96KM/H (0–60MPH)	N/A

BUGATTI TYPE 51

The Type 51 succeeded the Type 35 as Bugatti's premier racing car for the 1930s. However, unlike the dominant Type 35s of the prior decade, the Type 51 (and later Type 53, Type 54 and Type 59) were unable to compete with the government-supported German and Italian offerings.

COUNTRY OF ORIGIN	FRANCE
YEARS OF PRODUCTION	1931–32
DISPLACEMENT	2262CC (138CI)
CONFIGURATION	FRONT-MOUNTED 8-CYL
TRANSMISSION	4-SPEED MANUAL, REAR-WHEEL DRIVE
POWER	118KW (160BHP)
TORQUE	N/A
TOP SPEED	230KM/H (143MPH)
0–96KM/H (0–60MPH)	N/A

BUGATTI TYPE 55

The Type 55 was a road-going version of the Type 54 Grand Prix car. It was a roadster, and power came from the Type 51's 2262cc (138ci) straight-eight engine, which produced 99kW (135bhp) with a Roots-type supercharger attached. Just 38 examples were produced between 1932 and 1935.

COUNTRY OF ORIGIN	FRANCE
YEARS OF PRODUCTION	1932–35
DISPLACEMENT	2262CC (138CI)
CONFIGURATION	FRONT-MOUNTED 8-CYL
TRANSMISSION	4-SPEED MANUAL, REAR-WHEEL DRIVE
POWER	99KW (135BHP)
TORQUE	N/A
TOP SPEED	177KM/H (110MPH)
0–96KM/H (0–60MPH)	17.3SEC

ASTON MARTIN ULSTER

Introduced during one of Aston Martin's many periods of crisis, the Ulster was a road-going race car. Its 1.5-litre engine was much more powerful than similar Aston Martin units, thanks to bigger valves, a higher compression ratio and larger SU carburettors. With the right back-axle ratio, the car could top the magic 161km/h (100mph).

COUNTRY OF ORIGIN	UK
YEARS OF PRODUCTION	1934–36
DISPLACEMENT	1495CC (91CI)
CONFIGURATION	FRONT-MOUNTED 4-CYL
TRANSMISSION	4-SPEED MANUAL, REAR-WHEEL DRIVE
POWER	59KW (80BHP)
TORQUE	N/A
TOP SPEED	161KM/H (100MPH)
0–96KM/H (0–60MPH)	N/A

FERRARI 166 INTER

The 166 was Ferrari's first car, launched in 1947. The first cars were all racers; it wasn't until 1949 that there was a road car available, in the form of the 166 Inter. Construction was by Touring of Milan, with power supplied by a 2-litre V12 engine in the nose.

COUNTRY OF ORIGIN	ITALY
YEARS OF PRODUCTION	1949–51
DISPLACEMENT	1995CC (122CI)
CONFIGURATION	FRONT-MOUNTED V12
TRANSMISSION	5-SPEED MANUAL, REAR-WHEEL DRIVE
POWER	88KW (120BHP)
TORQUE	159NM (117LB FT)
TOP SPEED	171KM/H (106MPH)
0–96KM/H (0–60MPH)	10.0SEC

ROVER JET1

The two-seater JET1 had the engine positioned behind the seats, air intake grilles on either side of the car and exhaust outlets on the top of the tail. During tests, the car reached top speeds of nearly 244km/h (152mph). JET1 ran on petrol, paraffin or diesel, but fuel consumption problems proved insurmountable for a production car.

COUNTRY OF ORIGIN	UK
YEARS OF PRODUCTION	1950
DISPLACEMENT	N/A
CONFIGURATION	FRONT-MOUNTED GAS TURBINE
TRANSMISSION	REAR-WHEEL DRIVE
POWER	177KW (240BHP)
TORQUE	N/A
TOP SPEED	244KM/H (152MPH)
0–96KM/H (0–60MPH)	6.5SEC

JAGUAR C-TYPE

Otherwise known as the XK120C, this sleek two-seater with aero screens was built with just one aim – to win Le Mans, which it did in 1951. Along with a new tubular steel chassis and rack-and-pinion steering, there was an uprated cylinder head for the straight-six along with a higher compression ratio of 9:1.

COUNTRY OF ORIGIN	UK
YEARS OF PRODUCTION	1951–54
DISPLACEMENT	3442CC (210CI)
CONFIGURATION	FRONT-ENGINED STRAIGHT-SIX
TRANSMISSION	4-SPEED MANUAL, REAR-WHEEL DRIVE
POWER	150KW (204BHP)
TORQUE	298NM (220LB FT)
TOP SPEED	232KM/H (144MPH)
0–96KM/H (0–60MPH)	8.1SEC

JAGUAR D-TYPE

Built to win the Le Mans 24 Hours, the D-Type did so on no fewer than three occasions (1955–57) thanks to its advanced construction, aerodynamic design and powerful six-cylinder engine. The powerplant was Jaguar's XK unit, but with high-lift valves, dry-sump lubrication, triple Weber carburettors and bigger inlet valves.

COUNTRY OF ORIGIN	UK
YEARS OF PRODUCTION	1953–57
DISPLACEMENT	3442CC (210CI)
CONFIGURATION	FRONT-ENGINED STRAIGHT-SIX
TRANSMISSION	4-SPEED MANUAL, REAR-WHEEL DRIVE
POWER	184KW (250BHP)
TORQUE	328NM (242LB FT)
TOP SPEED	240KM/H (149MPH)
0–96KM/H (0–60MPH)	5.2SEC

PORSCHE 356 CARRERA

The 356 was the first production car to come from Porsche; it made its debut in 1949 while the first Carrera model went on sale in 1955. This is seen as the ultimate 356, with its four-cam engine and racing heritage – underneath there are still torsion bars and swing axles though.

COUNTRY OF ORIGIN	GERMANY
YEARS OF PRODUCTION	1956–57
DISPLACEMENT	1498CC (91CI)
CONFIGURATION	REAR-MOUNTED FLAT-4
TRANSMISSION	4-SPEED MANUAL, REAR-WHEEL DRIVE
POWER	74KW (100BHP)
TORQUE	119NM (88LB FT)
TOP SPEED	200KM/H (124MPH)
0–96KM/H (0–60MPH)	12.0SEC

PORSCHE 356 SPEEDSTER

Another highly desirable version of the 356, the Speedster featured a lower roofline than standard, to improve aerodynamics while also reducing weight. Some owners bought the cars for competition rather than road use, so there was a Super Tune option that increased the available power to 65kW (88bhp) instead of the usual 44kW (60bhp).

COUNTRY OF ORIGIN	GERMANY
YEARS OF PRODUCTION	1956–58
DISPLACEMENT	1582CC (97CI)
CONFIGURATION	REAR-MOUNTED FLAT-4
TRANSMISSION	4-SPEED MANUAL, REAR-WHEEL DRIVE
POWER	44KW (60BHP)
TORQUE	110NM (81LB FT)
TOP SPEED	159KM/H (99MPH)
0–96KM/H (0–60MPH)	16.5SEC

MERCEDES 300SL ROADSTER

After 1400 examples of the 300SL gull-wing had been built, Mercedes replaced it with a more civilized open-topped version of the same car. There were now low-pivot swing axles to improve handling, while the 3-litre engine was tuned to give more torque. A total of 1858 examples were made.

COUNTRY OF ORIGIN	GERMANY
YEARS OF PRODUCTION	1957–63
DISPLACEMENT	2996CC (183CI)
CONFIGURATION	FRONT-MOUNTED 6-CYL
TRANSMISSION	4-SPEED MANUAL, REAR-WHEEL DRIVE
POWER	177KW (240BHP)
TORQUE	294NM (217LB FT)
TOP SPEED	225KM/H (140MPH)
0–96KM/H (0–60MPH)	8.8 SEC

ASTON MARTIN DB4

The DB4 was a huge advance for Aston Martin. Gone was the old tubular chassis, replaced by a sheet steel affair that was much stronger. The bodyshell consisted of lightweight aluminium panelling, while there was a new six-cylinder double overhead-cam alloy powerplant, designed by Tadek Marek.

COUNTRY OF ORIGIN	UK
YEARS OF PRODUCTION	1958–63
DISPLACEMENT	3670CC (224CI)
CONFIGURATION	FRONT-MOUNTED 6-CYL
TRANSMISSION	4-SPEED MANUAL, REAR-WHEEL DRIVE
POWER	177KW (240BHP)
TORQUE	325NM (240LB FT)
TOP SPEED	227KM/H (141MPH)
0–96KM/H (0–60MPH)	8.5SEC

JAGUAR E-TYPE

Was there ever a car made that captured the imagination like the Jaguar E-Type? All those sensuous curves, the massive performance on offer, yet a price tag that was reasonably affordable meant Jaguar couldn't fail. Until 1964 a 3.8-litre engine was fitted; this was superseded by a 4.2-litre unit in 1965.

COUNTRY OF ORIGIN	UK
YEARS OF PRODUCTION	1961–64
DISPLACEMENT	3781CC (231CI)
CONFIGURATION	FRONT-MOUNTED 6-CYL
TRANSMISSION	4-SPEED MANUAL, REAR-WHEEL DRIVE
POWER	195KW (265BHP)
TORQUE	353NM (260LB FT)
TOP SPEED	240KM/H (149MPH)
0–96KM/H (0–60MPH)	7.1SEC

ASTON MARTIN DB5

One of the greatest grand tourers ever built, the DB5 is most famous for its starring role in various James Bond films. But it's much more talented than that: the hand-made alloy skin hid a 4-litre all-alloy straight-six that endowed the car with a top speed of over 225km/h (140mph).

COUNTRY OF ORIGIN	UK
YEARS OF PRODUCTION	1963–66
DISPLACEMENT	3995CC (244CI)
CONFIGURATION	FRONT-MOUNTED 6-CYL
TRANSMISSION	4-SPEED MANUAL, REAR-WHEEL DRIVE
POWER	207KW (282BHP)
TORQUE	390NM (288LB FT)
TOP SPEED	227KM/H (141MPH)
0–96KM/H (0–60MPH)	8.1SEC

MASERATI MISTRAL

Another Maserati based on the 3500GT, the Mistral used the same engine as the Sebring, later in fuel-injected form. At first there was just a coupé available, but from 1964 there was also a spyder version offered, both versions being styled by Frua and all cars being constructed by Maggiora.

COUNTRY OF ORIGIN	ITALY
YEARS OF PRODUCTION	1963–70
DISPLACEMENT	3692CC (225CI)
CONFIGURATION	FRONT-MOUNTED 6-CYL
TRANSMISSION	5-SPEED MANUAL, REAR-WHEEL DRIVE
POWER	180KW (245BHP)
TORQUE	343NM (253LB FT)
TOP SPEED	233KM/H (145MPH)
0–96KM/H (0–60MPH)	N/A

TVR GRIFFITH

Jack Griffith was an American motor trader who negotia deal with TVR to sell heavily modified Granturas with his o name on. The first cars were known as Griffith 200s; 4.7-litre V8 in a car originally fitted with a small four-c engine, hair-raising performance was guaranteed.

COUNTRY OF ORIGIN	UK
YEARS OF PRODUCTION	1963–65
DISPLACEMENT	4727CC (288CI)
CONFIGURATION	FRONT-MOUNTED V8
TRANSMISSION	4-SPEED MANUAL, REAR-WHEEL DRIVE
POWER	199KW (271BHP)
TORQUE	426NM (314LB FT)
TOP SPEED	249KM/H (155MPH)
0–96KM/H (0–60MPH)	5.7SEC

FERRARI 275GTB

One of the most sensuous shapes of all time, the 275GTB was penned by Pininfarina, who also designed the spyder version (the GTS). With a five-speed transaxle and nearly 250kW (340bhp) on tap, the 275 offered crushing performance. If this wasn't enough, however, there was a six-carburettor version available, with 235kW (320bhp).

COUNTRY OF ORIGIN	ITALY
YEARS OF PRODUCTION	1964–68
DISPLACEMENT	3286CC (201CI)
CONFIGURATION	FRONT-MOUNTED V12
TRANSMISSION	5-SPEED MANUAL, REAR-WHEEL DRIVE
POWER	206KW (280BHP)
TORQUE	255NM (188LB FT)
TOP SPEED	251KM/H (156MPH)
0–96KM/H (0–60MPH)	6.0SEC

ISO GRIFO

Designed by Giorgetto Giugiaro and powered by a Chevrolet Corvette V8, the Grifo combined Italian flair with American muscle. The car had come about because Renzo Rivolta wanted something to rival the cars of Ferrari and Lamborghini, but couldn't find anything – so he built his own.

COUNTRY OF ORIGIN	ITALY
YEARS OF PRODUCTION	1964–74
DISPLACEMENT	5359CC (327CI)
CONFIGURATION	FRONT-MOUNTED V8
TRANSMISSION	4-SPEED MANUAL, REAR-WHEEL DRIVE
POWER	257KW (350BHP)
TORQUE	488NM (360LB FT)
TOP SPEED	262KM/H (163MPH)
0–96KM/H (0–60MPH)	6.4SEC

PORSCHE 904

The 904 debuted in 1964 as a successor to the Porsche 718, and it was the first Porsche to use a fibreglass bodyshell. There were standard and GTS variants, both of which featured a mid-mounted engine along with a fibreglass body bonded to a steel chassis for extra rigidity.

COUNTRY OF ORIGIN	GERMANY
YEARS OF PRODUCTION	1964–65
DISPLACEMENT	1966CC (120CI)
CONFIGURATION	MID-MOUNTED FLAT-4
TRANSMISSION	4-SPEED MANUAL, REAR-WHEEL DRIVE
POWER	114KW (155BHP)
TORQUE	169NM (125LB FT)
TOP SPEED	(5.5MPH)
0–96KM/H (0–60MPH)	156SEC

ASTON MARTIN DB6

Very obviously an evolution of the DB5's design, the DB6 was a far more modern car thanks to its monocoque construction – although there was still an aluminium outer skin. That glorious 4-litre 'six' remained, but with more power. The wheelbase was also longer, to improve the ride without killing the handling.

COUNTRY OF ORIGIN	UK
YEARS OF PRODUCTION	1965–70
DISPLACEMENT	3995CC (244CI)
CONFIGURATION	FRONT-MOUNTED 6-CYL
TRANSMISSION	4-SPEED MANUAL, REAR-WHEEL DRIVE
POWER	207KW (282BHP)
TORQUE	390NM (288LB FT)
TOP SPEED	225KM/H (140MPH)
0–96KM/H (0–60MPH)	N/A

BIZZARINI GT STRADA

Giotto Bizzarini had worked for Ferrari, but when the two quarrelled the former ended up leaving to set up his own rival company. The 5300GT was the result, based on the Iso Grifo that Bizzarini had also designed while working for Renzo Rivolta. Power was provided by a Chevrolet V8.

COUNTRY OF ORIGIN	ITALY
YEARS OF PRODUCTION	1965–69
DISPLACEMENT	5354CC (327CI)
CONFIGURATION	FRONT-ENGINED V8
TRANSMISSION	4-SPEED MANUAL, REAR-WHEEL DRIVE
POWER	268KW (365BHP)
TORQUE	511NM (377LB FT)
TOP SPEED	275KM/H (171MPH)
0–96KM/H (0–60MPH)	6.0SEC

JAGUAR XJ13

The XJ13 was originally developed as a prototype race car, developed to compete at Le Mans in the 1960s. Using Jaguar's first ever V12 engine (mounted in the middle), the car was never taken seriously by the company's management and it was put into storage after just one was made.

COUNTRY OF ORIGIN	UK
YEARS OF PRODUCTION	1966
DISPLACEMENT	4991CC (305CI)
CONFIGURATION	MID-MOUNTED V12
TRANSMISSION	5-SPEED MANUAL, REAR-WHEEL DRIVE
POWER	369KW (502BHP)
TORQUE	495NM (365LB FT)
TOP SPEED	274KM/H (170MPH)
0–96KM/H (0–60MPH)	N/A

ALFA ROMEO 33 STRADALE

The 33 Stradale started out as a race car, but 18 road-going versions were also produced. They were usually clothed by independent coachbuilders such as Bertone and Giugiaro, although the factory version was designed by Franco Scaglione. Race and road versions used the same twin-cam V8, but it was detuned for the latter.

COUNTRY OF ORIGIN	ITALY
YEARS OF PRODUCTION	1967–69
DISPLACEMENT	1995CC (122CI)
CONFIGURATION	MID-MOUNTED V8
TRANSMISSION	6-SPEED MANUAL, REAR-WHEEL DRIVE
POWER	169KW (230BHP)
TORQUE	183NM (135LB FT)
TOP SPEED	261KM/H (162MPH)
0–96KM/H (0–60MPH)	N/A

DE TOMASO MANGUSTA

The first production car to come from De Tomaso, the Mangusta (Mongoose) was designed to eat Cobras – just as in real life. Sitting in the middle was a Ford-sourced V8 (the same as in AC's Cobra), and while the car was ferociously fast, its handling left a lot to be desired.

COUNTRY OF ORIGIN	ITALY
YEARS OF PRODUCTION	1967–72
DISPLACEMENT	4727CC (288CI)
CONFIGURATION	MID-MOUNTED V8
TRANSMISSION	5-SPEED MANUAL, REAR-WHEEL DRIVE
POWER	224KW (305BHP)
TORQUE	531NM (392LB FT)
TOP SPEED	249KM/H (155MPH)
0–96KM/H (0–60MPH)	6.3SEC

MASERATI GHIBLI

Perhaps the most stylish of all the classic Maseratis, the Ghibli was based on the defunct Mexico, although the chassis was shortened and the engine was enlarged to 4.7 litres. This powerplant was the most powerful that Maserati had ever built. At first just a coupé was offered, but from 1967 there was also a spyder.

COUNTRY OF ORIGIN	ITALY
YEARS OF PRODUCTION	1967–73
DISPLACEMENT	4719CC (288CI)
CONFIGURATION	FRONT-MOUNTED V8
TRANSMISSION	5-SPEED MANUAL, REAR-WHEEL DRIVE
POWER	250KW (340BHP)
TORQUE	442NM (326LB FT)
TOP SPEED	257KM/H (160MPH)
0–96KM/H (0–60MPH)	6.6SEC

TOYOTA 2000GT

Helping to make the 2000GT a true driver's car was a backbone chassis, built to the same principles as Lotus' Elan – the contemporary benchmark for dynamic ability. With disc brakes and unequal-length wishbones all round, the chassis allowed the car to excel. But overfussy styling and Toyota's lacklustre image ensured buyers looked elsewhere for their driving thrills.

COUNTRY OF ORIGIN	JAPAN
YEARS OF PRODUCTION	1967–70
DISPLACEMENT	1988CC (121CI)
CONFIGURATION	FRONT-MOUNTED 6-CYL
TRANSMISSION	5-SPEED MANUAL, REAR-WHEEL DRIVE
POWER	110KW (150BHP)
TORQUE	175NM (129LB FT)
TOP SPEED	220KM/H (137MPH)
0–96KM/H (0–60MPH)	8.4SEC

CHEVROLET CORVETTE

Although the third-generation Corvette wasn't very well received by critics when it was launched, the buying public loved it. They loved its brash looks and powerful engines, and even though the suspension continued to be rather crude, it was effective. Most importantly, though, the cars were affordable.

COUNTRY OF ORIGIN	USA
YEARS OF PRODUCTION	1968–84
DISPLACEMENT	6997CC (427CI)
CONFIGURATION	FRONT-MOUNTED V8
TRANSMISSION	3-SPEED AUTO, REAR-WHEEL DRIVE
POWER	316KW (430BHP)
TORQUE	624NM (460LB FT)
TOP SPEED	243KM/H (151MPH)
0–96KM/H (0–60MPH)	6.8SEC

FERRARI DAYTONA

While its greatest adversary Lamborghini resorted to putting the engine in the middle, Ferrari stuck with a front-engined design for its new supercar in 1968. That didn't make it any less desirable though, and despite the fact that Ferrari only ever called it the 365GTB/4, the car is better known by its Daytona nickname.

COUNTRY OF ORIGIN	ITALY
YEARS OF PRODUCTION	1968–73
DISPLACEMENT	4390CC (268CI)
CONFIGURATION	FRONT-MOUNTED V12
TRANSMISSION	5-SPEED MANUAL, REAR-WHEEL DRIVE
POWER	260KW (353BHP)
TORQUE	433NM (319LB FT)
TOP SPEED	280KM/H (174MPH)
0–96KM/H (0–60MPH)	5.4SEC

ASTON MARTIN V8

The first Aston Martin DBS model featured a six-cylinder powerplant, but from 1969 there was a new V8-engined version available – the DBS V8. From 1972 it was known simply as the V8, fitted with a Bosch fuel-injected quad-cam V8 that had been designed in-house by Tadek Marek.

COUNTRY OF ORIGIN	UK
YEARS OF PRODUCTION	1969–89
DISPLACEMENT	5340CC (326CI)
CONFIGURATION	FRONT-MOUNTED V8
TRANSMISSION	5-SPEED MANUAL, REAR-WHEEL DRIVE
POWER	N/A
TORQUE	N/A
TOP SPEED	261KM/H (162MPH)
0–96KM/H (0–60MPH)	6.0SEC

MASERATI INDY

When Maserati wanted to replace the Sebring, it opted for a car that was far sleeker and much more modern. Looking similar to the Ghibli, the Indy was a 2+2 that was based on the Quattroporte's chassis – it also used the same 4.1-litre V8 as the luxury saloon, although the capacity would increase to 4.9 litres in 1973.

COUNTRY OF ORIGIN	ITALY
YEARS OF PRODUCTION	1969–74
DISPLACEMENT	4136CC (252CI)
CONFIGURATION	FRONT-MOUNTED V8
TRANSMISSION	5-SPEED MANUAL, REAR-WHEEL DRIVE
POWER	191KW (260BHP)
TORQUE	363NM (268LB FT)
TOP SPEED	225KM/H (140MPH)
0–96KM/H (0–60MPH)	7.2SEC

BOLWELL NAGARI

You've probably never heard of Bolwell, yet this small Australian company produced no fewer than nine different designs over a two-decade period. Using Ford V8 power, the Nagari was an evolution of earlier Bolwell designs spanning Mark 1 to Mark 7. Just 127 coupés and 13 convertibles were made, however.

COUNTRY OF ORIGIN	AUSTRALIA
YEARS OF PRODUCTION	1969–74
DISPLACEMENT	4950CC (302CI)
CONFIGURATION	FRONT-MOUNTED V8
TRANSMISSION	4-SPEED MANUAL, REAR-WHEEL DRIVE
POWER	177KW (240BHP)
TORQUE	N/A
TOP SPEED	201KM/H (125MPH)
0–96KM/H (0–60MPH)	6.4SEC

MERCEDES C111

The C111 was a series of experimental cars produced by Mercedes-Benz in the 1960s and 1970s, experimenting with new engine technologies, such as rotary and diesel powerplants. Other experimental features included gullwing doors and luxurious interiors with leather trim and air conditioning.

COUNTRY OF ORIGIN	GERMANY
YEARS OF PRODUCTION	1969–79
DISPLACEMENT	1800CC (110CI)
CONFIGURATION	MID-MOUNTED ROTARY
TRANSMISSION	5-SPEED MANUAL, REAR-WHEEL DRIVE
POWER	206KW (280BHP)
TORQUE	293NM (216LB FT)
TOP SPEED	261KM/H (162MPH)
0–96KM/H (0–60MPH)	5.0SEC

Ultimate Dream Car 1:
Jaguar XK120

Introduced not long after the end of World War II, the XK120 offered an amazing insight into the future of motoring. When most cars available at the time were still using prewar technology and designs, the Jaguar XK was a breath of fresh air.

Designed as a stop-gap to show what Jaguar could do, the XK120 was hastily built on a shortened MkV chassis. The car was to act as a showcase for Jaguar's new XK engine, to be available in four and six-cylinder forms – in the end, though, the smaller unit was never offered.

The XK120 made its debut at the London Motor Show at the end of 1948, and caused a sensation. Here was a car that looked as though it had driven straight from the future, with its rakish lines and advanced specification. That twin-cam straight-six could take the car to an astonishing 120mph (193km/h) – which is how the car got its name. In fact, this was the world's first mass-production twin-cam unit, and it would ultimately survive for nearly five decades, powering Jaguars until almost the end of the twentieth century.

Nor was it just the engine that was cutting-edge; the front suspension was equally advanced. Double wishbones and torsion bars offered both handling and comfort – although the rear suspension was less impressive, unfortunately.

There were three key derivatives offered, the only closed one being a fixed-head coupé. There was also a roadster (the most popular variant) plus a drophead coupé – another open car but this time with a primitive roof to keep its occupants sheltered from the elements.

With such modern engineering under the skin, it was inevitable that the XK120 would prove successful in competition. By 1950 the car was already notching up victories; first came the Tourist Trophy of that year, swiftly followed by the RAC Rally in the following season.

COUNTRY OF ORIGIN	UK
YEARS OF PRODUCTION	1949–54
DISPLACEMENT	3442CC (210CI)
CONFIGURATION	FRONT-MOUNTED 6-CYL.
TRANSMISSION	4-SPEED MANUAL, REAR-WHEEL DRIVE
POWER	118kW (160BHP)
TORQUE	264Nm (195LB FT)
TOP SPEED	201KM/H (125MPH)
0–96KM/H (0–60MPH)	10.0SEC

ALFA ROMEO MONTREAL

Bertone displayed this car in concept form at the 1967 Montreal Motor Show; three years later, Alfa Romeo decided to put it into production. The car was powered by a detuned version of the twin-cam dry-sump V8 more usually seen in its type 33 race cars, complete with mechanical fuel injection.

COUNTRY OF ORIGIN	ITALY
YEARS OF PRODUCTION	1970–77
DISPLACEMENT	2593CC (158CI)
CONFIGURATION	FRONT-MOUNTED V8
TRANSMISSION	5-SPEED MANUAL, REAR-WHEEL DRIVE
POWER	147KW (200BHP)
TORQUE	235NM (173LB FT)
TOP SPEED	220KM/H (137MPH)
0–96KM/H (0–60MPH)	7.6SEC

MONTEVERDI HAI

When it comes to exclusive supercars, few are rarer than the Monteverdi Hai. Just two were built, and the cars were designed by Peter Monteverdi himself – despite his having no formal training. Although there was massive performance on offer, the cars were also luxurious, with air conditioning and leather trim throughout.

COUNTRY OF ORIGIN	SWITZERLAND
YEARS OF PRODUCTION	1970–90
DISPLACEMENT	6980CC (426CI)
CONFIGURATION	MID-MOUNTED V8
TRANSMISSION	5-SPEED MANUAL, REAR-WHEEL DRIVE
POWER	331KW (450BHP)
TORQUE	666NM (491LB FT)
TOP SPEED	290KM/H (180MPH)
0–96KM/H (0–60MPH)	4.8SEC

MASERATI BORA

The Bora was Maserati's first ever mid-engined car, meaning the company could compete with Lamborghini and Ferrari, which were both using this advanced new layout. It was unusual in that it featured a semi-monocoque construction while it was also incredibly aerodynamic, despite having had no wind-tunnel testing.

COUNTRY OF ORIGIN	ITALY
YEARS OF PRODUCTION	1971–78
DISPLACEMENT	4930CC (301CI)
CONFIGURATION	MID-MOUNTED V8
TRANSMISSION	5-SPEED MANUAL, REAR-WHEEL DRIVE
POWER	246KW (335BHP)
TORQUE	480NM (354LB FT)
TOP SPEED	280KM/H (174MPH)
0–96KM/H (0–60MPH)	6.0SEC

MASERATI MERAK

Looking very much like the Bora, the Merak was a cheaper, smaller-engined car than its bigger brother. Designed to take on Ferrari's Dino, the Merak was powered by the same V6 that was fitted to the Citroen SM, with the gearbox, braking system and hydraulics all taken from the same source.

COUNTRY OF ORIGIN	ITALY
YEARS OF PRODUCTION	1972–83
DISPLACEMENT	2965CC (181CI)
CONFIGURATION	MID-MOUNTED V6
TRANSMISSION	5-SPEED MANUAL, REAR-WHEEL DRIVE
POWER	153KW (208BHP)
TORQUE	255NM (188LB FT)
TOP SPEED	230KM/H (143MPH)
0–96KM/H (0–60MPH)	7.7SEC

FERRARI BOXER

The first Boxer, launched in 1973, was fitted with a 4.4-litre V12 powerplant, but from 1976 there was a 4.9-litre unit fitted, offering more power as well as more performance. From 1981 there was Bosch electronic fuel injection to give even more power, while also making the car more driveable.

COUNTRY OF ORIGIN	ITALY
YEARS OF PRODUCTION	1973–84
DISPLACEMENT	4942CC (302CI)
CONFIGURATION	MID-ENGINED FLAT-12
TRANSMISSION	5-SPEED MANUAL, REAR-WHEEL DRIVE
POWER	250kW (340BHP)
TORQUE	449NM (331LB FT)
TOP SPEED	262KM/H (163MPH)
0–96KM/H (0–60MPH)	6.2SEC

BMW 2002 TURBO

It wasn't the world's first turbocharged production car, but it was certainly one of the most aggressively styled. However, the nature of the 2002 Turbo's power delivery meant you had to be a committed enthusiast to be able to live with it on a day-to-day basis. Still, it was incredibly quick.

COUNTRY OF ORIGIN	GERMANY
YEARS OF PRODUCTION	1973–74
DISPLACEMENT	1990CC (121CI)
CONFIGURATION	FRONT-MOUNTED 4-CYL
TRANSMISSION	4-SPEED MANUAL, REAR-WHEEL DRIVE
POWER	125kW (170BHP)
TORQUE	240NM (177LB FT)
TOP SPEED	209KM/H (130MPH)
0–96KM/H (0–60MPH)	7.3SEC

MASERATI KHAMSIN

Replacing the Indy, the Khamsin didn't look as good and was flawed mechanically because of its 2+2 configuration. In a bid to free up space for the rear-seat occupants, the engine was moved to the front, spoiling the car's balance in the process. It was still very quick, though.

COUNTRY OF ORIGIN	ITALY
YEARS OF PRODUCTION	1973–82
DISPLACEMENT	4930CC (301CI)
CONFIGURATION	FRONT-MOUNTED V8
TRANSMISSION	5-SPEED MANUAL, REAR-WHEEL DRIVE
POWER	235kW (320BHP)
TORQUE	480NM (354LB FT)
TOP SPEED	257KM/H (160MPH)
0–96KM/H (0–60MPH)	8.1SEC

LOTUS ESPRIT

An all-time classic, the Esprit was originally styled by Giugiaro, although the car was updated in 1987 by styling maestro Peter Stevens. At first Lotus' own twin-cam four-cylinder engine was fitted, in 2-litre form. This was expanded to 2.2 litres in 1980 – the same year that the iconic Esprit Turbo hit the streets.

COUNTRY OF ORIGIN	UK
YEARS OF PRODUCTION	1976–2004
DISPLACEMENT	2174CC (133CI)
CONFIGURATION	MID-MOUNTED IN-LINE 4-CYL
TRANSMISSION	5-SPEED MANUAL, REAR-WHEEL DRIVE
POWER	194kW (264BHP)
TORQUE	354NM (261LB FT)
TOP SPEED	259KM/H (161MPH)
0–96KM/H (0–60MPH)	4.9SEC

PANTHER SIX

With just one example produced, and another cobbled together later from spare parts, it would be hard to argue that the Panther Six was really a production car. However, it's worthy of inclusion here simply because it was so outrageous, with its twin-turbo 8.2-litre Cadillac V8 and those six wheels.

COUNTRY OF ORIGIN	UK
YEARS OF PRODUCTION	1977
DISPLACEMENT	8193CC (500CI)
CONFIGURATION	MID-MOUNTED V8
TRANSMISSION	3-SPEED AUTO, REAR-WHEEL DRIVE
POWER	441KW (600BHP)
TORQUE	813NM (600LB FT)
TOP SPEED	323KM/H (200MPH) (CLAIMED)
0–96KM/H (0–60MPH)	N/A

PORSCHE 928

Intended as a replacement for the 911, the 928 addressed many of the failings of what should have been its predecessor. It was seen as an extra model, however, as it was more of a grand tourer due to its weight. A water-cooled V8 in the nose was also seen as too radical by Porsche purists.

COUNTRY OF ORIGIN	GERMANY
YEARS OF PRODUCTION	1977–86
DISPLACEMENT	4957CC (302CI)
CONFIGURATION	FRONT-MOUNTED V8
TRANSMISSION	5-SPEED MANUAL, REAR-WHEEL DRIVE
POWER	243KW (330BHP)
TORQUE	430NM (317LB FT)
TOP SPEED	266KM/H (165MPH)
0–96KM/H (0–60MPH)	5.7SEC

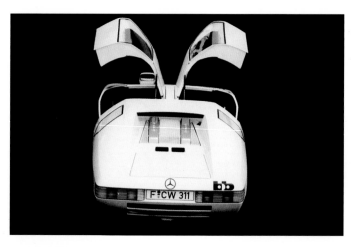

B+B CW311

Eberhard Schulz ran a successful tuning company in the 1970s called B+B. Focusing on upgrading Porsches, he decided to create his own car in 1978, called the CW311. Inspired by the Mercedes C111 prototypes, the car featured a mid-mounted AMG-tuned 6.3-litre V8 engine. The car would become the Isdera Imperator.

COUNTRY OF ORIGIN	GERMANY
YEARS OF PRODUCTION	1978
DISPLACEMENT	6300CC (384CI)
CONFIGURATION	MID-MOUNTED V8
TRANSMISSION	5-SPEED MANUAL, REAR-WHEEL DRIVE
POWER	294KW (400BHP)
TORQUE	587NM (433LB FT)
TOP SPEED	322KM/H (200MPH)
0–96KM/H (0–60MPH)	4.8SEC

BMW M1

The M1 project was a catalogue of disasters from start to finish; by the time it arrived, the series for which it had been created had been scrapped. It was a great car, though, with its ultra-smooth straight-six, from which up to 515kW (700bhp) could be extracted in race form.

COUNTRY OF ORIGIN	GERMANY
YEARS OF PRODUCTION	1979–80
DISPLACEMENT	3453CC (211CI)
CONFIGURATION	MID-MOUNTED STRAIGHT-SIX
TRANSMISSION	5-SPEED MANUAL, REAR-WHEEL DRIVE
POWER	204KW (277BHP) @ 6500RPM
TORQUE	324NM (239LB FT) @ 5000RPM
TOP SPEED	261KM/H (162MPH)
0–96KM/H (0–60MPH)	5.5SEC

AUDI QUATTRO

At the end of the 1970s, Audi needed to boost its image. The result was the Quattro, which was designed for rallying but with a road car spin-off. Using the five-cylinder engine usually seen in the 200, there was a four-wheel drive transmission while the floorpan was taken from the 80.

COUNTRY OF ORIGIN	GERMANY
YEARS OF PRODUCTION	1980–89
DISPLACEMENT	2144CC (131CI)
CONFIGURATION	FRONT-MOUNTED 5-CYL
TRANSMISSION	5-SPEED MANUAL, FOUR-WHEEL DRIVE
POWER	147kW (200BHP)
TORQUE	285NM (210LB FT)
TOP SPEED	222KM/H (138MPH)
0–96KM/H (0–60MPH)	6.5SEC

RENAULT 5 TURBO 2

In standard form, the Renault 5 was an innocuous little motor, but with a turbocharged powerplant in the middle mated to a Renault 30 transmission, the car was a formidable rally weapon. Aside from the exterior design, the car shared little with the standard car; suspension and braking were all bespoke.

COUNTRY OF ORIGIN	FRANCE
YEARS OF PRODUCTION	1980–86
DISPLACEMENT	1397CC (85CI)
CONFIGURATION	MID-MOUNTED 4-CYL
TRANSMISSION	5-SPEED MANUAL, REAR-WHEEL DRIVE
POWER	118kW (160BHP)
TORQUE	210NM (155LB FT)
TOP SPEED	200KM/H (124MPH)
0–96KM/H (0–60MPH)	7.8SEC

ISDERA SPYDER

The first car to come from the Isdera stable, the Spyder was also known as the 033. Clearly hailing from Germany with its muscular styling and silver paintwork, the Spyder was initially powered by a Mercedes 2.3-litre engine, although 2.5- or 3.0-litre items were optional from 1989.

COUNTRY OF ORIGIN	GERMANY
YEARS OF PRODUCTION	1983–90
DISPLACEMENT	2299CC (140CI)
CONFIGURATION	MID-MOUNTED 4-CYL
TRANSMISSION	5-SPEED MANUAL, REAR-WHEEL DRIVE
POWER	125kW (170BHP)
TORQUE	218NM (161LB FT)
TOP SPEED	232KM/H (144MPH)
0–96KM/H (0–60MPH)	N/A

ARGYLL GT TURBO

The work of Bob Henderson, the Argyll GT was one of Scotland's few cars – and a supercar at that. With its mid-mounted Rover V8, the car was claimed to top 241km/h (150mph), while suspension was from the Triumph 2500 and the five-speed gearbox was a ZF unit.

COUNTRY OF ORIGIN	UK
YEARS OF PRODUCTION	1984–90
DISPLACEMENT	3528CC (215CI)
CONFIGURATION	MID-MOUNTED V8
TRANSMISSION	5-SPEED MANUAL, REAR-WHEEL DRIVE
POWER	184kW (250BHP)
TORQUE	406NM (300LB FT)
TOP SPEED	241KM/H (150MPH)
0–96KM/H (0–60MPH)	6.4SEC

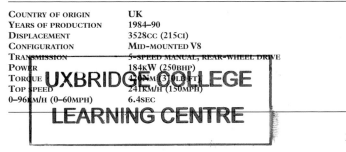

AUDI QUATTRO SPORT

The standard Quattro may have been astonishingly [...]
but a purpose-built weapon with which to contest th[e]
Group B series was essential if Audi was to take on [...]
Peugeot, Ford and the rest – and win. The Sport wa[s a]
shorter, kevlar-bodied version of the normal car, but [...]
more power.

COUNTRY OF ORIGIN	GERMANY
YEARS OF PRODUCTION	1984–85
DISPLACEMENT	2134CC (130CI)
CONFIGURATION	FRONT-ENGINED IN-LINE 5-CYL
TRANSMISSION	5-SPEED MANUAL, FOUR-WHEEL DRIVE
POWER	225KW (306BHP)
TORQUE	350NM (258LB FT)
TOP SPEED	249KM/H (155MPH)
0–96KM/H (0–60MPH)	4.8SEC

BMW M635CSI

Known as the M6 in the USA but the M635CSi
everywhere else, this was the fastest, most exclusive model in
BMW's range when it arrived in 1984. Compared with the car's
lesser siblings, the suspension was recalibrated for a sportier drive,
while the engine was taken from BMW's defunct M1 supercar.

COUNTRY OF ORIGIN	GERMANY
YEARS OF PRODUCTION	1984–90
DISPLACEMENT	2453CC (150CI)
CONFIGURATION	FRONT-MOUNTED 6-CYL
TRANSMISSION	5-SPEED MANUAL, REAR-WHEEL DRIVE
POWER	210KW (286BHP)
TORQUE	340NM (251LB FT)
TOP SPEED	241KM/H (150MPH)
0–96KM/H (0–60MPH)	6.0SEC

CHEVROLET CORVETTE C4

The C4 was a big step forward for the Corvette, with a
much sleeker body design, which was eminently practical
with that large glass tailgate. It also featured an electronic
dashboard, while braking was vastly improved thanks to the
adoption of alloy callipers that dissipated the heat better.

COUNTRY OF ORIGIN	USA
YEARS OF PRODUCTION	1984–96
DISPLACEMENT	5736CC (350CI)
CONFIGURATION	FRONT-MOUNTED V8
TRANSMISSION	4-SPEED MANUAL, REAR-WHEEL DRIVE
POWER	180KW (245BHP)
TORQUE	468NM (345LB FT)
TOP SPEED	257KM/H (160MPH)
0–96KM/H (0–60MPH)	5.6SEC

FERRARI TESTAROSSA

Whereas Ferraris had generally been elegantly desig[ned, the]
Testarossa took Ferrari in a new direction. Styled as [ever]
by Pininfarina, the Testarossa took its name from on[e of]
Ferrari's 1950s sports racers, and featured some ama[zing]
design elements – not the least of which were those s[lats]
down the side and across the back.

COUNTRY OF ORIGIN	ITALY
YEARS OF PRODUCTION	1984–92
DISPLACEMENT	4942CC (302CI)
CONFIGURATION	MID-ENGINED FLAT-12
TRANSMISSION	5-SPEED MANUAL, REAR-WHEEL DRIVE
POWER	287KW (390BHP)
TORQUE	491NM (362LB FT)
TOP SPEED	275KM/H (171MPH)
0–96KM/H (0–60MPH)	5.2SEC

MG METRO 6R4

For a brief period in the 1980s, everyone went Group B mad. The 6R4 was British Leyland's attempt at boosting the Metro's image; it packed a 3-litre V6 in the middle, based on the Rover V8. Road cars got 184kW (250bhp), but up to 441kW (600bhp) was on tap for the full-house rally versions.

COUNTRY OF ORIGIN	UK
YEARS OF PRODUCTION	1985
DISPLACEMENT	2991CC (183CI)
CONFIGURATION	MID-MOUNTED V6
TRANSMISSION	5-SPEED MANUAL, FOUR-WHEEL DRIVE
POWER	184KW (250BHP)
TORQUE	305NM (225LB FT)
TOP SPEED	225KM/H (140MPH)
0–96KM/H (0–60MPH)	4.5SEC

BMW M5 E28

For many years, BMW had the Q-car market pretty much to itself – and it was largely because of this car. The Bavarian firm had realized that not all fast drivers wanted to show off, so it fitted the M1's 210kW (286bhp) powerplant under the bonnet (less the dry-sump lubrication) and the rest is history.

COUNTRY OF ORIGIN	GERMANY
YEARS OF PRODUCTION	1986–88
DISPLACEMENT	3453CC (211CI)
CONFIGURATION	FRONT-MOUNTED 6-CYL
TRANSMISSION	5-SPEED MANUAL, REAR-WHEEL DRIVE
POWER	210KW (286BHP)
TORQUE	339NM (250LB FT)
TOP SPEED	243KM/H (151MPH)
0–96KM/H (0–60MPH)	6.2SEC

RENAULT GTA

Renault wanted to build a car that could compete with the Porsche 911, and while it achieved its aim the badge on the nose was always going to hold back buyers. Despite fabulous performance and handling, buyers shunned the GTA because of its lacklustre image and typical Renault plasticky interior.

COUNTRY OF ORIGIN	FRANCE
YEARS OF PRODUCTION	1985–91
DISPLACEMENT	2458CC (150CI)
CONFIGURATION	REAR-MOUNTED V6
TRANSMISSION	5-SPEED MANUAL, REAR-WHEEL DRIVE
POWER	147KW (200BHP)
TORQUE	290NM (214LB FT)
TOP SPEED	249KM/H (155MPH)
0–96KM/H (0–60MPH)	6.3SEC

FORD SIERRA COSWORTH

The standard Sierra may have been a humdrum family saloon, but Ford certainly breathed life into it when the decision was made to take it Group A racing. That meant 5000 road-going examples had to be built, each one with three doors, a whale-tail rear spoiler and a 150kW (204bhp) turbocharged 2-litre engine.

COUNTRY OF ORIGIN	GERMANY/UK
YEARS OF PRODUCTION	1986–90
DISPLACEMENT	1993CC (122CI)
CONFIGURATION	FRONT-MOUNTED 4-CYL
TRANSMISSION	5-SPEED MANUAL, REAR-WHEEL DRIVE
POWER	150KW (204BHP)
TORQUE	275NM (203LB FT)
TOP SPEED	233KM/H (145MPH)
0–96KM/H (0–60MPH)	6.2SEC

ISDERA IMPERATOR

Looking a little like the Mercedes C-111 concepts of the 1960s and 1970s, the Imperator was also known as the 108i. Fitted with a choice of Mercedes or Porsche power-plants, the gullwinged monster was fast and exclusive, and directly evolved from the B+B CW311 of 1978.

COUNTRY OF ORIGIN	GERMANY
YEARS OF PRODUCTION	1986
DISPLACEMENT	5547CC (338CI)
CONFIGURATION	MID-MOUNTED V8
TRANSMISSION	5-SPEED MANUAL, REAR-WHEEL DRIVE
POWER	287KW (390BHP)
TORQUE	525NM (387LB FT)
TOP SPEED	283KM/H (176MPH)
0–96KM/H (0–60MPH)	5.0SEC

NISSAN MID-4

The first of three generations of Mid-4 was unveiled in 1985, with the follow-up shown two years later. This latter edition featured a 3-litre V6 engine driving all four wheels via a five-speed manual gearbox. However, the final car in the series never even got off the drawing board to production.

COUNTRY OF ORIGIN	JAPAN
YEARS OF PRODUCTION	1987
DISPLACEMENT	2960CC (181CI)
CONFIGURATION	MID-MOUNTED V6, TWIN-TURBO
TRANSMISSION	5-SPEED MANUAL, FOUR-WHEEL DRIVE
POWER	243KW (330BHP)
TORQUE	382NM (282LB FT)
TOP SPEED	270KM/H (168MPH)
0–96KM/H (0–60MPH)	5.0SEC

VENTURI 260

A car that looked great and went even better, the Venturi was hindered by its lack of heritage – buyers chose Lotuses and TVRs instead. It used the PRV V6 from Renault in 2.8-litre guise, and there was a backbone chassis wrapped in a glassfibre bodyshell, with multi-link rear suspension and wishbones at the front.

COUNTRY OF ORIGIN	FRANCE
YEARS OF PRODUCTION	1987–95
DISPLACEMENT	2849CC (174CI)
CONFIGURATION	MID-MOUNTED V6
TRANSMISSION	5-SPEED MANUAL, REAR-WHEEL DRIVE
POWER	191KW (260BHP)
TORQUE	431NM (318LB FT)
TOP SPEED	270KM/H (168MPH)
0–96KM/H (0–60MPH)	5.3SEC

ASTON MARTIN VIRAGE

With the DBS having been launched two decades earlier, you'd think the Virage couldn't come soon enough. Yet it was seen as a retrograde step in many ways, not least of all thanks to those uninspiring lines. A stiffer bodyshell, however, meant that the car was better to drive, even if the mechanicals were largely carried over.

COUNTRY OF ORIGIN	UK
YEARS OF PRODUCTION	1988–96
DISPLACEMENT	5340CC (326CI)
CONFIGURATION	FRONT-MOUNTED V8
TRANSMISSION	5-SPEED MANUAL, REAR-WHEEL DRIVE
POWER	243KW (330BHP)
TORQUE	461NM (340LB FT)
TOP SPEED	253KM/H (157MPH)
0–96KM/H (0–60MPH)	6.8SEC

LANCIA DELTA INTEGRALE

Originally conceived as a homologation special for rallying, the Integrale was initially known as the Delta HF Turbo 4x4. Throughout production, the car retained its four-door hatchback bodyshell, but the wheelarches became ever fatter as power outputs rose. Fuel injection and forced induction were a constant; from 1989, there were also 16 valves.

COUNTRY OF ORIGIN	ITALY
YEARS OF PRODUCTION	1988–93
DISPLACEMENT	1995CC (122CI)
CONFIGURATION	FRONT-MOUNTED 4-CYL
TRANSMISSION	5-SPEED MANUAL, FOUR-WHEEL DRIVE
POWER	154KW (210BHP)
TORQUE	298NM (220LB FT)
TOP SPEED	220KM/H (137MPH)
0–96KM/H (0–60MPH)	5.7SEC

NISSAN 300ZX

Although the car before it was also known as the 300ZX, it had nothing in common with this all-new car. At first there was only a normally aspirated edition offered, but from 1990 there was also a twin-turbo car available. This was also the first ZX offered as a true convertible, rather than a targa.

COUNTRY OF ORIGIN	JAPAN
YEARS OF PRODUCTION	1989–2002
DISPLACEMENT	2960CC (181CI)
CONFIGURATION	FRONT-MOUNTED 6-CYL
TRANSMISSION	5-SPEED MANUAL, REAR-WHEEL DRIVE
POWER	206KW (280BHP)
TORQUE	373NM (275LB FT)
TOP SPEED	251KM/H (156MPH)
0–96KM/H (0–60MPH)	6.0SEC

TVR 450SEAC

The 450SEAC was the third in a hat-trick of wild 350i-derived roadsters from TVR, following on from the 400SE and 420SEAC. The name was short for Special Equipment Aramid Composite, giving away the fact that the car was made of kevlar instead of glassfibre to allow for a stronger bodyshell while keeping the weight down.

COUNTRY OF ORIGIN	UK
YEARS OF PRODUCTION	1988–89
DISPLACEMENT	4441CC (271CI)
CONFIGURATION	FRONT-MOUNTED V8
TRANSMISSION	5-SPEED MANUAL, REAR-WHEEL DRIVE
POWER	238KW (324BHP)
TORQUE	420NM (310LB FT)
TOP SPEED	257KM/H (160MPH)
0–96KM/H (0–60MPH)	4.7SEC

JIOTTO CASPITA

Produced by Japanese company Dome in 1989, the Caspita was manufactured for another Japanese company, Jiotto. At first it was equipped with a detuned Formula One V12 powerplant, but in 1990 a Judd V10 unit was fitted instead. Both engines were mounted transversely, driving the rear wheels via a six-speed manual gearbox.

COUNTRY OF ORIGIN	JAPAN
YEARS OF PRODUCTION	1989
DISPLACEMENT	3497CC (213CI)
CONFIGURATION	MID-MOUNTED FLAT-12
TRANSMISSION	6-SPEED MANUAL, REAR-WHEEL DRIVE
POWER	331KW (450BHP)
TORQUE	362NM (267LB FT)
TOP SPEED	320KM/H (199MPH)
0–96KM/H (0–60MPH)	4.7SEC

NISSAN SKYLINE R32

The R32 revived the GT-R tag that hadn't been offered since 1973. This was the new range-topper with all the technology thrown at it that Nissan could muster. Along with twin ceramic turbochargers, there was four-wheel steering and four-wheel drive – it was no surprise that the car was quickly nicknamed 'Godzilla'.

COUNTRY OF ORIGIN	JAPAN
YEARS OF PRODUCTION	1989–94
DISPLACEMENT	2658CC (162CI)
CONFIGURATION	FRONT-MOUNTED 6-CYL
TRANSMISSION	5-SPEED MANUAL, FOUR-WHEEL DRIVE
POWER	206KW (280BHP)
TORQUE	353NM (260LB FT)
TOP SPEED	249KM/H (155MPH)
0–96KM/H (0–60MPH)	5.1SEC

DE TOMASO PANTERA II

The year 1991 saw the introduction of a much-facelifted new Pantera. Designed by Marcello Gandini, it was wider with new suspension and brakes. But the project stalled before it had even got off the ground – just like the all-new Pantera that was proposed in 2001.

COUNTRY OF ORIGIN	ITALY
YEARS OF PRODUCTION	1990–92
DISPLACEMENT	4942CC (247CI)
CONFIGURATION	MID-ENGINED V8
TRANSMISSION	5-SPEED MANUAL, REAR-WHEEL DRIVE
POWER	224KW (305BHP)
TORQUE	445NM (328LB FT)
TOP SPEED	270KM/H (168MPH)
0–96KM/H (0–60MPH)	N/A

LAMBORGHINI DIABLO

The first Diablos used a 5.7-litre V12; as it evolved, there were four-wheel drive (VT) models, along with the Roadster from 1995. The SE30 of 1993 was built to commemorate 30 years of Lamborghini's existence, but the fruitiest was the 368kW (500bhp) SV of 1995 – at least until the 6-litre edition was launched in 2000, with 404kW (550bhp).

COUNTRY OF ORIGIN	ITALY
YEARS OF PRODUCTION	1990–2001
DISPLACEMENT	5729CC (350CI)
CONFIGURATION	MID-MOUNTED V12
TRANSMISSION	5-SPEED MANUAL, REAR-WHEEL DRIVE/FOUR-WHEEL DRIVE
POWER	362KW (492BHP)
TORQUE	580NM (428LB FT)
TOP SPEED	330KM/H (205MPH)
0–96KM/H (0–60MPH)	4.2SEC

MITSUBISHI 3000GT

Known as the GTO in some markets, the 3000GT was a technological tour de force. It packed all sorts of gadgetry into a sleek bodyshell: four-wheel steering, electronically adjustable shock absorbers and four-wheel drive with a torque split transfer system were all standard. The engine was just as advanced too.

COUNTRY OF ORIGIN	JAPAN
YEARS OF PRODUCTION	1990–2000
DISPLACEMENT	2972CC (181CI)
CONFIGURATION	FRONT-MOUNTED V6
TRANSMISSION	5-SPEED MANUAL, FOUR-WHEEL DRIVE
POWER	210KW (286BHP)
TORQUE	407NM (300LB FT)
TOP SPEED	254KM/H (158MPH)
0–96KM/H (0–60MPH)	5.6SEC

VAUXHALL LOTUS CARLTON

Ultra-fast saloons are common now, but when the Vauxhall Lotus Carlton was launched in 1990 its only rival was BMW's M5. With 277kW (377bhp) on tap and rear-wheel drive with no electronic aids, the Carlton could be quite a handful if you wanted to press on, but there was little to touch it with its top speed of 285km/h (177mph).

COUNTRY OF ORIGIN	GERMANY/UK
YEARS OF PRODUCTION	1990–93
DISPLACEMENT	3615CC (221CI)
CONFIGURATION	FRONT-MOUNTED STRAIGHT-SIX
TRANSMISSION	6-SPEED MANUAL, REAR-WHEEL DRIVE
POWER	277KW (377BHP)
TORQUE	568NM (419LB FT)
TOP SPEED	285KM/H (177MPH)
0–96KM/H (0–60MPH)	5.1SEC

ALPINE A610

Although it looks very much like the GTA that preceded it, 80 per cent of the A610 was new or at least heavily revised. There were now pop-up headlamps and more aggressive bumpers, and the brakes and suspension were upgraded. The chassis was also much stiffer to improve handling.

COUNTRY OF ORIGIN	FRANCE
YEARS OF PRODUCTION	1991–95
DISPLACEMENT	2975CC (182CI)
CONFIGURATION	REAR-MOUNTED V6
TRANSMISSION	5-SPEED MANUAL, REAR-WHEEL DRIVE
POWER	184KW (250BHP)
TORQUE	350NM (258LB FT)
TOP SPEED	256KM/H (159MPH)
0–96KM/H (0–60MPH)	5.8SEC

CALLAWAY CORVETTE SPEEDSTER

Reeves Callaway started out with a twin-turbo version of the Alfa Romeo GTV6, which caught the attention of Chevrolet's bosses. They asked Callaway to overhaul a Corvette, which was displayed at the 1991 Los Angeles Auto Show, where 50 orders were taken for the twin-turbo monster, complete with adjustable suspension and Brembo brakes.

COUNTRY OF ORIGIN	USA
YEARS OF PRODUCTION	1991
DISPLACEMENT	5700CC (348CI)
CONFIGURATION	FRONT-MOUNTED V8
TRANSMISSION	6-SPEED MANUAL, REAR-WHEEL DRIVE
POWER	309KW (420BHP)
TORQUE	762NM (562LB FT)
TOP SPEED	298KM/H (185MPH)
0–96KM/H (0–60MPH)	4.5SEC

FERRARI 512TR

Although clearly based on the Testarossa, the 512TR was a thoroughly re-engineered version of the car. As well as a heavily revised V12 powerplant and updated interior, there were also upgraded braking and suspension systems, while the centre of gravity was lowered to improve the handling.

COUNTRY OF ORIGIN	ITALY
YEARS OF PRODUCTION	1991–94
DISPLACEMENT	4942CC (302CI)
CONFIGURATION	MID-MOUNTED V12
TRANSMISSION	5-SPEED MANUAL, REAR-WHEEL DRIVE
POWER	310KW (422BHP)
TORQUE	488NM (360LB FT)
TOP SPEED	309KM/H (192MPH)
0–96KM/H (0–60MPH)	4.8SEC

MAZDA RX-7

Known as the FD generation, this third edition of the RX-7 was the biggest-selling derivative offered by Mazda and by far the most futuristic as well as the fastest and most powerful. With its twin-turbocharged rotary engine, the handling was faultless, but the cars were costly to buy as well as to run.

COUNTRY OF ORIGIN	JAPAN
YEARS OF PRODUCTION	1991–2002
DISPLACEMENT	2616CC (160CI)
CONFIGURATION	FRONT-MOUNTED ROTARY
TRANSMISSION	5-SPEED MANUAL, REAR-WHEEL DRIVE
POWER	188KW (255BHP)
TORQUE	293NM (216LB FT)
TOP SPEED	249KM/H (155MPH)
0–96KM/H (0–60MPH)	5.1SEC

MERCEDES C112

With its C111 series of concepts so well known, Mercedes cashed in on the brand by launching a new production supercar at the 1991 Frankfurt Motor Show. But with the global economy in meltdown, the last thing the world needed was another hypercar, so the plug was pulled.

COUNTRY OF ORIGIN	GERMANY
YEARS OF PRODUCTION	1991
DISPLACEMENT	5987CC (365CI)
CONFIGURATION	MID-MOUNTED V8
TRANSMISSION	6-SPEED MANUAL, REAR-WHEEL DRIVE
POWER	300KW (408BHP)
TORQUE	582NM (429LB FT)
TOP SPEED	311KM/H (193MPH)
0–96KM/H (0–60MPH)	4.9SEC

TVR GRIFFITH

With its hugely powerful V8 engine and lightweight glassfibre bodyshell, the Griffith was an extremely fearsome car to try to tame – it featured nothing in the way of electronics to save the driver. What it did have was a simply engineered Rover V8 driving the rear wheels via a limited-slip differential.

COUNTRY OF ORIGIN	UK
YEARS OF PRODUCTION	1991–2002
DISPLACEMENT	4988CC (304CI)
CONFIGURATION	FRONT-MOUNTED V8
TRANSMISSION	5-SPEED MANUAL, REAR-WHEEL DRIVE
POWER	250KW (340BHP)
TORQUE	475NM (350LB FT)
TOP SPEED	259KM/H (161MPH)
0–96KM/H (0–60MPH)	4.2SEC

BMW M3 E36

A much more usable car than the original M3, the E36 offered not only a six-cylinder powerplant, but there was also a four-door saloon to sell alongside the coupé and convertible. Initially there was 3-litre straight-six power, but from 1996 the displacement was increased to 3.2 litres when the Evo arrived.

COUNTRY OF ORIGIN	GERMANY
YEARS OF PRODUCTION	1992–99
DISPLACEMENT	3201CC (195CI)
CONFIGURATION	FRONT-MOUNTED 6-CYL
TRANSMISSION	5-SPEED MANUAL, REAR-WHEEL DRIVE
POWER	236KW (321BHP)
TORQUE	350NM (258LB FT)
TOP SPEED	249KM/H (155MPH)
0–96KM/H (0–60MPH)	5.4SEC

BUGATTI EB110

With the world's economy going into overdrive during the late 1980s, the time seemed right to revive the Bugatti marque and create something ultra-exclusive as well as hyper-quick. But by the time the EB110 was available, a recession had arrived, nobody wanted supercars any more and Bugatti went bust.

COUNTRY OF ORIGIN	ITALY
YEARS OF PRODUCTION	1992–95
DISPLACEMENT	3500CC (214CI)
CONFIGURATION	MID-MOUNTED V12, QUAD-TURBO
TRANSMISSION	6-SPEED MANUAL, FOUR-WHEEL DRIVE
POWER	412KW (560BHP)
TORQUE	611NM (451LB FT)
TOP SPEED	344KM/H (214MPH)
0–96KM/H (0–60MPH)	3.4SEC

FORD ESCORT RS COSWORTH

The Escort Cosworth was designed to become Ford's rallying weapon in place of the Sierra, so the company's Special Vehicle Engineering (SVE) division grafted the Escort's bodyshell onto the Sierra's mechanicals. While the new car was significantly shorter, its width was the same as Sierra's, for maximum grip and agility.

COUNTRY OF ORIGIN	GERMANY/UK
YEARS OF PRODUCTION	1992–96
DISPLACEMENT	1993CC (122CI)
CONFIGURATION	FRONT-MOUNTED 4-CYL
TRANSMISSION	5-SPEED MANUAL, FOUR-WHEEL DRIVE
POWER	167KW (227BHP)
TORQUE	304NM (224LB FT)
TOP SPEED	230KM/H (143MPH)
0–96KM/H (0–60MPH)	5.8SEC

JAGUAR XJ220

This was a dream car that proved to be a nightmare for Jaguar. In concept form it featured four-wheel drive and a V12 engine, but by the time it reached production it was rear-wheel drive and had a twin-turbo V6 fitted. It didn't matter, though; the car was still faster than anything else in production.

COUNTRY OF ORIGIN	UK
YEARS OF PRODUCTION	1992–95
DISPLACEMENT	3498CC (213CI)
CONFIGURATION	MID-MOUNTED V6, TWIN-TURBO
TRANSMISSION	5-SPEED MANUAL, REAR-WHEEL DRIVE
POWER	399KW (542BHP)
TORQUE	644NM (475LB FT)
TOP SPEED	340KM/H (211MPH)
0–96KM/H (0–60MPH)	3.6SEC

SPIESS C522

Designing a car to take on the McLaren F1, German company Spiess unveiled its TC522 in 1992. With a twin-turbocharged 5.7-litre V8, there was also carbon fibre bodywork and a bespoke six-speed gearbox by British company Xtrac. Unsurprisingly, because of its exorbitant price tag, the company sank without trace almost immediately.

COUNTRY OF ORIGIN	GERMANY
YEARS OF PRODUCTION	1992
DISPLACEMENT	5666CC (346CI)
CONFIGURATION	MID-MOUNTED V8
TRANSMISSION	6-SPEED MANUAL, REAR-WHEEL DRIVE
POWER	368KW (500BHP)
TORQUE	881NM (650LB FT)
TOP SPEED	306KM/H (190MPH)
0–96KM/H (0–60MPH)	4.0SEC

TVR CHIMAERA

For those who felt the Griffith was too fierce, the Chimaera was a slightly less wild version of the same car. As with the Griffith, the engine was set well back to balance the weight distribution, while the bodyshell was glassfibre once more to keep the car's weight down.

COUNTRY OF ORIGIN	UK
YEARS OF PRODUCTION	1992–2001
DISPLACEMENT	4988CC (304CI)
CONFIGURATION	FRONT-MOUNTED V8
TRANSMISSION	5-SPEED MANUAL, REAR-WHEEL DRIVE
POWER	250kW (340BHP)
TORQUE	475NM (350LB FT)
TOP SPEED	266KM/H (165MPH)
0–96KM/H (0–60MPH)	4.4SEC

YAMAHA OX99–11

The term 'race car for the road' is trotted out all too often where supercars are concerned, but it was a worthy tag in the case of the OX99–11. This was a car that really did use Formula One technology, but the sums didn't add up and Yamaha pulled out before the project really got going.

COUNTRY OF ORIGIN	JAPAN
YEARS OF PRODUCTION	1992
DISPLACEMENT	3498CC (213CI)
CONFIGURATION	MID-MOUNTED V12
TRANSMISSION	6-SPEED MANUAL, REAR-WHEEL DRIVE
POWER	309kW (420BHP)
TORQUE	N/A
TOP SPEED	306KM/H (190MPH)
0–96KM/H (0–60MPH)	3.7 SEC

DE TOMASO GUARA

Considering some of the gorgeous designs to have come from De Tomaso in earlier years, the Guara was not a thing of beauty. However, it was fast and undeniably exclusive; over a 'production' run that lasted more than a decade, just 40 coupés and 10 convertibles were constructed.

COUNTRY OF ORIGIN	ITALY
YEARS OF PRODUCTION	1993–2004
DISPLACEMENT	4601CC (281CI)
CONFIGURATION	MID-MOUNTED V8
TRANSMISSION	6-SPEED MANUAL, REAR-WHEEL DRIVE
POWER	224kW (305BHP)
TORQUE	401NM (296LB FT)
TOP SPEED	277KM/H (172MPH)
0–96KM/H (0–60MPH)	4.9SEC

LISTER STORM

It was no surprise that just four examples of the Storm were built – the car was fast and looked fabulous, but the Lister name didn't have the cachet of its rivals. There was a 7-litre Jaguar V12 in the middle, while the bodywork was made of carbon fibre and alloy honeycomb.

COUNTRY OF ORIGIN	UK
YEARS OF PRODUCTION	1993–94
DISPLACEMENT	6997CC (427CI)
CONFIGURATION	FRONT-MOUNTED V12
TRANSMISSION	6-SPEED MANUAL, REAR-WHEEL DRIVE
POWER	437kW (594BHP)
TORQUE	786NM (580LB FT)
TOP SPEED	306KM/H (190MPH)
0–96KM/H (0–60MPH)	4.7SEC

PORSCHE 968 CLUB SPORT

The 968 was a development of the 944, as it featured an upgraded version of that car's 3-litre four-cylinder engine, while there was a transaxle for optimum weight distribution. In Club Sport trim there were bigger wheels, while the rear seat and power windows were junked to keep the weight down.

COUNTRY OF ORIGIN	GERMANY
YEARS OF PRODUCTION	1993–95
DISPLACEMENT	2990CC (182CI)
CONFIGURATION	FRONT-MOUNTED 4-CYL
TRANSMISSION	6-SPEED MANUAL, REAR-WHEEL DRIVE
POWER	177KW (240BHP)
TORQUE	305NM (225LB FT)
TOP SPEED	253KM/H (157MPH)
0–96KM/H (0–60MPH)	6.5SEC

SUBARU IMPREZA TURBO

When it comes to understated looks with breathtaking ability, the Impreza Turbo is the master. Unassuming to look at, the boosted Impreza handles and accelerates like nothing else on Earth – except for its arch-rival the Mitsubishi Evo, of course. It's all down to the four-wheel drive, turbocharged engine and electronics galore…

COUNTRY OF ORIGIN	JAPAN
YEARS OF PRODUCTION	1993–2000
DISPLACEMENT	1994CC (122CI)
CONFIGURATION	FRONT-MOUNTED FLAT-4
TRANSMISSION	5-SPEED MANUAL, FOUR-WHEEL DRIVE
POWER	158KW (215BHP)
TORQUE	290NM (214LB FT)
TOP SPEED	232KM/H (144MPH)
0–96KM/H (0–60MPH)	5.4SEC

TOYOTA SUPRA

The Supra started out as a top-of-the-range Celica, but in 1986 Toyota decided to set up a separate range, with a completely restyled model, and by this fourth-generation edition the Supra was a true supercar. With a twin-turbocharged 3-litre straight-six, the car was ferociously quick, with handling to match.

COUNTRY OF ORIGIN	JAPAN
YEARS OF PRODUCTION	1993–2002
DISPLACEMENT	2997CC (183CI)
CONFIGURATION	FRONT-MOUNTED 6-CYL
TRANSMISSION	5-SPEED MANUAL, REAR-WHEEL DRIVE
POWER	243KW (330BHP)
TORQUE	427NM (315LB FT)
TOP SPEED	254KM/H (158MPH)
0–96KM/H (0–60MPH)	5.1SEC

VENTURI 400GT

Venturi had such a tumultuous short existence that it never really stood a chance, but you couldn't deny that its cars were thrilling. First came the Atlantique, then this twin-turbo monster that proved to be so exclusive that hardly anybody could afford it. It proved to be Venturi's swan song … or did it?

COUNTRY OF ORIGIN	FRANCE
YEARS OF PRODUCTION	1993–95
DISPLACEMENT	2975CC (182CI)
CONFIGURATION	MID-MOUNTED V6
TRANSMISSION	5-SPEED MANUAL, REAR-WHEEL DRIVE
POWER	300KW (408BHP)
TORQUE	521NM (384LB FT)
TOP SPEED	291KM/H (181MPH)
0–96KM/H (0–60MPH)	4.7SEC

AUDI RS2

Take selected parts from Porsche's parts bin and fit them to an Audi 80 Avant, and the RS2 is the result. With its 432mm (17in) 911 wheels, plus a six-speed close-ratio gearbox and four-pot braking system from the 968, the RS2 was quite a car – especially as Porsche coaxed 232kW (315bhp) from the 2.2-litre engine.

COUNTRY OF ORIGIN	GERMANY
YEARS OF PRODUCTION	1994–95
DISPLACEMENT	2226CC (136CI)
CONFIGURATION	FRONT-MOUNTED 5-CYL
TRANSMISSION	6-SPEED MANUAL, FOUR-WHEEL DRIVE
POWER	232kW (315BHP)
TORQUE	409NM (302LB FT)
TOP SPEED	261KM/H (162MPH)
0–96KM/H (0–60MPH)	4.8SEC

CALLAWAY CAMARO C8

Already well-known for his heavily modified Corvettes, Callaway turned his attention to the new Camaro in 1994. He stiffened the bodyshell as well as the suspension. Fresh brakes came from Brembo and the bodywork was redesigned for a smoother look. It was topped off by a stroked version of Chevrolet's small-block V8.

COUNTRY OF ORIGIN	USA
YEARS OF PRODUCTION	1994
DISPLACEMENT	6276CC (383CI)
CONFIGURATION	FRONT-MOUNTED V8
TRANSMISSION	6-SPEED MANUAL, REAR-WHEEL DRIVE
POWER	297kW (404BHP)
TORQUE	559NM (412LB FT)
TOP SPEED	277KM/H (172MPH)
0–96KM/H (0–60MPH)	4.7SEC

FERRARI F355

It wasn't going to prove much of a challenge trying to improve on the 348, which had never been very well received. Compared with that car, the F355 was faster and handled far better; this was partly down to an aerodynamic undertray that reduced lift at high speed.

COUNTRY OF ORIGIN	ITALY
YEARS OF PRODUCTION	1994–99
DISPLACEMENT	3496CC (213CI)
CONFIGURATION	MID-MOUNTED V8
TRANSMISSION	6-SPEED MANUAL, REAR-WHEEL DRIVE
POWER	279kW (380BHP)
TORQUE	363NM (268LB FT)
TOP SPEED	278KM/H (173MPH)
0–96KM/H (0–60MPH)	4.6SEC

FERRARI F512M

The final chapter in the Testarossa story, the F512M (for Modificata) was the last standard production Ferrari to be fitted with a mid-mounted V12 engine. There were also fixed headlamps in place of the previous pop-up units, and the straked rear lights were replaced with four circular items.

COUNTRY OF ORIGIN	ITALY
YEARS OF PRODUCTION	1994–96
DISPLACEMENT	4943CC (302CI)
CONFIGURATION	MID-MOUNTED FLAT-12
TRANSMISSION	5-SPEED MANUAL, REAR-WHEEL DRIVE
POWER	324kW (440BHP)
TORQUE	499NM (368LB FT)
TOP SPEED	315KM/H (196MPH)
0–96KM/H (0–60MPH)	4.8SEC

DODGE VIPER GTS-R

From the point when Dodge showed a fixed-head Viper in
1993, it was obvious that the company had to build the car.
From 1996 it was available, so the next step was to create a
racer: the GTS-R, which appeared in prototype form in
1995. With carbon fibre bodywork, the GTS-R could top
327km/h (203mph).

COUNTRY OF ORIGIN	USA
YEARS OF PRODUCTION	1995–
DISPLACEMENT	7996CC (488CI)
CONFIGURATION	FRONT-MOUNTED V10
TRANSMISSION	6-SPEED MANUAL, REAR-WHEEL DRIVE
POWER	478KW (650BHP)
TORQUE	881NM (650LB FT)
TOP SPEED	327KM/H (203MPH)
0–96KM/H (0–60MPH)	3.1SEC

JIMENEZ NOVIA

Created by Ramon Jimenez, the Novia had a specification
to make any schoolboy go weak at the knees. An engine
with 16 cylinders and 80 valves was surely the stuff of
dreams – along with the 412kW (560bhp) it generated.
The four cylinder heads were courtesy of Yamaha. The
project sank before things had even got going.

COUNTRY OF ORIGIN	SPAIN
YEARS OF PRODUCTION	1995
DISPLACEMENT	4118CC (251CI)
CONFIGURATION	MID-MOUNTED W16
TRANSMISSION	6-SPEED MANUAL, REAR-WHEEL DRIVE
POWER	412KW (560BHP)
TORQUE	433NM (319LB FT)
TOP SPEED	380KM/H (236MPH) (CLAIMED)
0–96KM/H (0–60MPH)	3.0SEC (CLAIMED)

NISSAN SKYLINE R33

Continuing the tradition for labelling the range-topper the
GT-R, the R33 packed in the technology once more, but this
time it was also available as a rare four-door saloon as well as
a two-door coupé. There was even an R33-based estate offered,
called the Stagea.

COUNTRY OF ORIGIN	JAPAN
YEARS OF PRODUCTION	1995–98
DISPLACEMENT	2658CC (162CI)
CONFIGURATION	FRONT-MOUNTED 6-CYL
TRANSMISSION	5-SPEED MANUAL, FOUR-WHEEL DRIVE
POWER	203KW (276BHP)
TORQUE	367NM (271LB FT)
TOP SPEED	249KM/H (155MPH)
0–96KM/H (0–60MPH)	5.4SEC

FERRARI 550/575 MARANELLO

When you compare it with its 512TR/Testarossa
predecessor, the 500 is far more modern and far more
elegant – although not all Ferrari buyers want to be
anonymous. With an all-alloy V12 in the nose, weight
distribution was an issue, but the Maranello handled
much better than its forebear.

COUNTRY OF ORIGIN	ITALY
YEARS OF PRODUCTION	1996–2006
DISPLACEMENT	5474CC (334CI)
CONFIGURATION	FRONT-MOUNTED V12
TRANSMISSION	6-SPEED MANUAL, REAR-WHEEL DRIVE
POWER	352KW (479BHP)
TORQUE	568NM (419LB FT)
TOP SPEED	320KM/H (199MPH)
0–96KM/H (0–60MPH)	4.6SEC

Mercedes 300SL Gullwing

The 300SL was initially seen in 1952, appearing as a lightweight sports racer. The 300 denoted the engine's 3.0-litre capacity while the SL stood for Super-Leicht, or super-lightweight. Being a race car, the issue of cost didn't really figure in the 300SL's development, so when the decision was made to produce a road-going version, it was decided that building costs wouldn't be too much of a factor.

The 300SL's running gear was largely borrowed from the 300-series of saloons, albeit with some very significant changes along the way. The 3.0-litre straight-six mounted up front featured a single overhead camshaft, and in standard form it was capable of producing a healthy 128kW (174bhp). When tuned it was possible to extract well over 147kW (200bhp) from the same engine, and by 1957 around 1400 examples had been built, which is when the 300SL Roadster superseded the coupé. To allow for conventional doors, the chassis had to be redesigned, although losing the roof meant there had to be considerable stiffness on offer. Strengthening the chassis took its toll on the kerb weight, but partly to compensate the powerplant was retuned to liberate a few more horses – however, the open car was never as quick as the coupé.

To make the high-speed handling much safer, the rear suspension was redesigned, although it still incorporated swing axles in its design. By the time the Roadster appeared, the 300SL was getting outdated in some ways – it was now seen as a tourer rather than a sportscar. Disc brakes were fitted all round in 1961, but the writing was on the wall, and from 1963 there would be an all-new, much more modern (and affordable) range of SLs on offer.

COUNTRY OF ORIGIN	GERMANY
YEARS OF PRODUCTION	1954–57
DISPLACEMENT	2996CC (183CI)
CONFIGURATION	FRONT-MOUNTED 6-CYL
TRANSMISSION	4-SPEED MANUAL, REAR-WHEEL DRIVE
POWER	177KW (240BHP)
TORQUE	294NM (217LB FT)
TOP SPEED	225KM/H (140MPH)
0–96KM/H (0–60MPH)	8.8 SEC

LOTUS ESPRIT V8

Ever since its introduction in 1976, the Esprit was only ever fitted with four-cylinder powerplants. Some of these were incredibly powerful, but there's no substitute for cubic inches, so Lotus fitted its own 3.5-litre V8 from 1996. At the same time, the bodyshell was beefed up, with flared wheelarches and a huge rear wing.

COUNTRY OF ORIGIN	UK
YEARS OF PRODUCTION	1996–2004
DISPLACEMENT	3506CC (214CI)
CONFIGURATION	MID-MOUNTED V8
TRANSMISSION	5-SPEED MANUAL, REAR-WHEEL DRIVE
POWER	257KW (349BHP)
TORQUE	400NM (295LB FT)
TOP SPEED	249KM/H (155MPH)
0–96KM/H (0–60MPH)	5.9SEC

TVR CERBERA

The Cerbera was unusual for TVR, in that it was offered as a fixed-head only – other than that it was typical for the company. That meant a steel backbone chassis clothed in glassfibre panelling, with a V8 in the nose. It didn't use the old Rover unit, though; here was TVR's own AJP8 powerplant.

COUNTRY OF ORIGIN	UK
YEARS OF PRODUCTION	1996–2003
DISPLACEMENT	4185CC (255CI)
CONFIGURATION	FRONT-MOUNTED V8
TRANSMISSION	5-SPEED MANUAL, REAR-WHEEL DRIVE
POWER	257KW (350BHP)
TORQUE	434NM (320LB FT)
TOP SPEED	249KM/H (180MPH)
0–96KM/H (0–60MPH)	4.2SEC

FERRARI F50

Built to celebrate its 50th birthday in 1997 (hence the name), the F50 was intended to be the most outrageous road-going supercar ever devised by Ferrari. However, while the car looked as though it was from another planet, it was easier to drive than most of the Ferraris before it.

COUNTRY OF ORIGIN	ITALY
YEARS OF PRODUCTION	1997
DISPLACEMENT	4698CC (287CI)
CONFIGURATION	MID-MOUNTED V12
TRANSMISSION	6-SPEED MANUAL, REAR-WHEEL DRIVE
POWER	382KW (520BHP)
TORQUE	470NM (347LB FT)
TOP SPEED	323KM/H (201MPH)
0–96KM/H (0–60MPH)	3.7SEC

VOLKSWAGEN W12

If only Volkswagen had found the courage to put it into production, the W12 would have been one of the most amazing supercars ever built, with its mid-mounted W12 powerplant. But with the Audi R8, Bugatti Veyron and Lamborghini Gallardo all under development, the VW/Audi Group had enough supercars on its hands.

COUNTRY OF ORIGIN	GERMANY
YEARS OF PRODUCTION	1997–2001
DISPLACEMENT	5998CC (266CI)
CONFIGURATION	MID-MOUNTED W12
TRANSMISSION	6-SPEED MANUAL, FOUR-WHEEL DRIVE
POWER	434KW (590BHP)
TORQUE	620NM (457LB FT)
TOP SPEED	349KM/H (217MPH)
0–96KM/H (0–60MPH)	3.5SEC

AC SUPERBLOWER

It was a shame that AC had to give up on a name as iconic as the Cobra, but that's what happened when it adopted the Superblower tag for its venerable supercar. There was still an all-alloy bodyshell, now powered by a supercharged Ford V8 to give a potent 235kW (320bhp).

COUNTRY OF ORIGIN	UK
YEARS OF PRODUCTION	1998–
DISPLACEMENT	4942CC (302CI)
CONFIGURATION	FRONT-MOUNTED V8
TRANSMISSION	5-SPEED MANUAL, REAR-WHEEL DRIVE
POWER	235KW (320BHP)
TORQUE	522NM (385LB FT)
TOP SPEED	249KM/H (155MPH)
0–96KM/H (0–60MPH)	4.2SEC

ASTON MARTIN VANTAGE 600

Although the standard Vantage offered 404kW (550bhp), Aston Martin decided to produce an even more powerful edition in 1998, with an extra 37kW (50bhp). This was more than just a special edition Vantage, though; it was the final coachbuilt car to come from the famous British company, and the last traditional V8.

COUNTRY OF ORIGIN	UK
YEARS OF PRODUCTION	1998–2000
DISPLACEMENT	5340CC (326CI)
CONFIGURATION	FRONT-MOUNTED V8, TWIN SUPERCHARGERS
TRANSMISSION	5-SPEED MANUAL, REAR-WHEEL DRIVE
POWER	441KW (600BHP)
TORQUE	813NM (600LB FT)
TOP SPEED	322KM/H (200MPH)
0–96KM/H (0–60MPH)	3.9SEC

CALLAWAY C12

Take one Corvette C5, completely re-engineer its LS1 5.7-litre V8, then restyle the car so it's much more slippery, and you've got a Callaway C12. Well, you have once you've also upgraded the brakes with dustbin-lid-sized discs wrapped with wheels and tyres to suit.

COUNTRY OF ORIGIN	USA
YEARS OF PRODUCTION	1998–2002
DISPLACEMENT	5680CC (347CI)
CONFIGURATION	FRONT-MOUNTED V8
TRANSMISSION	6-SPEED MANUAL, REAR-WHEEL DRIVE
POWER	324KW (440BHP)
TORQUE	569NM (420LB FT)
TOP SPEED	303KM/H (188MPH)
0–96KM/H (0–60MPH)	4.6SEC

JAGUAR XKR

The XJS had never captured the imagination like the E-Type had done for Jaguar – what was needed was something with jaw-dropping looks and fabulous performance. The XK was that car, and in XKR, or supercharged form, it was even faster. There was a choice of coupé or cabriolet bodystyles.

COUNTRY OF ORIGIN	UK
YEARS OF PRODUCTION	1998–2006
DISPLACEMENT	4196CC (256CI)
CONFIGURATION	FRONT-MOUNTED V8
TRANSMISSION	AUTOMATIC, REAR-WHEEL DRIVE
POWER	294KW (400BHP)
TORQUE	553NM (408LB FT)
TOP SPEED	249KM/H (155MPH)
0–96KM/H (0–60MPH)	5.2SEC

MASERATI 3200GT

Another Italdesign masterpiece, this was the first Maserati to be built by Ferrari, the then-new owner of the marque. The car with perhaps the most memorable tail-lights ever, those slender boomerang-shaped LEDs were the epitome of elegance – but Maserati soon lost its nerve and fitted more conventional units, watering down the design in the process.

COUNTRY OF ORIGIN	ITALY
YEARS OF PRODUCTION	1998–2001
DISPLACEMENT	3217CC (196CI)
CONFIGURATION	FRONT-MOUNTED V8
TRANSMISSION	6-SPEED MANUAL, REAR-WHEEL DRIVE
POWER	272KW (370 BHP)
TORQUE	490NM (362LB FT)
TOP SPEED	280KM/H (174MPH)
0–96KM/H (0–60MPH)	5.1SEC

ASTON MARTIN DB7 VANTAGE

Considering the Jaguar XJS appeared in 1975, it was rather disappointing that an Aston Martin making its debut a quarter of a century later should be based on the same floorpan. That mattered little, though; the DB7 looked fantastic, had performance to match and proved to be a big leap forward over the DBS.

COUNTRY OF ORIGIN	UK
YEARS OF PRODUCTION	1999–2004
DISPLACEMENT	5935CC (362CI)
CONFIGURATION	FRONT-MOUNTED V12
TRANSMISSION	6-SPEED MANUAL, REAR-WHEEL DRIVE
POWER	309KW (420BHP)
TORQUE	542NM (400LB FT)
TOP SPEED	298KM/H (185MPH); VOLANTE 266KM/H (165MPH)
0–96KM/H (0–60MPH)	5.0SEC

NISSAN SKYLINE R34

With an even more aggressive look than before, the R34 GT-R featured a revised chassis compared with the R33, while the turbochargers were now steel turbine units and there was a stronger manual gearbox – this time with an extra ratio, so there were now six gears to choose from.

COUNTRY OF ORIGIN	JAPAN
YEARS OF PRODUCTION	1999–2002
DISPLACEMENT	2658CC (162CI)
CONFIGURATION	FRONT-MOUNTED 6-CYL
TRANSMISSION	6-SPEED MANUAL, FOUR-WHEEL DRIVE
POWER	203KW (276BHP)
TORQUE	392NM (289LB FT)
TOP SPEED	266KM/H (165MPH)
0–96KM/H (0–60MPH)	4.7SEC

ARIEL ATOM

It can be a real pain getting panels and doors to fit properly – which is why the Ariel Atom dispensed with these and featured a chassis that was almost entirely exposed to the elements. In fact, the Atom was effectively just a chassis with an engine; its power-to-weight ratio was consequently phenomenal.

COUNTRY OF ORIGIN	UK
YEARS OF PRODUCTION	2000–03
DISPLACEMENT	1998CC (122CI)
CONFIGURATION	MID-MOUNTED 4-CYL
TRANSMISSION	6-SPEED MANUAL, REAR-WHEEL DRIVE
POWER	221KW (300BHP)
TORQUE	220NM (162LB FT)
TOP SPEED	249KM/H (155MPH)
0–96KM/H (0–60MPH)	3.3SEC

BMW Z8

Originally seen as the Z07 concept, the Z8 started out as a styling exercise that updated the legendary 507 from the same company. But when the concept caused a sensation at the 1997 Tokyo Motor Show, the car was put into production, with an M5 engine and an all-alloy bodyshell.

COUNTRY OF ORIGIN	GERMANY
YEARS OF PRODUCTION	2000–03
DISPLACEMENT	4941CC (302CI)
CONFIGURATION	FRONT-MOUNTED V8
TRANSMISSION	6-SPEED MANUAL, REAR-WHEEL DRIVE
POWER	294KW (400BHP)
TORQUE	500NM (369LB FT)
TOP SPEED	249KM/H (155MPH)
0–96KM/H (0–60MPH)	4.8SEC

MERCEDES CLK55 AMG

Another monster from the AMG stable, the CLK55 was created by transplanting AMG's heavily reworked 5.5-litre V8 into Mercedes' regular CLK. Offered as a coupé or convertible, the car was superseded by the revised CLK in 2002 – which in turn was replaced by the CLK63 in 2006.

COUNTRY OF ORIGIN	GERMANY
YEARS OF PRODUCTION	2000–02
DISPLACEMENT	5439CC (332CI)
CONFIGURATION	FRONT-MOUNTED V8
TRANSMISSION	6-SPEED SEMI-AUTO, REAR-WHEEL DRIVE
POWER	252KW (342BHP)
TORQUE	510NM (376LB FT)
TOP SPEED	249KM/H (155MPH)
0–96KM/H (0–60MPH)	5.1SEC

MORGAN AERO 8

With a range of cars that looked as though they were decades old – largely because they were – what Morgan needed was something new. It had a reputation, however, for producing cars that looked ancient, so the BMW-engined Aero 8 was the solution, as it looked old but featured cutting-edge construction.

COUNTRY OF ORIGIN	UK
YEARS OF PRODUCTION	2000–
DISPLACEMENT	4398CC (268CI)
CONFIGURATION	FRONT-MOUNTED V8
TRANSMISSION	6-SPEED MANUAL, REAR-WHEEL DRIVE
POWER	245KW (333BHP)
TORQUE	449NM (331LB FT)
TOP SPEED	274KM/H (170MPH)
0–96KM/H (0–60MPH)	4.3SEC

PANOZ ESPERANTE

The second car to come from Panoz, after the Roadster, the Esperante was more of a grand tourer than a no-frills sportscar. However, due to its hand-built nature, pretty much any specification was possible, with various engine swaps offered. The car was based around alloy body and chassis units.

COUNTRY OF ORIGIN	USA
YEARS OF PRODUCTION	2000–
DISPLACEMENT	4601CC (281CI)
CONFIGURATION	FRONT-MOUNTED V8
TRANSMISSION	5-SPEED MANUAL, REAR-WHEEL DRIVE
POWER	235KW (320BHP)
TORQUE	427NM (315LB FT)
TOP SPEED	249KM/H (155MPH)
0–96KM/H (0–60MPH)	4.2SEC

SUBARU IMPREZA P1

While most Imprezas were four-door saloons or five-door estates, the P1 was based on Subaru's two-door saloon bodyshell and was available only with metallic blue paintwork. Not only was this bodyshell much stiffer than its four-door counterpart, but it also looked far more sporting.

COUNTRY OF ORIGIN	JAPAN
YEARS OF PRODUCTION	2000–01
DISPLACEMENT	1994CC (122CI)
CONFIGURATION	FRONT-MOUNTED FLAT-4
TRANSMISSION	5-SPEED MANUAL, FOUR-WHEEL DRIVE
POWER	203KW (276BHP)
TORQUE	353NM (260LB FT)
TOP SPEED	241KM/H (150MPH)
0–96KM/H (0–60MPH)	4.9SEC

TVR TUSCAN SPEED SIX

TVR's Tuscan was a force to be reckoned with on the roads of the 1960s and on the race tracks of the 1990s, so the brand was revived for a new supercar that went on sale in 2000. Powered by TVR's own straight-six, the Tuscan received a minor facelift in 2005.

COUNTRY OF ORIGIN	UK
YEARS OF PRODUCTION	2000–
DISPLACEMENT	3996CC (244CI)
CONFIGURATION	FRONT-MOUNTED 6-CYL
TRANSMISSION	5-SPEED MANUAL, REAR-WHEEL DRIVE
POWER	287KW (390BHP)
TORQUE	420NM (310LB FT)
TOP SPEED	314KM/H (195MPH)
0–96KM/H (0–60MPH)	3.8SEC

ULTIMA GTR

Available as a fully built car or in kit form, the Ultima GTR broke the world record for the fastest accelerating car, as it was capable of sprinting to 161km/h (100mph) from a standstill in just 5.3 seconds. Available in open or closed versions, up to 592kW (720bhp) was available.

COUNTRY OF ORIGIN	UK
YEARS OF PRODUCTION	2000–
DISPLACEMENT	6277CC (383CI)
CONFIGURATION	MID-MOUNTED V8
TRANSMISSION	5-SPEED MANUAL, REAR-WHEEL DRIVE
POWER	393KW (534BHP)
TORQUE	716NM (528LB FT)
TOP SPEED	372KM/H (231MPH)
0–96KM/H (0–60MPH)	2.7SEC

ASTON MARTIN VANQUISH

It looked like a souped-up DB7, but the Vanquish was far more than that because it was a completely new car. It was also the fastest car ever to come out of the gates of Aston Martin, thanks to a 48-valve quad-cam V12 powerplant that offered 338kW (460bhp) – or 382kW (520bhp) in Vanquish S form.

COUNTRY OF ORIGIN	UK
YEARS OF PRODUCTION	2001–07
DISPLACEMENT	5935CC (362CI)
CONFIGURATION	FRONT-MOUNTED V12
TRANSMISSION	6-SPEED MANUAL, REAR-WHEEL DRIVE
POWER	382KW (520BHP)
TORQUE	578NM (426LB FT)
TOP SPEED	322KM/H (200MPH)
0–96KM/H (0–60MPH)	4.8SEC

B-ENGINEERING EDONIS

You'd think a Bugatti EB110 Super Sport didn't need too much in the way of improvements, but that isn't what B-Engineering thought. This company comprehensively re-engineered the Bugatti and restyled it into oblivion, effectively carrying over little more than the original carbon fibre bodytub and V12 powerplant.

COUNTRY OF ORIGIN	ITALY
YEARS OF PRODUCTION	2001
DISPLACEMENT	3760CC (229CI)
CONFIGURATION	MID-MOUNTED V12
TRANSMISSION	6-SPEED MANUAL, REAR-WHEEL DRIVE
POWER	500KW (680BHP)
TORQUE	735NM (542LB FT)
TOP SPEED	365KM/H (227MPH)
0–96KM/H (0–60MPH)	3.9SEC

BMW M3 E46

Looking less understated than the second-generation M3, the E46, or third-generation car, was powered by a 3.2-litre version of the straight-six powerplant of its predecessor. However, power was increased while the four-door saloon option was dropped; BMW focused on coupé and convertible sales instead.

COUNTRY OF ORIGIN	GERMANY
YEARS OF PRODUCTION	2001–
DISPLACEMENT	3241CC (198CI)
CONFIGURATION	FRONT-MOUNTED 6-CYL
TRANSMISSION	5-SPEED MANUAL, REAR-WHEEL DRIVE
POWER	252KW (343BHP)
TORQUE	365NM (269LB FT)
TOP SPEED	249KM/H (155MPH)
0–96KM/H (0–60MPH)	4.8SEC

LAMBORGHINI MURCIELAGO

The key requirements behind the Murcielago were top-notch performance and handling, with the only significant component carried over from the Diablo being the powerplant. It didn't take long for Roadster, 40th Anniversary and R-GT versions to appear, while the LP640 appeared in 2006, a new derivative even more extreme than before.

COUNTRY OF ORIGIN	ITALY
YEARS OF PRODUCTION	2001–
DISPLACEMENT	6192CC (378CI)
CONFIGURATION	MID-MOUNTED V12
TRANSMISSION	5-SPEED MANUAL, FOUR-WHEEL DRIVE
POWER	427KW (580BHP)
TORQUE	649NM (479LB FT)
TOP SPEED	330KM/H (205MPH)
0–96KM/H (0–60MPH)	3.6SEC

SALEEN S7

Saleen made its name tuning Mustangs for the road and track, but in 2001 it launched its own supercar to take on the greats. Designed to be more usable and less costly to run than the typical supercar, the S7 featured a simple all-alloy V8 supplied by Ford but heavily reworked by Saleen.

COUNTRY OF ORIGIN	USA
YEARS OF PRODUCTION	2001–
DISPLACEMENT	6998CC (427CI)
CONFIGURATION	MID-MOUNTED V8
TRANSMISSION	6-SPEED MANUAL, REAR-WHEEL DRIVE
POWER	405KW (550BHP)
TORQUE	712NM (525LB FT)
TOP SPEED	386KM/H (240MPH) (CLAIMED)
0–96KM/H (0–60MPH)	3.3SEC

Ultimate Dream Car 3:
Lotus Seven

The car that inspired hundreds of replicas, the Lotus Seven is one of the most highly focused driver's cars ever. Not only did it put its occupants close to the action with a minimum of cosseting, but it also reduced mass to a minimum in a bid to offer the best possible power-to-weight ratio. Most importantly though, it brought in much-needed cash for Lotus, which was losing money on every Elite it was also producing at the same time.

The Seven was clearly a development of the Six, which was also fitted with cycle wings and offered no concessions to the comfort of its occupants. The Six may have been basic, but when it came to handling there was nothing that could touch it – and the Seven was dynamically even better.

The Seven consisted of a multi-tubular frame, around which was an aluminium body shell. There were cycle wings and no doors; the sides were cut away instead for easier access. Weather protection was little more than an afterthought; the idea was that as long as you could keep moving, you'd stay dry enough!

All Sevens were supplied as kits, with Lotus providing a chassis and bodyshell, along with all the mechanical parts for the car to be assembled at home. This meant the Seven could be bought far more cheaply, with purchase tax not being levied on home-built cars.

Lotus bought all the mechanical components in, with a multitude of engines being used. These ranged from Ford's ancient side-valve unit through to all-alloy Coventry-Climax racing units. The front suspension was independent, while at the rear there was a rear axle that was controlled by coil springs, radius arms and a Panhard rod.

Between 1957 and 1973 there were four basic series of Seven, with all sorts of different mechanical specifications being offered. Even when Lotus stopped building the car it could still be bought new though, thanks to Caterham acquiring the rights.

COUNTRY OF ORIGIN	UK
YEARS OF PRODUCTION	1957–73
DISPLACEMENT	1172CC (72CI)
CONFIGURATION	FRONT-MOUNTED 4-CYL
TRANSMISSION	4-SPEED MANUAL, REAR-WHEEL DRIVE
POWER	29KW (40BHP)
TORQUE	79NM (58LB FT)
TOP SPEED	122KM/H (76MPH)
0–96KM/H (0–60MPH)	17.8SEC

FARBOUD GTS

Continuing where the Farboud GT had left off, the GTS was also powered by a twin-turbo V6 from the Audi stable. The car's design was toned down from the GT, but still there were major production issues, which led to the project being sold to Chris Marsh in 2005.

COUNTRY OF ORIGIN	UK
YEARS OF PRODUCTION	2005–
DISPLACEMENT	2968CC (181CI)
CONFIGURATION	MID-MOUNTED V6
TRANSMISSION	6-SPEED MANUAL, REAR-WHEEL DRIVE
POWER	276KW (375BHP)
TORQUE	407NM (300LB FT)
TOP SPEED	274KM/H (170MPH)
0–96KM/H (0–60MPH)	3.8SEC

FERRARI FXX

Just 20 FXXs were built, with buyers able to use the cars on race tracks only, as it was not homologated for road use. To boost power to 588kW (800bhp), the V12 engine was taken up to 6.3 litres while the paddle-shift gearbox could swap ratios in just a tenth of a second.

COUNTRY OF ORIGIN	ITALY
YEARS OF PRODUCTION	2005
DISPLACEMENT	6262CC (382CI)
CONFIGURATION	MID-MOUNTED FLAT-12
TRANSMISSION	6-SPEED SEMI-AUTO, REAR-WHEEL DRIVE
POWER	588KW (800BHP)
TORQUE	690NM (509LB FT)
TOP SPEED	N/A
0–96KM/H (0–60MPH)	N/A

FORD GT

Launched to mark a hundred years of Ford, the GT was an updated edition of perhaps its most iconic car ever – the GT40. However, while it looked much the same, the car was entirely new, with a fresh V8 engine and ultra-modern construction methods. Just 4038 examples were built.

COUNTRY OF ORIGIN	USA
YEARS OF PRODUCTION	2005–06
DISPLACEMENT	5409CC (330CI)
CONFIGURATION	MID-MOUNTED V8
TRANSMISSION	5-SPEED MANUAL, REAR-WHEEL DRIVE
POWER	405KW (550BHP)
TORQUE	678NM (500LB FT)
TOP SPEED	330KM/H (205MPH)
0–96KM/H (0–60MPH)	3.8SEC

INVICTA S1

Reviving a badge that had not been seen since the 1940s, the Invicta was claimed to incorporate the world's first single-piece carbon-fibre monocoque. That gave it strength and lightness, while power with reliability were offered thanks to Ford's quad-cam 4.6-litre V8 installed in the nose – which could be tuned to give 600bhp.

COUNTRY OF ORIGIN	GB
YEARS OF PRODUCTION	2005–
DISPLACEMENT	4601CC (280CC)
CONFIGURATION	FRONT-MOUNTED V8
TRANSMISSION	5-SPEED MANUAL, REAR-WHEEL DRIVE
POWER	239KW (325BHP)
TORQUE	300LB FT
TOP SPEED	273KM/H (170MPH)
0–96KM/H (0–60MPH)	5.0SEC

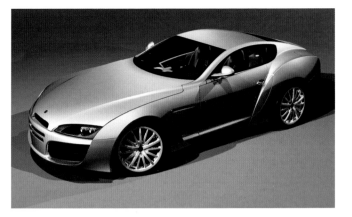

LARAKI BORAC

The Borac was Laraki's take on the grand tourer theme, powered by the same Mercedes-sourced 6-litre V12 as the Fulgura. However, while the Fulgura had 500kW (680bhp) on tap, the Borac's unit was normally aspirated so it could muster no more than a rather weedy 397kW (540bhp).

COUNTRY OF ORIGIN	MOROCCO
YEARS OF PRODUCTION	2005–
DISPLACEMENT	6000CC (366CI)
CONFIGURATION	MID-MOUNTED V12, QUAD-TURBO
TRANSMISSION	6-SPEED MANUAL, REAR-WHEEL DRIVE
POWER	397KW (540BHP)
TORQUE	750NM (553LB FT)
TOP SPEED	311KM/H (193MPH) (CLAIMED)
0–100KM/H (0–62MPH)	4.5SEC (CLAIMED)

LARAKI FULGURA

You could be forgiven for never having heard of the Moroccan supercar company Laraki, because it's debatable whether or not any of its cars were ever actually delivered to paying customers. However, the Fulgura was fast, stylish and beautifully built – if rather lacking in heritage for the money asked.

COUNTRY OF ORIGIN	MOROCCO
YEARS OF PRODUCTION	2005–
DISPLACEMENT	6000CC (366CI)
CONFIGURATION	MID-MOUNTED V12, QUAD-TURBO
TRANSMISSION	6-SPEED MANUAL, REAR-WHEEL DRIVE
POWER	500KW (680BHP)
TORQUE	750NM (553LB FT)
TOP SPEED	352KM/H (219MPH) (CLAIMED)
0–100KM/H (0–62MPH)	3.4SEC (CLAIMED)

MASERATI MC12

Produced to allow Maserati to compete in the FIA GT championship, the MC12 was based on the Ferrari Enzo but was longer, wider and taller. There were 50 cars built: 25 for competition and a further 25 for sale to customers who wanted to use them on the road.

COUNTRY OF ORIGIN	ITALY
YEARS OF PRODUCTION	2005
DISPLACEMENT	5998CC (366CI)
CONFIGURATION	MID-MOUNTED V12
TRANSMISSION	6-SPEED SEQUENTIAL MANUAL, REAR-WHEEL DRIVE
POWER	457KW (622BHP)
TORQUE	651NM (480LB FT)
TOP SPEED	330KM/H (205MPH)
0–96KM/H (0–60MPH)	3.8SEC

MAYBACH EXELERO

It looks like something from a Batman film, but the Exelero was actually a test bed for tyre manufacturer Fulda to develop its products. Based on a Maybach 57S platform, the Exelero's twin-turbo V12 powerplant was upgraded to generate a massive 515kW (700bhp), allowing the car to top 352km/h (219mph).

COUNTRY OF ORIGIN	GERMANY
YEARS OF PRODUCTION	2005
DISPLACEMENT	5908CC (361CI)
CONFIGURATION	FRONT-MOUNTED V12
TRANSMISSION	5-SPEED AUTO
POWER	515KW (700BHP)
TORQUE	1020NM (752LB FT)
TOP SPEED	352KM/H (219MPH)
0–96KM/H (0–60MPH)	4.4SEC

MERCEDES CL65 AMG

Looking much like the entry-level CL500, the CL65 was one of the most understated yet overpowered cars available in the Mercedes range. With a hand-built twin-turbocharged 6-litre V12 in the nose, the CL65 could sprint to 96km/h (60mph) in under four seconds, with four occupants along for the ride.

COUNTRY OF ORIGIN	GERMANY
YEARS OF PRODUCTION	2005–06
DISPLACEMENT	5980CC (365CI)
CONFIGURATION	FRONT-MOUNTED V12
TRANSMISSION	6-SPEED SEMI-AUTO, REAR-WHEEL DRIVE
POWER	450KW (612BHP)
TORQUE	999NM (737LB FT)
TOP SPEED	249KM/H (155MPH)
0–96KM/H (0–60MPH)	3.8SEC

MITSUBISHI EVO IX FQ360

The first few generations of Mitsubishi Evo were a well-kept secret, but by the time the ninth generation was unveiled, this was well and truly the company's halo model. The Evo seemed able to defy the laws of physics, such was its ability to cover ground at an apparently impossible rate.

COUNTRY OF ORIGIN	JAPAN
YEARS OF PRODUCTION	2005–
DISPLACEMENT	1997CC (121CI)
CONFIGURATION	FRONT-MOUNTED 4-CYL
TRANSMISSION	6-SPEED MANUAL, FOUR-WHEEL DRIVE
POWER	269KW (366BHP)
TORQUE	492NM (363LB FT)
TOP SPEED	252KM/H (157MPH)
0–96KM/H (0–60MPH)	3.9SEC

PAGANI ZONDA F

The Zonda F (for Fangio) featured a 7.3-litre engine with 437kW (594bhp) and 759Nm (560lb ft) of torque. But it wasn't all about power; 50kg (110lb) was taken from the weight, while there was a ceramic braking system, and a one-piece rear spoiler that dramatically increased rear downforce at high speed.

COUNTRY OF ORIGIN	ITALY
YEARS OF PRODUCTION	2005–
DISPLACEMENT	7291CC (445CI)
CONFIGURATION	MID-MOUNTED V12
TRANSMISSION	6-SPEED MANUAL, REAR-WHEEL DRIVE
POWER	437KW (594BHP)
TORQUE	759NM (560LB FT)
TOP SPEED	344KM/H (214MPH)
0–96KM/H (0–60MPH)	3.5SEC

TVR SAGARIS

Based on the TVR T350, the Sagaris first appeared in 2003 but wasn't offered for sale until 2005. As with all other cars from this tiny British company, there were no driver aids to help put the power down, while anti-lock brakes and airbags were also conspicuously absent from the spec sheets.

COUNTRY OF ORIGIN	UK
YEARS OF PRODUCTION	2005–
DISPLACEMENT	3996CC (244CI)
CONFIGURATION	FRONT-MOUNTED 6-CYL
TRANSMISSION	5-SPEED MANUAL, REAR-WHEEL DRIVE
POWER	294KW (400BHP)
TORQUE	475NM (350LB FT)
TOP SPEED	274KM/H (170MPH)
0–96KM/H (0–60MPH)	3.9SEC

BMW M6

Mechanically the same as the contemporary M5, the M6 was even faster thanks to a lower kerb weight. This was in part due to a carbon fibre roof that also helped to reduce the centre of gravity, ensuring that rolls in the corners were less of an issue than they might otherwise have been.

COUNTRY OF ORIGIN	GERMANY
YEARS OF PRODUCTION	2006–
DISPLACEMENT	4999CC (305CI)
CONFIGURATION	FRONT-MOUNTED V10
TRANSMISSION	6-SPEED SEMI-AUTO, REAR-WHEEL DRIVE
POWER	373KW (507BHP)
TORQUE	519NM (383LB FT)
TOP SPEED	249KM/H (155MPH)
0–96KM/H (0–60MPH)	4.6SEC

BMW Z4M COUPÉ

While the Z3 Coupé had been an acquired taste – at least as far as the design was concerned – BMW was keen to make the Z4 Coupé much more mainstream. Porsche needed some healthy competition for its Cayman, so BMW created a car that was more of a coupé than an estate.

COUNTRY OF ORIGIN	GERMANY
YEARS OF PRODUCTION	2006–
DISPLACEMENT	3246CC (198CI)
CONFIGURATION	FRONT-MOUNTED 6-CYL
TRANSMISSION	6-SPEED SEMI-AUTO, REAR-WHEEL DRIVE
POWER	249KW (338BHP)
TORQUE	365NM (269LB FT)
TOP SPEED	249KM/H (155MPH)
0–96KM/H (0–60MPH)	5.0SEC

CHEVROLET CORVETTE Z06

The 2006 Corvette Z06 was the fastest Corvette ever to come out of Chevrolet. With a 377kW (512bhp) V8 installed in the nose of this glassfibre supercar, 322km/h (200mph) was almost within reach. This performance was partly down to a strict diet; the Z06 was built around an alloy backbone chassis in place of the usual steel affair.

COUNTRY OF ORIGIN	USA
YEARS OF PRODUCTION	2006–
DISPLACEMENT	7011CC (428CI)
CONFIGURATION	FRONT-MOUNTED V8
TRANSMISSION	6-SPEED MANUAL, REAR-WHEEL DRIVE
POWER	377KW (512BHP)
TORQUE	637NM (470LB FT)
TOP SPEED	320KM/H (199MPH)
0–96KM/H (0–60MPH)	3.9SEC

GUMPERT APOLLO

The name may have been unfortunate, but that didn't make the Gumpert any less desirable. With a twin-turbo Audi-sourced V8 shoehorned into the middle of a carbon fibre bodyshell, the Apollo was searingly quick – as it needed to be if it was to beat the contemporary crop of established supercar names.

COUNTRY OF ORIGIN	GERMANY
YEARS OF PRODUCTION	2006–
DISPLACEMENT	4163CC (254CI)
CONFIGURATION	MID-MOUNTED V8
TRANSMISSION	6-SPEED SEMI-AUTO, REAR-WHEEL DRIVE
POWER	478KW (650BHP)
TORQUE	850NM (627LB FT)
TOP SPEED	359KM/H (223MPH)
0–96KM/H (0–60MPH)	3.0SEC

JAGUAR XKR

The original XK looked great but was never very involving to drive – this second-generation car addressed that issue while also offering much better packaging and a far more exciting soundtrack. With its ultra-rigid alloy spaceframe and supercharged V8, performance and agility came in spades.

COUNTRY OF ORIGIN	UK
YEARS OF PRODUCTION	2006–
DISPLACEMENT	4196CC (256CI)
CONFIGURATION	FRONT-MOUNTED V8
TRANSMISSION	6-SPEED SEMI-AUTO, REAR-WHEEL DRIVE
POWER	304KW (414BHP)
TORQUE	560NM (413LB FT)
TOP SPEED	249KM/H (155MPH)
0–96KM/H (0–60MPH)	4.9SEC

NOBLE M15

Noble was already used to producing extremely fast supercars, and some of them were rather costly, but the M15 launched the company into a whole new area. Competing with the likes of Porsche and even Ferrari, the M15 was certainly quick but had just a V6 engine and no heritage to draw on.

COUNTRY OF ORIGIN	UK
YEARS OF PRODUCTION	2006–
DISPLACEMENT	2968CC (181CI)
CONFIGURATION	MID-MOUNTED V6
TRANSMISSION	6-SPEED MANUAL, REAR-WHEEL DRIVE
POWER	335KW (455BHP)
TORQUE	617NM (455LB FT)
TOP SPEED	278KM/H (173MPH)
0–96KM/H (0–60MPH)	3.5SEC

ALFA ROMEO 8C COMPETIZIONE

Alfa Romeo originally unveiled the 8C Competizione in concept form at the 2003 Frankfurt Motor Show. Then everything went quiet, but in 2006 the company announced that it would build 500 coupé versions while a convertible would follow later, all fitted with the same Maserati-sourced 4.7-litre V8.

COUNTRY OF ORIGIN	ITALY
YEARS OF PRODUCTION	2007–
DISPLACEMENT	4691CC (286CI)
CONFIGURATION	FRONT-MOUNTED V8
TRANSMISSION	6-SPEED MANUAL, REAR-WHEEL DRIVE
POWER	327KW (444BHP)
TORQUE	470NM (347LB FT)
TOP SPEED	N/A
0–96KM/H (0–60MPH)	N/A

AUDI R8

If Lamborghini hadn't been part of the Audi stable, the R8 almost certainly wouldn't have happened. That's because the R8 was a more highly developed version of the Lamborghini Gallardo, although it didn't initially feature that car's 5-litre V10 engine; there was a 4.2-litre V8 unit fitted instead.

COUNTRY OF ORIGIN	GERMANY
YEARS OF PRODUCTION	2007–
DISPLACEMENT	4163CC (254CI)
CONFIGURATION	MID-MOUNTED V10
TRANSMISSION	6-SPEED SEMI-AUTO, REAR-WHEEL DRIVE
POWER	304KW (414BHP)
TORQUE	430NM (317LB FT)
TOP SPEED	301KM/H (187MPH)
0–96KM/H (0–60MPH)	4.6SEC

CAPARO T1

Set up by a team that was involved in the development of the McLaren F1, the Caparo T1 was a supercar like no other. There was never any suggestion of any kind of practicality – this was a no-frills car designed to go as fast as possible, with its bespoke V8 engine and carbon fibre/alloy monocoque.

COUNTRY OF ORIGIN	UK
YEARS OF PRODUCTION	2007–
DISPLACEMENT	2400CC (148CI)
CONFIGURATION	MID-MOUNTED V8
TRANSMISSION	6-SPEED SEMI-AUTO, REAR-WHEEL DRIVE
POWER	353kW (480BHP)
TORQUE	N/A
TOP SPEED	322KM/H (200MPH)
0–96KM/H (0–60MPH)	2.5SEC

MASERATI GRANTURISMO

The GranTurismo may have borrowed all sorts of elements from various other grand tourers, but its looks remained sensational. With its sensuous curves, long bonnet and muscular haunches, the Maserati had the show – and the go too, courtesy of the 4.2-litre V8 up front.

COUNTRY OF ORIGIN	GB
YEARS OF PRODUCTION	2007–
DISPLACEMENT	4244CC (259CI)
CONFIGURATION	FRONT-MOUNTED V8
TRANSMISSION	6-SPEED SEMI-AUTO, REAR-WHEEL DRIVE
POWER	294kW (400BHP)
TORQUE	460NM (339LB FT)
TOP SPEED	284KM/H (177MPH)
0–96KM/H (0–60MPH)	5.2SEC

TRAMONTANA

Tramontana burst onto the scene at the 2005 Geneva Motor Show, with its oddly styled supercar. Featuring a mid-mounted V12 with two turbochargers, the company claimed the car was good for around 299km/h (186mph) – which seemed rather conservative when you consider that it was claimed to have 530kW (720bhp) on tap.

COUNTRY OF ORIGIN	SPAIN
YEARS OF PRODUCTION	2007–
DISPLACEMENT	5500CC (336CI)
CONFIGURATION	MID-MOUNTED V12
TRANSMISSION	AUTOMATIC, REAR-WHEEL DRIVE
POWER	530kW (720BHP)
TORQUE	824NM (608LB FT)
TOP SPEED	299KM/H (186MPH)
0–96KM/H (0–60MPH)	3.9SEC

Mass Market

Mass-produced cars should, in theory, be at the opposite end of the scale from anything that somebody might dream about, but that's definitely not the case. Many of the most common cars of decades ago have become incredibly collectible; sometimes it's because there are now few survivors or it may be because the car in question rewrote the rules or created a new type of car. Then there's simply the nostalgia factor; many people who grow up with a mainstream car will try to track down an example of the same make and model in later years.

Think about this latter category and key vehicles such as the Ford Model T and Austin Seven are ripe for the picking; millions of people grew up with these icons, and while they were mere transport when new, their classic status makes them far more desirable in the twenty-first century. With more and more of us buying a classic because of its ability to transport us to a bygone age, it's entirely predictable that great numbers of mainstream classics such as the Volkswagen Beetle and Citroen 2CV will make an appearance.

While vehicles such as the 2CV and Beetle must be included because of their mass appeal, some of the other selections are here because they truly broke down the barriers. When Citroen's Traction Avant was introduced in 1934, the concept of a mass-production front-wheel drive car was truly fantastic. It may not have been the world's first car to have drive to the front, but it was the first one that people could go out and buy in significant numbers – if they could afford it, of course. For while the Citroen was a mass-produced vehicle, buying any sort of car before World War II was financially out of reach for most.

This is why models like the Morris Bullnose and Ford Model A were so important; these were true economy cars that put the world on wheels. In the other chapters, you'll find cars that were contemporaries of the Ford and Morris, which were much more exclusive and far more desirable. But it was the Model A and the Bullnose that made dreams come true in the 1920s and 1930s; purchasing a car of any kind was out of reach for many, but these were the cars that ensured more people than ever could buy a car of their own.

It's not just about sheer numbers, though; many of the cars in this chapter were innovators. We've already mentioned the Traction Avant, but there were also the Ford Model T, Land Rover, Renault 16 and Plymouth Voyager. All radically different from each other, they each changed the automotive landscape forever, in their own ways.

The Ford Model T wasn't the world's first mass-produced car, but Henry Ford did make massive strides in building the perfect production line, with the Model T available at a far more affordable price than anyone else could afford to charge. It's the same story where Land Rover is concerned; its four-wheel drive Series 1 of 1948 wasn't the first car to have drive to each corner, but it was tough, practical and capable of going just about anywhere, creating a new niche in the process. That's why the Renault 16 and Plymouth Voyager are also included; they introduced car buyers to the concept of the hatchback and the people carrier respectively, proving that mainstream needn't mean staid.

The R360 was Mazda's first car; the company previously focused on motorbikes.

FORD MODEL T

If it hadn't been for the Model T, many Americans of the 1920s would have had extremely limited mobility. The car put America on wheels, thanks to its affordability and reliability, while there was also a wide range of bodystyles offered, from two- and four-door saloons to tourers, coupés and even pick-ups.

COUNTRY OF ORIGIN	USA
YEARS OF PRODUCTION	1911–27
DISPLACEMENT	2890CC (176CI)
CONFIGURATION	FRONT-MOUNTED 4-CYL
TRANSMISSION	2-SPEED MANUAL, REAR-WHEEL DRIVE
POWER	15kW (20BHP)
TORQUE	111Nm (82LB FT)
TOP SPEED	68KM/H (42MPH)
0–96KM/H (0–60MPH)	N/A

MORRIS BULLNOSE

Officially badged the 'Oxford' and 'Cowley', the Bullnose earned its nickname because of the distinctive rounded cowling on top of the radiator. The Cowley was the cheaper car of the two, but both were designed to bring motoring to the masses.

COUNTRY OF ORIGIN	UK
YEARS OF PRODUCTION	1913–26
DISPLACEMENT	1495CC (91CI)
CONFIGURATION	FRONT-MOUNTED 4-CYL
TRANSMISSION	3-SPEED MANUAL, REAR-WHEEL DRIVE
POWER	18kW (24BHP)
TORQUE	N/A
TOP SPEED	89KM/H (55MPH)
0–96KM/H (0–60MPH)	N/A

AUSTIN SEVEN

The car that launched both Nissan and BMW, Austin's Seven was an amazingly important vehicle because of the number of people to which it gave mobility. Herbert Austin realized that there was a need for a small, basic, affordable car – he was right, because demand for the Seven was overwhelming.

COUNTRY OF ORIGIN	UK
YEARS OF PRODUCTION	1922–39
DISPLACEMENT	747CC (46CI)
CONFIGURATION	FRONT-MOUNTED 4-CYL
TRANSMISSION	3-SPEED MANUAL, REAR-WHEEL DRIVE
POWER	7kW (10BHP)
TORQUE	N/A
TOP SPEED	83KM/H (52MPH)
0–96KM/H (0–60MPH)	N/A

BMW DIXI

Dixi was originally an independent car maker, which started production in 1904. It was sold to BMW in 1928, a year after it had acquired the rights to build the Austin Seven under licence. This car was officially known as the 3/15 DA-1, and saloon, roadster tourer and coupé versions were offered.

COUNTRY OF ORIGIN	GERMANY
YEARS OF PRODUCTION	1927–31
DISPLACEMENT	747CC (46CI)
CONFIGURATION	FRONT-MOUNTED 4-CYL
TRANSMISSION	3-SPEED MANUAL, REAR-WHEEL DRIVE
POWER	11kW (15BHP)
TORQUE	N/A
TOP SPEED	72KM/H (45MPH)
0–96KM/H (0–60MPH)	N/A

FORD MODEL A

The Model T may have put the world on wheels, but it couldn't go on forever. The Model A succeeded it, and it was a far more advanced car with its all-new engine, four-wheel braking and an electric starter as standard. The cars were built in the USA as well as the UK.

COUNTRY OF ORIGIN	USA
YEARS OF PRODUCTION	1928–32
DISPLACEMENT	3293CC (201CI)
CONFIGURATION	FRONT-MOUNTED 4-CYL
TRANSMISSION	3-SPEED MANUAL, REAR-WHEEL DRIVE
POWER	29KW (40BHP)
TORQUE	174NM (128LB FT)
TOP SPEED	105KM/H (65MPH)
0–96KM/H (0–60MPH)	32.0SEC

HUDSON TERRAPLANE

It was difficult for Hudson to compete with the big US car makers, but it did so by producing cars that were more technically advanced. The Terraplane featured a bodyshell welded to the chassis for better stiffness, while there were hydraulic brakes all round, with a mechanical back-up brake in case of main brakes failure.

COUNTRY OF ORIGIN	USA
YEARS OF PRODUCTION	1932–39
DISPLACEMENT	3474CC (212CI)
CONFIGURATION	FRONT-MOUNTED 6-CYL
TRANSMISSION	3-SPEED MANUAL, REAR-WHEEL DRIVE
POWER	65KW (88BHP)
TORQUE	N/A
TOP SPEED	129KM/H (80MPH)
0–96KM/H (0–60MPH)	23.2SEC

ADLER TRUMPF JUNIOR

Taking its name from the German word for eagle (Adler), the Adler Trumpf Junior was an economy car that was equipped with front-wheel drive, something that was highly unusual for the time.

COUNTRY OF ORIGIN	GERMANY
YEARS OF PRODUCTION	1934–41
DISPLACEMENT	995CC (61CI)
CONFIGURATION	FRONT-MOUNTED 4-CYL
TRANSMISSION	4-SPEED MANUAL, FRONT-WHEEL DRIVE
POWER	18KW (25BHP)
TORQUE	N/A
TOP SPEED	96KM/H (60MPH)
0–96KM/H (0–60MPH)	N/A

CITROEN TRACTION AVANT

Citroen never used to be shy about producing truly innovative cars, and it was the Traction Avant that gave the company this reputation. Here was the world's first mass-produced car with front-wheel drive. Citroen also dispensed with the chassis; there was monocoque construction instead, complete with air-cushioned engine mountings.

COUNTRY OF ORIGIN	FRANCE
YEARS OF PRODUCTION	1935–57
DISPLACEMENT	1911CC (117CI)
CONFIGURATION	FRONT-MOUNTED 4-CYL
TRANSMISSION	3-SPEED MANUAL, FRONT-WHEEL DRIVE
POWER	41KW (56BHP)
TORQUE	119NM (88LB FT)
TOP SPEED	117KM/H (73MPH)
0–96KM/H (0–60MPH)	23.4SEC

DKW F5 ROADSTER

DKW's origins were given away by its initials, which stood for Dampf Kraft Wagen (Steam Powered Vehicle). By 1935 the company had teamed up with Horch and Wanderer to form Auto Union, resulting in the petrol-powered front-wheel drive F5 economy car.

COUNTRY OF ORIGIN	GERMANY
YEARS OF PRODUCTION	1935–37
DISPLACEMENT	690CC (42CI)
CONFIGURATION	FRONT-MOUNTED 2-CYL
TRANSMISSION	3-SPEED MANUAL, FRONT-WHEEL DRIVE
POWER	13KW (18BHP)
TORQUE	N/A
TOP SPEED	80KM/H (50MPH)
0–96KM/H (0–60MPH)	N/A

FIAT TOPOLINO

Designed to bring motoring to Italy's masses, the 500, or Topolino, was an astonishingly successful small car. During a 12-year production run (including six years of war), there were virtually no changes, with 110,000 units sold by the time production ceased in 1948 (although the car was directly replaced with another 500).

COUNTRY OF ORIGIN	ITALY
YEARS OF PRODUCTION	1936–48
DISPLACEMENT	569CC (35CI)
CONFIGURATION	REAR-MOUNTED 4-CYL
TRANSMISSION	4-SPEED MANUAL, REAR-WHEEL DRIVE
POWER	10KW (13BHP)
TORQUE	28NM (21LB FT)
TOP SPEED	84KM/H (52MPH)
0–96KM/H (0–60MPH)	N/A

LANCIA APRILIA

The Aprilia was amazingly advanced for its time; it was more like a car from the 1950s than the 1930s. It had a monocoque construction, and there was also independent suspension all round, along with hydraulic brakes. While the V4 engine was small, it was free-revving and gave the car quite a turn of speed.

COUNTRY OF ORIGIN	ITALY
YEARS OF PRODUCTION	1936–49
DISPLACEMENT	1352CC (83CI)
CONFIGURATION	FRONT-MOUNTED V4
TRANSMISSION	4-SPEED MANUAL, REAR-WHEEL DRIVE
POWER	35KW (48BHP)
TORQUE	N/A
TOP SPEED	132KM/H (82MPH)
0–96KM/H (0–60MPH)	22.8SEC

STUDEBAKER CHAMPION

The Champion was launched to take Studebaker slightly downmarket and introduce a new type of customer to the company's products. Despite this policy, the Champion was more expensive than its direct competitors, but there weren't enough cars to go round in the immediate post-war years so Studebaker still sold every car it could build.

COUNTRY OF ORIGIN	USA
YEARS OF PRODUCTION	1939–57
DISPLACEMENT	5899CC (360CI)
CONFIGURATION	FRONT-MOUNTED V8
TRANSMISSION	3-SPEED AUTO, REAR-WHEEL DRIVE
POWER	179KW (244BHP)
TORQUE	393NM (290LB FT)
TOP SPEED	185KM/H (115MPH)
0–96KM/H (0–60MPH)	9.8SEC

VOLKSWAGEN BEETLE

The Beetle started out as a pet project of Ferdinand Porsche; the car's origins reach back to 1934, when the Nazi government requested that a peoples' car be designed and built. The end result was the rear-engined Volkswagen (People's Car), which went on to sell more than 22 million copies over a 58-year production span.

COUNTRY OF ORIGIN	GERMANY
YEARS OF PRODUCTION	1945–2003
DISPLACEMENT	1131CC (68CI)
CONFIGURATION	REAR-MOUNTED FLAT-FOUR
TRANSMISSION	4-SPEED MANUAL, REAR-WHEEL DRIVE
POWER	18kW (25BHP)
TORQUE	66NM (49LB FT)
TOP SPEED	101KM/H (63MPH)
0–96KM/H (0–60MPH)	N/A

CROSLEY

Powel Crosley entered into car production in 1939 with the same ambitions as Volkswagen – to create a people's car. He started out with a two-cylinder car and progressed to this four-cylinder model in 1946. The car sold well for three years, but was then quickly overtaken by more competent rivals.

COUNTRY OF ORIGIN	USA
YEARS OF PRODUCTION	1946–49
DISPLACEMENT	721CC (44CI)
CONFIGURATION	FRONT-MOUNTED 4-CYL
TRANSMISSION	3-SPEED MANUAL, REAR-WHEEL DRIVE
POWER	20kW (27BHP)
TORQUE	N/A
TOP SPEED	129KM/H (80MPH)
0–96KM/H (0–60MPH)	20.0SEC

WILLYS JEEP

The ultimate utility vehicle, the Jeep took its name from the abbreviation for General Purpose, or GP. Originally engineered by Bantam, the Jeep was produced by Ford, Willys and Bantam. The tough four-cylinder engine and revolutionary four-wheel drive transmission allowed the car to go just about anywhere.

COUNTRY OF ORIGIN	USA
YEARS OF PRODUCTION	1941–46
DISPLACEMENT	2195CC (134CI)
CONFIGURATION	FRONT-MOUNTED 4-CYL
TRANSMISSION	3-SPEED MANUAL, FOUR-WHEEL DRIVE
POWER	44kW (60BHP)
TORQUE	142NM (105LB FT)
TOP SPEED	100KM/H (62MPH)
0–96KM/H (0–60MPH)	30.0SEC

MERCURY SPORTSMAN

It may have been called the Sportsman, but there wasn't very much that was sporty about this Mercury. What it did have was plenty of style, with the wood panelling behind the doors. It also packed a 3.9-litre V8, but being a flat-head unit there wasn't much power on offer.

COUNTRY OF ORIGIN	USA
YEARS OF PRODUCTION	1946
DISPLACEMENT	3916CC (239CI)
CONFIGURATION	FRONT-MOUNTED V8
TRANSMISSION	3-SPEED AUTO, REAR-WHEEL DRIVE
POWER	74kW (100BHP)
TORQUE	N/A
TOP SPEED	132KM/H (82MPH)
0–96KM/H (0–60MPH)	21.2SEC

TRIUMPH RENOWN

Using the same mechanicals and a broadly similar chassis as the Roadster, the Renown was a rather conservative saloon. When launched in 1946 the car was known as the 1800 or 2000 Saloon, but the Renown tag was adopted shortly after. Power was provided by the Standard Vanguard's 2088cc engine.

COUNTRY OF ORIGIN	UK
YEARS OF PRODUCTION	1946–54
DISPLACEMENT	2088CC (127CI)
CONFIGURATION	FRONT-MOUNTED 4-CYL
TRANSMISSION	3-SPEED MANUAL O/D, REAR-WHEEL DRIVE
POWER	50kW (68BHP)
TORQUE	146NM (108LB FT)
TOP SPEED	121KM/H (75MPH)
0–96KM/H (0–60MPH)	25.1SEC

GMC STEPSIDE

Perhaps the best-looking pick-up ever created, the Stepside was new for 1947 and it was a big advance over its CC and EC predecessors. The engineering was very simple, but buyers didn't care about that; they were more concerned with the reliability and brilliant ride quality when carting stuff about.

COUNTRY OF ORIGIN	USA
YEARS OF PRODUCTION	1947–54
DISPLACEMENT	3736CC (230CI)
CONFIGURATION	FRONT-MOUNTED 6-CYL
TRANSMISSION	4-SPEED MANUAL, REAR-WHEEL DRIVE
POWER	74kW (100BHP)
TORQUE	267NM (187LB FT)
TOP SPEED	134KM/H (83MPH)
0–96KM/H (0–60MPH)	22.0SEC

RENAULT 4CV

France's answer to the Volkswagen Beetle, the 4CV featured a rear-mounted engine that drove the rear wheels, wrapped in a bodyshell full of compound curves. However, while the VW offered just two doors, the Renault had four – but it was constantly outsold by Citroen's 2CV and the Beetle.

COUNTRY OF ORIGIN	FRANCE
YEARS OF PRODUCTION	1947–61
DISPLACEMENT	760CC (46CI)
CONFIGURATION	REAR-MOUNTED 4-CYL
TRANSMISSION	3-SPEED MANUAL, REAR-WHEEL DRIVE
POWER	14kW (19BHP)
TORQUE	45NM (33LB FT)
TOP SPEED	92KM/H (57MPH)
0–96KM/H (0–60MPH)	N/A

VOLVO PV444/544

The PV444 was the car that put Volvo on the map. Developed during World War II, it didn't go on sale until 1947. The styling was inspired by US themes, something that continued when the PV544 was announced in 1958. This featured a bigger engine and more equipment, along with a single-piece windscreen.

COUNTRY OF ORIGIN	SWEDEN
YEARS OF PRODUCTION	1947–65
DISPLACEMENT	1583CC (97CI)
CONFIGURATION	FRONT-MOUNTED 4-CYL
TRANSMISSION	4-SPEED MANUAL, REAR-WHEEL DRIVE
POWER	63kW (85BHP)
TORQUE	145NM (107LB FT)
TOP SPEED	137KM/H (85MPH)
0–96KM/H (0–60MPH)	N/A

CITROEN 2CV

The 2CV was known as the 'umbrella on wheels', and was utilitarian motoring at its best in post-war France. The original brief was to come up with a car that could cross a ploughed field with a basket of eggs on the back seat – and they had to arrive intact. C'est magnifique!

COUNTRY OF ORIGIN	FRANCE
YEARS OF PRODUCTION	1948–90
DISPLACEMENT	602CC (37CI)
CONFIGURATION	FRONT-MOUNTED 2-CYL.
TRANSMISSION	4-SPEED MANUAL, FRONT-WHEEL DRIVE
POWER	21KW (29BHP)
TORQUE	39NM (29LB FT)
TOP SPEED	108KM/H (67MPH)
0–96KM/H (0–60MPH)	32.8SEC

HUDSON SUPER SIX

When the 'Stepdown' range was launched by Hudson in the late 1940s, the Super Six car went down a storm. Its unitary construction meant the bodyshell was stiff for superior handling, while the straight-six powerplant in the nose helped reduce the centre of gravity to limit roll on the corners.

COUNTRY OF ORIGIN	USA
YEARS OF PRODUCTION	1948–51
DISPLACEMENT	4287CC (262CI)
CONFIGURATION	FRONT-MOUNTED 6-CYL.
TRANSMISSION	3-SPEED AUTO, REAR-WHEEL DRIVE
POWER	89KW (121BHP)
TORQUE	N/A
TOP SPEED	N/A
0–96KM/H (0–60MPH)	N/A

LAND ROVER SERIES I

Maurice Wilks, Rover's chief designer in the post-war period, needed a Jeep-type vehicle to use around his Welsh holiday home, so he copied America's four-wheel drive icon and created an off-shoot company, which he called Land Rover. With selectable four-wheel drive, leaf springs and a ladder frame chassis, the Series I was an instant hit.

COUNTRY OF ORIGIN	UK
YEARS OF PRODUCTION	1948–58
DISPLACEMENT	1595CC (97CI)
CONFIGURATION	FRONT-MOUNTED 4-CYL.
TRANSMISSION	4-SPEED MANUAL, FOUR-WHEEL DRIVE
POWER	37KW (50BHP)
TORQUE	108NM (80LB FT)
TOP SPEED	89KM/H (55MPH)
0–96KM/H (0–60MPH)	N/A

MORRIS MINOR TOURER

One of the most recognizable and classic shapes ever, the Morris Minor was introduced at the 1948 British motor show with a 918cc (56ci) side-valve engine. In time the engine grew, but only to 1098cc (67ci). One of the most collectable Minors is the convertible, otherwise known as the Tourer.

COUNTRY OF ORIGIN	UK
YEARS OF PRODUCTION	1948–71
DISPLACEMENT	1098CC (67CI)
CONFIGURATION	FRONT-MOUNTED 4-CYL.
TRANSMISSION	4-SPEED MANUAL, REAR-WHEEL DRIVE
POWER	35KW (48BHP)
TORQUE	81NM (60LB FT)
TOP SPEED	119KM/H (74MPH)
0–96KM/H (0–60MPH)	24.8SEC

STANDARD VANGUARD PHASE I

Announced to the public in July 1947, the Vanguard was Britain's first post-war all-new British car. Government export rules meant that most Vanguards found their way to the USA, something foreseen when the car was designed: not only was the exterior styling trans-Atlantic, so too was the column-change gearbox.

COUNTRY OF ORIGIN	UK
YEARS OF PRODUCTION	1948–52
DISPLACEMENT	2088CC (127CI)
CONFIGURATION	FRONT-MOUNTED 4-CYL
TRANSMISSION	3-SPEED MANUAL REAR-WHEEL DRIVE
POWER	50kW (68BHP)
TORQUE	146NM (108LB FT)
TOP SPEED	124KM/H (77MPH)
0–96KM/H (0–60MPH)	22.0SEC

BOND MINICAR

Available in no fewer than seven guises during its 17-year production run, the Minicar featured three distinct designs, all with three wheels. The Minicar offered minimal motoring – along with minimal comfort and performance too, but the cars sold well. When it comes to quirky microcars, the Bond takes some beating.

COUNTRY OF ORIGIN	UK
YEARS OF PRODUCTION	1949–66
DISPLACEMENT	249CC (15CI)
CONFIGURATION	FRONT-MOUNTED 2-CYL
TRANSMISSION	4-SPEED MANUAL, FRONT-WHEEL DRIVE
POWER	11kW (15BHP)
TORQUE	N/A
TOP SPEED	97KM/H (60MPH)
0–96KM/H (0–60MPH)	N/A

CHEVROLET FLEETLINE

During the 1940s, the Fleetline had been Chevrolet's big money-spinner, and 1948 marked the last year of the Fleetline as a separate model (during this year it was Chevy's most popular car). From 1949, though, the Fleetline badge denoted a fastback design for Chevrolet's mainstream models.

COUNTRY OF ORIGIN	USA
YEARS OF PRODUCTION	1949–52
DISPLACEMENT	3548CC (216CI)
CONFIGURATION	FRONT-MOUNTED 6-CYL
TRANSMISSION	3-SPEED MANUAL, REAR-WHEEL DRIVE
POWER	66kW (90BHP)
TORQUE	238NM (176LB FT)
TOP SPEED	N/A
0–96KM/H (0–60MPH)	N/A

KAISER VIRGINIAN

Take a look at the Frazer Manhattan, and you'll see that this is exactly the same car. Well nearly, because aside from a slightly different nose and tail treatment, there was very little to separate the Virginian from the Manhattan with its straight-six powerplant and three-speed manual transmission.

COUNTRY OF ORIGIN	USA
YEARS OF PRODUCTION	1949–50
DISPLACEMENT	3707CC (226CI)
CONFIGURATION	FRONT-MOUNTED 6-CYL
TRANSMISSION	3-SPEED MANUAL O/D, REAR-WHEEL DRIVE
POWER	82kW (112BHP)
TORQUE	N/A
TOP SPEED	145KM/H (90MPH)
0–96KM/H (0–60MPH)	20.0SEC

PONTIAC CHIEFTAIN

Successor to the Torpedo Eight, the Chieftain featured incredibly modern styling when it went on sale in 1949. There was a new, stiffer chassis design, while the straight-eight engine received a capacity boost to improve torque and power. Independent suspension remained at the front with leaf springs at the rear.

COUNTRY OF ORIGIN	USA
YEARS OF PRODUCTION	1949–1958
DISPLACEMENT	4080CC (249CI)
CONFIGURATION	FRONT-MOUNTED 8-CYL
TRANSMISSION	4-SPEED AUTO, REAR-WHEEL DRIVE
POWER	76KW (104BHP)
TORQUE	255NM (188LB FT)
TOP SPEED	143KM/H (89MPH)
0–96KM/H (0–60MPH)	19.0SEC

CROSLEY HOT SHOT

Powel Crosley tried to build on the success of his earlier cars by launching a new model that looked more modern, while also offering both performance and economy. The Hot Shot achieved that, but it didn't offer much in the way of comfort.

COUNTRY OF ORIGIN	USA
YEARS OF PRODUCTION	1950–52
DISPLACEMENT	721CC (44CI)
CONFIGURATION	FRONT-MOUNTED 4-CYL
TRANSMISSION	3-SPEED MANUAL, REAR-WHEEL DRIVE
POWER	20KW (27BHP)
TORQUE	N/A
TOP SPEED	129KM/H (80MPH)
0–96KM/H (0–60MPH)	20.0SEC

DODGE WAYFARER SPORTABOUT

The Wayfarers were Dodge's smallest cars of the early post-war period and were built principally around price considerations. Yet they had more style than most of their contemporaries, if not much in the way of performance. They weren't very technically advanced either, with two-speed gearboxes and L-head engines – but they looked fabulous.

COUNTRY OF ORIGIN	USA
YEARS OF PRODUCTION	1950–51
DISPLACEMENT	3771CC (230CI)
CONFIGURATION	FRONT-MOUNTED V8
TRANSMISSION	2-SPEED AUTO, REAR-WHEEL DRIVE
POWER	76KW (103BHP)
TORQUE	N/A
TOP SPEED	137KM/H (85MPH)
0–96KM/H (0–60MPH)	24.5SEC

FORD CRESTLINER

In the early 1950s, the 'hardtop convertible' was becoming fashionable, but Ford was still quite a conservative company. Instead of embracing the trend wholeheartedly, Ford came up with the Crestliner; it was a two-door coupé that retained B-pillars, while others were creating pillarless designs.

COUNTRY OF ORIGIN	USA
YEARS OF PRODUCTION	1950–51
DISPLACEMENT	3921CC (239CI)
CONFIGURATION	FRONT-MOUNTED V8
TRANSMISSION	3-SPEED MANUAL, REAR-WHEEL DRIVE
POWER	74KW (100BHP)
TORQUE	N/A
TOP SPEED	161KM/H (100MPH)
0–96KM/H (0–60MPH)	14.0SEC

Ultimate Dream Car 4:
AC Cobra 427

Carroll Shelby created the Cobra in 1962, when he put a 4260cc (260ci) Ford V8 into an AC Ace. It was a simple formula; take one civilized British sportscar and shoehorn a powerful V8 into it, creating a machine that was far more than the sum of its parts. When Shelby wanted a car to beat Ferrari in circuit racing during the 1960s, he could see the Ace's potential. Shelby had already been at the sharp end of motor racing; by 1960 he'd been forced to retire from racing, so he set himself two goals. The first was to construct a successful V8-powered European-styled sportscar – and the second was to beat Enzo Ferrari at his own game.

When Shelby retired from racing, he had no idea how he'd put his V8-engined car into production. He approached AC, suggesting that he transplant an eight-cylinder engine into the Ace. AC was keen to progress the project, even though Shelby had no idea whose engine he'd use. That conundrum was soon solved when Shelby acquired some examples of Ford's all-new V8, which had been introduced in the 1961 Fairlane.

With the engine sorted, it was a case of beefing-up the Ace's bodywork and coming up with a chassis that could take the torque. By January 1962 the prototype was ready and within a year the car had won its first races. That was when the Cobra went on sale in Ford dealerships, in a bid to boost the company's image – although the really big boost came in October 1963, when the 427 (7-litre) engine was first installed.

These first 427-powered cars were virtually impossible to drive, thanks to huge power and an incredibly crude chassis. The answer was to introduce an overhauled design, with much more strengthening and coil-spring suspension. It was still a brute, but at least it was slightly more driveable!

COUNTRY OF ORIGIN	UK/USA
YEARS OF PRODUCTION	1962–1968
DISPLACEMENT	4727CC (288CI)
CONFIGURATION	FRONT-MOUNTED V8
TRANSMISSION	4-SPEED MANUAL, REAR-WHEEL DRIVE
POWER	199KW (271BHP)
TORQUE	426NM (314LB FT)
TOP SPEED	222KM/H (138MPH)
0–96KM/H (0–60MPH)	5.5SEC

FORD VICTORIA

Ford couldn't make enough of the 1951 Victoria, such was its popularity. One of the new-fangled hardtop coupés, the car was stylish and utterly contemporary and Ford sold more than 110,000 of them in a single season – before promptly canning it to make way for newer models.

COUNTRY OF ORIGIN	USA
YEARS OF PRODUCTION	1951
DISPLACEMENT	3921CC (239CI)
CONFIGURATION	FRONT-MOUNTED V8
TRANSMISSION	3-SPEED MANUAL, REAR-WHEEL DRIVE
POWER	74kW (100BHP)
TORQUE	N/A
TOP SPEED	153KM/H (95MPH)
0–96KM/H (0–60MPH)	17.8SEC

HENRY J

The Henry J rose from the ashes of a defunct Kaiser-Frazer, and was intended as a car for the people – a modern-day Model T for those on a tight budget. Able to accommodate four in comfort, the car had a strong performance but spartan interiors, and although it sold well initially the success was short-lived.

COUNTRY OF ORIGIN	USA
YEARS OF PRODUCTION	1951–54
DISPLACEMENT	2637CC (161CI)
CONFIGURATION	FRONT-MOUNTED 6-CYL
TRANSMISSION	3-SPEED MANUAL, REAR-WHEEL DRIVE
POWER	59kW (80BHP)
TORQUE	N/A
TOP SPEED	137KM/H (85MPH)
0–96KM/H (0–60MPH)	14.0SEC

HUDSON HORNET

The Hornet was based on Hudson's 'Stepdown' design, introduced for the 1948 model year. There was a choice of two- or four-door saloon, convertible or coupé. The Hornet's floorpan was recessed between the chassis rails so occupants stepped down into the car, thus ensuring as low a centre of gravity as possible.

COUNTRY OF ORIGIN	USA
YEARS OF PRODUCTION	1951–54
DISPLACEMENT	5047CC (308CI)
CONFIGURATION	FRONT-MOUNTED 6-CYL
TRANSMISSION	4-SPEED MANUAL, REAR-WHEEL DRIVE
POWER	107kW (145BHP)
TORQUE	348NM (257LB FT)
TOP SPEED	150KM/H (93MPH)
0–96KM/H (0–60MPH)	11.0SEC

MORRIS MINOR TRAVELLER

If you want a classic car that can be tuned, yet remains eminently practical, you won't do better than a Morris Minor estate, otherwise known as the Traveller. The car offers space aplenty and the original A-Series engine can easily be upgraded. That wood framing also gives the car loads of character.

COUNTRY OF ORIGIN	UK
YEARS OF PRODUCTION	1952–71
DISPLACEMENT	1098CC (67CI)
CONFIGURATION	FRONT-MOUNTED 4-CYL
TRANSMISSION	4-SPEED MANUAL, REAR-WHEEL DRIVE
POWER	35kW (48BHP)
TORQUE	81NM (60LB FT)
TOP SPEED	119KM/H (74MPH)
0–96KM/H (0–60MPH)	24.8SEC

STUDEBAKER STARLINER

Studebaker celebrated its 100th anniversary in 1952, so it had to do something special to mark the occasion. The Korean War got in the way, however, as the company was kept busy building military equipment, so a sixth facelift of the original 1947 model was what buyers actually received.

COUNTRY OF ORIGIN	USA
YEARS OF PRODUCTION	1952
DISPLACEMENT	3810CC (233CI)
CONFIGURATION	FRONT-MOUNTED V8
TRANSMISSION	3-SPEED MANUAL, REAR-WHEEL DRIVE
POWER	88KW (120BHP)
TORQUE	258NM (190LB FT)
TOP SPEED	161KM/H (100MPH)
0–96KM/H (0–60MPH)	13.0SEC

HOLDEN FJ

The FJ was the car that all Australians wanted when it was unveiled back in 1953. Here was a comfortable and spacious family saloon that was also affordable. It was also possible to tailor the FJ's specifications to the buyer's needs, while for the first time ever Holden offered two-tone paintwork.

COUNTRY OF ORIGIN	AUSTRALIA
YEARS OF PRODUCTION	1953–56
DISPLACEMENT	2160CC (132CI)
CONFIGURATION	FRONT-MOUNTED 6-CYL
TRANSMISSION	3-SPEED MANUAL, REAR-WHEEL DRIVE
POWER	44KW (60BHP)
TORQUE	136NM (100LB FT)
TOP SPEED	129KM/H (80MPH)
0–96KM/H (0–60MPH)	19.0SEC

HUDSON JET

If ever a car deserved to succeed, it was the Hudson Jet. It was nicely engineered, well built and modern in its design, but buyers just didn't want to know, thanks to aggressive marketing from GM, Ford and Chrysler. It also didn't help that the car was rather more costly than its rivals.

COUNTRY OF ORIGIN	USA
YEARS OF PRODUCTION	1953–54
DISPLACEMENT	3309CC (202CI)
CONFIGURATION	FRONT-MOUNTED 6-CYL
TRANSMISSION	3-SPEED MANUAL, REAR-WHEEL DRIVE
POWER	84KW (114BHP)
TORQUE	210NM (155LB FT)
TOP SPEED	153KM/H (95MPH)
0–96KM/H (0–60MPH)	14.0SEC

LANCIA APPIA

Built to replace the Ardea, the Appia sat below the Aurelia in Lancia's pecking order. That's why it featured a relatively small V4 engine, but thanks to the doors, bonnet, boot lid and rear wings being made of aluminium, performance was much more lively than you might expect.

COUNTRY OF ORIGIN	ITALY
YEARS OF PRODUCTION	1953–63
DISPLACEMENT	1090CC (67CI)
CONFIGURATION	FRONT-MOUNTED V4
TRANSMISSION	4-SPEED MANUAL, REAR-WHEEL DRIVE
POWER	28KW (38BHP)
TORQUE	71NM (52LB FT)
TOP SPEED	122KM/H (76MPH)
0–96KM/H (0–60MPH)	32.5SEC

NASH METROPOLITAN

Perhaps the cutest car ever made, the Metropolitan was a caricature on wheels thanks to the narrow track and short wheelbase. Built in England for the US market (at least initially), the Metropolitan proved reasonably popular despite its tiny proportions, with 104,000 being built over a seven-year production run.

COUNTRY OF ORIGIN	USA
YEARS OF PRODUCTION	1953–61
DISPLACEMENT	1489CC (91CI)
CONFIGURATION	FRONT-MOUNTED 4-CYL
TRANSMISSION	3-SPEED MANUAL, REAR-WHEEL DRIVE
POWER	35kW (47BHP)
TORQUE	100NM (74LB FT)
TOP SPEED	121KM/H (75MPH)
0–96KM/H (0–60MPH)	24.8SEC

NASH RAMBLER

The 1953 Rambler was an odd beast: it wasn't an economy car but it wasn't a full-sized one either. Offering a bigger body than was usual for such a fuel-efficient car, the Rambler was offered with a choice of estate, convertible and hardtop bodystyles.

COUNTRY OF ORIGIN	USA
YEARS OF PRODUCTION	1953–55
DISPLACEMENT	3204CC (195CI)
CONFIGURATION	FRONT-MOUNTED 6-CYL
TRANSMISSION	3-SPEED MANUAL O/D, REAR-WHEEL DRIVE
POWER	74kW (100BHP)
TORQUE	N/A
TOP SPEED	137KM/H (85MPH)
0–96KM/H (0–60MPH)	18.0SEC

BMW ISETTA

Although the design originated in Italy, the Isetta was what kept BMW alive in the 1950s – not that it made the company much money. BMW re-engineered the car to take a range of 250, 300 and 600cc (15, 18 and 36ci) powerplants, although the basic concept remained intact, with the single side-hinged door on the front.

COUNTRY OF ORIGIN	GERMANY
YEARS OF PRODUCTION	1955–62
DISPLACEMENT	250CC (15CI)
CONFIGURATION	REAR-MOUNTED 1-CYL
TRANSMISSION	4-SPEED MANUAL, REAR-WHEEL DRIVE
POWER	9kW (12BHP)
TORQUE	15NM (11LB FT)
TOP SPEED	82KM/H (51MPH)
0–96KM/H (0–60MPH)	N/A

CHEVROLET 3100 SERIES

Chevrolet was on a high in the mid-1950s, with its Bel Air and Corvette selling well, largely on the strength of an all-new V8. The obvious thing to do was to transplant the unit into its freshly redesigned 3100 Stepside pick-up truck, transforming the vehicle in the process.

COUNTRY OF ORIGIN	USA
YEARS OF PRODUCTION	1955–57
DISPLACEMENT	4341CC (265CI)
CONFIGURATION	FRONT-MOUNTED V8
TRANSMISSION	3-SPEED MANUAL, REAR-WHEEL DRIVE
POWER	107kW (145BHP)
TORQUE	N/A
TOP SPEED	129KM/H (80MPH)
0–96KM/H (0–60MPH)	7.3SEC

CITROEN DS19

Even now, the Citroen DS looks as though it's from another planet; when it debuted back in 1955, it must have seemed that the martians had landed. With its hydropneumatic suspension, inboard disc brakes and swivelling headlamps, the car really pushes the boundaries – the rest of the world is still playing catch-up.

COUNTRY OF ORIGIN	FRANCE
YEARS OF PRODUCTION	1955–77
DISPLACEMENT	1911CC (117CI)
CONFIGURATION	FRONT-MOUNTED 4-CYL
TRANSMISSION	4-SPEED MANUAL, FRONT-WHEEL DRIVE
POWER	55KW (75BHP)
TORQUE	137NM (101LB FT)
TOP SPEED	140KM/H (87MPH)
0–96KM/H (0–60MPH)	23.3SEC

DODGE CORONET

When Dodge launched the Coronet in 1949, it was the company's most prestigious model line, but from 1955 it became the entry-level model, with a choice of six- or eight-cylinder powerplants. Buyers could also choose between a hardtop coupé, an estate or a saloon, with a choice of two or four doors.

COUNTRY OF ORIGIN	USA
YEARS OF PRODUCTION	1955–57
DISPLACEMENT	5326CC (325CI)
CONFIGURATION	FRONT-MOUNTED V8
TRANSMISSION	3-SPEED AUTO, REAR-WHEEL DRIVE
POWER	191KW (260BHP)
TORQUE	N/A
TOP SPEED	N/A
0–96KM/H (0–60MPH)	N/A

GLAS GOGGOMOBIL

The Goggomobil was the first car to come from Hans Glas' newly formed car-manufacturing company. With two cylinders and four seats, the car was cheap and practical, so it could undercut the VW Beetle. There wasn't enough power with the original 250cc (15ci) engine, however, so it consequently increased in capacity several times.

COUNTRY OF ORIGIN	GERMANY
YEARS OF PRODUCTION	1955–69
DISPLACEMENT	293CC (18CI)
CONFIGURATION	REAR-MOUNTED 2-CYL
TRANSMISSION	4-SPEED MANUAL, REAR-WHEEL DRIVE
POWER	11KW (15BHP)
TORQUE	23NM (17LB FT)
TOP SPEED	84KM/H (52MPH)
0–96KM/H (0–60MPH)	N/A

LLOYD 600

A product of the Borgward empire, the Lloyd had a bodyshell that consisted of fabric panels stretched over a wooden frame, a design chosen because of a lack of steel in post-war Germany. Its construction helped to keep the weight down, which was essential with just a two-stroke, two-cylinder, air-cooled engine in the nose offering a mere 14kW (19bhp).

COUNTRY OF ORIGIN	GERMANY
YEARS OF PRODUCTION	1955–59
DISPLACEMENT	596CC (36CI)
CONFIGURATION	FRONT-MOUNTED 2-CYL
TRANSMISSION	4-SPEED MANUAL, FRONT-WHEEL DRIVE
POWER	14kW (19BHP)
TORQUE	38NM (28LB FT)
TOP SPEED	100KM/H (62MPH)
0–96KM/H (0–60MPH)	N/A

VOLVO AMAZON

Never officially called the Amazon anywhere, this Volvo was significant in that it was the world's first car sold with seat belts. While it looked big and heavy, the Amazon was strong but surprisingly light to drive, which is why the cars are so popular today with those who take part in historic rallying.

COUNTRY OF ORIGIN	SWEDEN
YEARS OF PRODUCTION	1956–69
DISPLACEMENT	1778CC (109CI)
CONFIGURATION	FRONT-MOUNTED 4-CYL
TRANSMISSION	4-SPEED MANUAL, REAR-WHEEL DRIVE
POWER	59kW (80BHP)
TORQUE	142NM (105LB FT)
TOP SPEED	153KM/H (95MPH)
0–96KM/H (0–60MPH)	14.2SEC

HEINKEL H1

With demand for bubble cars unable to be satisfied, Ernst Heinkel set about producing his own with several improvements over BMW's Isetta. Firstly there was space for four people (supposedly), while the H1 was also lighter and better looking. Production ceased in 1958, but the car later went on sale as the Trojan in the UK.

COUNTRY OF ORIGIN	GERMANY
YEARS OF PRODUCTION	1956–65
DISPLACEMENT	204CC (12CI)
CONFIGURATION	FRONT-MOUNTED 1-CYL
TRANSMISSION	4-SPEED MANUAL, REAR-WHEEL DRIVE
POWER	7KW (10BHP)
TORQUE	N/A
TOP SPEED	80KM/H (50MPH)
0–96KM/H (0–60MPH)	N/A

OLDSMOBILE 88 HOLIDAY COUPÉ

The 88 Holiday Coupé was one of the best-looking cars to come out of America during the 1950s, with all its curves and lashings of chrome. The panoramic windscreen at the front was duplicated at the back, and with nearly 400,000 examples sold in 1956 alone, Oldsmobile clearly got it right.

COUNTRY OF ORIGIN	USA
YEARS OF PRODUCTION	1956
DISPLACEMENT	6079CC (371CI)
CONFIGURATION	FRONT-MOUNTED V8
TRANSMISSION	3-SPEED MANUAL, REAR-WHEEL DRIVE
POWER	229kW (312BHP)
TORQUE	556NM (410LB FT)
TOP SPEED	195KM/H (121MPH)
0–96KM/H (0–60MPH)	N/A

RENAULT DAUPHINE

It wasn't much to look at, but the Renault Dauphine was a fabulous car for so many reasons. Eminently practical and affordable, it was great to drive as well, thanks to independent suspension at the front and an optional hydro-pneumatic system at the rear. Some versions could even top 161km/h (100mph).

COUNTRY OF ORIGIN	FRANCE
YEARS OF PRODUCTION	1956–58
DISPLACEMENT	845CC (52CI)
CONFIGURATION	REAR-MOUNTED 4-CYL
TRANSMISSION	4-SPEED MANUAL, REAR-WHEEL DRIVE
POWER	22KW (30BHP)
TORQUE	58NM (43LB FT)
TOP SPEED	106KM/H (66MPH)
0–96KM/H (0–60MPH)	45.7SEC

FIAT NUOVA 500

It's already 30 years since the last Nuova 500 was built, yet they're still on every street corner in Italy. Thanks to the car's charm, practicality and economy, the 500 makes a brilliant ownership proposition in the 21st century, which is why the cars are so collectable and have built up such a following.

COUNTRY OF ORIGIN	ITALY
YEARS OF PRODUCTION	1957–77
DISPLACEMENT	499CC (30CI)
CONFIGURATION	FRONT-MOUNTED 2-CYL
TRANSMISSION	4-SPEED MANUAL, REAR-WHEEL DRIVE
POWER	13KW (18BHP)
TORQUE	30NM (22LB FT)
TOP SPEED	97KM/H (60MPH)
0–96KM/H (0–60MPH)	N/A

FORD EDSEL

Rushed into production and plagued with quality-control problems as a result, the Edsel has gone down in history as the biggest motoring flop of all time. Once its initial problems had been sorted, however, the Edsel wasn't such a bad car at all – but the damage had already been done.

COUNTRY OF ORIGIN	USA
YEARS OF PRODUCTION	1957–60
DISPLACEMENT	5915CC (361CI)
CONFIGURATION	FRONT-MOUNTED V8
TRANSMISSION	3-SPEED AUTO, REAR-WHEEL DRIVE
POWER	223KW (303BHP)
TORQUE	542NM (400LB FT)
TOP SPEED	174KM/H (108MPH)
0–96KM/H (0–60MPH)	11.8SEC

FORD RANCHERO

In an attempt to match GM's product line model for model, Ford introduced a pick-up version of its Ranch Wagon, with a bench seat and more style than anything GM could muster. Offering the comfort of a saloon with the practicality of a pick-up, the Ranchero name survived until 1979.

COUNTRY OF ORIGIN	USA
YEARS OF PRODUCTION	1957–59
DISPLACEMENT	5766CC (352CI)
CONFIGURATION	FRONT-MOUNTED V8
TRANSMISSION	3-SPEED MANUAL, REAR-WHEEL DRIVE
POWER	221KW (300BHP)
TORQUE	N/A
TOP SPEED	169KM/H (105MPH)
0–96KM/H (0–60MPH)	9.5SEC

Ultimate Dream Car 5:
Ford GT40

Ford built the GT40 with one aim in mind – to put an end to Ferrari's domination of endurance racing. When Ford approached Ferrari in a takeover bid during 1963, things were going very well until the last minute. Assuming the deal was in the bag, Ford's directors were furious when everything fell through, which is why they determined then and there that Ferrari would have to be taken down a peg or two.

It was decided from the outset that the car would be built in the UK, because that's where the most talented race car engineers and designers were located. The car would be powered by an American Ford V8 engine, which would be the usual large, unstressed unit that could easily be tuned to develop huge amounts of power for the circuit. The GT40 was designed at Ford's American design centre in Dearborn, but its construction took place in the UK; the glassfibre body panels were constructed in England while the cars were assembled in Slough, at Ford's Advanced Vehicle factory.

Sitting in the middle of the GT40 was a 4.7-litre Ford V8. There was double-wishbone suspension all round, along with coil springs and damper units. An anti-roll bar was also fitted front and rear, while disc brakes hauled the car down from the 322km/h (200mph) top speeds that the racers could achieve. Although the GT40 was designed as a race car, Ford realized the PR potential of making some road cars available for wealthy customers. While the GT40 didn't make an especially civilized road car, it did offer immense performance as well as jaw-dropping looks. However, despite the GT40's Le Mans success throughout the 1960s, sales were very hard to come by – not helped very much by the list price of £6450 ($17,996). This was at a time when a decent house would have cost around the same.

COUNTRY OF ORIGIN	USA
YEARS OF PRODUCTION	1964–69
DISPLACEMENT	4738CC (289CI)
CONFIGURATION	MID-MOUNTED V8
TRANSMISSION	5-SPEED MANUAL, REAR-WHEEL DRIVE
POWER	225KW (306BHP)
TORQUE	446NM (329LB FT)
TOP SPEED	264KM/H (164MPH)
0–96KM/H (0–60MPH)	5.3SEC

CHECKER MARATHON

Forever inextricably linked with New York, Checker's Marathon was officially known as the A11 and it made its debut way back in 1961. Initially available was the Chevrolet 3.7-litre straight-six power, but the small-block V8 was also available later on. Bizarrely, there was an eight-door version called the Aero Cab – few were made.

COUNTRY OF ORIGIN	USA
YEARS OF PRODUCTION	1961–82
DISPLACEMENT	4998CC (305CI)
CONFIGURATION	FRONT-MOUNTED V8
TRANSMISSION	3-SPEED AUTO, REAR-WHEEL DRIVE
POWER	85KW (155BHP)
TORQUE	339NM (250LB FT)
TOP SPEED	158KM/H (98MPH)
0–96KM/H (0–60MPH)	15.5SEC

RENAULT 4

France's best-selling car for nearly two decades, the Renault 4 was the first production car in the world to feature a sealed cooling system. It was amazingly versatile and surprisingly good to drive – although there was so little power available that maintaining momentum was an essential part of piloting a 4.

COUNTRY OF ORIGIN	FRANCE
YEARS OF PRODUCTION	1961–92
DISPLACEMENT	845CC (52CI)
CONFIGURATION	FRONT-MOUNTED 4-CYL
TRANSMISSION	4-SPEED MANUAL, FRONT-WHEEL DRIVE
POWER	21KW (28BHP)
TORQUE	66NM (49LB FT)
TOP SPEED	109KM/H (68MPH)
0–96KM/H (0–60MPH)	40.5SEC

BMW 1500

If it hadn't been for the 1500 'Neue Klasse', there's a good chance BMW wouldn't be here now. It was this car that gave BMW a secure financial footing, with its crisp styling, excellent build quality and superb driving experience, with things getting even better later on, thanks to ever larger engines.

COUNTRY OF ORIGIN	GERMANY
YEARS OF PRODUCTION	1962–72
DISPLACEMENT	1499CC (91CI)
CONFIGURATION	FRONT-MOUNTED 4-CYL
TRANSMISSION	4-SPEED MANUAL, REAR-WHEEL DRIVE
POWER	59KW (80BHP)
TORQUE	118NM (87LB FT)
TOP SPEED	148KM/H (92MPH)
0–96KM/H (0–60MPH)	14SECS

CHEVROLET SUBURBAN

Believe it or not, the Suburban tag has been in continuous use since 1933. It started out gracing an estate car, but within two years it was to be found on a pick-up. By 1960, the Suburban had been restyled, although it would be another two years before it became a truly desirable SUV.

COUNTRY OF ORIGIN	USA
YEARS OF PRODUCTION	1962–66
DISPLACEMENT	4638CC (283CI)
CONFIGURATION	FRONT-MOUNTED V8
TRANSMISSION	3-SPEED MANUAL, REAR-WHEEL DRIVE
POWER	143KW (195BHP)
TORQUE	386NM (285LB FT)
TOP SPEED	167KM/H (104MPH)
0–96KM/H (0–60MPH)	14.2SEC

ROVER P6

Rover may have had a dowdy image in the early 1960s, but its P6 dispelled any myths about the conservatism of this British car maker. With its revolutionary construction, in-board rear brakes and De Dion independent rear suspension, it was no wonder that this was the first ever Car of the Year in 1964.

COUNTRY OF ORIGIN	UK
YEARS OF PRODUCTION	1963–76
DISPLACEMENT	3528CC (215CI)
CONFIGURATION	FRONT-MOUNTED V8
TRANSMISSION	4-SPEED MANUAL, REAR-WHEEL DRIVE
POWER	106KW (144BHP)
TORQUE	267NM (197LB FT)
TOP SPEED	188KM/H (117MPH)
0–96KM/H (0–60MPH)	9.5SEC

FIAT 850

The 850 was hugely important to Fiat during the 1960s, and there was a whole family of cars built on the model's platform. As well as a two-door saloon, there was a coupé and a highly covetable Spider, and while none of the cars had much power, they were all fun to drive.

COUNTRY OF ORIGIN	ITALY
YEARS OF PRODUCTION	1965–73
DISPLACEMENT	843CC (51CI)
CONFIGURATION	REAR-MOUNTED 4-CYL
TRANSMISSION	4-SPEED MANUAL, REAR-WHEEL DRIVE
POWER	35KW (47BHP)
TORQUE	60NM (44LB FT)
TOP SPEED	140KM/H (87MPH)
0–96KM/H (0–60MPH)	18.2SEC

RENAULT 16

Largely forgotten nowadays, the Renault 16 was significant because of its hatchback design, complete with fold-flat seats. There was also independent suspension all round, with disc brakes at the front along with front-wheel drive. It created a template that would be copied worldwide by every single major car maker.

COUNTRY OF ORIGIN	FRANCE
YEARS OF PRODUCTION	1965–79
DISPLACEMENT	1565CC (96CI)
CONFIGURATION	FRONT-MOUNTED 4-CYL
TRANSMISSION	4-SPEED MANUAL, FRONT-WHEEL DRIVE
POWER	49KW (67BHP)
TORQUE	114NM (84LB FT)
TOP SPEED	145KM/H (90MPH)
0–96KM/H (0–60MPH)	15.7SEC

CHEVROLET BLAZER

SUVs may be big news in the USA in the 21st century, but back in the 1960s nobody could have foreseen just how popular they would become. Chevrolet launched its K5 Blazer way back in 1969 with a choice of 5.0 or 5.7-litre V8s; the cars were not impressive on-road, but were virtually unbeatable off it.

COUNTRY OF ORIGIN	USA
YEARS OF PRODUCTION	1969–73
DISPLACEMENT	5735CC (350CI)
CONFIGURATION	FRONT-MOUNTED V8
TRANSMISSION	3-SPEED AUTO, FOUR-WHEEL DRIVE
POWER	121KW (165BHP)
TORQUE	346NM (255LB FT)
TOP SPEED	158KM/H (98MPH)
0–96KM/H (0–60MPH)	15.0SEC

ALFA ROMEO ALFASUD

The Alfasud was incredibly important to Alfa Romeo throughout the 1970s and well into the 1980s. Here was an ultra-modern small sporting car that was also astonishingly practical. With its front-wheel drive and boxer engine, it was great to drive, but a nightmare to own thanks to frequently appalling build quality.

COUNTRY OF ORIGIN	ITALY
YEARS OF PRODUCTION	1972–84
DISPLACEMENT	1350CC (82CI)
CONFIGURATION	FRONT-MOUNTED FLAT-4
TRANSMISSION	5-SPEED MANUAL, FRONT-WHEEL DRIVE
POWER	58kW (79BHP)
TORQUE	110NM (81LB FT)
TOP SPEED	158KM/H (98MPH)
0–96KM/H (0–60MPH)	12.2SEC

CHEVROLET C10

Chevrolet made some big changes to its light truck designs in 1973, with the C10 representing a new, smoother set of lines. There was now curved side glass, while there was also a sculpted curve that ran down the truck's waist. Thanks to a massive engine bay, the C10 proved popular with hot-rodders.

COUNTRY OF ORIGIN	USA
YEARS OF PRODUCTION	1973
DISPLACEMENT	7439CC (454CI)
CONFIGURATION	FRONT-MOUNTED V8
TRANSMISSION	3-SPEED AUTO, REAR-WHEEL DRIVE
POWER	313kW (425BHP)
TORQUE	678NM (500LB FT)
TOP SPEED	196KM/H (122MPH)
0–96KM/H (0–60MPH)	7.8SEC

CHRYSLER VOYAGER

A people carrier may not be everyone's idea of a dream car, but when this car made its debut in 1983, a whole new market sector was born. Based on Chrysler's K-cars, the Voyagers were space-efficient, cheap to buy and styled so well that hardly any design changes were required for over a decade.

COUNTRY OF ORIGIN	USA
YEARS OF PRODUCTION	1983–96
DISPLACEMENT	2972CC (181CI)
CONFIGURATION	FRONT-MOUNTED V6
TRANSMISSION	4-SPEED AUTO, FRONT-WHEEL DRIVE
POWER	105kW (143BHP)
TORQUE	232NM (171LB FT)
TOP SPEED	172KM/H (107MPH)
0–96KM/H (0–60MPH)	13.5SEC

RENAULT ESPACE

Beaten only by the Chrysler Voyager, the Espace was the first people carrier to come from Europe. Even though it was no longer than a conventional car, there was space for seven people, with three rows of seats being offered. Few people understood it at first, but it didn't take long for the idea to catch on.

COUNTRY OF ORIGIN	FRANCE
YEARS OF PRODUCTION	1985–91
DISPLACEMENT	1995CC (122CI)
CONFIGURATION	FRONT-MOUNTED 4-CYL
TRANSMISSION	5-SPEED MANUAL, FRONT-WHEEL DRIVE
POWER	76kW (103BHP)
TORQUE	161NM (119LB FT)
TOP SPEED	166KM/H (103MPH)
0–96KM/H (0–60MPH)	12.9SEC

FORD F150

Ford's F-Series was introduced in 1948; by the time this edition broke cover, it was the tenth-generation model. Available with a huge array of engines and configurations, the F150 was America's best-selling pick-up truck for year after year. In 2001 alone, there were more than 900,000 sold.

COUNTRY OF ORIGIN	USA
YEARS OF PRODUCTION	1997–2003
DISPLACEMENT	5400CC (329CI)
CONFIGURATION	FRONT-MOUNTED V8
TRANSMISSION	4-SPEED AUTO, FOUR-WHEEL DRIVE
POWER	191kW (260BHP)
TORQUE	468NM (345LB FT)
TOP SPEED	N/A
0–96KM/H (0–60MPH)	N/A

DODGE DURANGO

It may have looked like a truck, but the Durango didn't drive like one thanks to a much stiffer chassis than usual along with the double-wishbone front suspension. There was a choice of rear or front-wheel drive and there were three engines available: a V6 or two V8s, the largest displacing 5.9 litres.

COUNTRY OF ORIGIN	USA
YEARS OF PRODUCTION	1998–2003
DISPLACEMENT	5898CC (360CI)
CONFIGURATION	FRONT-MOUNTED V8
TRANSMISSION	6-SPEED MANUAL, FOUR-WHEEL DRIVE
POWER	184kW (250BHP)
TORQUE	454NM (335LB FT)
TOP SPEED	185KM/H (115MPH)
0–96KM/H (0–60MPH)	8.7SEC

SMART FORTWO

Perhaps the funkiest city car ever, the ForTwo was initially known as the Coupé. Then along came the ForFour so a new name had to be found. With its clever packaging and beautiful engineering, the ForTwo was a masterpiece – but its maker struggled to make any money on it at all.

COUNTRY OF ORIGIN	GERMANY
YEARS OF PRODUCTION	1998–2006
DISPLACEMENT	698CC (43CI)
CONFIGURATION	REAR-MOUNTED 3-CYL
TRANSMISSION	SEQUENTIAL 6-SPEED, REAR-WHEEL DRIVE
POWER	45kW (61BHP)
TORQUE	95NM (70LB FT)
TOP SPEED	135KM/H (84MPH)
0–96KM/H (0–60MPH)	15.5SEC

Luxury Cars

No matter how much equipment is shoehorned into a cabin, or how much power an engine offers, there's always room for more. Whatever the state of the global economy, there will always be people who can afford to buy a luxurious car, no matter how exclusively it's priced. The cars in this chapter were among the most luxurious of their day, usually available only to the upwardly mobile, if not the very wealthy. However, while all these cars offer luxury they were usually a rung below those cars at the very top of the pile, as these are covered in the ultra-exclusive chapter.

While these cars were generally more affordable than some of their contemporaries, that doesn't make them any less desirable – then or now. Who would turn their nose up at a Bentley MkVI or Riley RM, never mind a Jaguar Mk10 or Cadillac Seville? However, while there are plenty of mainstream manufacturers represented here, it's perhaps the marques that disappeared long ago which provide the most interesting reading. Take a closer look at the Tatra Type 77 or the Tucker Torpedo, and it's no wonder the manufacturers ultimately failed to survive; innovation is great in its place, but it does have to be profitable.

However, luxurious cars are often not especially innovative; they're frequently the opposite. The luxurious cars of the immediate post-war years were usually rather staid in their design and construction; they just offered more of everything in terms of space, equipment and performance to justify their over-sized price tags. That's exactly how it was for the Jaguar MkVII, Wolseley 25 and Rover P3, which were all very conservative in their design, but which were extremely luxurious nonetheless.

Not all luxury cars have to be sedate, four-door saloons, though; read on and you'll see there were also plenty of grand tourers deserving of the luxury tag. Models such as the Fiat 2300S, Jensen CV-8 and Iso Rivolta were far more stylish than contemporary luxury saloons, yet they could offer as much of everything – except rear-seat space, perhaps. Once more, though, it's the long-dead marques that are the most absorbing; Studebaker, Gordon Keeble and Vanden Plas haven't produced a car between them for decades, yet their cars have more of a following than ever.

Read through this chapter and you'll see that there's probably more diversity here than in any of the others. As well as established and long-defunct marques, there are obscurities such as the Zimmer Quicksilver and Borgward Big Six. Then there are the unfamiliar takes on more familiar cars, such as the Jaguar XJS-derived Lynx Eventer or Ferrari-engined Lancia Thema 8.32 – both completely mad cars but loveable all the same for their idiosyncratic charm. And what about the Lamborghini LM-002 and Citroen SM? Perhaps the SM shouldn't be too much of a surprise, with Citroen frequently making mad-cap decisions that were doomed to fail. But Lamborghini making a V12-engined off-roader? What's all that about?

With more choice than ever in the twenty-first century, it's perhaps the luxury market that's most under attack. As smaller, more fuel efficient (and affordable) cars offer so much more of everything, it's hard to justify spending a lot of money on a luxury car. That's why these are the cars that will be made in smaller numbers – or not made at all – ensuring an even greater rarity, and collectability.

Lancia's Thesis ushered in a new era for the company.

REO FLYING CLOUD

Taking part of its name from the initials of its founder (Ransom Eli Olds), the Flying Cloud was the first car to use Lockheed's new internal expanding brake system. The car featured styling by Fabio Segardi, and its name was meant to evoke thoughts of speed and lightness. It was the final model from the company.

COUNTRY OF ORIGIN	USA
YEARS OF PRODUCTION	1927–36
DISPLACEMENT	3735CC (228CI)
CONFIGURATION	FRONT-MOUNTED 6-CYL
TRANSMISSION	4-SPEED MANUAL, REAR-WHEEL DRIVE
POWER	N/A
TORQUE	N/A
TOP SPEED	N/A
0–96KM/H (0–60MPH)	N/A

LANCIA LAMBDA

The original Lambda was revolutionary in that it featured monocoque construction, making the bodyshell much stiffer and so improving the handling. Performance was also good, thanks to a strong V4 engine. However, cars built between 1928 and 1931 featured a separate chassis so they could more easily be bodied by independent coachbuilders.

COUNTRY OF ORIGIN	ITALY
YEARS OF PRODUCTION	1928–31
DISPLACEMENT	2569CC (157CI)
CONFIGURATION	FRONT-MOUNTED V4
TRANSMISSION	4-SPEED MANUAL, REAR-WHEEL DRIVE
POWER	51KW (69BHP)
TORQUE	N/A
TOP SPEED	121KM/H (75MPH)
0–96KM/H (0–60MPH)	N/A

BENTLEY 8-LITRE

The 8-Litre was the largest and most luxurious Bentley made prior to the purchase of the marque by Rolls-Royce. It used a massive 7982cc (487ci) straight-six engine and was available in short- (3.65m/144in) or long-wheelbase (3.96m/156in) guises, making it the largest car produced in the UK up to that time.

COUNTRY OF ORIGIN	UK
YEARS OF PRODUCTION	1930–31
DISPLACEMENT	7982CC (487CI)
CONFIGURATION	FRONT-MOUNTED 6-CYL
TRANSMISSION	4-SPEED MANUAL, REAR-WHEEL DRIVE
POWER	162KW (220BHP)
TORQUE	N/A
TOP SPEED	163KM/H (101MPH)
0–96KM/H (0–60MPH)	N/A

PACKARD TWIN SIX

The world's first car with a V12 powerplant, the Twin Six brand was first seen in 1915. This later version of the car didn't surface until 1932, however, by which time the Depression was biting. Packard decided to try to compete with Cadillac's V16; the company did well to sell 5744 examples of the car.

COUNTRY OF ORIGIN	USA
YEARS OF PRODUCTION	1932–39
DISPLACEMENT	7299CC (445CI)
CONFIGURATION	FRONT-MOUNTED V12
TRANSMISSION	3-SPEED MANUAL, REAR-WHEEL DRIVE
POWER	118KW (160BHP)
TORQUE	N/A
TOP SPEED	145KM/H (90MPH)
0–96KM/H (0–60MPH)	N/A

CHRYSLER AIRFLOW

There was so much that was revolutionary about the Airflow, from its wind-tunnel-tested lines to its aircraft-inspired construction. But it was over-advanced for America's car buyers, who thought it was too radical with its puncture-proof tyres and automatically engaging overdrive. The car was restyled within a year, but it made no difference to poor sales.

COUNTRY OF ORIGIN	USA
YEARS OF PRODUCTION	1934–1937
DISPLACEMENT	4883CC (298CI)
CONFIGURATION	FRONT-MOUNTED 8-CYL
TRANSMISSION	3-SPEED MANUAL, REAR-WHEEL DRIVE
POWER	82KW (122BHP)
TORQUE	N/A
TOP SPEED	142KM/H (88MPH)
0–96KM/H (0–60MPH)	19.5SEC

TATRA TYPE 77

Compare the Tatra Type 77 with its contemporaries, and it seems like it's from another planet. Even Citroen's Traction Avant looked dated alongside this Czech marvel. With full-width styling and masses of interior space, the Type 77 was truly ahead of its time, so it's a shame that the car was out of reach for everyone except Communist Party leaders.

COUNTRY OF ORIGIN	CZECHOSLOVAKIA
YEARS OF PRODUCTION	1934–37
DISPLACEMENT	2970CC (181CI)
CONFIGURATION	REAR-MOUNTED V8
TRANSMISSION	4-SPEED MANUAL, REAR-WHEEL DRIVE
POWER	55KW (75BHP)
TORQUE	133NM (98LB FT)
TOP SPEED	137KM/H (85MPH)
0–96KM/H (0–60MPH)	14.0SEC

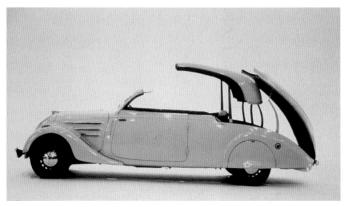

PEUGEOT 402 ECLIPSE

The car that's generally credited with starting the folding hardtop craze, the 402 of 1935 was actually beaten to it by the Peugeot 401 of the previous year. As with the rest of the 402 range, the Eclipse featured a 1991cc (121ci) four-cylinder engine, but the big news was that retractable roof, which disappeared into the boot.

COUNTRY OF ORIGIN	FRANCE
YEARS OF PRODUCTION	1935–37
DISPLACEMENT	1991CC (121CI)
CONFIGURATION	FRONT-MOUNTED 4-CYL
TRANSMISSION	5-SPEED MANUAL, REAR-WHEEL DRIVE
POWER	51KW (70BHP)
TORQUE	N/A
TOP SPEED	N/A
0–96KM/H (0–60MPH)	N/A

LINCOLN ZEPHYR

With its V12 powerplant, the Zephyr was powerful and refined, and advanced too with its unitary construction. It didn't prove especially reliable at first, however, with all manner of problems afflicting that engine. One neat touch was the two-speed rear axle, which effectively gave the car six forward gears.

COUNTRY OF ORIGIN	USA
YEARS OF PRODUCTION	1936–42
DISPLACEMENT	4375CC (269CI)
CONFIGURATION	FRONT-MOUNTED V12
TRANSMISSION	3-SPEED MANUAL, REAR-WHEEL DRIVE
POWER	81KW (110BHP)
TORQUE	244NM (180LB FT)
TOP SPEED	140KM/H (87MPH)
0–96KM/H (0–60MPH)	16.0SEC

TATRA TYPE 87

With many lessons learned from the Type 77, the 87 was fitted with an alloy engine that was both lighter and quieter than the unit it replaced. Once again fitted out the back, the powerplant gave the car very odd handling characteristics; in fact, many German army officers were banned from driving them.

COUNTRY OF ORIGIN	CZECHOSLOVAKIA
YEARS OF PRODUCTION	1937–50
DISPLACEMENT	2968CC (181CI)
CONFIGURATION	REAR-MOUNTED V8
TRANSMISSION	4-SPEED MANUAL, REAR-WHEEL DRIVE
POWER	55KW (75BHP)
TORQUE	N/A
TOP SPEED	161KM/H (100MPH)
0–96KM/H (0–60MPH)	N/A

DAIMLER DB18

First seen before the war, the DB18 was revived by Daimler once the hostilities were over, although there were fewer bodystyles offered. Carried over was the 2.5-litre straight-six, complete with Daimler's unique pre-selector gearbox with fluid flywheel, the ratios swapped by pressing the clutch pedal. This model became the Consort in 1949.

COUNTRY OF ORIGIN	UK
YEARS OF PRODUCTION	1938–50
DISPLACEMENT	2522CC (154CI)
CONFIGURATION	FRONT-MOUNTED 6-CYL
TRANSMISSION	4-SPEED MANUAL, REAR-WHEEL DRIVE
POWER	51KW (70BHP)
TORQUE	148NM (109LB FT)
TOP SPEED	116KM/H (72MPH)
0–96KM/H (0–60MPH)	28.3SEC

GRAHAM HOLLYWOOD

When Auburn-Cord-Duesenberg went out of business in the late 1930s, it was Graham-Paige that stepped in, turning the front-wheel drive Cord 810 into a rear-wheel drive saloon. There wasn't much performance on offer, but the refinement and ride were superb, although the car wasn't enough to ensure the survival of the company.

COUNTRY OF ORIGIN	USA
YEARS OF PRODUCTION	1941
DISPLACEMENT	218CC (3572CI)
CONFIGURATION	FRONT-MOUNTED 6-CYL
TRANSMISSION	3-SPEED MANUAL, REAR-WHEEL DRIVE
POWER	91KW (124BHP)
TORQUE	247NM (182LB FT)
TOP SPEED	143KM/H (89MPH)
0–96KM/H (0–60MPH)	14.6SEC

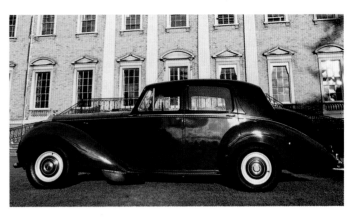

PONTIAC TORPEDO EIGHT

Intended to leave Buick behind for good, the Torpedo Eight looked futuristic when it was unveiled in 1941, although its separate-chassis construction wasn't particularly cutting-edge at the time. The wide grille, sealed beam headlights and independent front suspension pointed the way forward, while the straight-eight offered superb refinement.

COUNTRY OF ORIGIN	USA
YEARS OF PRODUCTION	1941–48
DISPLACEMENT	4817CC (294CI)
CONFIGURATION	FRONT-MOUNTED 8-CYL
TRANSMISSION	3-SPEED AUTO, REAR-WHEEL DRIVE
POWER	76KW (103BHP)
TORQUE	258NM (190LB FT)
TOP SPEED	142KM/H (88MPH)
0–96KM/H (0–60MPH)	18.9SEC

BENTLEY MKVI

Before the war, Bentleys had been available only to the most wealthy. The company decided to change that by producing a car that was less labour-intensive to build, and while it was still costly it was certainly cheaper. It was advanced too, with servo-assisted brakes, independent front suspension and a four-speed manual gearbox.

COUNTRY OF ORIGIN	UK
YEARS OF PRODUCTION	1946–55
DISPLACEMENT	4256CC (260CI)
CONFIGURATION	FRONT-MOUNTED 6-CYL
TRANSMISSION	4-SPEED MANUAL, REAR-WHEEL DRIVE
POWER	N/A
TORQUE	N/A
TOP SPEED	161KM/H (100MPH)
0–96KM/H (0–60MPH)	15.2SEC

INVICTA BLACK PRINCE

When it came to innovation, the Black Prince offered more than most, with independent suspension all round and no gearbox as such – power was transmitted via a Brockhouse hydraulic torque converter. There were also built-in hydraulic jacks, but the cars were too expensive and Invicta folded in 1950.

COUNTRY OF ORIGIN	UK
YEARS OF PRODUCTION	1946–50
DISPLACEMENT	2999CC (183CI)
CONFIGURATION	FRONT-MOUNTED 6-CYL
TRANSMISSION	AUTOMATIC, REAR-WHEEL DRIVE
POWER	88KW (120BHP)
TORQUE	214NM (158LB FT)
TOP SPEED	145KM/H (90MPH)
0–96KM/H (0–60MPH)	N/A

RILEY RM

It looked rather antiquated when launched just after the war, but the Riley RM was quite advanced in some ways. While its construction was old-fashioned, with a separate chassis and an ash frame for the bodyshell, there was a free-revving twin-cam four-cylinder engine and hydraulic brakes all round.

COUNTRY OF ORIGIN	UK
YEARS OF PRODUCTION	1946–53
DISPLACEMENT	2443CC (149CI)
CONFIGURATION	FRONT-MOUNTED 4-CYL
TRANSMISSION	4-SPEED MANUAL, REAR-WHEEL DRIVE
POWER	74KW (100BHP)
TORQUE	184NM (136LB FT)
TOP SPEED	153KM/H (95MPH)
0–96KM/H (0–60MPH)	15.2SEC

FORD V8 PILOT

Although it was officially a new post-war model, the V8 Pilot was based heavily on the prewar V8–62. The exterior styling was barely updated, but at least there was a new 2.5-litre engine. This powerplant didn't provide enough power, however, so Ford quickly switched to the flat-head V8 that it had previously used in military applications.

COUNTRY OF ORIGIN	USA
YEARS OF PRODUCTION	1947–51
DISPLACEMENT	3622CC (221CI)
CONFIGURATION	FRONT-MOUNTED V8
TRANSMISSION	3-SPEED MANUAL, REAR-WHEEL DRIVE
POWER	63KW (85BHP)
TORQUE	N/A
TOP SPEED	134KM/H (83MPH)
0–96KM/H (0–60MPH)	20.5SEC

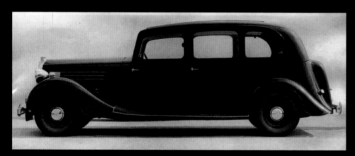

WOLSELEY 25

When it comes to oddballs, few are more strange than the Wolseley 25. Clearly a prewar car, it was introduced by Wolseley in 1947 to use up surplus stocks of parts. However, while it was hopelessly outdated it was also extremely luxurious, as it was available as a seven-seater limousine only.

COUNTRY OF ORIGIN	UK
YEARS OF PRODUCTION	1947–48
DISPLACEMENT	3485CC (213CI)
CONFIGURATION	FRONT-MOUNTED 6-CYL
TRANSMISSION	4-SPEED MANUAL, REAR-WHEEL DRIVE
POWER	76KW (104BHP)
TORQUE	225NM (166LB FT)
TOP SPEED	137KM/H (85MPH)
0–96KM/H (0–60MPH)	20.4SEC

AUSTIN SHEERLINE

Imposing cars that were very exclusive, the Sheerlines sat at the top of the Austin range, with lines penned by Dick Burzi that were reminiscent of contemporary Bentleys. They were powered by overhead-valve six-cylinder engines that had previously been used to power Austin's trucks before the war.

COUNTRY OF ORIGIN	UK
YEARS OF PRODUCTION	1947–54
DISPLACEMENT	3993CC (244CI)
CONFIGURATION	FRONT-MOUNTED 6-CYL
TRANSMISSION	4-SPEED MANUAL, REAR-WHEEL DRIVE
POWER	92KW (125BHP)
TORQUE	N/A
TOP SPEED	130KM/H (81MPH)
0–96KM/H (0–60MPH)	19.4SEC

AUSTIN A90 ATLANTIC

Even though Austin could have sold its entire output to British customers, all its cars had to be exported to earn much-needed cash after the war. That's why the A90 Atlantic looked like it did; it was styled for American buyers. Its performance was too leisurely and just 8000 were sold in four years.

COUNTRY OF ORIGIN	UK
YEARS OF PRODUCTION	1948–52
DISPLACEMENT	2660CC (162CI)
CONFIGURATION	FRONT-MOUNTED 4-CYL
TRANSMISSION	4-SPEED MANUAL, REAR-WHEEL DRIVE
POWER	65KW (88BHP)
TORQUE	190NM (140LB FT)
TOP SPEED	146KM/H (91MPH)
0–96KM/H (0–60MPH)	16.6SEC

BRISTOL 401
The BMW-based 400 had shown that Bristol could produce exclusive sporting cars, and the 401 reinforced that reputation. This new car was much more sophisticated, though, with lightweight aluminium body panels wrapped around a spaceframe chassis. The styling was much more aerodynamic, helped by Bristol's background of manufacturing aircraft.

COUNTRY OF ORIGIN	UK
YEARS OF PRODUCTION	1948–53
DISPLACEMENT	1971CC (120CI)
CONFIGURATION	FRONT-MOUNTED 6-CYL
TRANSMISSION	4-SPEED MANUAL, REAR-WHEEL DRIVE
POWER	63kW (85BHP)
TORQUE	145NM (107LB FT)
TOP SPEED	156KM/H (97MPH)
0–96KM/H (0–60MPH)	15.1SEC

LAGONDA 2.6-LITRE
Lagonda designed and engineered a completely new car for the post-war years, but couldn't afford to put it on sale. Aston Martin's David Brown rescued Lagonda and brought the car to market, the 2.6-Litre featuring a cruciform-shaped chassis with all-independent suspension, in-board rear brakes and a twin overhead-cam engine.

COUNTRY OF ORIGIN	UK
YEARS OF PRODUCTION	1948–53
DISPLACEMENT	2580CC (157CI)
CONFIGURATION	FRONT-MOUNTED 6-CYL
TRANSMISSION	4-SPEED MANUAL, REAR-WHEEL DRIVE
POWER	77kW (105BHP)
TORQUE	180NM (133LB FT)
TOP SPEED	145KM/H (90MPH)
0–96KM/H (0–60MPH)	17.6SEC

ROVER P3
The P3 was the first of Rover's post-war cars, but you wouldn't think so to look at it. It appeared much like Rover's prewar P2 but it was wider and shorter, and the bodyshell was steel whereas its predecessor had an ash frame. Power was provided by either four- or six-cylinder engines.

COUNTRY OF ORIGIN	UK
YEARS OF PRODUCTION	1948–49
DISPLACEMENT	2103CC (128CI)
CONFIGURATION	FRONT-MOUNTED 6-CYL
TRANSMISSION	4-SPEED MANUAL, REAR-WHEEL DRIVE
POWER	53kW (72BHP)
TORQUE	150NM (111LB FT)
TOP SPEED	121KM/H (75MPH)
0–96KM/H (0–60MPH)	29.4SEC

TUCKER TORPEDO
If ever a car deserved to succeed, it was Preston Tucker's 48 Torpedo. With imaginative styling and engineering, the car was first shown in 1948, and alongside the predictable offerings of the more familiar American car makers the Torpedo was a breath of fresh air, but it was just too far ahead of its time.

COUNTRY OF ORIGIN	USA
YEARS OF PRODUCTION	1948
DISPLACEMENT	5491CC (335CI)
CONFIGURATION	REAR-MOUNTED FLAT-SIX
TRANSMISSION	4-SPEED MANUAL, REAR-WHEEL DRIVE
POWER	122kW (166BHP)
TORQUE	N/A
TOP SPEED	193KM/H (120MPH)
0–96KM/H (0–60MPH)	10.1SEC

WOLSELEY 6/80

The archetypal British police car of the 1950s, the 6/80 was the fastest and most highly specified of Wolseley's offerings at the time. Based on the same monocoque as the cheaper Six, the 6/80 was much more powerful, with its 2.2-litre twin-carburetted overhead-cam engine.

COUNTRY OF ORIGIN	UK
YEARS OF PRODUCTION	1948–54
DISPLACEMENT	2215CC (135CI)
CONFIGURATION	FRONT-MOUNTED 4-CYL
TRANSMISSION	4-SPEED MANUAL, REAR-WHEEL DRIVE
POWER	53KW (72BHP)
TORQUE	138NM (102LB FT)
TOP SPEED	124KM/H (77MPH)
0–96KM/H (0–60MPH)	27.8SEC

BUICK ROADMASTER

As soon as World War II was over, Buick pressed ahead with car production, its first all-new model being the Roadmaster. With its ultra-modern full-width styling, the car proved an immediate hit. Yet under the skin it wasn't so advanced; most of the suspension dated from a decade earlier.

COUNTRY OF ORIGIN	USA
YEARS OF PRODUCTION	1949–58
DISPLACEMENT	5243CC (320CI)
CONFIGURATION	FRONT-MOUNTED V8
TRANSMISSION	2-SPEED AUTO, REAR-WHEEL DRIVE
POWER	110KW (150BHP)
TORQUE	353NM (260LB FT)
TOP SPEED	161KM/H (100MPH)
0–96KM/H (0–60MPH)	17.1SEC

CADILLAC SERIES 62

When Chrysler started fitting fins to all its cars in the 1950s, GM wanted to respond with the same treatment. The answer was the Series 62, which would go on to have the biggest ever fins of any car during the 1959 season. Things would never be the same again!

COUNTRY OF ORIGIN	USA
YEARS OF PRODUCTION	1949
DISPLACEMENT	6390CC (225CI)
CONFIGURATION	FRONT-MOUNTED V8
TRANSMISSION	3-SPEED AUTO, REAR-WHEEL DRIVE
POWER	240KW (325BHP)
TORQUE	590NM (435LB FT)
TOP SPEED	195KM/H (121MPH)
0–96KM/H (0–60MPH)	11.0SEC

FRAZER MANHATTAN CONVERTIBLE

When it comes to white elephants, they don't come much bigger than the Manhattan Convertible from an ailing Kaiser-Frazer. Beautifully built and opulently finished, these massive four-door dropheads were costly but underpowered with their side-valve straight-sixes – which is why just 253 were produced.

COUNTRY OF ORIGIN	USA
YEARS OF PRODUCTION	1949–51
DISPLACEMENT	3705CC (226CI)
CONFIGURATION	FRONT-MOUNTED 6-CYL
TRANSMISSION	3-SPEED MANUAL, REAR-WHEEL DRIVE
POWER	82KW (112BHP)
TORQUE	94NM (69LB FT)
TOP SPEED	145KM/H (90MPH)
0–96KM/H (0–60MPH)	22.0SEC

ROVER P4

The classic 'Auntie' Rover, the P4 was the first truly new post-war design for Rover, influenced by the American designs of the time. Early cars were known as 'Cyclops' models because of their single, auxiliary light in the grille, but a restyle in 1952 saw a more conventional nose in keeping with Rover's conservative image.

COUNTRY OF ORIGIN	UK
YEARS OF PRODUCTION	1949–64
DISPLACEMENT	2625CC (160CI)
CONFIGURATION	FRONT-MOUNTED 6-CYL
TRANSMISSION	4-SPEED MANUAL, REAR-WHEEL DRIVE
POWER	75KW (102BHP)
TORQUE	190NM (140LB FT)
TOP SPEED	151KM/H (94MPH)
0–96KM/H (0–60MPH)	18.0SEC

ALVIS TA/TC21

The first new post-war car from Alvis was the traditionally styled TA21, powered by a new 2993cc (182ci) straight-six – hence the car's official name of Alvis 3-Litre. For 1953 there was a minor facelift, so the car was redesignated the TC21; the TB21 had been a low-volume roadster built in 1951 only.

COUNTRY OF ORIGIN	UK
YEARS OF PRODUCTION	1950–55
DISPLACEMENT	2993CC (182CI)
CONFIGURATION	FRONT-MOUNTED 6-CYL
TRANSMISSION	4-SPEED MANUAL, REAR-WHEEL DRIVE
POWER	66KW (90BHP)
TORQUE	203NM (150LB FT)
TOP SPEED	138KM/H (86MPH)
0–96KM/H (0–60MPH)	19.8SEC

CHRYSLER IMPERIAL

Built to celebrate its 50th anniversary, the Imperial was little more than a reheated New Yorker. The problem was that it was meant to compete with the best that Cadillac, Packard and Lincoln could offer. Just 10,650 examples of the car were built before the plug was pulled.

COUNTRY OF ORIGIN	USA
YEARS OF PRODUCTION	1950–54
DISPLACEMENT	5422CC (331CI)
CONFIGURATION	FRONT-MOUNTED V8
TRANSMISSION	4-SPEED AUTO, REAR-WHEEL DRIVE
POWER	132KW (180BHP)
TORQUE	423NM (312LB FT)
TOP SPEED	161KM/H (100MPH)
0–96KM/H (0–60MPH)	13.0SEC

HUDSON COMMODORE

The most expensive and exclusive offering that Hudson had, the Commodore was also the most popular of the company's designs during the 1950 model year. Thanks to its innovative 'step-down' construction, the car would prove to be impossible to facelift on an annual basis – something the customer demanded.

COUNTRY OF ORIGIN	USA
YEARS OF PRODUCTION	1950
DISPLACEMENT	4161CC (254CI)
CONFIGURATION	FRONT-MOUNTED 8-CYL
TRANSMISSION	3-SPEED MANUAL, REAR-WHEEL DRIVE
POWER	94KW (128BHP)
TORQUE	268NM (198LB FT)
TOP SPEED	145KM/H (90MPH)
0–96KM/H (0–60MPH)	15.0SEC

Ultimate Dream Car 6:
Lamborghini Miura

Ferruccio Lamborghini wanted to show that supercars could be modern and based on then-current race-car technology. With the most successful race cars having their powerplants mounted behind the driver, it made sense that the most dynamic road cars should also be using this layout. Bearing in mind that the Miura was only the second model line to come out of the fledgling company, it was even more impressive that Lamborghini managed to pull it off successfully.

The Miura was first shown at the 1966 Geneva Motor Show, creating a storm because it borrowed nothing from existing supercars. Sitting behind the two occupants was a transversely mounted V12 that featured a quartet of camshafts and was capable of generating 258kW (350bhp). Throughout the Miura, Lamborghini's aim was to replicate race-car practice for the road as much as possible. That's why there was double-wishbone suspension all round, as well as massive disc brakes. The car also featured a semi-monocoque, which was strong enough to protect the occupants in the event of a crash. Getting a V12 engine to fit into the available space, along with a gearbox and final drive, was no mean feat; it involved mounting the powerplant sideways and incorporating the gearbox into the sump. Once this had been done, it was relatively simple to position the final drive behind the engine/gearbox combination, with the whole shooting match then sitting between the cabin and the rear axle.

The first incarnation of the Miura was known as the TP400, for Trasversale Posteriore 4-litre. By 1970 it was time to upgrade the car, the result being the 272kW (370bhp) Miura S. This had a far more flexible powerplant, with a flatter torque curve so it wasn't as peaky. It was the final incarnation of the breed, however, that's now the most sought-after – the SV. Not only did it have a very fruity 283kW (385bhp), enabling it to allegedly crack 282km/h (175mph), but the gearbox arrangement was significantly improved.

COUNTRY OF ORIGIN	ITALY
YEARS OF PRODUCTION	1966–72
DISPLACEMENT	3929CC (240CI)
CONFIGURATION	MID-MOUNTED V12
TRANSMISSION	5-SPEED MANUAL, REAR-WHEEL DRIVE
POWER	272KW (370BHP)
TORQUE	388NM (286LB FT)
TOP SPEED	277KM/H (172MPH)
0–96KM/H (0–60MPH)	6.7SEC

OLDSMOBILE 88

With a model name that lasted the lifetime of Oldsmobile, the first 88s started out as big, brash luxury cars dripping with chrome. The 88 was also the first true muscle car, firing the starting gun for the horsepower wars that would break out in Detroit in the early 1950s.

COUNTRY OF ORIGIN	USA
YEARS OF PRODUCTION	1950
DISPLACEMENT	4975CC (304CI)
CONFIGURATION	FRONT-MOUNTED V8
TRANSMISSION	3-SPEED MANUAL, REAR-WHEEL DRIVE
POWER	99KW (135BHP)
TORQUE	N/A
TOP SPEED	156KM/H (97MPH)
0–96KM/H (0–60MPH)	12.0SEC

PACKARD

The 1950 Packards marked the beginning of the end for a company that couldn't compete with America's Big Three. Luxurious but without the glamorous looks needed to charge big bucks, these final cars were available as woody-bodied estates as well as rather bland-looking saloons.

COUNTRY OF ORIGIN	USA
YEARS OF PRODUCTION	1950
DISPLACEMENT	5831CC (356CI)
CONFIGURATION	FRONT-MOUNTED V8
TRANSMISSION	3-SPEED MANUAL O/D, REAR-WHEEL DRIVE
POWER	118KW (160BHP)
TORQUE	N/A
TOP SPEED	153KM/H (95MPH)
0–96KM/H (0–60MPH)	20.0SEC

CHRYSLER NEW YORKER

The New Yorker was generally Chrysler's most popular car in the 1950s, partly because of its brilliantly efficient Hemi cylinder heads. Another reason was because it could be ordered with a choice of Fluid-Matic or Fluid-Torque automatic transmissions, which were sportier than their rivals.

COUNTRY OF ORIGIN	USA
YEARS OF PRODUCTION	1951–54
DISPLACEMENT	5430CC (331CI)
CONFIGURATION	FRONT-MOUNTED V8
TRANSMISSION	3-SPEED AUTO, REAR-WHEEL DRIVE
POWER	132KW (180BHP)
TORQUE	423NM (312LB FT)
TOP SPEED	172KM/H (107MPH)
0–96KM/H (0–60MPH)	13.6SEC

FORD COMETE

The Comete started out as a Ford, but ended up badged as a Simca when the French company took over the American outfit's European subsidiary. Power was initially provided by a 2.2-litre V8, but there wasn't enough of it so Ford slotted in a 3.9-litre truck unit – but buyers still shunned the car.

COUNTRY OF ORIGIN	FRANCE
YEARS OF PRODUCTION	1951–54
DISPLACEMENT	2158CC (133CI)
CONFIGURATION	FRONT-MOUNTED V8
TRANSMISSION	4-SPEED MANUAL, REAR-WHEEL DRIVE
POWER	46KW (63BHP)
TORQUE	128NM (94LB FT)
TOP SPEED	135KM/H (84MPH)
0–96KM/H (0–60MPH)	24.5SEC

FRAZER

This was the last car to be sold by Frazer before the company finally closed its doors – and while its cars were unpopular before 1951, the dealers couldn't get enough in its final years. The 1951 Frazers may have been merely reheated 1949 models, but they had style and are now collectable.

COUNTRY OF ORIGIN	USA
YEARS OF PRODUCTION	1951
DISPLACEMENT	3705CC (226CI)
CONFIGURATION	FRONT-MOUNTED 6-CYL
TRANSMISSION	3-SPEED MANUAL, REAR-WHEEL DRIVE
POWER	85kW (115BHP)
TORQUE	94Nm (69LB FT)
TOP SPEED	145KM/H (90MPH)
0–96KM/H (0–60MPH)	22.0

JAGUAR MK VII

Bizarrely, the Mk VII saloon arrived long before the iconic Mk II, and was Jaguar's first all-new post-war saloon. Early cars offered the option of an awful two-speed automatic gearbox, but most featured a manual unit. From 1955 the car became the Mk VIIM; it lasted in this form until 1957, when the Mk I was launched.

COUNTRY OF ORIGIN	UK
YEARS OF PRODUCTION	1951–54
DISPLACEMENT	3442CC (210CI)
CONFIGURATION	FRONT-MOUNTED 6-CYL
TRANSMISSION	4-SPEED MANUAL, REAR-WHEEL DRIVE
POWER	118kW (160BHP)
TORQUE	264Nm (195LB FT)
TOP SPEED	163KM/H (101MPH)
0–96KM/H (0–60MPH)	13.7SEC

KAISER DRAGON

Looking much like the Traveler and also the Manhattan, the Dragon focused on daring colours and materials to try to distance it from the crowd. Kaiser had looked to home furnishings to differentiate its cars, but many found them too gaudy or costly and sales were hard to come by.

COUNTRY OF ORIGIN	USA
YEARS OF PRODUCTION	1951–53
DISPLACEMENT	3707CC (226CI)
CONFIGURATION	FRONT-MOUNTED 6-CYL
TRANSMISSION	3-SPEED MANUAL O/D, REAR-WHEEL DRIVE
POWER	87kW (118BHP)
TORQUE	N/A
TOP SPEED	145KM/H (90MPH)
0–96KM/H (0–60MPH)	15.0SEC

KAISER TRAVELER

Many people didn't realize it but the Traveler was a revolutionary car, because in essence it was a hatchback. With its two-piece tailgate and fold-down rear seats, there was practicality like never before. At first there were two- or four-door models offered, but the former soon disappeared from the price lists.

COUNTRY OF ORIGIN	USA
YEARS OF PRODUCTION	1951–53
DISPLACEMENT	3707CC (226CI)
CONFIGURATION	FRONT-MOUNTED 6-CYL
TRANSMISSION	3-SPEED MANUAL O/D, REAR-WHEEL DRIVE
POWER	87kW (118BHP)
TORQUE	N/A
TOP SPEED	145KM/H (90MPH)
0–96KM/H (0–60MPH)	15.0SEC

PACKARD MAYFAIR

The hardtop coupé was one of the biggest smash hits of the post-war era, so all of America's car makers had to jump on the bandwagon if they were to compete. Packard's take was the Mayfair, a latecomer that offered straight-eight power but sold fewer than most of its key rivals.

COUNTRY OF ORIGIN	USA
YEARS OF PRODUCTION	1951–53
DISPLACEMENT	5356CC (327CI)
CONFIGURATION	FRONT-MOUNTED 8-CYL
TRANSMISSION	3-SPEED MANUAL O/D, REAR-WHEEL DRIVE
POWER	132KW (180BHP)
TORQUE	N/A
TOP SPEED	145KM/H (90MPH)
0–96KM/H (0–60MPH)	15.0SEC

PACKARD PATRICIAN

Titled after the Roman name for an aristocrat, the Patrician looks great now but was outdated even when launched. Its straight-eight powerplant couldn't rival the V8s offered elsewhere, and the Packard was constantly outsold by the Big Three – which is why Packard got radical for 1955...

COUNTRY OF ORIGIN	USA
YEARS OF PRODUCTION	1951–54
DISPLACEMENT	5880CC (358CI)
CONFIGURATION	FRONT-MOUNTED 8-CYL
TRANSMISSION	3-SPEED AUTO, REAR-WHEEL DRIVE
POWER	156KW (212BHP)
TORQUE	N/A
TOP SPEED	153KM/H (95MPH)
0–96KM/H (0–60MPH)	16.0SEC

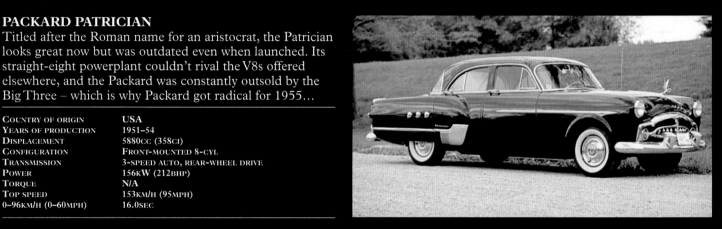

DESOTO FIREDOME

Occupying the top slot in DeSoto's 1952 range, the Firedome marked a return to V8 power for the company. Introduced in time to celebrate DeSoto's 25th anniversary, the Firedome replaced the Custom and was available as a saloon, estate, coupé or convertible. Over 64,000 were sold in its first year.

COUNTRY OF ORIGIN	USA
YEARS OF PRODUCTION	1952–54
DISPLACEMENT	4524CC (276CI)
CONFIGURATION	FRONT-MOUNTED V8
TRANSMISSION	3-SPEED AUTO, REAR-WHEEL DRIVE
POWER	118KW (160BHP)
TORQUE	339NM (250LB FT)
TOP SPEED	161KM/H (100MPH)
0–96KM/H (0–60MPH)	15.5SEC

LINCOLN CAPRI

All-new for 1952, the Capri proved an instant hit, thanks to its tunability, refined V8 and the stiff chassis that helped handling. The car was successful in racing too: it won the Carrera Panamericana three years in a row. It was also luxurious, with powered seats, windows, steering and brakes.

COUNTRY OF ORIGIN	USA
YEARS OF PRODUCTION	1952–55
DISPLACEMENT	5194CC (317CI)
CONFIGURATION	FRONT-MOUNTED V8
TRANSMISSION	3-SPEED AUTO, REAR-WHEEL DRIVE
POWER	151KW (205BHP)
TORQUE	380NM (280LB FT)
TOP SPEED	174KM/H (108MPH)
0–96KM/H (0–60MPH)	13.4SEC

PACKARD CARIBBEAN

Packard needed to shed its conservative image, so it debuted a show car called the Pan American, which proved a hit. Production swiftly followed, with the car called the Caribbean. It featured a flat-head straight-eight, two-tone paint and partially enclosed rear wheels. Suddenly Packard was no longer stuck in the past.

COUNTRY OF ORIGIN	USA
YEARS OF PRODUCTION	1952–54
DISPLACEMENT	5882CC (359CI)
CONFIGURATION	FRONT-MOUNTED 8-CYL
TRANSMISSION	3-SPEED AUTO, REAR-WHEEL DRIVE
POWER	156KW (212BHP)
TORQUE	420NM (310LB FT)
TOP SPEED	163KM/H (101MPH)
0–96KM/H (0–60MPH)	15.8SEC

BRISTOL 403

A direct descendant of the 401, the 403 featured a much-improved version of the straight-six seen in the earlier car. With 74kW (100bhp) on tap, the car was the first Bristol to breach the magic 161km/h (100mph) barrier, while there was also a new gearbox with free-wheel capability on first gear.

COUNTRY OF ORIGIN	UK
YEARS OF PRODUCTION	1953–55
DISPLACEMENT	1971CC (120CI)
CONFIGURATION	FRONT-MOUNTED 6-CYL
TRANSMISSION	4-SPEED MANUAL, REAR-WHEEL DRIVE
POWER	63KW (85BHP)
TORQUE	145NM (107LB FT)
TOP SPEED	156KM/H (97MPH)
0–96KM/H (0–60MPH)	15.1SEC

BUICK SKYLARK

To celebrate half a century of car production, Buick came up with the Skylark. Designed by Harley Earl, the Skylark was the company's range-topper, so it was as highly specified as possible. That's why there was a wraparound windscreen, plenty of chrome trim and a powered convertible fabric roof.

COUNTRY OF ORIGIN	USA
YEARS OF PRODUCTION	1953
DISPLACEMENT	5276CC (322CI)
CONFIGURATION	FRONT-MOUNTED V8
TRANSMISSION	2-SPEED AUTO, REAR-WHEEL DRIVE
POWER	147KW (200BHP)
TORQUE	N/A
TOP SPEED	169KM/H (105MPH)
0–96KM/H (0–60MPH)	11.5SEC

DAIMLER CONQUEST

The Conquest proved to be something of a gamble for Daimler, as it was designed to succeed the Consort, but nothing was carried over. An all-new bodyshell was equipped with a new six-cylinder engine, but there wasn't enough power on offer – at least not until the 74kW (100bhp) Conquest Century of 1954 (specifications given).

COUNTRY OF ORIGIN	UK
YEARS OF PRODUCTION	1953–58
DISPLACEMENT	2433CC (148CI)
CONFIGURATION	FRONT-MOUNTED 6-CYL
TRANSMISSION	4-SPEED PRE-SELECTOR, REAR-WHEEL DRIVE
POWER	74KW (100BHP)
TORQUE	153NM (131LB FT)
TOP SPEED	140KM/H (87MPH)
0–96KM/H (0–60MPH)	16.3SEC

FORD THUNDERBIRD

The Thunderbird was never intended to be a fully fledged sportscar – Ford claimed it was a 'personal luxury car' that offered the comfort of a grand tourer with a decent turn of speed when necessary. With a 4.8-litre V8 up front, there was certainly no shortage of go when it was needed.

COUNTRY OF ORIGIN	USA
YEARS OF PRODUCTION	1955–57
DISPLACEMENT	4783CC (292CI)
CONFIGURATION	FRONT-MOUNTED V8
TRANSMISSION	3-SPEED MANUAL, REAR-WHEEL DRIVE
POWER	156KW (212BHP)
TORQUE	403NM (297LB FT)
TOP SPEED	196KM/H (122MPH)
0–96KM/H (0–60MPH)	9.5SEC

JENSEN 541

When the 541 was unveiled in 1953, it was envisaged that the car would be constructed in steel. By the time it reached production in 1955, however, the bodyshell was made of glassfibre, while motive power was provided by an Austin-built 4-litre straight-six, giving 96kW (130bhp) and a top speed of well over 161km/h (100mph).

COUNTRY OF ORIGIN	UK
YEARS OF PRODUCTION	1955–63
DISPLACEMENT	3993CC (244CI)
CONFIGURATION	FRONT-MOUNTED 6-CYL
TRANSMISSION	4-SPEED MANUAL, REAR-WHEEL DRIVE
POWER	96KW (130BHP)
TORQUE	N/A
TOP SPEED	187KM/H (116MPH)
0–96KM/H (0–60MPH)	10.8SEC

PONTIAC SAFARI

Pontiac's version of the Chevy Nomad, the Safari was made in fewer numbers and thus has become even more collectable. However, while much of the bodyshell was carried over from its cousin, the mechanicals were pure Pontiac, with a choice of V8s mated to GM Hydra-Matic automatic transmissions.

COUNTRY OF ORIGIN	USA
YEARS OF PRODUCTION	1955–57
DISPLACEMENT	5684CC (347CI)
CONFIGURATION	FRONT-MOUNTED V8
TRANSMISSION	3-SPEED AUTO, REAR-WHEEL DRIVE
POWER	235KW (320BHP)
TORQUE	N/A
TOP SPEED	185KM/H (115MPH)
0–96KM/H (0–60MPH)	10.5SEC

STUDEBAKER SPEEDSTER

Laden with chrome, the Speedster was based on a Studebaker President, which was then treated to a two-tone paint job and acres of polished metal. Even in standard form the cars were fast, but they could also be ordered with a supercharged powerplant, guaranteeing electrifying performance.

COUNTRY OF ORIGIN	USA
YEARS OF PRODUCTION	1955
DISPLACEMENT	4246CC (259CI)
CONFIGURATION	FRONT-MOUNTED V8
TRANSMISSION	3-SPEED MANUAL, REAR-WHEEL DRIVE
POWER	136KW (185BHP)
TORQUE	N/A
TOP SPEED	177KM/H (110MPH)
0–96KM/H (0–60MPH)	9.0SEC

ALVIS TD/TE/TF

Alvis desperately needed to update its cars by the mid-1950s, so it turned to Swiss designer Graber to do the job. The result was one of the most beautifully understated classics ever, with slim pillars and discreet lines. Starting out as the TC108/G, the car gradually evolved, with more power and better brakes, to the TF.

COUNTRY OF ORIGIN	UK
YEARS OF PRODUCTION	1956–67
DISPLACEMENT	2993CC (183CI)
CONFIGURATION	FRONT-MOUNTED 6-CYL
TRANSMISSION	5-SPEED MANUAL, REAR-WHEEL DRIVE
POWER	96KW (130BHP)
TORQUE	233NM (172LB FT)
TOP SPEED	171KM/H (106MPH)
0–96KM/H (0–60MPH)	12.5SEC

DESOTO FIREFLITE

The most charismatic model in DeSoto's range, the Fireflite was designed by Virgil Exner, who was noted for his off-the-wall thinking. Under the bonnet was a 188kW (255bhp) V8 that endowed the car with a decent turn of speed, while there were saloon, coupé and estate versions offered, the latter with up to nine seats.

COUNTRY OF ORIGIN	USA
YEARS OF PRODUCTION	1956–61
DISPLACEMENT	5424CC (331CI)
CONFIGURATION	FRONT-MOUNTED V8
TRANSMISSION	3-SPEED AUTO, REAR-WHEEL DRIVE
POWER	188KW (255BHP)
TORQUE	461NM (340LB FT)
TOP SPEED	190KM/H (118MPH)
0–96KM/H (0–60MPH)	8.2SEC

FORD FAIRLANE SKYLINER

This wasn't the first folding hardtop, but it was the first one produced in any quantity. With seven electric motors, 13 switches, 10 solenoids, eight circuit breakers and more than 183m (600ft) of wiring, the mechanism was a work of art – especially as it all worked well and proved to be reliable.

COUNTRY OF ORIGIN	USA
YEARS OF PRODUCTION	1956–59
DISPLACEMENT	5768CC (351CI)
CONFIGURATION	FRONT-MOUNTED V8
TRANSMISSION	3-SPEED AUTO, REAR-WHEEL DRIVE
POWER	221KW (300BHP)
TORQUE	517NM (381LB FT)
TOP SPEED	180KM/H (112MPH)
0–96KM/H (0–60MPH)	10.5SEC

FORD ZODIAC CONVERTIBLE

The Zodiac was always the top of the Consul/Zephyr/Zodiac range, with a choice of saloon, convertible or estate editions to choose from. Built by Carbodies, the convertible is one of the most evocative of the 1960s classics – and now highly sought after in six-cylinder form.

COUNTRY OF ORIGIN	UK
YEARS OF PRODUCTION	1956–62
DISPLACEMENT	2553CC (156CI)
CONFIGURATION	FRONT-MOUNTED 6-CYL
TRANSMISSION	3-SPEED AUTO, REAR-WHEEL DRIVE
POWER	63KW (85BHP)
TORQUE	180NM (133LB FT)
TOP SPEED	142KM/H (88MPH)
0–96KM/H (0–60MPH)	17.1SEC

LANCIA FLAMINIA

Originally intended to replace the Aurelia, the Flaminia sold alongside it for the first two years. Styled by Pininfarina, the car was influenced by contemporary American design trends. It was powered at first by a new 2.5-litre V6, although from 1963 there was a larger, 2775cc (169ci) unit fitted.

COUNTRY OF ORIGIN	ITALY
YEARS OF PRODUCTION	1956–70
DISPLACEMENT	2775CC (169CI)
CONFIGURATION	FRONT-MOUNTED V6
TRANSMISSION	4-SPEED MANUAL, REAR-WHEEL DRIVE
POWER	103KW (140BHP)
TORQUE	221NM (163LB FT)
TOP SPEED	180KM/H (112MPH)
0–96KM/H (0–60MPH)	12.7SEC

BUICK CABALLERO ESTATE

The all-steel estate car, along with the pillarless saloon, were two of the most innovative bodystyles of the post-war era, so it was only a matter of time before the two were combined. Although American Motors was first with the Rambler Custom Cross Country in 1956, Buick swiftly followed suit with the Caballero.

COUNTRY OF ORIGIN	USA
YEARS OF PRODUCTION	1957–58
DISPLACEMENT	5962CC (364CI)
CONFIGURATION	FRONT-MOUNTED V8
TRANSMISSION	3-SPEED MANUAL, REAR-WHEEL DRIVE
POWER	221KW (300BHP)
TORQUE	N/A
TOP SPEED	177KM/H (110MPH)
0–96KM/H (0–60MPH)	10.0SEC

CHEVROLET BEL AIR

One of the all-time great motoring icons, the Bel Air was inspired by the aircraft of the time – it was all down to Harley Earl, who was obsessed with the jet age. The Bel Air was more than a pretty face, though. While its chassis was simple, the car was great to drive with its 4.6-litre small-block V8.

COUNTRY OF ORIGIN	USA
YEARS OF PRODUCTION	1957
DISPLACEMENT	4637CC (283CI)
CONFIGURATION	FRONT-MOUNTED V8
TRANSMISSION	3-SPEED MANUAL, REAR-WHEEL DRIVE
POWER	162KW (220BHP)
TORQUE	366NM (270LB FT)
TOP SPEED	185KM/H (115MPH)
0–96KM/H (0–60MPH)	8.5SEC

CHRYSLER NEW YORKER

Launching Chrysler's 'Look Forward' policy, the sensational 1957 New Yorker looked great but was well out of the reach of most Americans. With Hemi power, modern suspension and those fabulous lines, the car ruffled a lot of feathers in Detroit – but just 10,948 saloons were made.

COUNTRY OF ORIGIN	USA
YEARS OF PRODUCTION	1957
DISPLACEMENT	6421CC (392CI)
CONFIGURATION	FRONT-MOUNTED V8
TRANSMISSION	3-SPEED AUTO, REAR-WHEEL DRIVE
POWER	239KW (325BHP)
TORQUE	610NM (450LB FT)
TOP SPEED	185KM/H (115MPH)
0–96KM/H (0–60MPH)	12.3SEC

STUDEBAKER GOLDEN HAWK

The Golden Hawk, like its sister models the Sky Hawk and Flight Hawk, was based on Studebaker's Starlight, first seen in 1953. Sitting at the top of the range, the Golden Hawk was the most powerful of all Studebaker's models; from 1957 it was even more powerful as the engine was supercharged to give over 221kW (300bhp).

COUNTRY OF ORIGIN	USA
YEARS OF PRODUCTION	1957–58
DISPLACEMENT	5768CC (352CI)
CONFIGURATION	FRONT-MOUNTED V8
TRANSMISSION	3-SPEED AUTO, REAR-WHEEL DRIVE
POWER	202kW (275BHP)
TORQUE	407NM (300LB FT)
TOP SPEED	175KM/H (109MPH)
0–96KM/H (0–60MPH)	9.5SEC

TATRA 603

Able to trace its heritage back to Ledwinka's first T77, with its trademark rear-mounted air-cooled V8 and room inside for six passengers, the 603 used a hemi-head 2.5-litre V8. To ensure the powerplant didn't overheat, there were air scoops in the rear wings and a thermostatically operated air vent in the front bumper.

COUNTRY OF ORIGIN	CZECHOSLOVAKIA
YEARS OF PRODUCTION	1957–75
DISPLACEMENT	2472CC (151CI)
CONFIGURATION	REAR-MOUNTED V8
TRANSMISSION	4-SPEED MANUAL, REAR-WHEEL DRIVE
POWER	77kW (105BHP)
TORQUE	N/A
TOP SPEED	159KM/H (99MPH)
0–96KM/H (0–60MPH)	15.2SEC

VAUXHALL CRESTA PA

Vauxhall's parent company was American-owned – something that was all too apparent in the design of some of its post-war cars. Large fins, wraparound windscreens and heavy chrome-laden bumpers front and rear were all styling cues inspired by the American cars of the time. In place of a V8, however, there were just six cylinders up front.

COUNTRY OF ORIGIN	UK
YEARS OF PRODUCTION	1957–62
DISPLACEMENT	2262CC (138CI)
CONFIGURATION	FRONT-MOUNTED 6-CYL
TRANSMISSION	3-SPEED MANUAL O/D, REAR-WHEEL DRIVE
POWER	60kW (82BHP)
TORQUE	168NM (124LB FT)
TOP SPEED	145KM/H (90MPH)
0–96KM/H (0–60MPH)	16.8SEC

ARMSTRONG SIDDELEY STAR SAPPHIRE

In 1952 the Sapphire 346 limousine had been launched; the Star Sapphire was the replacement for this in 1958. There was now a 121kW (165bhp) 4-litre engine as standard, hooked up to an automatic gearbox as standard, although it was still possible to specify a four-speed manual if required.

COUNTRY OF ORIGIN	UK
YEARS OF PRODUCTION	1958–60
DISPLACEMENT	3990CC (243CI)
CONFIGURATION	FRONT-MOUNTED 6-CYL
TRANSMISSION	4-SPEED MANUAL, REAR-WHEEL DRIVE
POWER	121kW (165BHP)
TORQUE	353NM (260LB FT)
TOP SPEED	161KM/H (100MPH)
0–96KM/H (0–60MPH)	14.8SEC

CHEVROLET IMPALA

The Impala started out in 1958 as an upmarket trim package for Chevrolet's Bel Air, but by 1959 it had become a model in its own right, with a choice of two or four-door saloons. By 1960 the Impala was the biggest-selling car in the US, and by 1966 it had notched up a remarkable 13 million sales.

COUNTRY OF ORIGIN	USA
YEARS OF PRODUCTION	1959–60
DISPLACEMENT	5702CC (348CI)
CONFIGURATION	FRONT-MOUNTED V8
TRANSMISSION	3-SPEED AUTO, REAR-WHEEL DRIVE
POWER	184KW (250BHP)
TORQUE	481NM (355LB FT)
TOP SPEED	185KM/H (115MPH)
0–96KM/H (0–60MPH)	10.5SEC

PONTIAC BONNEVILLE

Pontiac's cars were usually seen as dependable but rather boring – its 1959 Bonneville set out to change that. With its lower, sleeker lines, the new Bonneville offered up to 254kW (345bhp) and an ultra-smooth ride thanks to an increase in track. Buyers could choose from a range of coupés and convertibles.

COUNTRY OF ORIGIN	USA
YEARS OF PRODUCTION	1959–60
DISPLACEMENT	6372CC (224CI)
CONFIGURATION	FRONT-MOUNTED V8
TRANSMISSION	3-SPEED AUTO, REAR-WHEEL DRIVE
POWER	254KW (345BHP)
TORQUE	610NM (450LB FT)
TOP SPEED	193KM/H (120MPH)
0–96KM/H (0–60MPH)	8.1SEC

STUDEBAKER SILVER HAWK

Stung by the fact that buyers were shunning the costly Golden Hawk, Studebaker came up with a cheaper alternative in a bid to up the showroom traffic. There was now a straight-six offered as well as the V8, and while the smaller powerplant ensured the car wasn't fast, it still looked great.

COUNTRY OF ORIGIN	USA
YEARS OF PRODUCTION	1959
DISPLACEMENT	4246CC (259CI)
CONFIGURATION	FRONT-MOUNTED V8
TRANSMISSION	3-SPEED MANUAL, REAR-WHEEL DRIVE
POWER	143KW (195BHP)
TORQUE	N/A
TOP SPEED	161KM/H (100MPH)
0–96KM/H (0–60MPH)	12.0SEC

JAGUAR MK II

Jaguar is lucky enough to have many icons in its past; the Mk II is just one of them. During the car's lifetime it was offered with a choice of 2.4-, 3.4- or 3.8-litre powerplants. Compared with its Mk I predecessor, there were disc brakes fitted, along with a larger rear window and a wider rear track.

COUNTRY OF ORIGIN	UK
YEARS OF PRODUCTION	1960–68
DISPLACEMENT	3442CC (210CI)
CONFIGURATION	FRONT-MOUNTED 6-CYL
TRANSMISSION	4-SPEED MANUAL, REAR-WHEEL DRIVE
POWER	154KW (210BHP)
TORQUE	293NM (216LB FT)
TOP SPEED	193KM/H (120MPH)
0–96KM/H (0–60MPH)	9.1SEC

CHRYSLER 300G

Chrysler had a hot one on its hands with its 'letter series'.
Each year there was a new car, with the 300G marking
quite a leap forward over its predecessor in terms of design.
There was still amazing opulence, though – from a push-
button transmission to a self-seeking radio, the owner
wanted for nothing.

COUNTRY OF ORIGIN	USA
YEARS OF PRODUCTION	1961
DISPLACEMENT	6767CC (413CI)
CONFIGURATION	FRONT-MOUNTED V8
TRANSMISSION	3-SPEED AUTO, REAR-WHEEL DRIVE
POWER	224KW (305BHP)
TORQUE	671NM (495LB FT)
TOP SPEED	209KM/H (130MPH)
0–96KM/H (0–60MPH)	8.4SEC

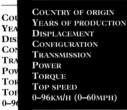

FIAT 2300S COUPÉ

With gorgeous lines designed by Ghia, the 2300S Coupé was dubbed
'the poor man's Ferrari' by many, although it wasn't aimed at people
who were especially poverty-stricken, as it was a costly vehicle. Inside,
it was luxuriously appointed, while there were servo-assisted disc
brakes all round.

COUNTRY OF ORIGIN	ITALY
YEARS OF PRODUCTION	1961–68
DISPLACEMENT	2279CC (139CI)
CONFIGURATION	FRONT-MOUNTED 6-CYL
TRANSMISSION	4-SPEED MANUAL, REAR-WHEEL DRIVE
POWER	77KW (105BHP)
TORQUE	167NM (123LB FT)
TOP SPEED	161KM/H (100MPH)
0–96KM/H (0–60MPH)	12.3SEC

FORD THUNDERBIRD

The Thunderbird had been launched as a rival to the
Corvette, but Ford reckoned that for its second-generation
edition it should adopt a four-seater layout. It was a strategy
that worked; sales subsequently doubled. There was also a
move to monocoque construction, which improved the
handling immeasurably.

COUNTRY OF ORIGIN	USA
YEARS OF PRODUCTION	1961–63
DISPLACEMENT	7046CC (430CI)
CONFIGURATION	FRONT-MOUNTED V8
TRANSMISSION	3-SPEED AUTO, REAR-WHEEL DRIVE
POWER	257KW (350BHP)
TORQUE	664NM (490LB FT)
TOP SPEED	195KM/H (121MPH)
0–96KM/H (0–60MPH)	8.2SEC

JENSEN CV-8

The CV-8's exclusivity was guaranteed thanks to a high
price and the hand-built nature of the car. With its unusual
styling, it was something of an acquired taste aesthetically,
but you couldn't argue with the luxurious interior or huge
performance available from the 5.9-litre Chrysler V8 in
the front.

COUNTRY OF ORIGIN	UK
YEARS OF PRODUCTION	1961–66
DISPLACEMENT	5916CC (364CI)
CONFIGURATION	FRONT-MOUNTED V8
TRANSMISSION	4-SPEED MANUAL, REAR-WHEEL DRIVE
POWER	224KW (305BHP)
TORQUE	536NM (395LB FT)
TOP SPEED	211KM/H (131MPH)
0–96KM/H (0–60MPH)	8.4SEC

FORD THUNDERBIRD

For 1965 the Thunderbird was restyled to look less sporty and more of a grown-up grand tourer; it was obvious by this stage that the car was no sportscar, with its soft suspension and high kerb weight. Despite being outclassed by its rivals, the Thunderbird continued to outsell all of them.

COUNTRY OF ORIGIN	USA
YEARS OF PRODUCTION	1964–66
DISPLACEMENT	6391CC (390CI)
CONFIGURATION	FRONT-MOUNTED V8
TRANSMISSION	3-SPEED MANUAL, REAR-WHEEL DRIVE
POWER	221KW (300BHP)
TORQUE	579NM (427LB FT)
TOP SPEED	185KM/H (115MPH)
0–96KM/H (0–60MPH)	10.3SEC

GORDON KEEBLE

Gordon Keeble claimed this was 'the car built to aircraft standards'. It made its debut in 1960 but didn't go on sale until 1964, designed by Giorgetto Giugiaro and powered by a 5.4-litre Chevrolet Corvette V8. While there was always a steady demand for the car, parts supply issues led to the company going under in 1966.

COUNTRY OF ORIGIN	UK
YEARS OF PRODUCTION	1964–66
DISPLACEMENT	5355CC (327CI)
CONFIGURATION	FRONT-MOUNTED V8
TRANSMISSION	4-SPEED MANUAL, REAR-WHEEL DRIVE
POWER	221KW (300BHP)
TORQUE	488NM (360LB FT)
TOP SPEED	219KM/H (136MPH)
0–96KM/H (0–60MPH)	7.5SEC

VANDEN PLAS 4-LITRE R

When Rolls-Royce and BMC decided to collaborate on a relatively affordable luxury saloon, this was the result. Based on the 3-litre A110 Westminster, the Vanden Plas used a 4-litre Rolls-Royce six-cylinder engine mated to a Borg-Warner automatic gearbox. The 129kW (175bhp) engine offered refinement and torque aplenty, but it was thirsty and the running costs were high.

COUNTRY OF ORIGIN	UK
YEARS OF PRODUCTION	1964–68
DISPLACEMENT	3909CC (239CI)
CONFIGURATION	FRONT-MOUNTED 6-CYL
TRANSMISSION	4-SPEED MANUAL, REAR-WHEEL DRIVE
POWER	129KW (175BHP)
TORQUE	296NM (218LB FT)
TOP SPEED	180KM/H (112MPH)
0–96KM/H (0–60MPH)	12.7SEC

BENTLEY T-SERIES

The first Bentley to feature unitary construction, the T-Series was nothing more than a badge-engineered version of the Rolls-Royce Silver Shadow. That was no bad thing, though, as it meant there was luxury and power, with a choice of two- or four-door bodystyles. Later there would also be a convertible, the Continental.

COUNTRY OF ORIGIN	UK
YEARS OF PRODUCTION	1965–80
DISPLACEMENT	6750CC (412CI)
CONFIGURATION	FRONT-MOUNTED V8
TRANSMISSION	3-SPEED AUTO, REAR-WHEEL DRIVE
POWER	N/A
TORQUE	N/A
TOP SPEED	188KM/H (117MPH)
0–96KM/H (0–60MPH)	10.2SEC

BUICK GRAN SPORT

Although Buick wasn't seen as much of a contender in the muscle-car wars of the 1960s, the Gran Sport packed quite a punch thanks to the installation of GM's 401 'Nail-head' V8 up front. However, it wasn't all about speed; the Gran Sport was more of a luxury cruiser.

COUNTRY OF ORIGIN	USA
YEARS OF PRODUCTION	1965
DISPLACEMENT	6600CC (403CI)
CONFIGURATION	FRONT-MOUNTED V8
TRANSMISSION	3-SPEED AUTO, REAR-WHEEL DRIVE
POWER	239KW (325BHP)
TORQUE	N/A
TOP SPEED	187KM/H (116MPH)
0–96KM/H (0–60MPH)	8.0SEC

GLAS 2600 V8

Looking like a shrunken Maserati, the 2600 V8 earned its maker the nickname 'Glaserati', with its semi-fastback silhouette and headlights inset either side of the grille. The V8 was created by joining two 1300cc (79ci) four-cylinder units together, but the vehicle was to prove the company's undoing, with BMW taking Glas over in 1966.

COUNTRY OF ORIGIN	GERMANY
YEARS OF PRODUCTION	1965–67
DISPLACEMENT	2580CC (157CI)
CONFIGURATION	FRONT-MOUNTED V8
TRANSMISSION	5-SPEED MANUAL, REAR-WHEEL DRIVE
POWER	103KW (140BHP)
TORQUE	206NM (152LB FT)
TOP SPEED	195KM/H (121MPH)
0–96KM/H (0–60MPH)	8.7SEC

RAMBLER MARLIN

The Marlin was a personal luxury car that wore Rambler badges for the 1965 season, but switched to AMC items for its final two seasons. Larger than a Ford Mustang, the Marlin was well equipped and available only as a two-door fastback. Only around 16,500 were made across the three seasons it was offered.

COUNTRY OF ORIGIN	USA
YEARS OF PRODUCTION	1965–67
DISPLACEMENT	5356CC (327CI)
CONFIGURATION	FRONT-MOUNTED V8
TRANSMISSION	3-SPEED AUTO, REAR-WHEEL DRIVE
POWER	199KW (270BHP)
TORQUE	488NM (360LB FT)
TOP SPEED	N/A
0–96KM/H (0–60MPH)	11.2SEC

Ultimate Dream Car 7:
Dodge Charger Daytona

Chrysler unveiled its Hemi powerplant in February 1964, and it allowed Chrysler to win one race after another that season. As a result, NASCAR officials decided that any engine that powered a race car would have to be available (in some form) in a road car. That's where the Charger came in. Launched in 1966, this was a fastback version of the medium-sized Coronet, with a choice of 5.3- or 6.3-litre V8 engines. For 1967 there were initially few changes to the fastback Charger, but then in August of that year came the news – there was to be a new model, headed by a R/T (Road and Track) version that packed a 7.2-litre engine. That model was the Magnum, but there was also a 7-litre Hemi option available, with a four-barrel carburettor.

These top two engines were only available when the car was ordered in R/T specification, which meant they were thinly disguised racers for the road. They also didn't carry the normal warranties, and the cost was a whopping extra 30 per cent over the standard models. All this was because the R/T cars were what Chrysler termed speciality vehicles, which were effectively homologation specials. And they were certainly outrageously fast; as well as topping nearly 257km/h (160mph), they could sprint to 96km/h (60mph) in less than five seconds.

Then came the knock-out punch – the Charger Daytona of 1969. The previous year hadn't been a good race season for Chrysler, so the company resolved to build something more aerodynamic – and the Daytona was the result. With its lengthened (and more slippery) nose, plus a 0.6m (2ft) high rear wing, the car certainly had presence. It also offered success to a certain degree, but not as much as Ford's cars – the blue oval took 29 wins against Chrysler's 22. At this point Chrysler gave up, ushering in a new era in conservatism with its cars.

COUNTRY OF ORIGIN	USA
YEARS OF PRODUCTION	1969–71
DISPLACEMENT	7211CC (440CI)
CONFIGURATION	FRONT-MOUNTED V8
TRANSMISSION	4-SPEED MANUAL, REAR-WHEEL DRIVE
POWER	276KW (375BHP)
TORQUE	651NM (480LB FT)
TOP SPEED	321KM/H (200MPH)
0–96KM/H (0–60MPH)	4.8SEC

ZIL 114

Replacing the Zil 111, the 114 still featured a pushrod V8 in the nose, but the car's design was much more up to date and so were the rest of the mechanicals. There were now servo-assisted disc brakes all round, while air conditioning was fitted as standard.

COUNTRY OF ORIGIN	RUSSIA
YEARS OF PRODUCTION	1970–79
DISPLACEMENT	6962CC (425CI)
CONFIGURATION	FRONT-MOUNTED V8
TRANSMISSION	2-SPEED AUTO, REAR-WHEEL DRIVE
POWER	224kW (304BHP)
TORQUE	560NM (413LB FT)
TOP SPEED	192KM/H (119MPH)
0–96KM/H (0–60MPH)	N/A

BUICK RIVIERA GRAN SPORT

With that dramatic swept-back rear, it was no surprise that the Gran Sport was quickly nicknamed the 'boat-tail'. Only the 1971–72 examples had the really dramatic tail; the lines were toned down for 1973. Of more interest, though, was the engine – in the nose was a 7.5-litre V8, offering 243kW (330bhp).

COUNTRY OF ORIGIN	USA
YEARS OF PRODUCTION	1971–73
DISPLACEMENT	7453CC (455CI)
CONFIGURATION	FRONT-MOUNTED V8
TRANSMISSION	3-SPEED AUTO, REAR-WHEEL DRIVE
POWER	243kW (330BHP)
TORQUE	617NM (455LB FT)
TOP SPEED	193KM/H (120MPH)
0–96KM/H (0–60MPH)	8.1SEC

DAIMLER DOUBLE SIX

After its acquisition by Jaguar in 1960, Daimlers became rebadged products of the parent company. As a result, the Double Six was no more than a Jaguar XJ12 with a fluted grille and different badges – although it was no less desirable for that. Between 1975 and 1977, a coupé version of the Double Six was also offered.

COUNTRY OF ORIGIN	UK
YEARS OF PRODUCTION	1972–92
DISPLACEMENT	5343CC (326CI)
CONFIGURATION	FRONT-MOUNTED V12
TRANSMISSION	AUTOMATIC, REAR-WHEEL DRIVE
POWER	220kW (299BHP)
TORQUE	431NM (318LB FT)
TOP SPEED	241KM/H (150MPH)
0–96KM/H (0–60MPH)	8.1SEC

DE TOMASO LONGCHAMP

De Tomaso had no qualms about copying other people's ideas, with the Longchamp heavily inspired by the then-new Mercedes 450SLC. The idea was to build a car that was more agile than the Deauville, while also being faster, but build quality was never good enough to compete with the more mainstream car makers.

COUNTRY OF ORIGIN	ITALY
YEARS OF PRODUCTION	1972–89
DISPLACEMENT	5763CC (352CI)
CONFIGURATION	FRONT-MOUNTED V8
TRANSMISSION	5-SPEED MANUAL, REAR-WHEEL DRIVE
POWER	243KW (330BHP)
TORQUE	441NM (325LB FT)
TOP SPEED	240KM/H (149MPH)
0–96KM/H (0–60MPH)	6.7SEC

MERCEDES S-CLASS

Challenging Rolls-Royce for maker of the best car in the world, the W116 S-Class had everything; handling, refinement, build quality and performance. Even with a six-cylinder engine, the car was fast, but there was also a choice of V8 units, the largest of which displaced a massive 6.9 litres.

COUNTRY OF ORIGIN	GERMANY
YEARS OF PRODUCTION	1972–80
DISPLACEMENT	4520CC (276CI)
CONFIGURATION	FRONT-MOUNTED V8
TRANSMISSION	AUTOMATIC, REAR-WHEEL DRIVE
POWER	165KW (225BHP)
TORQUE	378NM (279LB FT)
TOP SPEED	216KM/H (134MPH)
0–96KM/H (0–60MPH)	N/A

TRIUMPH DOLOMITE SPRINT

The Dolomite range was confusing since it looked much like Triumph's Toledo, as well as the 1300 and 1500 models. However, time has shown that there's only one model worth coveting: the 2-litre 16-valve Sprint. Poor reliability gave the car a bad reputation, but if properly looked after the cars are fabulous.

COUNTRY OF ORIGIN	UK
YEARS OF PRODUCTION	1973–80
DISPLACEMENT	1998CC (122CI)
CONFIGURATION	FRONT-MOUNTED 4-CYL
TRANSMISSION	4-SPEED MANUAL O/D, REAR-WHEEL DRIVE
POWER	93KW (127BHP)
TORQUE	168NM (124LB FT)
TOP SPEED	185KM/H (115MPH)
0–96KM/H (0–60MPH)	8.7SEC

CITROEN CX

The DS had been so far ahead of its time that, when the time came to replace it, everyone else was still trying to catch up. That didn't stop Citroen pushing the boundaries ever further – the hydropneumatic suspension and hydraulic brakes were developed further ,while the outer skin was even more slippery.

COUNTRY OF ORIGIN	FRANCE
YEARS OF PRODUCTION	1974–91
DISPLACEMENT	2473CC (151CI)
CONFIGURATION	FRONT-MOUNTED 4-CYL
TRANSMISSION	5-SPEED MANUAL, FRONT-WHEEL DRIVE
POWER	124KW (168BHP)
TORQUE	294NM (217LB FT)
TOP SPEED	203KM/H (126MPH)
0–96KM/H (0–60MPH)	8.6SEC

PEUGEOT 504 CABRIOLET

While the saloon and estate 504s were mere workhorses, the coupé and cabriolet versions were stylish sportscars designed by Pininfarina. The cabriolet could seat four, while the retractable cloth roof could stow flush with the rear deck. Power was provided by a fuel-injected four-cylinder engine, while a V6 was available later.

COUNTRY OF ORIGIN	FRANCE
YEARS OF PRODUCTION	1974–83
DISPLACEMENT	1971CC (120CI)
CONFIGURATION	FRONT-MOUNTED 4-CYL
TRANSMISSION	5-SPEED MANUAL, REAR-WHEEL DRIVE
POWER	81KW (110BHP)
TORQUE	178NM (131LB FT)
TOP SPEED	179KM/H (111MPH)
0–96KM/H (0–60MPH)	12.0SEC

TATRA 613

Tatra had never built conventional cars, and the T613 was no exception. It didn't matter that it was costly to build and expensive to buy; this was a car for government officials and the seriously wealthy only. With its air-cooled quad-cam V8 mounted in the back, the car's handling was best described as 'interesting'.

COUNTRY OF ORIGIN	CZECHOSLOVAKIA
YEARS OF PRODUCTION	1974–97
DISPLACEMENT	3495CC (213CI)
CONFIGURATION	REAR-MOUNTED V8
TRANSMISSION	5-SPEED MANUAL, REAR-WHEEL DRIVE
POWER	121KW (165BHP)
TORQUE	213NM (150LB FT)
TOP SPEED	185KM/H (115MPH)
0–96KM/H (0–60MPH)	12.0SEC

CADILLAC SEVILLE

Signalling a move to smaller, more fuel-efficient and nimble Cadillacs, the Seville was designed to take on European cars that were selling in ever greater numbers in the USA. With its Oldsmobile-derived 5.7-litre V8, the Seville may have been a smaller Cadillac, but it was as luxurious as ever.

COUNTRY OF ORIGIN	USA
YEARS OF PRODUCTION	1975–79
DISPLACEMENT	5736CC (350CI)
CONFIGURATION	FRONT-MOUNTED V8
TRANSMISSION	3-SPEED AUTO, REAR-WHEEL DRIVE
POWER	132KW (180BHP)
TORQUE	373NM (275LB FT)
TOP SPEED	185KM/H (115MPH)
0–96KM/H (0–60MPH)	11.5SEC

JAGUAR XJ COUPÉ

First seen in 1973, the XJ Coupé didn't go on sale until 1975. Based on the floorpan of the XJ saloon, the running gear was carried over; the car just lost two doors and gained a different roof line. But the Coupé was costlier than the saloon, which is what most buyers bought.

COUNTRY OF ORIGIN	UK
YEARS OF PRODUCTION	1975–77
DISPLACEMENT	5343CC (326CI)
CONFIGURATION	FRONT-MOUNTED V12
TRANSMISSION	3-SPEED AUTO, REAR-WHEEL DRIVE
POWER	210KW (285BHP)
TORQUE	399NM (294LB FT)
TOP SPEED	238KM/H (148MPH)
0–96KM/H (0–60MPH)	7.6SEC

TATRA T600 TATRAPLAN

By the time the 613 was launched by Tatra in the mid-1970s, rear-engined cars were almost extinct. But Tatra had built rear-engined cars for decades, and it could see no reason to change just because nobody else was doing it. Demand was always low, but the T613 soldiered on until 1998, built as the T700 from 1996.

COUNTRY OF ORIGIN	CZECHOSLOVAKIA
YEARS OF PRODUCTION	1975–96
DISPLACEMENT	3495CC (213CI)
CONFIGURATION	REAR-MOUNTED V8
TRANSMISSION	5-SPEED MANUAL, REAR-WHEEL DRIVE
POWER	121KW (165BHP)
TORQUE	N/A
TOP SPEED	185KM/H (115MPH)
0–96KM/H (0–60MPH)	12.0SEC

LANCIA GAMMA

Built to compete with luxury cars such as the Ford Granada and Citroen CX, the Gamma should have been a world beater. However, because of a tendency to rot and an engine that frequently shed its cam belt, destroying itself in the process, the car is now remembered for all the wrong reasons.

COUNTRY OF ORIGIN	ITALY
YEARS OF PRODUCTION	1976–84
DISPLACEMENT	2484CC (152CI)
CONFIGURATION	FRONT-MOUNTED FLAT-4
TRANSMISSION	5-SPEED MANUAL, FRONT-WHEEL DRIVE
POWER	103KW (140BHP)
TORQUE	207NM (153LB FT)
TOP SPEED	201KM/H (125MPH)
0–96KM/H (0–60MPH)	9.2SEC

ASTON MARTIN LAGONDA

In the history of over-ambitious cars, the Lagonda surely deserves a prize. With its space-age digital dash and complex central locking, the car was too complicated for its own good and the first cars were a complete nightmare to own. It survived 14 years, though, so there was clearly no shortage of fans.

COUNTRY OF ORIGIN	UK
YEARS OF PRODUCTION	1977–90
DISPLACEMENT	5340CC (326CI)
CONFIGURATION	FRONT-MOUNTED V8
TRANSMISSION	AUTOMATIC, REAR-WHEEL DRIVE
POWER	221KW (300BHP)
TORQUE	N/A
TOP SPEED	233KM/H (145MPH)
0–96KM/H (0–60MPH)	8.4SEC

OPEL MONZA

Using the same mechanicals as the Senator executive saloon, the Monza was a superb coupé built for crossing continents with ease. With its 3-litre straight-six and manual or automatic transmissions, the Monza offered refinement and masses of equipment, with good handling and performance despite rather too much bulk.

COUNTRY OF ORIGIN	GERMANY
YEARS OF PRODUCTION	1978–86
DISPLACEMENT	2968CC (181CI)
CONFIGURATION	FRONT-MOUNTED 6-CYL
TRANSMISSION	5-SPEED MANUAL, REAR-WHEEL DRIVE
POWER	132KW (180BHP)
TORQUE	243NM (179LB FT)
TOP SPEED	214KM/H (133MPH)
0–96KM/H (0–60MPH)	8.5SEC

BMW M535I

The M535i was the first road car developed by BMW's Motorsport division, after the ill-fated M1. True to form, the M535i didn't look very fast, but was ferociously quick thanks to its 3.5-litre straight-six, more usually seen in the 635CSi. There was also a close-ratio gearbox and Bilstein suspension to spice up the handling.

COUNTRY OF ORIGIN	GERMANY
YEARS OF PRODUCTION	1979–81
DISPLACEMENT	3453CC (211CI)
CONFIGURATION	FRONT-MOUNTED 6-CYL
TRANSMISSION	5-SPEED MANUAL, REAR-WHEEL DRIVE
POWER	160KW (218BHP)
TORQUE	309NM (228LB FT)
TOP SPEED	224KM/H (139MPH)
0–96KM/H (0–60MPH)	7.1SEC

ROLLS-ROYCE SILVER SPIRIT

Although the Silver Spirit replaced the Silver Shadow, it was effectively the same car but with a new set of clothes – which weren't as attractive. With Bentley badges this car was known as the Mulsanne, while there were standard- and long-wheelbase versions offered, the latter known as the Silver Spur.

COUNTRY OF ORIGIN	UK
YEARS OF PRODUCTION	1980–97
DISPLACEMENT	6750CC (412CI)
CONFIGURATION	FRONT-MOUNTED V8
TRANSMISSION	3-SPEED AUTO, REAR-WHEEL DRIVE
POWER	N/A
TORQUE	N/A
TOP SPEED	192KM/H (119MPH)
0–96KM/H (0–60MPH)	10.0SEC

CADILLAC SEVILLE

When Cadillac created its new Seville for 1980, it made a silly mistake – it made a move to front-wheel drive while also ditching the availability of a V8. The company quickly learned the error of its ways, but even more stupidly then introduced a diesel engine while allowing build quality to slip.

COUNTRY OF ORIGIN	USA
YEARS OF PRODUCTION	1980–86
DISPLACEMENT	4097CC (250CI)
CONFIGURATION	FRONT-MOUNTED V8
TRANSMISSION	3-SPEED AUTO, REAR-WHEEL DRIVE
POWER	99KW (135BHP)
TORQUE	258NM (190LB FT)
TOP SPEED	164KM/H (102MPH)
0–96KM/H (0–60MPH)	N/A

MASERATI BITURBO

Alessandro De Tomaso bailed out Maserati after it had gone bust in 1975; his plan was to produce a sporting four-seater that could compete with BMW's 3-Series. During a 10-year production span, there were two- and four-door saloons available along with a convertible; the Biturbo would also spawn the Ghibli and Shamal.

COUNTRY OF ORIGIN	ITALY
YEARS OF PRODUCTION	1981–1991
DISPLACEMENT	2491CC (152CI)
CONFIGURATION	FRONT-MOUNTED V6
TRANSMISSION	5-SPEED MANUAL, REAR-WHEEL DRIVE
POWER	136KW (185BHP)
TORQUE	282NM (208LB FT)
TOP SPEED	206KM/H (128MPH)
0–96KM/H (0–60MPH)	7.2SEC

BITTER SC

At first glance the SC looked like a Ferrari 400, but underneath that sleek skin the mechanicals were much more mundane. Instead of a V12 there was a 3-litre V6, taken from the Opel Senator, along with the rest of the running gear. Bitter offered two and four-door saloons along with a convertible.

COUNTRY OF ORIGIN	GERMANY
YEARS OF PRODUCTION	1982–86
DISPLACEMENT	2969CC (181CI)
CONFIGURATION	FRONT-MOUNTED 6-CYL
TRANSMISSION	5-SPEED MANUAL, REAR-WHEEL DRIVE
POWER	132KW (180BHP)
TORQUE	243NM (179LB FT)
TOP SPEED	214KM/H (133MPH)
0–96KM/H (0–60MPH)	9.2SEC

BRISTOL BRIGAND

Bristol did a spot of mixing and matching with the Brigand – it took the two-door coupé bodyshell of the Britannia and equipped it with the turbocharged 5.9-litre V8 of the Beaufighter. The result was an ultra-rapid gentleman's carriage that was understated in a way that only Bristol could manage.

COUNTRY OF ORIGIN	UK
YEARS OF PRODUCTION	1982–93
DISPLACEMENT	5898CC (360CI)
CONFIGURATION	FRONT-MOUNTED V8
TRANSMISSION	AUTOMATIC, REAR-WHEEL DRIVE
POWER	N/A
TORQUE	N/A
TOP SPEED	225KM/H (140MPH)
0–96KM/H (0–60MPH)	N/A

ROVER SD1 VITESSE

When the Rover SD1 was introduced in 1976, it was available solely with a 3.5-litre V8, so it was only natural that this would be the mainstay of the range. At first there was the V8-S, but in 1983 the Vitesse tag was revived, the car getting recalibrated suspension and steering, plus uprated brakes.

COUNTRY OF ORIGIN	UK
YEARS OF PRODUCTION	1982–87
DISPLACEMENT	3528CC (215CI)
CONFIGURATION	FRONT-MOUNTED V8
TRANSMISSION	5-SPEED MANUAL, REAR-WHEEL DRIVE
POWER	140KW (190BHP)
TORQUE	298NM (220LB FT)
TOP SPEED	212KM/H (132MPH)
0–96KM/H (0–60MPH)	7.1SEC

AUDI 100CD

In the late 1970s, Audi decided that it would focus on high-quality engineering and new technologies to distance its cars from everybody else's. The 100CD was the result of that strategy, with an amazingly low drag coefficient of just 0.30 – something that had previously been assumed impossible for this class of car.

COUNTRY OF ORIGIN	GERMANY
YEARS OF PRODUCTION	1983–91
DISPLACEMENT	2144CC (131CI)
CONFIGURATION	FRONT-MOUNTED 5-CYL
TRANSMISSION	5-SPEED MANUAL, FRONT-WHEEL DRIVE
POWER	100KW (136BHP)
TORQUE	180NM (133LB FT)
TOP SPEED	206KM/H (128MPH)
0–96KM/H (0–60MPH)	9.5SEC

HUMMER H1

One of the most iconic vehicles of the 21st century – and for all the wrong reasons – is General Motors' Hummer. The project started out in 1980 as the High Mobility Multi-Purpose Wheeled Vehicle (HMMWV), or Humvee, with a Chevrolet petrol engine. By 1994 the powerplant had been changed to a 6.4-litre GM V8 turbodiesel.

COUNTRY OF ORIGIN	USA
YEARS OF PRODUCTION	1983–
DISPLACEMENT	6472CC (395CI)
CONFIGURATION	FRONT-MOUNTED V8
TRANSMISSION	4-SPEED AUTO, FOUR-WHEEL DRIVE
POWER	143KW (195BHP)
TORQUE	583NM (430LB FT)
TOP SPEED	140KM/H (87MPH)
0–96KM/H (0–60MPH)	17.3SEC

ALFA ROMEO 90

Designed by Bertone and introduced at the 1984 Turin Motor Show, the 90 was pitched between Alfa Romeo's Alfetta and Six, both of which were discontinued after the 90's launch. The 90 used the Alfetta chassis (including its rear-mounted transaxle) and took its engines from the Six.

COUNTRY OF ORIGIN	ITALY
YEARS OF PRODUCTION	1984–87
DISPLACEMENT	1492CC (91CI)
CONFIGURATION	FRONT-MOUNTED V6
TRANSMISSION	5-SPEED MANUAL, REAR-WHEEL DRIVE
POWER	115KW (156BHP)
TORQUE	210NM (155LB FT)
TOP SPEED	203KM/H (126MPH)
0–96KM/H (0–60MPH)	9.0SEC

JEEP CHEROKEE

The XJ-series of Cherokee was launched in 1984 as the first monocoque vehicle to come from Jeep. Unusually, while most American SUVs were based on a pick-up sibling, the Cherokee was designed from scratch as a stand-alone product. The car lasted for 13 years before it was facelifted.

COUNTRY OF ORIGIN	USA
YEARS OF PRODUCTION	1984–96
DISPLACEMENT	2837CC (173CI)
CONFIGURATION	FRONT-MOUNTED V8
TRANSMISSION	3-SPEED AUTO, REAR-WHEEL DRIVE
POWER	81KW (110BHP)
TORQUE	197NM (145LB FT)
TOP SPEED	148KM/H (92MPH)
0–96KM/H (0–60MPH)	N/A

BENTLEY TURBO R

It may look like a drawing room on wheels, but this is one fast car. Powered by Bentley's ancient 6750cc (142ci) V8, the Turbo R was phenomenally fast, thanks to the addition of a Garrett turbocharger. Despite a weight of well over 2 tonnes (2.2 tons), the Turbo R could sprint to 96km/h (60mph) in under seven seconds.

COUNTRY OF ORIGIN	UK
YEARS OF PRODUCTION	1985–96
DISPLACEMENT	6750CC (142CI)
CONFIGURATION	FRONT-MOUNTED V8
TRANSMISSION	AUTOMATIC, REAR-WHEEL DRIVE
POWER	N/A
TORQUE	N/A
TOP SPEED	217KM/H (135MPH)
0–96KM/H (0–60MPH)	6.7SEC

BMW 325I CONVERTIBLE

This second-generation 3-Series was the first of the series to be offered in drop-top form, courtesy of BMW. Earlier cars had been converted by Baur, but this factory-built solution was much neater with its flush-fitting roof. With the 2.5-litre straight-six, it offered creamy smooth power and aural delights too.

COUNTRY OF ORIGIN	GERMANY
YEARS OF PRODUCTION	1985–93
DISPLACEMENT	2494CC (152CI)
CONFIGURATION	FRONT-MOUNTED 6-CYL
TRANSMISSION	5-SPEED MANUAL, REAR-WHEEL DRIVE
POWER	126KW (171BHP)
TORQUE	306NM (226LB FT)
TOP SPEED	217KM/H (135MPH)
0–96KM/H (0–60MPH)	8.5SEC

LANCIA THEMA 8.32

When it comes to barking mad saloons, the Thema 8.32 is up there at the top, thanks to its Ferrari V8 driving the front wheels. There were eight cylinders and 32 valves, and with 215 horses scrabbling for traction it was easy to wreck the tyres in a single burst.

COUNTRY OF ORIGIN	ITALY
YEARS OF PRODUCTION	1985–90
DISPLACEMENT	2926CC (179CI)
CONFIGURATION	FRONT-MOUNTED V8
TRANSMISSION	5-SPEED MANUAL, FRONT-WHEEL DRIVE
POWER	158KW (215BHP)
TORQUE	283NM (209LB FT)
TOP SPEED	224KM/H (139MPH)
0–96KM/H (0–60MPH)	7.2SEC

ZIMMER QUICKSILVER

The Quicksilver looked as though it should have had a huge V8 in its nose, but in reality there was a relatively small V6 just ahead of the rear wheels. The configuration came from the fact that the car was based on the Pontiac Fiero, which meant handling was good while the car was cheap to run.

COUNTRY OF ORIGIN	USA
YEARS OF PRODUCTION	1985–88
DISPLACEMENT	2834CC (173CI)
CONFIGURATION	MID-MOUNTED V6
TRANSMISSION	3-SPEED AUTO, REAR-WHEEL DRIVE
POWER	103KW (140BHP)
TORQUE	230NM (170LB FT)
TOP SPEED	195KM/H (121MPH)
0–96KM/H (0–60MPH)	9.7SEC

LAMBORGHINI LM002

If you thought the performance SUV was a recent phenomenon, prepare to rethink. Even now, it's not possible to buy a factory-built SUV with a V12 petrol engine – but you could have done in the 1990s. Initially developed for military use, the LM002 featured a Countach engine and seating for up to 11 in military layout.

COUNTRY OF ORIGIN	ITALY
YEARS OF PRODUCTION	1986–93
DISPLACEMENT	5167CC (315CI)
CONFIGURATION	FRONT-MOUNTED V12
TRANSMISSION	5-SPEED MANUAL, FOUR-WHEEL DRIVE
POWER	327KW (444BHP)
TORQUE	461NM (340LB FT)
TOP SPEED	187KM/H (116MPH)
0–96KM/H (0–60MPH)	8.5SEC

CADILLAC ELDORADO TOURING COUPÉ

The first Eldorado joined Cadillac's range as long ago as 1953, so the Touring Coupé had a lot to live up to. One of a whole new range of Eldorados, the ETC was fitted with the excellent Northstar V8. The new Eldorado range generally proved popular, but buyers were no longer keen on two-door cars.

COUNTRY OF ORIGIN	USA
YEARS OF PRODUCTION	1992–2003
DISPLACEMENT	4467CC (273CI)
CONFIGURATION	FRONT-MOUNTED V8
TRANSMISSION	4-SPEED AUTO, REAR-WHEEL DRIVE
POWER	132KW (180BHP)
TORQUE	325NM (240LB FT)
TOP SPEED	201KM/H (125MPH)
0–96KM/H (0–60MPH)	8.5SEC

FERRARI 456GT

Ferrari had decided to stick with a mid-engined layout for its four-seater when it launched the Mondial, but the 456 signalled a return to the classic front-engined V12 formula. In 1998 a facelifted car was launched, the 456 M (Modificata), with improved aerodynamics and a revised interior.

COUNTRY OF ORIGIN	ITALY
YEARS OF PRODUCTION	1992–2003
DISPLACEMENT	5474CC (334CI)
CONFIGURATION	FRONT-MOUNTED V12
TRANSMISSION	6-SPEED MANUAL, REAR-WHEEL DRIVE
POWER	325KW (442BHP)
TORQUE	549NM (405LB FT)
TOP SPEED	311KM/H (193MPH)
0–96KM/H (0–60MPH)	5.1SEC

JEEP GRAND CHEROKEE

With one of the most iconic names in motoring, Jeep felt it was time to expand in 1992 by producing a four-wheel drive suitable for the family and offering space, comfort and performance. The Grand Cherokee featured lots of equipment, plus a four-wheel drive system that could direct the torque to whichever axle could cope best.

COUNTRY OF ORIGIN	USA
YEARS OF PRODUCTION	1993–98
DISPLACEMENT	5899CC (360CI)
CONFIGURATION	FRONT-MOUNTED V8
TRANSMISSION	4-SPEED AUTO, FOUR-WHEEL DRIVE
POWER	174KW (237BHP)
TORQUE	468NM (345LB FT)
TOP SPEED	200KM/H (124MPH)
0–96KM/H (0–60MPH)	8.2SEC

AUDI A8

It may not have looked especially radical, but the A8 was built like virtually no other car because its bodyshell was constructed entirely of aluminium. That meant a weight saving of around 300kg (660lb) over a conventional steel car, as well as greater refinement and better crash safety.

COUNTRY OF ORIGIN	GERMANY
YEARS OF PRODUCTION	1994–2002
DISPLACEMENT	4172CC (255CI)
CONFIGURATION	FRONT-MOUNTED V8
TRANSMISSION	5-SPEED SEMI-AUTO, FOUR-WHEEL DRIVE
POWER	221KW (300BHP)
TORQUE	400NM (295LB FT)
TOP SPEED	249KM/H (155MPH)
0–96KM/H (0–60MPH)	7.3SEC

FORD EXPLORER

The first Explorers were seen in 1991, but by 1995 there had been a major facelift, making the car look far more modern while also introducing much better suspension. More importantly, though, power was now provided by the Windsor V8, and there was also a five-speed automatic transmission available.

COUNTRY OF ORIGIN	USA
YEARS OF PRODUCTION	1995–2001
DISPLACEMENT	4601CC (281CI)
CONFIGURATION	FRONT-MOUNTED V8
TRANSMISSION	5-SPEED AUTO, FOUR-WHEEL DRIVE
POWER	179KW (243BHP)
TORQUE	397NM (293LB FT)
TOP SPEED	171KM/H (106MPH)
0–96KM/H (0–60MPH)	11.0SEC

FORD EXPEDITION

SUVs were big business in the late 1990s, and few came bigger than the Expedition – although Ford's Excursion was even larger. Designed to take on the Chevy Suburban and Toyota Land Cruiser, the Expedition replaced Ford's Bronco and offered seating for up to eight.

COUNTRY OF ORIGIN	USA
YEARS OF PRODUCTION	1997–2003
DISPLACEMENT	5403CC (330CI)
CONFIGURATION	FRONT-MOUNTED V8
TRANSMISSION	4-SPEED AUTO, FOUR-WHEEL DRIVE
POWER	194KW (264BHP)
TORQUE	466NM (344LB FT)
TOP SPEED	182KM/H (113MPH)
0–96KM/H (0–60MPH)	10.0SEC

ISUZU VEHI-CROSS

Although it looked radical on the outside, the Vehi-cross was little more than a dressed-up Isuzu Trooper. That meant there was a four-wheel drive chassis equipped with either a 3.2- or 3.5-litre V6 engine, although it was the first ever car to offer computer-controlled all-wheel drive for off-roading.

COUNTRY OF ORIGIN	JAPAN
YEARS OF PRODUCTION	1997–2001
DISPLACEMENT	3494CC (213CI)
CONFIGURATION	FRONT-ENGINED V6
TRANSMISSION	4-SPEED AUTO, REAR-WHEEL DRIVE
POWER	158KW (215BHP)
TORQUE	312NM (230LB FT)
TOP SPEED	171KM/H (106MPH)
0–96KM/H (0–60MPH)	N/A

Ultimate Dream Car 8:
De Tomaso Pantera

Having enjoyed huge success in the showroom on the back of its Le Mans successes with the GT40, Ford realized that as the 1970s dawned what it needed was an image booster. The fastest and easiest way of getting a completely new car into production was to outsource its development. The two key people at Ford (Henry Ford II and newly appointed company president Lee Iacocca) both knew Alejandro De Tomaso, and they reckoned he could engineer a car for them and get it into production. In 1967, De Tomaso had bought the Ghia design house. This move allowed him to design and engineer low-volume production cars quickly, which is why he was commissioned to come up with the goods. Because the project was bankrolled by Ford, there was no question as to who would supply the engines; a 5.7-litre V8 was selected from the outset, mated to a ZF five-speed manual gearbox.

By 1970 a prototype car was on show at the New York auto show. Called simply the 351, it had been styled by Ghia's Tom Tjaarda, with the chassis development carried out by ex-Lamborghini engineer Gianpaolo Dallara. The longitudinally installed V8 was placed ahead of the rear axle line but behind the driver, while the brakes were all-disc. Following race-car practice, there were double-wishbones and coil springs at both ends along with rack-and-pinion steering to keep everything as sharp as possible.

The car went on sale in 1971, christened Pantera (Panther) by Ford. Development continued, with impact bumpers fitted in 1972. In the same year, the Pantera L (for Luxury) made its debut. Next was the GT5, introduced in 1982; this was joined by the GT5-S in 1984. The GT5 featured all the body addenda of the GTS, but in metal instead of plastic, and the wheelarch extensions were riveted to the wings. The wheelarch extensions were integrated into the GT5-S's bodywork.

COUNTRY OF ORIGIN	ITALY/US
YEARS OF PRODUCTION	1971–93
DISPLACEMENT	5763CC (352CI)
CONFIGURATION	MID-ENGINED V8
TRANSMISSION	5-SPEED MANUAL, REAR-WHEEL DRIVE
POWER	257KW (350BHP)
TORQUE	451NM (333LB FT)
TOP SPEED	266KM/H (165MPH)
0–96KM/H (0–60MPH)	5.0SEC

PEUGEOT 406 COUPÉ V6

Whichever version of the 406 you bought, the car was a looker, but in coupé form the car was something really special. Designed by Pininfarina, the coupé looked fabulous from every angle, but the car was costly and the interior wasn't special enough for such a low-volume vehicle.

COUNTRY OF ORIGIN	FRANCE
YEARS OF PRODUCTION	1997–2003
DISPLACEMENT	2946CC (180CI)
CONFIGURATION	FRONT-MOUNTED V6
TRANSMISSION	5-SPEED MANUAL, FRONT-WHEEL DRIVE
POWER	143KW (194BHP)
TORQUE	273NM (201LB FT)
TOP SPEED	230KM/H (143MPH)
0–96KM/H (0–60MPH)	7.9SEC

CADILLAC STS

Cadillac has had to reinvent itself on many occasions in an attempt to hold its own against more youthful marques. With the Germans making inroads into America's luxury car market during the 1990s, Cadillac came up with the STS to keep them at bay. It even tried to turn the tables by selling the STS in Europe, but there were few takers.

COUNTRY OF ORIGIN	USA
YEARS OF PRODUCTION	1998–2005
DISPLACEMENT	4571CC (279CI)
CONFIGURATION	FRONT-MOUNTED V8
TRANSMISSION	4-SPEED AUTO, REAR-WHEEL DRIVE
POWER	224KW (305BHP)
TORQUE	401NM (295LB FT)
TOP SPEED	245KM/H (152MPH)
0–96KM/H (0–60MPH)	6.9SEC

LINCOLN NAVIGATOR

Loved by rap stars and footballers alike, the Lincoln Navigator was based on the super-sized Ford Expedition, which in turn could trace its roots back to the company's F150 pick-up. With air suspension, the car was both capable off road and very comfortable when on the road, especially as the suspension height was adjustable.

COUNTRY OF ORIGIN	USA
YEARS OF PRODUCTION	1998–2002
DISPLACEMENT	5400CC (330CI)
CONFIGURATION	FRONT-MOUNTED V8
TRANSMISSION	4-SPEED AUTO, FOUR-WHEEL DRIVE
POWER	169KW (230BHP)
TORQUE	441NM (325LB FT)
TOP SPEED	175KM/H (109MPH)
0–96KM/H (0–60MPH)	11.4SEC

MERCEDES E55 AMG

BMW's M5 had ruled the supersaloon roost for well over a decade, while Audi's S6 was also making in-roads into the market. Mercedes needed its own contender, and the E55 AMG was it. With a 260kW (354bhp) V8 in the nose, but the looks of a regular base-model E-Class, this was one hell of a Q-car.

COUNTRY OF ORIGIN	GERMANY
YEARS OF PRODUCTION	1998–2002
DISPLACEMENT	5439CC (332CI)
CONFIGURATION	FRONT-MOUNTED V8
TRANSMISSION	6-SPEED AUTO, REAR-WHEEL DRIVE
POWER	260KW (354BHP)
TORQUE	529NM (390LB FT)
TOP SPEED	249KM/H (155MPH)
0–96KM/H (0–60MPH)	5.5SEC

BMW X5

Proving that BMW could do nothing to tarnish its sporting reputation, the X5 was launched in 1999 and was instantly acclaimed for its dynamic abilities. Despite the car's massive popularity, BMW then offered a smaller version, the X3, while from 2007 there was an all-new seven-seater X5.

COUNTRY OF ORIGIN	GERMANY
YEARS OF PRODUCTION	1999–2006
DISPLACEMENT	4398CC (268CI)
CONFIGURATION	FRONT-MOUNTED V8
TRANSMISSION	5-SPEED MANUAL, FOUR-WHEEL DRIVE
POWER	235KW (320BHP)
TORQUE	439NM (324LB FT)
TOP SPEED	201KM/H (125MPH)
0–96KM/H (0–60MPH)	7.2SEC

JAGUAR XJR

There was little to give away the fact that this supersaloon from Jaguar packed a supercharged V8 engine that offered 272kW (370bhp). Looking much like any other XJ saloon, the XJR was built to take on the BMW M5; but while it was quick, it was a very different animal.

COUNTRY OF ORIGIN	UK
YEARS OF PRODUCTION	2000–03
DISPLACEMENT	3996CC (244CI)
CONFIGURATION	FRONT-MOUNTED V8
TRANSMISSION	AUTOMATIC, REAR-WHEEL DRIVE
POWER	272KW (370BHP)
TORQUE	525NM (387LB FT)
TOP SPEED	249KM/H (155MPH)
0–96KM/H (0–60MPH)	5.6SEC

MERCEDES ML55 AMG

With the G-Wagen hopelessly outdated by 2000, Mercedes launched an all-new SUV that was supposedly capable of taking on the BMW X5 and Range Rover. It was poorly built, however, and badly received – in ML55 guise it was laughably overpowered for its relatively crude chassis.

COUNTRY OF ORIGIN	GERMANY
YEARS OF PRODUCTION	2000–05
DISPLACEMENT	5439CC (332CI)
CONFIGURATION	FRONT-MOUNTED V8
TRANSMISSION	5-SPEED AUTO, FOUR-WHEEL DRIVE
POWER	260KW (354BHP)
TORQUE	510NM (376LB FT)
TOP SPEED	241KM/H (150MPH)
0–96KM/H (0–60MPH)	6.4SEC

FORD THUNDERBIRD

Ford was doing badly at the end of the last century, so in a bid to revive its fortunes it decided to cash in on its heritage in a big way. This Thunderbird was intended to be reminiscent of the original, and while the car was originally the hottest property in the USA, sales quickly tailed off.

COUNTRY OF ORIGIN	USA
YEARS OF PRODUCTION	2001–05
DISPLACEMENT	3950CC (241CI)
CONFIGURATION	FRONT-MOUNTED V8
TRANSMISSION	5-SPEED AUTO, REAR-WHEEL DRIVE
POWER	188KW (256BHP)
TORQUE	362NM (267LB FT)
TOP SPEED	222KM/H (138MPH)
0–96KM/H (0–60MPH)	7.0SEC

LANCIA THESIS

It started out as the Dialogos concept in 1999, and when it was shown Lancia just had to put it into production. Sure enough, the Thesis appeared in 2001, much watered down inside but still looking fabulous on the outside. There was a choice of five- or six-cylinder powerplants giving up to 169kW (230bhp).

COUNTRY OF ORIGIN	ITALY
YEARS OF PRODUCTION	2001
DISPLACEMENT	2959CC (181CI)
CONFIGURATION	FRONT-MOUNTED V6
TRANSMISSION	5-SPEED AUTO, FRONT-WHEEL DRIVE
POWER	158KW (215BHP)
TORQUE	263NM (194LB FT)
TOP SPEED	233KM/H (145MPH)
0–96KM/H (0–60MPH)	9.1SEC

RANGE ROVER MK 3

No matter how hard other premium manufacturers try to beat the Range Rover, they just can't produce an off-roader with the same sense of occasion. Initially offered with a choice of BMW V8 petrol or straight-six diesel engines, the air-sprung Range Rover received a V8 diesel in 2006.

COUNTRY OF ORIGIN	UK
YEARS OF PRODUCTION	2001–
DISPLACEMENT	4394CC (268CI)
CONFIGURATION	FRONT-MOUNTED V8
TRANSMISSION	5-SPEED AUTO, FOUR-WHEEL DRIVE
POWER	225KW (306BHP)
TORQUE	439NM (324LB FT)
TOP SPEED	200KM/H (124MPH)
0–96KM/H (0–60MPH)	8.3SEC

VOLKSWAGEN PASSAT W8

With Ferdinand Piech at the helm, Volkswagen was very good at answering questions that nobody had asked. For some inexplicable reason, Piech decided that an eight-cylinder Passat was what the world wanted, developing an engine specially for the job. Needless to say, nobody bought them.

COUNTRY OF ORIGIN	GERMANY
YEARS OF PRODUCTION	2001–04
DISPLACEMENT	3999CC (244CI)
CONFIGURATION	FRONT-MOUNTED W8
TRANSMISSION	6-SPEED SEMI-AUTO, FOUR-WHEEL DRIVE
POWER	202KW (275BHP)
TORQUE	370NM (273LB FT)
TOP SPEED	249KM/H (155MPH)
0–96KM/H (0–60MPH)	6.5SEC

CADILLAC ESCALADE

Ever keen to jump on a bandwagon, GM created a Cadillac SUV once it had seen that the fad for full-sized off-roaders wasn't going to disappear. The car was introduced in response to a whole raft of rivals, initially based on the GMC Yukon Denali with 5.7-litre, then 6-litre V8 power.

COUNTRY OF ORIGIN	USA
YEARS OF PRODUCTION	2002–06
DISPLACEMENT	5967CC (364CI)
CONFIGURATION	FRONT-MOUNTED V8
TRANSMISSION	4-SPEED AUTO, FOUR-WHEEL DRIVE
POWER	254KW (345BHP)
TORQUE	515NM (380LB FT)
TOP SPEED	N/A
0–96KM/H (0–60MPH)	N/A

BENTLEY CONTINENTAL GT

The Continental GT was incredibly significant for Bentley because it marked a parting with Rolls-Royce, while also being the first all-new car from the company in half a century, with totally fresh mechanicals. At first, just a coupé was offered, then a saloon and a convertible.

COUNTRY OF ORIGIN	UK
YEARS OF PRODUCTION	2003–
DISPLACEMENT	5998CC (366CI)
CONFIGURATION	FRONT-MOUNTED W12
TRANSMISSION	6-SPEED AUTO/SEQUENTIAL MANUAL, FOUR-WHEEL DRIVE
POWER	406kW (552BHP)
TORQUE	649NM (479LB FT)
TOP SPEED	319KM/H (198MPH)
0–96KM/H (0–60MPH)	4.7SEC

HUMMER H2

Whereas the H1 was the full-fat Hummer for military use, the H2 was an attempt at making a car that was more usable on the public road. Although it was lighter and slimmer, however, it was longer and taller and did little to stem the huge tide of criticism against such 'gas-guzzling' SUVs.

COUNTRY OF ORIGIN	USA
YEARS OF PRODUCTION	2003–
DISPLACEMENT	5967CC (364CI)
CONFIGURATION	FRONT-MOUNTED V8
TRANSMISSION	4-SPEED AUTO, FOUR-WHEEL DRIVE
POWER	232kW (316BHP)
TORQUE	515NM (380LB FT)
TOP SPEED	N/A
0–96KM/H (0–60MPH)	N/A

INFINITI FX45

Replacing the QX4, Infiniti's FX series was available in 3.5-litre V6 (FX35) or 4.5-litre V8 (FX45) guises. This SUV carried Infiniti badges but was engineered by Nissan, which needed to create a new luxury brand because of the high cost of its cars – just like Toyota with Lexus.

COUNTRY OF ORIGIN	USA/JAPAN
YEARS OF PRODUCTION	2003–
DISPLACEMENT	4494CC (274CI)
CONFIGURATION	FRONT-MOUNTED V8
TRANSMISSION	5-SPEED AUTO, FOUR-WHEEL DRIVE
POWER	235kW (320BHP)
TORQUE	454NM (335LB FT)
TOP SPEED	220KM/H (137MPH)
0–96KM/H (0–60MPH)	6.3SEC

LINCOLN AVIATOR

Ford introduced the Aviator to take on Infiniti's FX and Cadillac's SRX, but it lasted just two years. The car was big, brash and incredibly luxurious, but it was also very costly and buyers stayed away. With so many other SUVs available from the Ford group, the decision was made to can it.

COUNTRY OF ORIGIN	USA
YEARS OF PRODUCTION	2003–05
DISPLACEMENT	4605CC (281CI)
CONFIGURATION	FRONT-MOUNTED V8
TRANSMISSION	5-SPEED AUTO, FOUR-WHEEL DRIVE
POWER	222kW (302BHP)
TORQUE	407NM (300LB FT)
TOP SPEED	182KM/H (113MPH)
0–96KM/H (0–60MPH)	10.0SEC

143

MASERATI QUATTROPORTE
If you're not Italian, the Quattroporte sounds very exotic
– but it simply means 'four-door'. However, while the
name might not be that exciting, the specification most
certainly is. Packing a 4.2-litre V8, the Quattroporte
could serve up a healthy 294kW (400bhp) – enough to
take the car to 296km/h (167mph).

COUNTRY OF ORIGIN	ITALY
YEARS OF PRODUCTION	2003–
DISPLACEMENT	4244CC (259CI)
CONFIGURATION	FRONT-MOUNTED V8
TRANSMISSION	6-SPEED MANUAL, REAR-WHEEL DRIVE
POWER	294kW (400BHP)
TORQUE	451NM (333LB FT)
TOP SPEED	269KM/H (167MPH)
0–96KM/H (0–60MPH)	5.2SEC

VOLKSWAGEN PHAETON W12
Volkswagen offered Phaeton buyers all sorts of engines,
along with a choice of long or standard wheelbases. But the
car didn't have the prestige to appeal to badge-conscious
buyers – which was a tragedy because it was a genuinely
capable machine, and astonishingly fast in W12 form.

COUNTRY OF ORIGIN	GERMANY
YEARS OF PRODUCTION	2003–
DISPLACEMENT	5998CC (366CI)
CONFIGURATION	FRONT-MOUNTED W12
TRANSMISSION	5-SPEED AUTO, FOUR-WHEEL DRIVE
POWER	331kW (450BHP)
TORQUE	560NM (413LB FT)
TOP SPEED	249KM/H (155MPH)
0–96KM/H (0–60MPH)	6.1SEC

MG ZT V8
Although it was in dire straits financially, MG Rover wanted
to create a sports saloon that could take on the Germans.
With hardly any money to spend, the front-wheel drive MG
ZT was turned into a rear-wheel drive V8-powered monster.
Few cars were made before MG Rover went bust in 2005.

COUNTRY OF ORIGIN	UK
YEARS OF PRODUCTION	2003–05
DISPLACEMENT	4601CC (281CI)
CONFIGURATION	FRONT-MOUNTED V8
TRANSMISSION	6-SPEED MANUAL, REAR-WHEEL DRIVE
POWER	188kW (256BHP)
TORQUE	409NM (302LB FT)
TOP SPEED	249KM/H (155MPH)
0–96KM/H (0–60MPH)	6.5SEC

PORSCHE CAYENNE TURBO S
Developed in conjunction with Volkswagen, the
Cayenne was the vehicle that Porsche purists
were hoping the company would never build.
However, while it's hard to argue that any SUV
can be truly sporty, Porsche managed to create
an off-roader that had better dynamics than any
of its rivals.

COUNTRY OF ORIGIN	GERMANY
YEARS OF PRODUCTION	2003–07
DISPLACEMENT	4511CC (275CI)
CONFIGURATION	FRONT-MOUNTED V8
TRANSMISSION	6-SPEED SEMI-AUTO, FOUR-WHEEL DRIVE
POWER	331kW (450BHP)
TORQUE	620NM (457LB FT)
TOP SPEED	266KM/H (165MPH)
0–96KM/H (0–60MPH)	5.6SEC

CADILLAC CTS-V

Designed to compete with BMW's M3 and the C55 AMG from Mercedes, the CTS-V was the range-topper for Cadillac's CTS. Packing a 5.7-litre V8 punch, with an engine borrowed from the Corvette C5, the CTS-V was the first car to be launched under Cadillac's V-Series performance brand.

COUNTRY OF ORIGIN	USA
YEARS OF PRODUCTION	2004–07
DISPLACEMENT	5666CC (346CI)
CONFIGURATION	FRONT-MOUNTED V8
TRANSMISSION	6-SPEED MANUAL, REAR-WHEEL DRIVE
POWER	294KW (400BHP)
TORQUE	529NM (390LB FT)
TOP SPEED	264KM/H (164MPH)
0–96KM/H (0–60MPH)	5.0SEC

INFINITI QX56

Designed to take on the Cadillac Escalade and Lincoln Navigator at their own game, the QX56 was Infiniti's take on the full-sized SUV. However, while it was undeniably well built, fast, comfortable, refined and astonishingly well specified, the car's challenging looks were a barrier to sales.

COUNTRY OF ORIGIN	USA/JAPAN
YEARS OF PRODUCTION	2004–
DISPLACEMENT	5552CC (339CI)
CONFIGURATION	FRONT-MOUNTED V8
TRANSMISSION	5-SPEED AUTO, FOUR-WHEEL DRIVE
POWER	235KW (320BHP)
TORQUE	533NM (393LB FT)
TOP SPEED	N/A
0–96KM/H (0–60MPH)	N/A

MERCEDES G-WAGEN

The G-Wagen was properly known as the Gelandewagen, or Cross-Country Vehicle. First offered in 1979, the G-Wagen was one of the most sophisticated and durable off-roaders available at the time, but it was transformed in 2004 with the launch of the barking-mad G55 AMG.

COUNTRY OF ORIGIN	GERMANY
YEARS OF PRODUCTION	2004–
DISPLACEMENT	5439CC (332CI)
CONFIGURATION	FRONT-MOUNTED V8
TRANSMISSION	5-SPEED AUTO, FOUR-WHEEL DRIVE
POWER	363KW (493BHP)
TORQUE	700NM (516LB FT)
TOP SPEED	209KM/H (130MPH)
0–96KM/H (0–60MPH)	5.6SEC

NISSAN TITAN

In the USA, full-sized pick-ups are big business. With Ford, Chevrolet and Dodge having the market sewn up, Nissan decided to muscle in on the action by introducing the Titan, an XXL-sized pick-up that didn't take any prisoners. With its 5.5-litre V8 and aircraft-carrier dimensions, the Titan was quite a car.

COUNTRY OF ORIGIN	JAPAN
YEARS OF PRODUCTION	2004–
DISPLACEMENT	5552CC (339CI)
CONFIGURATION	FRONT-MOUNTED V8
TRANSMISSION	5-SPEED MANUAL, REAR-WHEEL DRIVE
POWER	233KW (317BHP)
TORQUE	522NM (385LB FT)
TOP SPEED	N/A
0–96KM/H (0–60MPH)	N/A

CHRYSLER 300C

Chrysler showed the world in 2005 that a big executive saloon didn't have to look boring, with its daringly styled 300C. Based on the Mercedes E-Class platform, the car was also available as an estate, with a choice of petrol or diesel engines – including a monster 6.1-litre V8 in the SRT-8.

COUNTRY OF ORIGIN	USA
YEARS OF PRODUCTION	2005–
DISPLACEMENT	5654CC (345CI)
CONFIGURATION	FRONT-MOUNTED V8
TRANSMISSION	5-SPEED AUTO, REAR-WHEEL DRIVE
POWER	250KW (340BHP)
TORQUE	525NM (387LB FT)
TOP SPEED	249KM/H (155MPH)
0–96KM/H (0–60MPH)	6.4SEC

LAND ROVER RANGE ROVER SPORT

When it was first shown in three-door concept form in 2004, the Sport was known as the Range Stormer. By the time the production car was unveiled in 2005, something had been lost in translation, but it was still a fabulous car to drive – and even more so in supercharged V8 form.

COUNTRY OF ORIGIN	UK
YEARS OF PRODUCTION	2005–
DISPLACEMENT	4196CC (256CI)
CONFIGURATION	FRONT-MOUNTED V8
TRANSMISSION	6-SPEED MANUAL, FOUR-WHEEL DRIVE
POWER	291KW (396BHP)
TORQUE	560NM (413LB FT)
TOP SPEED	225KM/H (140MPH)
0–96KM/H (0–60MPH)	7.5SEC

AUDI ALLROAD

With off-roaders becoming all the rage, Audi hit on the bright idea of creating a pseudo off-roader without increasing the ride height quite so much. The design helped the dynamics enormously while also allowing people to drive in the rough if they wanted to. This was Audi's second take on the Allroader theme.

COUNTRY OF ORIGIN	GERMANY
YEARS OF PRODUCTION	2006–
DISPLACEMENT	4163CC (254CI)
CONFIGURATION	FRONT-MOUNTED V8
TRANSMISSION	6-SPEED SEMI-AUTO, FOUR-WHEEL DRIVE
POWER	257KW (350BHP)
TORQUE	441NM (325LB FT)
TOP SPEED	249KM/H (155MPH)
0–96KM/H (0–60MPH)	6.3SEC

AUDI S8

If you want space and luxury but don't want to shout about it, you buy one of Audi's S or RS models. With understated lines and four-wheel drive to help drive the massive power down, the S8 was fitted with a V10 engine closely related to the one usually found in the middle of Lamborghini's Gallardo.

COUNTRY OF ORIGIN	GERMANY
YEARS OF PRODUCTION	2006–
DISPLACEMENT	5204CC (318CI)
CONFIGURATION	FRONT-MOUNTED V10
TRANSMISSION	6-SPEED SEMI-AUTO, FOUR-WHEEL DRIVE
POWER	331KW (450BHP)
TORQUE	579NM (427LB FT)
TOP SPEED	249KM/H (155MPH)
0–96KM/H (0–60MPH)	5.1SEC

CITROEN C6

You couldn't accuse Citroen of not trying. Despite the fact that Germany had cornered the executive car market by the time of the C6's introduction in 2006, Citroen still decided to introduce its own contender for the segment. Needless to say, the car was universally shunned as buyers chose BMWs and Audis instead.

COUNTRY OF ORIGIN	FRANCE
YEARS OF PRODUCTION	2006–
DISPLACEMENT	2946CC (180CI)
CONFIGURATION	FRONT-MOUNTED V6
TRANSMISSION	6-SPEED AUTO, FRONT-WHEEL DRIVE
POWER	158KW (215BHP)
TORQUE	290NM (214LB FT)
TOP SPEED	230KM/H (143MPH)
0–96KM/H (0–60MPH)	9.4SEC

MERCEDES CL600

Sitting almost at the top of the Mercedes range, the CL600 was a coupé version of the ultra-high-tech S-Class. Fitted with far more technology than most owners would ever realise, the CL600 featured a twin-turbocharged 5.5-litre V12, offering phenomenal performance with unbelievable refinement.

COUNTRY OF ORIGIN	GERMANY
YEARS OF PRODUCTION	2006–
DISPLACEMENT	5513CC (336CI)
CONFIGURATION	FRONT-MOUNTED V12
TRANSMISSION	5-SPEED AUTO, REAR-WHEEL DRIVE
POWER	380KW (517BHP)
TORQUE	829NM (612LB FT)
TOP SPEED	249KM/H (155MPH)
0–96KM/H (0–60MPH)	4.4SEC

MERCEDES CLS63 AMG

It was getting ever harder to come up with something genuinely new by 2004, but that's just what Mercedes did with its CLS, which was somewhere between a coupé and a saloon. Although all CLS derivatives are fast and well-equipped, the ridiculously powerful CLS63 AMG was the ultimate incarnation.

COUNTRY OF ORIGIN	GERMANY
YEARS OF PRODUCTION	2006–
DISPLACEMENT	6208CC (379CI)
CONFIGURATION	FRONT-MOUNTED V8
TRANSMISSION	7-SPEED SEMI-AUTO, REAR-WHEEL DRIVE
POWER	378KW (514BHP)
TORQUE	629NM (464LB FT)
TOP SPEED	249KM/H (155MPH)
0–96KM/H (0–60MPH)	4.5SEC

LEXUS LS600H

With fuel consumption becoming such a big issue in the early twenty-first century, and with big cars invariably consuming huge quantities of fuel, Lexus decided to get clever and reduce the thirst of its largest vehicles. Which is why the 5-litre engine was supplemented by an electric hybrid system.

COUNTRY OF ORIGIN	JAPAN
YEARS OF PRODUCTION	2006–
DISPLACEMENT	5001CC (305CI)
CONFIGURATION	FRONT-MOUNTED V8
TRANSMISSION	8-SPEED MANUAL, REAR-WHEEL DRIVE
POWER	316KW (430BHP)
TORQUE	494NM (364LB FT)
TOP SPEED	249KM/H (155MPH)
0–96KM/H (0–60MPH)	5.7SEC

Oddballs

Take a look at the cars in this chapter and you might be forgiven for thinking you've picked up the wrong book. After all, many of the cars included here would be more at home in a book called Glorious Automotive Failures, Rubbish Cars or similar. While it's hard to deny that many of the models included here frequently fell short of expectations – in terms of production numbers, ability or reliability – that doesn't make them any less desirable now. That's the great thing about time; as it passes, just about anything becomes collectable for one reason or another.

Some of the cars in this chapter were only ever intended to be built in tiny numbers, while others were simply so awful that few buyers would ever be tempted into parting with their money. The Alfa Romeo Bimotore sits in the former category; the idea of building a series of twin-engined racers is so fantastic that not even this charismatic Italian car builder would ever entertain it. However, cars like the Gaylord, Citroen Bijou and Lightburn Zeta Sports were not meant to be all that exclusive – they just turned out to be, for a variety of reasons.

All of the cars assembled here share a small number of traits, which is what makes them all highly unusual. A combination of quirky styling, flawed (but often innovative) engineering or an initial purchase cost far in excess of the car's true value are what made these vehicles fail. But that's what makes them so fascinating now; the idea of making a car that can drive on water or along metalled roads seems pointless in the extreme – at least for civilian use. But that didn't stop Hans Trippel from building the Amphicar or Gibbs from creating the Aquada. Then there's the concept of building a production car with an engine at each end, as Citroen did with the 2CV Sahara – just what was the point?

Sometimes the ideas weren't at all far-fetched though; they just seemed like the right way to go at the time. Many of the microcars of the 1950s and 1960s are now very desirable for their quirkiness, but when new they were highly sought after simply because they were the cheapest way of getting mobile. Cars like the Fuldamobil or Messerschmitt may seem incredibly basic now, and laughably uncomfortable, but when new they represented freedom and independence at an affordable rate. Then the Austin Mini came along and the microcar market collapsed virtually overnight.

With the car now well into its second century of production, and the world becoming increasingly sanitised, you'd think the completely mad cars would have all but disappeared. Far from it! There will always be a place for individuals, whether it's as car builders or as buyers. That can only be good news, because it ensures a steady supply of oddball cars such as the Smart Crossblade, Grinnall Scorpion and Carver One. As you'll see once you start delving, all of these cars look completely insane and are generally an acquired taste when it comes to driving them. However, they're all real cars that can be bought – in the case of the latter two on a new basis. So while production cars get ever more boring with their design, let's raise a glass to those who are prepared to stick their neck above the parapet and do something completely mad.

The Messerschmitt KR200 looked like an aircraft canopy.

ALLSTATE

For those who found visiting a car showroom too arduous, Sears Roebuck offered this rehashed Kaiser-Frazer Henry J in its catalogue, so you could order it from the comfort of your own home. Few people did, though, with just 2400 of the vehicles finding owners across two seasons.

COUNTRY OF ORIGIN	USA
YEARS OF PRODUCTION	1952–53
DISPLACEMENT	2637CC (161CI)
CONFIGURATION	FRONT-MOUNTED 6-CYL
TRANSMISSION	3-SPEED MANUAL, REAR-WHEEL DRIVE
POWER	59KW (80BHP)
TORQUE	N/A
TOP SPEED	129KM/H (80MPH)
0–96KM/H (0–60MPH)	20.0SEC

WOODILL WILDFIRE

Robert Woodill became one of America's most successful Dodge dealers in the early 1950s, and with his new-found wealth he couldn't resist trying to become a car maker. He created the Wildfire, a glassfibre sportscar inspired by the Jaguar XK120, powered by a Willy straight-six.

COUNTRY OF ORIGIN	USA
YEARS OF PRODUCTION	1952–56
DISPLACEMENT	2641CC (161CI)
CONFIGURATION	FRONT-MOUNTED 6-CYL
TRANSMISSION	4-SPEED MANUAL, REAR-WHEEL DRIVE
POWER	67KW (91BHP)
TORQUE	183NM (135LB FT)
TOP SPEED	177KM/H (110MPH)
0–96KM/H (0–60MPH)	N/A

KAISER-DARRIN

Produced by boatbuilders Glasspar, the Kaiser-Darrin was unnecessarily innovative. The oddest feature was the door design, as they slid forwards into the front wings – something that proved to be problematic throughout production. Power came from a Willys six-cylinder engine, although the last 100 cars featured supercharged Cadillac V8 power.

COUNTRY OF ORIGIN	USA
YEARS OF PRODUCTION	1954–55
DISPLACEMENT	2638CC (161CI)
CONFIGURATION	FRONT-MOUNTED 6-CYL
TRANSMISSION	3-SPEED MANUAL O/D, REAR-WHEEL DRIVE
POWER	66KW (90BHP)
TORQUE	N/A
TOP SPEED	158KM/H (98MPH)
0–96KM/H (0–60MPH)	15.1SEC

PANHARD DYNA 54

Panhard made a decision in the post-war years to sell cars
that were more affordable, but without losing its reputation
for innovation and flair. The Dyna 54 was ultra-modern,
with its independent suspension, hydraulic brakes and
alloy bodyshell, but it looked too weird for it to sell in
big numbers.

COUNTRY OF ORIGIN	FRANCE
YEARS OF PRODUCTION	1954–59
DISPLACEMENT	851CC (52CI)
CONFIGURATION	FRONT-MOUNTED 2-CYL
TRANSMISSION	4-SPEED MANUAL, FRONT-WHEEL DRIVE
POWER	30KW (41BHP)
TORQUE	64NM (47LB FT)
TOP SPEED	129KM/H (80MPH)
0–96KM/H (0–60MPH)	24.2SEC

FIAT MULTIPLA

This car is so outlandish, you'd think it was a French
creation, but the Multipla is an Italian design through and through.
Based on the 600, with its rear-mounted engine, the Multipla could
have highly unpredictable handling once it was loaded up, but Fiat
still sold 160,000 of them.

COUNTRY OF ORIGIN	ITALY
YEARS OF PRODUCTION	1955–66
DISPLACEMENT	633CC (39CI)
CONFIGURATION	REAR-MOUNTED 4-CYL
TRANSMISSION	4-SPEED MANUAL, REAR-WHEEL DRIVE
POWER	21KW (29BHP)
TORQUE	39NM (29LB FT)
TOP SPEED	106KM/H (66MPH)
0–96KM/H (0–60MPH)	54.0SEC

GAYLORD

The Gaylord brothers Jim and Ed liked their fast cars, but they liked their
luxury too. In 1954 they set about creating the most refined luxury car
ever, with variable-ratio power steering, Cadillac V8 power and a retractable
roof. It was certainly a masterpiece, but just two cars were made.

COUNTRY OF ORIGIN	USA
YEARS OF PRODUCTION	1955–57
DISPLACEMENT	5979CC (365CI)
CONFIGURATION	FRONT-MOUNTED V8
TRANSMISSION	4-SPEED AUTO, REAR-WHEEL DRIVE
POWER	224KW (305BHP)
TORQUE	N/A
TOP SPEED	201KM/H (125MPH)
0–96KM/H (0–60MPH)	9.0SEC

MESSERSCHMITT KR200

The 'Kabinroller' was the brainchild of aircraft engineer Fritz Fend,
who wanted to bring cheap mobility to the masses. He came up with
the aircraft canopy-like KR200, and the Messerschmitt aircraft
company decided to put the car into production, with two seats, a
single-cylinder engine and cable-operated brakes.

COUNTRY OF ORIGIN	GERMANY
YEARS OF PRODUCTION	1955–64
DISPLACEMENT	191CC (12CI)
CONFIGURATION	REAR-MOUNTED 1-CYL
TRANSMISSION	4-SPEED MANUAL, REAR-WHEEL DRIVE
POWER	7KW (10BHP)
TORQUE	N/A
TOP SPEED	100KM/H (62MPH)
0–96KM/H (0–60MPH)	N/A

BERKELEY B95/B105

The most powerful of the Berkeleys, the B95 and B105 were equipped with four-stroke engines in place of the two-stroke units usually fitted to the company's cars, although there was still chain drive to the front wheels. These Royal Enfield motorcycle units could propel the cars at speeds of up to 169km/h (105mph) – hence the car's name.

COUNTRY OF ORIGIN	UK
YEARS OF PRODUCTION	1956–61
DISPLACEMENT	328CC (20CI)
CONFIGURATION	FRONT-MOUNTED 2-CYL
TRANSMISSION	3-SPEED MANUAL, REAR-WHEEL DRIVE
POWER	13KW (18BHP)
TORQUE	30NM (22LB FT)
TOP SPEED	169KM/H (105MPH)
0–96KM/H (0–60MPH)	38.3SEC

BRUTSCH MOPETTA

Egon Brutsch had a dream to build the smallest car the world had ever seen – the Mopetta was the result. It's rumoured that the prototype was created overnight, with the single-cylinder ILO kick-start engine fitted later on. Unsurprisingly, production numbers were on the low side, with just 14 examples made.

COUNTRY OF ORIGIN	GERMANY
YEARS OF PRODUCTION	1956–58
DISPLACEMENT	49CC (3CI)
CONFIGURATION	FRONT-MOUNTED 1-CYL
TRANSMISSION	3-SPEED MANUAL, REAR-WHEEL DRIVE
POWER	1.7KW (2.3BHP)
TORQUE	N/A
TOP SPEED	45KM/H (28MPH)
0–96KM/H (0–60MPH)	N/A

VOLVO P1900

In 1953 Volvo boss Assar Gabrielsson visited America, where he saw how popular European sports cars had become. He resolved to build a Volvo sports car, so he commissioned California-based Glasspar to design, engineer and build one. Costs were too high and the quality too poor, however, so the plug was pulled after just 57 cars were built.

COUNTRY OF ORIGIN	SWEDEN
YEARS OF PRODUCTION	1956–57
DISPLACEMENT	1414CC (86CI)
CONFIGURATION	FRONT-MOUNTED 4-CYL
TRANSMISSION	3-SPEED MANUAL, REAR-WHEEL DRIVE
POWER	51KW (70BHP)
TORQUE	103NM (76LB FT)
TOP SPEED	N/A
0–96KM/H (0–60MPH)	N/A

MEADOWS FRISKY SPORT

Originally conceived as a gull-winged fixed-head, the Frisky Sport entered production as a convertible but was later offered as a coupé. The rear wheels were so close to each other that no differential was considered necessary. The car evolved into the three-wheeled Family Three.

COUNTRY OF ORIGIN	UK
YEARS OF PRODUCTION	1957–59
DISPLACEMENT	325CC (20CI)
CONFIGURATION	MID-MOUNTED 2-CYL
TRANSMISSION	4-SPEED MANUAL, REAR-WHEEL DRIVE
POWER	12KW (16BHP)
TORQUE	24NM (18LB FT)
TOP SPEED	90KM/H (56MPH)
0–96KM/H (0–60MPH)	N/A

ZUNDAPP JANUS

Zundapp originally produced motorcycles, but in 1954 a decision was made to build a weather-proof vehicle. Instead of developing its own car, Zundapp bought in a design from Dornier. However, within six months Zundapp had given up, selling the project on to Bosch; just 6902 Januses were made.

COUNTRY OF ORIGIN	GERMANY
YEARS OF PRODUCTION	1957–58
DISPLACEMENT	248CC (15CI)
CONFIGURATION	MID-MOUNTED 1-CYL
TRANSMISSION	4-SPEED MANUAL, REAR-WHEEL DRIVE
POWER	10KW (14BHP)
TORQUE	22NM (16LB FT)
TOP SPEED	80KM/H (50MPH)
0–96KM/H (0–60MPH)	N/A

MESSERSCHMITT TG500

Unofficially known as the Tiger, the TG500 was a big advance over the KR200, thanks to its four wheels, two cylinders and hydraulic brakes. Its light weight meant that it was also faster than many of the full-sized cars that were on sale at the time – but it was strictly a two-seater.

COUNTRY OF ORIGIN	GERMANY
YEARS OF PRODUCTION	1958–64
DISPLACEMENT	490CC (30CI)
CONFIGURATION	REAR-MOUNTED 2-CYL
TRANSMISSION	4-SPEED MANUAL, REAR-WHEEL DRIVE
POWER	15KW (20BHP)
TORQUE	34NM (25LB FT)
TOP SPEED	121KM/H (75MPH)
0–96KM/H (0–60MPH)	18.7SEC

BERKELEY T60

While Berkeley's four-wheelers were popular, the company's designer, Laurie Bond, was a big fan of three-wheelers, so it was inevitable that a three-wheeler would be introduced at some point. The T60 of 1958 was a development of the four-wheeled B60, with a 328cc (20ci) Excelsior motorcycle engine that powered the front wheels.

COUNTRY OF ORIGIN	UK
YEARS OF PRODUCTION	1959–60
DISPLACEMENT	328CC (20CI)
CONFIGURATION	FRONT-MOUNTED 2-CYL
TRANSMISSION	4-SPEED MANUAL, FRONT-WHEEL DRIVE
POWER	13KW (18BHP)
TORQUE	30NM (22LB FT)
TOP SPEED	97KM/H (60MPH)
0–96KM/H (0–60MPH)	N/A

Ultimate Dream Car 9:
Lamborghini Countach

The Countach was unveiled in 1971 at the Geneva Motor Show in early prototype form. It was another creation from Marcello Gandini's pen, and where the Miura was aggressive and striking, the Countach was just plain brutal. But if the Countach really scored over its predecessor, it was in the driveability stakes. The Miura was twitchy on the limit, while the Countach would prove to be much more balanced.

Lamborghini gave the Countach another outing at the 1973 Geneva show, this time in more or less production form, but it would still be another year before the finished article was to be seen. When the production-ready car did emerge, it was badged LP400 Countach, denoting its 4-litre V12 and the fact that the powerplant was hung out the back (LP being short for Longitudinale Posteriore). This first iteration of the Countach had a claimed 276kW (375bhp), which was supposedly enough to allow a top speed of over 306km/h (190mph) – but nobody ever verified it officially. Still, it certainly looked the part and it went even better in 1978 , when the LP400S arrived. The car had wider, stickier tyres along with rejigged suspension, so the handling and roadholding were significantly improved, even if the car was no faster.

As part of Lamborghini's bid to stay one step ahead of Ferrari, there was an increase in the V12's capacity for 1982, when the LP500S appeared. The engine grew to 4.8 litres but the power remained at a quoted 276kW (375bhp); it was the driveability that increased, instead. New for 1985 was the LP500S QV – the Quattrovalvole, or four valves per cylinder. This configuration allowed better breathing for the mighty V12 engine, which also grew to 5.2 litres at the same time. The result of all this work was a power output of 335kW (455bhp), enough to deliver a 0–96km/h (0–60mph) time of just 4.9 seconds. The final incarnation of the Countach was in 1988, with the rather overblown Anniversary edition.

COUNTRY OF ORIGIN	ITALY
YEARS OF PRODUCTION	1974–90
DISPLACEMENT	5167CC (513CI)
CONFIGURATION	MID-MOUNTED V12
TRANSMISSION	5-SPEED MANUAL, REAR-WHEEL DRIVE
POWER	335KW (455BHP)
TORQUE	500NM (369LB FT)
TOP SPEED	286KM/H (178MPH)
0–96KM/H (0–60MPH)	4.9SEC

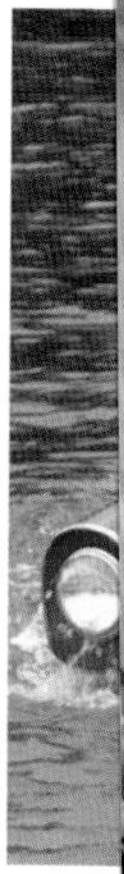

PEE
With
was t
or ref
extinc

COUNTR
YEARS
DISPLAC
CONFIG
TRANSM
POWER
TORQU
TOP SPE
0–96KM/

CHRY
Chrysl
so it p
Ameri
the ab
cars w
voracio

COUNTRY
YEARS OF
DISPLAC
CONFIGU
TRANSMI
POWER
TORQUE
TOP SPEE
0–96KM/H

LIGHTBURN ZETA SPORTS

Having acquired the rights to the Meadows Frisky, Harold Lightburn developed the car into the Zeta Sports. Dispensing with the doors to increase bodyshell stiffness, the car featured a 494cc (30ci) two-cylinder engine, as found in the FMR Tiger microcar. The car proved unpopular, with just 28 examples sold.

COUNTRY OF ORIGIN	AUSTRALIA
YEARS OF PRODUCTION	1964
DISPLACEMENT	494CC (30CI)
CONFIGURATION	FRONT-MOUNTED 2-CYL
TRANSMISSION	4-SPEED MANUAL, REAR-WHEEL DRIVE
POWER	15KW (21BHP)
TORQUE	N/A
TOP SPEED	126KM/H (78MPH)
0–96KM/H (0–60MPH)	N/A

MINI MOKE

The Moke was BMC's attempt at building an off-road military vehicle, based on the Mini. It was a disaster, as the car didn't have enough ground clearance or traction, so it was sold to the public as a fun car. For a brief time, however, it enjoyed cult status.

COUNTRY OF ORIGIN	UK
YEARS OF PRODUCTION	1964–68
DISPLACEMENT	848CC (52CI)
CONFIGURATION	FRONT-MOUNTED 4-CYL
TRANSMISSION	4-SPEED MANUAL, FRONT-WHEEL DRIVE
POWER	25KW (34BHP)
TORQUE	60NM (44LB FT)
TOP SPEED	135KM/H (84MPH)
0–96KM/H (0–60MPH)	27.9SEC

NSU WANKEL SPIDER

It looks great, but NSU's Wankel Spider was much more than just a pretty face – it was the world's first rotary-engined production car. Based on the more conventionally engineered Prinz Sport Coupé, the Spider was a good performer but suffered from a poor reliability that killed sales before they got going.

COUNTRY OF ORIGIN	GERMANY
YEARS OF PRODUCTION	1964–67
DISPLACEMENT	500CC (31CI)
CONFIGURATION	REAR-MOUNTED ROTARY
TRANSMISSION	4-SPEED MANUAL, REAR-WHEEL DRIVE
POWER	47KW (64BHP)
TORQUE	73NM (54LB FT)
TOP SPEED	148KM/H (92MPH)
0–96KM/H (0–60MPH)	16.7SEC

PANHARD 24CT

Based on the PL17, the 24CT was yet another quirky car to come from Panhard. Despite being fitted with a mere 848cc (52ci) and two cylinders' worth of raw power, the 24CT felt sprightly. It looked too odd, however, so buyers snapped up its rivals although they were generally less advanced.

COUNTRY OF ORIGIN	FRANCE
YEARS OF PRODUCTION	1964–67
DISPLACEMENT	848CC (52CI)
CONFIGURATION	FRONT-MOUNTED 2-CYL
TRANSMISSION	4-SPEED MANUAL, FRONT-WHEEL DRIVE
POWER	37KW (50BHP)
TORQUE	73NM (54LB FT)
TOP SPEED	143KM/H (89MPH)
0–96KM/H (0–60MPH)	22.3SEC

NSU RO80

It may have been the Car of the Year, but that was no guarantee of success for the Ro80. Although it offered superb high-speed refinement, the Ro80's rotary engine proved to be horrifically unreliable and the semi-automatic transmission was unpopular. The company went bust and was absorbed into the VW/Audi empire.

COUNTRY OF ORIGIN	GERMANY
YEARS OF PRODUCTION	1968–77
DISPLACEMENT	1990CC (121CI)
CONFIGURATION	FRONT-MOUNTED ROTARY
TRANSMISSION	3-SPEED SEMI-AUTO, FRONT-WHEEL DRIVE
POWER	85KW (115BHP)
TORQUE	164NM (121LB FT)
TOP SPEED	177KM/H (110MPH)
0–96KM/H (0–60MPH)	13.1SEC

ADAMS PROBE 15

Dennis and Peter Adams, who were also behind the Marcos GT, were responsible for the Probe 15. There can't be many cars made that are lower than this utterly crazy contraption, which went on to become the Concept Centaur, with a revised upper body. The car's engine was derived from that of the Hillman Imp.

COUNTRY OF ORIGIN	UK
YEARS OF PRODUCTION	1969
DISPLACEMENT	875CC (53CI)
CONFIGURATION	MID-MOUNTED 4-CYL
TRANSMISSION	4-SPEED MANUAL, REAR-WHEEL DRIVE
POWER	31KW (42BHP)
TORQUE	76NM (56LB FT)
TOP SPEED	N/A
0–96KM/H (0–60MPH)	N/A

BOND BUG

Reliant acquired Bond in 1969, closed its factory down, then set about having some fun. The result was the Bug, which was built by Reliant but carried Bond badges in case it was a flop. It actually sold rather well, though, initially with a 701cc (43ci) engine, then a 748cc (46ci) unit from 1973.

COUNTRY OF ORIGIN	UK
YEARS OF PRODUCTION	1970–74
DISPLACEMENT	701CC (43CI)
CONFIGURATION	FRONT-MOUNTED 4-CYL
TRANSMISSION	4-SPEED MANUAL, REAR-WHEEL DRIVE
POWER	23KW (31BHP)
TORQUE	64NM (47LB FT)
TOP SPEED	121KM/H (75MPH)
0–96KM/H (0–60MPH)	23.2SEC

CLAN CRUSADER

Good looking and even better to drive, the Clan Crusader should have been a winner. With Sunbeam Imp Sport power and a four-speed all-synchromesh gearbox, the car was light and reasonably powerful, as well as refined and comfortable. It was expensive too, which is why just 315 examples were produced.

COUNTRY OF ORIGIN	UK
YEARS OF PRODUCTION	1971–74
DISPLACEMENT	875CC (53CI)
CONFIGURATION	REAR-MOUNTED 4-CYL
TRANSMISSION	4-SPEED MANUAL, REAR-WHEEL DRIVE
POWER	38KW (51BHP)
TORQUE	71NM (52LB FT)
TOP SPEED	161KM/H (100MPH)
0–96KM/H (0–60MPH)	12.5SEC

DAF 55 MARATHON

The 55 was Daf's first car with a four-cylinder engine, and after the company entered two examples in the 1968 London to Sydney Marathon the Daf 55 Marathon coupé was born. Over the standard car there were alloy wheels, a rev counter and upgraded suspension, plus a free-flow exhaust.

COUNTRY OF ORIGIN	THE NETHERLANDS
YEARS OF PRODUCTION	1971–72
DISPLACEMENT	1289CC (79CI)
CONFIGURATION	FRONT-MOUNTED 4-CYL
TRANSMISSION	CVT, REAR-WHEEL DRIVE
POWER	40KW (55BHP)
TORQUE	83NM (61LB FT)
TOP SPEED	135KM/H (84MPH)
0–96KM/H (0–60MPH)	23.0SEC

CITROEN GS BIROTOR

Citroen embraced the rotary engine like virtually nobody else, developing an almost entirely new car that just happened to look like the GS. With a more upmarket interior than that car, just 847 cars were built before Citroen started buying them back to scrap, thanks to the car's horrific thirst.

COUNTRY OF ORIGIN	FRANCE
YEARS OF PRODUCTION	1973–75
DISPLACEMENT	TWIN-ROTOR WANKEL
CONFIGURATION	FRONT-MOUNTED ROTARY
TRANSMISSION	3-SPEED SEMI-AUTO, FRONT-WHEEL DRIVE
POWER	78KW (106BHP)
TORQUE	137NM (101LB FT)
TOP SPEED	177KM/H (110MPH)
0–96KM/H (0–60MPH)	14.0SEC

PANTHER RIO

Look closely, and you'll see that the Rio was little more than a tarted-up Triumph Dolomite. That meant the mechanicals were carried over unchanged, but after Panther had done its work there were alloy panels and much more standard equipment. Just 34 were made because of the high cost.

COUNTRY OF ORIGIN	UK
YEARS OF PRODUCTION	1975–77
DISPLACEMENT	1998CC (122CI)
CONFIGURATION	FRONT-MOUNTED 4-CYL
TRANSMISSION	4-SPEED MANUAL, REAR-WHEEL DRIVE
POWER	95KW (129BHP)
TORQUE	168NM (124LB FT)
TOP SPEED	185KM/H (115MPH)
0–96KM/H (0–60MPH)	9.9SEC

MIDAS

The first Midas coupé was shown in 1978; a facelifted version appeared in 1981 and for 1985 there were further tweaks. In 1989 a convertible was launched, but a factory fire led to the demise of Midas, with Pastiche taking over the project. That floundered, but the car was relaunched as the Cortez by Alternative Cars.

COUNTRY OF ORIGIN	UK
YEARS OF PRODUCTION	1978
DISPLACEMENT	1400CC (85CI)
CONFIGURATION	FRONT-MOUNTED 4-CYL
TRANSMISSION	4-SPEED MANUAL, FRONT-WHEEL DRIVE
POWER	75KW (102BHP)
TORQUE	N/A
TOP SPEED	200KM/H (124MPH)
0–96KM/H (0–60MPH)	8.8SEC

CRAYFORD ARGOCAT

Okay, so it's hard to argue that this is a car as such, but this amphibious beast must be just the ticket when trying to escape somebody in a conventional vehicle. Simply drive to the nearest river and dive straight in; the Argocat may not have been fast, but it was certainly flexible.

COUNTRY OF ORIGIN	UK
YEARS OF PRODUCTION	1982–
DISPLACEMENT	700CC (43CI)
CONFIGURATION	FRONT-MOUNTED FLAT-TWIN
TRANSMISSION	2-SPEED AUTO, ALL-WHEEL DRIVE
POWER	13KW (17BHP)
TORQUE	41NM (30LB FT)
TOP SPEED	N/A
0–96KM/H (0–60MPH)	N/A

SUBARU XT

Known as the XT, the Alcyone or the Vortex depending on the market, Subaru's oddly styled sportscar was offered with a choice of flat-four or flat-six engines. It may have looked challenging, but the bodyshell was undeniably slippery while the interior was undoubtedly hi-tech – too much so for most potential buyers.

COUNTRY OF ORIGIN	JAPAN
YEARS OF PRODUCTION	1985–91
DISPLACEMENT	2672CC (163CI)
CONFIGURATION	FRONT-MOUNTED FLAT-6
TRANSMISSION	5-SPEED MANUAL, FOUR-WHEEL DRIVE
POWER	107KW (145BHP)
TORQUE	212NM (156LB FT)
TOP SPEED	209KM/H (130MPH)
0–96KM/H (0–60MPH)	9.0SEC

Ultimate Dream Car 10:
Ferrari 288 GTO

The 288 GTO was Ferrari's technological tour de force, built specially for Group B racing. The bodywork was built largely of reinforced plastics, with carbon fibre and kevlar in some key areas. The bonnet was made of a kevlar glassfibre honeycomb composite, as was the bulkhead between the engine bay and cabin. Using the best Formula One technology available at the time, this construction offered massive rigidity with light weight.

The powerplant was a development of the V8, which usually nestled transversely in the 308 GTB's engine bay. The Group B formula carried a displacement limit of 4 litres, which is why the GTO's engine was taken down to 2855cc (174ci). Adding two turbochargers had the effect of multiplying the capacity by 1.4, so the effective displacement for the engine became 3997cc (244ci). This was the first time that Ferrari had turbocharged a production car, apart from the Italy-only tax-break special, the 208 GTB. But, of course, the powerplant wasn't just a blown GTB engine – it was much more than that. There was a pair of overhead camshafts for each bank of cylinders, with each combustion chamber having four valves. The crankshaft was machined from a solid billet of steel and there were two intercoolers that helped boost the available power to 294kW (400bhp) at 7000rpm. There was also 496Nm (366lb ft) of torque at 3800rpm – enough to take the car from a standstill to 96km/h (60mph) in just 4.8 seconds, before running out of steam at 304km/h (189mph).

The powerplant was positioned longitudinally, with the five-speed transaxle slung out behind it. Only the rear wheels were driven, while the suspension consisted of unequal-length wishbones at each corner, with coil springs, Koni dampers and anti-roll bars. Each front suspension unit connected with the lower portion of its hub carrier to feed loads into the body between the wishbone mounts, so that the overall height of the suspension could be kept to a minimum.

COUNTRY OF ORIGIN	ITALY
YEARS OF PRODUCTION	1984–87
DISPLACEMENT	2855CC (174CI)
CONFIGURATION	MID-MOUNTED V8, TWIN-TURBO
TRANSMISSION	5-SPEED MANUAL, REAR-WHEEL DRIVE
POWER	294KW (400BHP) @ 7000RPM
TORQUE	496NM (366LB FT) @ 3800RPM
TOP SPEED	304KM/H (189MPH)
0–96KM/H (0–60MPH)	4.8SEC

CATERHAM 21

Caterham's attempt at updating its Seven wasn't entirely successful. The 21 was supposed to be a more usable sportscar without the compromises of the Lotus cast-off, but the car was launched at the same time as Lotus unveiled its Elise; as a result, just 50 or so 21s were built.

COUNTRY OF ORIGIN	UK
YEARS OF PRODUCTION	1995–99
DISPLACEMENT	1588CC (97CI)
CONFIGURATION	FRONT-MOUNTED 4-CYL
TRANSMISSION	5-SPEED MANUAL, REAR-WHEEL DRIVE
POWER	100kW (136BHP)
TORQUE	156NM (115LB FT)
TOP SPEED	204KM/H (127MPH)
0–96KM/H (0–60MPH)	6.7SEC

GENERAL MOTORS EV-1

The EV-1 was the first purpose-built electric vehicle produced by GM and, at the time, was the only vehicle in the history of the company to bear a General Motors badge. GM built them to satisfy California's zero-emissions mandate issued in 1991, and leased over 800 examples from the 1117 manufactured.

COUNTRY OF ORIGIN	USA
YEARS OF PRODUCTION	1996–99
DISPLACEMENT	N/A
CONFIGURATION	FRONT-MOUNTED MOTOR
TRANSMISSION	1-SPEED FIXED, FRONT-WHEEL DRIVE
POWER	101kW (137BHP)
TORQUE	150NM (111LB FT)
TOP SPEED	129KM/H (80MPH)
0–96KM/H (0–60MPH)	N/A

CARVER ONE

It's not easy to come up with a design that'll allow your car to stand out from the crowd. However, perhaps the most obvious is to cut down on the wheel count, then make the car tilt at crazy angles as it corners. That way, you're guaranteed to get people looking.

COUNTRY OF ORIGIN	THE NETHERLANDS
YEARS OF PRODUCTION	1997–
DISPLACEMENT	659CC (40CI)
CONFIGURATION	MID-MOUNTED 4-CYL
TRANSMISSION	6-SPEED SEMI-AUTO, REAR-WHEEL DRIVE
POWER	50kW (68BHP)
TORQUE	100NM (74LB FT)
TOP SPEED	185KM/H (115MPH)
0–96KM/H (0–60MPH)	8.2SEC

DARE DZ

After leaving Ginetta, Ivor and Trevers Walklett set up Design And Research Engineering, or Dare, to build the DZ. Available as a convertible or coupé, power was provided by a Ford 2-litre engine – with the optional supercharger, this meant the car was good for over 232km/h (144mph).

COUNTRY OF ORIGIN	UK
YEARS OF PRODUCTION	1999
DISPLACEMENT	2000CC (122CI)
CONFIGURATION	MID-MOUNTED 4-CYL
TRANSMISSION	5-SPEED MANUAL, REAR-WHEEL DRIVE
POWER	96kW (130BHP)
TORQUE	172NM (127LB FT)
TOP SPEED	232KM/H (144MPH)
0–96KM/H (0–60MPH)	4.7SEC

HONDA INSIGHT

While everyone else was building heavy cars with ever-larger engines, Honda was trying to build the ultimate in lightweight, ultra-frugal cars. With its hybrid powertrain and hyper-slippery bodyshell, the Insight was truly innovative, but Toyota's Prius was much more practical with its five-door hatchback bodystyle.

COUNTRY OF ORIGIN	JAPAN
YEARS OF PRODUCTION	1999–2006
DISPLACEMENT	995CC (61CI)
CONFIGURATION	FRONT-MOUNTED 3-CYL
TRANSMISSION	5-SPEED MANUAL, FRONT-WHEEL DRIVE
POWER	54KW (73BHP)
TORQUE	107NM (79LB FT)
TOP SPEED	180KM/H (112MPH)
0–96KM/H (0–60MPH)	10.6SEC

BMW X5 LE MANS

In an attempt to prove that an SUV isn't inherently slow or unable to handle corners, BMW unveiled its X5 Le Mans at the 2000 Geneva Motor Show. With a V12 engine generating 515kW (700bhp), the car was ludicrously fast but also able to put the power down in an unbelievably civilized manner.

COUNTRY OF ORIGIN	GERMANY
YEARS OF PRODUCTION	2000
DISPLACEMENT	5990CC (366CI)
CONFIGURATION	FRONT-MOUNTED V12
TRANSMISSION	5-SPEED MANUAL, FOUR-WHEEL DRIVE
POWER	515KW (700BHP)
TORQUE	720NM (531LB FT)
TOP SPEED	278KM/H (173MPH)
0–96KM/H (0–60MPH)	4.7SEC

BOWLER WILDCAT 200

Bowler had been building Land-Rover-based cars since 1984, but it wasn't until 2000 that the first Wildcat 200 hit the streets. With its 4.6-litre V8, long-travel suspension and steel-tubed roll cage, the car had enough performance to tackle even the toughest off-road course – and quickly.

COUNTRY OF ORIGIN	UK
YEARS OF PRODUCTION	2000–
DISPLACEMENT	4601CC (281CI)
CONFIGURATION	FRONT-MOUNTED V8
TRANSMISSION	5-SPEED MANUAL, FOUR-WHEEL DRIVE
POWER	160KW (218BHP)
TORQUE	400NM (295LB FT)
TOP SPEED	N/A
0–96KM/H (0–60MPH)	N/A

RENAULT AVANTIME

Only a French company would come up with a car that was a cross between a coupé and a limousine. That's what Renault created with the Avantime, based on the Espace but with just one double-hinged door on each side. It was innovative, but early build-quality issues soon put paid to the car.

COUNTRY OF ORIGIN	FRANCE
YEARS OF PRODUCTION	2001–03
DISPLACEMENT	2946CC (180CI)
CONFIGURATION	FRONT-MOUNTED V6
TRANSMISSION	6-SPEED MANUAL, FRONT-WHEEL DRIVE
POWER	152KW (207BHP)
TORQUE	285NM (210LB FT)
TOP SPEED	220KM/H (137MPH)
0–96KM/H (0–60MPH)	8.6SEC

NISSAN CUBE

The first Cube, available in Japan only, was offered between 1998 and 2002. Like its successor, this Cube was based on the contemporary Micra; the newer model featured a more spacious interior and much more daring styling. Both models were available with four-wheel drive and continuously variable transmissions.

COUNTRY OF ORIGIN	JAPAN
YEARS OF PRODUCTION	2002–
DISPLACEMENT	1386CC (85CI)
CONFIGURATION	FRONT-MOUNTED 4-CYL
TRANSMISSION	4-SPEED AUTO, FRONT-WHEEL DRIVE
POWER	71KW (96BHP)
TORQUE	137NM (101LB FT)
TOP SPEED	161KM/H (100MPH)
0–96KM/H (0–60MPH)	N/A

SMART CROSSBLADE

Smart reckoned it would have a riot on its hands when it made 2002 examples of the Crossblade available in 2002. The car was certainly distinctive, but it was also madly impractical and laughably expensive – although there weren't many cars that could boast a hose-down interior…

COUNTRY OF ORIGIN	GERMANY
YEARS OF PRODUCTION	2002
DISPLACEMENT	599CC (37CI)
CONFIGURATION	REAR-MOUNTED 3-CYL
TRANSMISSION	6-SPEED SEQUENTIAL, REAR-WHEEL DRIVE
POWER	51KW (70BHP)
TORQUE	108NM (80LB FT)
TOP SPEED	135KM/H (84MPH)
0–96KM/H (0–60MPH)	17.0SEC

GIBBS AQUADA

Amphibious cars have never been big business – even the all-time most popular, the Amphicar, sold barely more than 8000. However, the Gibbs Aquada was never designed to sell in huge numbers; this was a showcase for the talents of a company that did these things because it could.

COUNTRY OF ORIGIN	UK
YEARS OF PRODUCTION	2003–
DISPLACEMENT	2500CC (153CI)
CONFIGURATION	MID-MOUNTED V6
TRANSMISSION	5-SPEED AUTO, REAR-WHEEL DRIVE
POWER	129KW (175BHP)
TORQUE	N/A
TOP SPEED	161KM/H (100MPH)
0–96KM/H (0–60MPH)	10.0SEC

MATRA M72

First shown at the 2000 Paris Motor Show in prototype form, the M72 was supposed to be offered from 2003 – but Matra's demise meant it never happened. Offering funky transport for two, the M72 was designed to be a low-cost fun car that could be driven by 16-year-olds.

COUNTRY OF ORIGIN	FRANCE
YEARS OF PRODUCTION	2003
DISPLACEMENT	750CC (46CI)
CONFIGURATION	REAR-MOUNTED 2-CYL
TRANSMISSION	4-SPEED AUTOMATIC, REAR-WHEEL DRIVE
POWER	37KW (50BHP)
TORQUE	N/A
TOP SPEED	N/A
0–96KM/H (0–60MPH)	14.0SEC

BOLLORE BLUECAR

The Bollore Group had no record of making cars, but it knew a thing or two about producing efficient batteries. On the strength of this, Bollore decided to create an electrically powered city car to showcase its products; it hadn't reached production by the time of writing, but you never know.

COUNTRY OF ORIGIN	FRANCE
YEARS OF PRODUCTION	2005
DISPLACEMENT	N/A
CONFIGURATION	FRONT-MOUNTED ELECTRIC MOTOR
TRANSMISSION	1-SPEED FIXED, FRONT-WHEEL DRIVE
POWER	49KW (67BHP)
TORQUE	169NM (125LB FT)
TOP SPEED	135KM/H (84MPH)
0–96KM/H (0–60MPH)	6.3SEC

VENTURI FETISH

Think of electric vehicles and it's milk floats that usually spring to mind. Venturi had plans to change all that, with its electrically propelled two-seater sportscar looking somewhat like a Vauxhall VX220 that had melted in the sun. The Fetish cost an astonishing $460,000 when unveiled in 2006.

COUNTRY OF ORIGIN	FRANCE
YEARS OF PRODUCTION	2007–
DISPLACEMENT	N/A
CONFIGURATION	MID-MOUNTED ELECTRIC MOTOR
TRANSMISSION	REAR-WHEEL DRIVE
POWER	184KW (250BHP)
TORQUE	220NM (162LB FT)
TOP SPEED	161KM/H (100MPH)
0–96KM/H (0–60MPH)	4.5SEC

Sportscars

Few would turn down the chance to have an ultimate car, but even fewer are in a position to own one. That's where the cars in this chapter come in; they're the models that people can actually afford to buy and run, yet they offer a thrill every time the engine is fired up. Sure, many of the cars here were for relatively wealthy enthusiasts only, but none of them were so fantastically priced that virtually nobody could afford them. Quite the reverse in fact; you'll find many sportscars in this chapter that became icons because of their affordability and their consequent ubiquity.

Cars like the Triumph TR2, MG TA and Austin Healey 100/4 were turning points in the evolution of the sportscar, as well as their respective makers. It's also no coincidence that all of these cars were just the start of a long line of models to come from their respective creators, culminating in the TR8, TF and 3000 MkIII respectively; in every case, the car manufacturer in question knew that it was onto a good thing. Decades after production ended, all of the aforementioned cars are highly collectable because they put the fun back into motoring – something they share with other models in this group.

Not all of the cars here are mainstream though; the most interesting are those that were made in limited numbers because the companies that produced them simply couldn't make them any faster. Such cars include the Facel Vega Facellia, Ginetta G4 and Elva Courier, along with the Sovam and Intermeccanica Italia. It's no coincidence that all of these marques have long since disappeared; making cars may be a glamorous pastime, but doing it profitably is a trick that passes most companies by.

Even established and well-respected companies can find it tricky making money out of enthusiasts' cars; Lotus and Lamborghini are just two of the many marques that have teetered on the brink of disaster time and time again; on several occasions it has seemed that the companies were about to breathe their last when salvation would arrive – usually in the shape of a much bigger company that swallowed these tiny outfits whole.

However, sportscars aren't the preserve of cottage industries of course; some of the greatest and most affordable drivers' cars ever made have been built by some of the biggest car manufacturers around. While BMW's M Coupé or Honda's S2000 might appear somewhat familiar because of their mainstream badges, nobody could deny that these are some of the best-resolved sportscars ever made, thanks to their bullet-proof build quality, fabulous chassis design and strong practicality – as well as the ability to put a huge grin on their drivers faces each time the engine is started.

Some of the greatest sportscars though, are the ones created by mass-market car makers as halo models. Take one Ford Fiesta-based sports coupé, give it a thorough overhaul, and voila – the Racing Puma. It's the same with the Renault Clio V6, Ford Focus RS and Alfa Romeo 147GTA; hot versions of ordinary cars. Sure, the basic cars are hardly what you'd call automotive dogs, but these halo models took a car that was already okay, and in each case transformed it into something truly special – something worth putting on a poster on the bedroom wall. Indeed, in each case, the car manufacturer in question created a true dream car.

Built for Honda's 50th anniversary, the S2000 was a revelation to drive.

VAUXHALL PRINCE HENRY

The C-type, as it was originally called, was first shown at the 1910 London Motor Show. As the car had four seats but no doors, the emphasis was on speed and handling. Sure enough, it soon gained a reputation for being one of the greatest sporting cars of its day, thanks to a top speed of 121km/h (75mph) and excellent engine flexibility.

COUNTRY OF ORIGIN	UK
YEARS OF PRODUCTION	1910–15
DISPLACEMENT	3054CC (186CI)
CONFIGURATION	FRONT-MOUNTED 4-CYL
TRANSMISSION	4-SPEED MANUAL, REAR-WHEEL DRIVE
POWER	44KW (60BHP)
TORQUE	N/A
TOP SPEED	121KM/H (75MPH)
0–96KM/H (0–60MPH)	N/A

MORGAN SUPER SPORTS AERO

The Morgan wasn't the only three-wheeler of its day, but it must rank as the most recognizable and the most fun to drive. With its two-cylinder engines stuck out front, and single rear wheel, the Aero was offered with a choice of Matchless, Blackburne, Ford or JAP powerplants.

COUNTRY OF ORIGIN	UK
YEARS OF PRODUCTION	1927–32
DISPLACEMENT	1098CC (67CI)
CONFIGURATION	FRONT-MOUNTED 2-CYL
TRANSMISSION	2-SPEED MANUAL, REAR-WHEEL DRIVE
POWER	33KW (45BHP)
TORQUE	N/A
TOP SPEED	121KM/H (75MPH)
0–96KM/H (0–60MPH)	N/A

MG MIDGET

Until the Midget came along, MG had focused on large sporting saloons and racing specials. Using the 847cc (52ci) overhead-cam engine designed for the Morris Minor, the Midget was an affordable sportscar for the masses. It used the same chassis as the Minor, but with lowered suspension and fabric body panels.

COUNTRY OF ORIGIN	UK
YEARS OF PRODUCTION	1929–34
DISPLACEMENT	847CC (52CI)
CONFIGURATION	FRONT-MOUNTED 4-CYL
TRANSMISSION	4-SPEED MANUAL, REAR-WHEEL DRIVE
POWER	24KW (32BHP)
TORQUE	N/A
TOP SPEED	105KM/H (65MPH)
0–96KM/H (0–60MPH)	N/A

ALVIS SPEED 20

Introduced at the 1931 Scottish Motor Show, the Speed 20 was initially fitted with beam axles, but from 1934 it was equipped with independent front suspension along with a new four-speed gearbox, which was equipped with synchromesh on all forward ratios. There were 1165 Speed 20s made in total, of the four different types.

COUNTRY OF ORIGIN	UK
YEARS OF PRODUCTION	1932–36
DISPLACEMENT	2511CC (153CI)
CONFIGURATION	FRONT-MOUNTED 6-CYL
TRANSMISSION	4-SPEED MANUAL, REAR-WHEEL DRIVE
POWER	53KW (72BHP)
TORQUE	169NM (125LB FT)
TOP SPEED	129KM/H (80MPH)
0–96KM/H (0–60MPH)	22.0SEC

TRIUMPH GLORIA

Triumph started its move upmarket with the Gloria, with a choice of four- or six-cylinder engines for this stylish sportscar. From 1935, Triumph focused exclusively on the Gloria, offering new bodystyles and engine options, but sales were never strong enough to sustain the company and production ceased in 1937.

COUNTRY OF ORIGIN	UK
YEARS OF PRODUCTION	1934–37
DISPLACEMENT	1991CC (121CI)
CONFIGURATION	FRONT-MOUNTED 6-CYL
TRANSMISSION	4-SPEED MANUAL O/D, REAR-WHEEL DRIVE
POWER	40KW (55BHP)
TORQUE	N/A
TOP SPEED	121KM/H (75MPH)
0–96KM/H (0–60MPH)	22SEC

MG TA

Replacing the MG PB in 1936, the TA was an evolution of its predecessor, with a longer wheelbase, wider track and greater length. The previous overhead-cam engine was swapped for a more conventional overhead-valve unit, while there were now hydraulic brakes all round.

COUNTRY OF ORIGIN	UK
YEARS OF PRODUCTION	1936–39
DISPLACEMENT	1292CC (79CI)
CONFIGURATION	FRONT-MOUNTED 4-CYL
TRANSMISSION	4-SPEED MANUAL, REAR-WHEEL DRIVE
POWER	37KW (50BHP)
TORQUE	N/A
TOP SPEED	129KM/H (80MPH)
0–96KM/H (0–60MPH)	23.1SEC

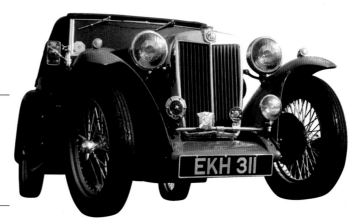

JAGUAR SS100

Launched officially as the Jaguar 3.5-Litre, this was a car that was never truly appreciated until years after it had gone out of production. At first there was a 2663cc (162ci) side-valve Standard engine fitted, but Jaguar's own 3485cc (213ci) unit transformed the car's performance, with a genuine 161km/h (100mph) attainable – hence the car's SS100 nickname.

COUNTRY OF ORIGIN	UK
YEARS OF PRODUCTION	1938–41
DISPLACEMENT	3485CC (213CI)
CONFIGURATION	FRONT-MOUNTED 6-CYL
TRANSMISSION	4-SPEED MANUAL, REAR-WHEEL DRIVE
POWER	92KW (125BHP)
TORQUE	N/A
TOP SPEED	161KM/H (100MPH)
0–96KM/H (0–60MPH)	10.4SEC

MG TC

As the first post-war car to come from MG, the TC featured the same engine as its prewar TB predecessor, but the bodyshell was wider to give more cabin space. All TCs were built with right-hand drive, despite the fact that most were exported to the USA.

COUNTRY OF ORIGIN	UK
YEARS OF PRODUCTION	1945–49
DISPLACEMENT	1250CC (76CI)
CONFIGURATION	FRONT-MOUNTED 4-CYL
TRANSMISSION	4-SPEED MANUAL, REAR-WHEEL DRIVE
POWER	40KW (54BHP)
TORQUE	87NM (64LB FT)
TOP SPEED	121KM/H (75MPH)
0–96KM/H (0–60MPH)	22.7SEC

TRIUMPH ROADSTER

Triumph was purchased by the Standard Motor Company in 1944, which was looking to project a more sporting image. Within two years the Roadster was launched, with a choice of 1.8-litre side-valve or 2.1-litre Standard Vanguard engines. The car was designed in-house, based on an all-new tubular steel chassis.

COUNTRY OF ORIGIN	UK
YEARS OF PRODUCTION	1946–49
DISPLACEMENT	2088CC (127CI)
CONFIGURATION	FRONT-MOUNTED 4-CYL
TRANSMISSION	3-SPEED MANUAL, REAR-WHEEL DRIVE
POWER	50kW (68BHP)
TORQUE	146NM (108LB FT)
TOP SPEED	124KM/H (77MPH)
0–96KM/H (0–60MPH)	24.8SEC

DENZEL

Ex-motorcycle racer Wolfgang Denzel started out using Volkswagen parts for his cars, but as production increased he began making more of his own components. His cars, however, were invariably inspired by the products of Volkswagen and Porsche, from their exterior design to their engineering.

COUNTRY OF ORIGIN	AUSTRIA
YEARS OF PRODUCTION	1948–60
DISPLACEMENT	1488CC (91CI)
CONFIGURATION	REAR-MOUNTED FLAT-4
TRANSMISSION	4-SPEED MANUAL, REAR-WHEEL DRIVE
POWER	63kW (85BHP)
TORQUE	113NM (83LB FT)
TOP SPEED	185KM/H (115MPH)
0–96KM/H (0–60MPH)	N/A

HEALEY SILVERSTONE

Unveiled in the summer of 1949, the Healey Silverstone was a truly focused sportscar, with cycle wings and a lightweight alloy bodyshell. To help aerodynamics, the headlamps were positioned behind the grille, while the windscreen could be retracted into the scuttle, with a small section standing proud to act as a spoiler.

COUNTRY OF ORIGIN	UK
YEARS OF PRODUCTION	1949–50
DISPLACEMENT	2443CC (149CI)
CONFIGURATION	FRONT-MOUNTED 4-CYL
TRANSMISSION	4-SPEED MANUAL, REAR-WHEEL DRIVE
POWER	76kW (104BHP)
TORQUE	179NM (132LB FT)
TOP SPEED	170KM/H (105MPH)
0–96KM/H (0–60MPH)	11.0SEC

MG TD

More than half a century after its introduction, the TD may look pretty antiquated, but after the TC it was a big step forward. As well as a much more spacious interior, there was a quieter, more reliable rear axle along with rack-and-pinion steering and independent suspension.

COUNTRY OF ORIGIN	UK
YEARS OF PRODUCTION	1949–53
DISPLACEMENT	1250CC (76CI)
CONFIGURATION	FRONT-MOUNTED 4-CYL
TRANSMISSION	4-SPEED MANUAL, REAR-WHEEL DRIVE
POWER	40KW (54BHP)
TORQUE	87NM (64LB FT)
TOP SPEED	129KM/H (80MPH)
0–96KM/H (0–60MPH)	19.4SEC

ASTON MARTIN DB2

There wasn't officially a DB1, as the first of the DB models was called simply the 2-Litre. That wasn't a popular car, but the DB2 was a huge advance. It featured beautiful exterior lines by Frank Feeley, while the engine was a work of art – even if early examples did tend to self-destruct.

COUNTRY OF ORIGIN	UK
YEARS OF PRODUCTION	1950–53
DISPLACEMENT	2580CC (157CI)
CONFIGURATION	FRONT-MOUNTED 6-CYL
TRANSMISSION	4-SPEED MANUAL, REAR-WHEEL DRIVE
POWER	92KW (125BHP)
TORQUE	169NM (125LB FT)
TOP SPEED	187KM/H (116MPH)
0–96KM/H (0–60MPH)	11.2SEC

JOWETT JUPITER

One of the most advanced cars of its day, the Jupiter featured a spaceframe chassis that was dressed with alloy panels to offer the optimum balance between stiffness and low weight. Power was provided by the same flat-four unit as the Javelin, which also allowed a lower centre of gravity than usual.

COUNTRY OF ORIGIN	UK
YEARS OF PRODUCTION	1950–54
DISPLACEMENT	1486CC (91CI)
CONFIGURATION	FRONT-MOUNTED 4-CYL
TRANSMISSION	4-SPEED MANUAL, REAR-WHEEL DRIVE
POWER	46KW (63BHP)
TORQUE	114NM (84LB FT)
TOP SPEED	135KM/H (84MPH)
0–96KM/H (0–60MPH)	16.8SEC

MUNTZ JET

Frank Kurtis decided to build his own car in 1948; he then sold the project to car salesman Earl Muntz, who put the car into production. Initially there was Cadillac 5.4-litre power, but this was superseded by a 5.5-litre Lincoln powerplant later on. Despite the Jet's odd looks, 394 were sold.

COUNTRY OF ORIGIN	USA
YEARS OF PRODUCTION	1950–54
DISPLACEMENT	5424CC (331CI)
CONFIGURATION	FRONT-MOUNTED V8
TRANSMISSION	3-SPEED AUTO, REAR-WHEEL DRIVE
POWER	118KW (160BHP)
TORQUE	N/A
TOP SPEED	180KM/H (112MPH)
0–96KM/H (0–60MPH)	12.3SEC

Ultimate Dream Car 11:
Ferrari F40

Despite its arresting looks, the F40 wasn't especially advanced under the skin. There was no four-wheel drive or even anti-lock brakes. But generous specification levels wasn't what the F40 was about – it was built to show how hard-core a road car Ferrari could produce. The two keys to the F40's astonishing performance were its low weight and huge power. To keep the weight down as much as possible, the bodyshell was built entirely from carbon fibre and kevlar. There was still a tubular chassis underneath the skin, but this was constructed from various steel alloys for maximum strength and lightness. By paying such attention to detail, the F40 tipped the scales at just 1102kg (2425lb). The all-alloy V8 engine was boosted by a pair of IHI turbochargers, the maximum power being delivered at 7000rpm, with 576kW (425lb ft) of torque from 4000rpm.

The F40 wasn't just about outright power and performance, though – there were also things such as balance and stability to be taken into account. That's why the weight distribution was as even as Ferrari could make it, while great attention to detail had been paid where the aerodynamics were concerned. When Pininfarina was briefed to come up with an extreme road car to commemorate Ferrari's 40th birthday, it also had to come up with a shape that had a drag co-efficient of just 0.34. This was achieved, partly by smoothing the underpan as much as possible.

The suspension was classic race car, with double wishbones and coil springs and adjustable Koni damper units. There was also height adjustment built into the system, with a standard setting, then a lower setting for high-speed cruising, which dropped the car 20mm (0.78in) closer to the ground. The final setting was for urban use, where the car could be raised to 20mm (0.78in) above standard. Cast-iron brake discs measuring 328mm (12.9in) across were fitted at each corner, with no ABS or servo assistance. Wheels were 432mm (17in) in diameter, the rear ones measuring 330mm (13in) across.

COUNTRY OF ORIGIN	ITALY
YEARS OF PRODUCTION	1987–92
DISPLACEMENT	2936CC (179CI)
CONFIGURATION	MID-MOUNTED V8
TRANSMISSION	5-SPEED MANUAL, REAR-WHEEL DRIVE
POWER	352kW (478BHP)
TORQUE	576NM (425LB FT)
TOP SPEED	323KM/H (201MPH)
0–96KM/H (0–60MPH)	4.5SEC

MG MGA

After the ancient T-Series MGs, the
modern, with its independent front
and-pinion steering. It was also far
it still featured a separate chassis, w
blunted performance. At first there
but from 1956 a coupé was offered

COUNTRY OF ORIGIN	UK
YEARS OF PRODUCTION	1955–62
DISPLACEMENT	1622CC (99CI)
CONFIGURATION	FRONT-MOUNTED 4
TRANSMISSION	4-SPEED MANUAL, I
POWER	63KW (86BHP)
TORQUE	132NM (97LB FT)
TOP SPEED	163KM/H (101MPH)
0–96KM/H (0–60MPH)	13.7SEC

VOLKSWAGEN KARMANN-GH

Karmann started talking to Volkswa
about building a sportscar. It wasn't
however, that the car first saw the lig
Ghia had been approached to design
prototype. The car was a hit despite
price and mere Beetle mechanicals u
stylish body.

COUNTRY OF ORIGIN	GERMANY
YEARS OF PRODUCTION	1955–74
DISPLACEMENT	1192CC (73CI)
CONFIGURATION	REAR-MOUNTED FLA
TRANSMISSION	4-SPEED MANUAL, R
POWER	22KW (30BHP)
TORQUE	76NM (56LB FT)
TOP SPEED	116KM/H (72MPH)
0–96KM/H (0–60MPH)	N/A

ASTON MARTIN DB MK III

Aston Martin had already built a race car called the DB3, so when the DB2 had to be replaced, the clumsy DB Mk III name was chosen. The car looked much sleeker, while the lighting was much more modern – so were the brakes, as there were now discs fitted at the front.

COUNTRY OF ORIGIN	UK
YEARS OF PRODUCTION	1957–59
DISPLACEMENT	2922CC (178CI)
CONFIGURATION	FRONT-MOUNTED 6-CYL
TRANSMISSION	4-SPEED MANUAL, REAR-WHEEL DRIVE
POWER	119KW (162BHP)
TORQUE	244NM (180LB FT)
TOP SPEED	192KM/H (119MPH)
0–96KM/H (0–60MPH)	9.3SEC

ALFA ROMEO GIULIETTA

First came the coupé, then ther Alfa Romeo made the most of i with a choice of 1290cc (79ci) cylinder engines. In Veloce form of these were built and even fev

COUNTRY OF ORIGIN	ITALY
YEARS OF PRODUCTION	1954–65
DISPLACEMENT	1290CC (79CI
CONFIGURATION	FRONT-MOUN
TRANSMISSION	4-SPEED MAN
POWER	66KW (90BHI
TORQUE	108NM (80LB
TOP SPEED	180KM/H (112
0–96KM/H (0–60MPH)	11.8SEC

AUTO UNION 1000SP

Looking like a Ford Thunderbird that had shrunk in the wash, the 1000SP was one of the best-looking affordable classics of the post-war era. It was first shown as a coupé in 1957, and a convertible version followed in 1961, both powered by a 980cc (60ci) three-cylinder, two-stroke engine that was also used by Saab.

COUNTRY OF ORIGIN	GERMANY
YEARS OF PRODUCTION	1957–65
DISPLACEMENT	980CC (60CI)
CONFIGURATION	FRONT-MOUNTED 3-CYL
TRANSMISSION	4-SPEED MANUAL, FRONT-WHEEL DRIVE
POWER	40KW (55BHP)
TORQUE	88NM (65LB FT)
TOP SPEED	132KM/H (82MPH)
0–96KM/H (0–60MPH)	23.2SEC

SWALLOW DORETTI

When William Lyons decided t on Jaguar, it was Tube Investm company. It decided to create a Triumph TR2 mechanicals, bu high thanks to the car's hand-b that production would quickly were made.

COUNTRY OF ORIGIN	UK
YEARS OF PRODUCTION	1954–55
DISPLACEMENT	1991CC (121C
CONFIGURATION	FRONT-MOUN
TRANSMISSION	4-SPEED MAN
POWER	66KW (90BHI
TORQUE	159NM (117L
TOP SPEED	156KM/H (97I
0–96KM/H (0–60MPH)	13.4SEC

JAGUAR XK150

The final version of the XK before the E-Type superseded it, the XK150 featured a single-piece windscreen. Once again there were three bodystyles, but the Roadster didn't arrive until nearly a year after the others. Initially there was a 3.4-litre straight-six fitted; this became the 3.8-litre unit later on.

COUNTRY OF ORIGIN	UK
YEARS OF PRODUCTION	1957–61
DISPLACEMENT	3781CC (231CI)
CONFIGURATION	FRONT-MOUNTED 6-CYL
TRANSMISSION	4-SPEED MANUAL, REAR-WHEEL DRIVE
POWER	162KW (220BHP)
TORQUE	325NM (240LB FT)
TOP SPEED	201KM/H (125MPH)
0–96KM/H (0–60MPH)	7.6SEC

AUSTIN HEALEY SPRITE

Donald Healey saw a gap in the market at the end of the 1950s – for a cheap, small sportscar. The 'Frogeye' Sprite was the result, another collaboration with Austin that used the 948 A-Series engine from the A35, along with that car's gearbox, back axle and front and rear suspension.

COUNTRY OF ORIGIN	UK
YEARS OF PRODUCTION	1958–61
DISPLACEMENT	948CC (58CI)
CONFIGURATION	FRONT-MOUNTED 4-CYL
TRANSMISSION	4-SPEED MANUAL, REAR-WHEEL DRIVE
POWER	32KW (43BHP)
TORQUE	71NM (52LB FT)
TOP SPEED	138KM/H (86MPH)
0–96KM/H (0–60MPH)	20.5SEC

ELVA COURIER

This was Frank Nichols' attempt at producing a low-cost sportscar for those who also wanted to go racing. It was initially fitted with Riley 1.5-litre engines, but MGA units were later fitted. Trojan took the company over in 1962, redesigning the car and wrecking the handling in the process; the company folded in 1965.

COUNTRY OF ORIGIN	USA
YEARS OF PRODUCTION	1958–65
DISPLACEMENT	1798CC (110CI)
CONFIGURATION	FRONT-MOUNTED 4-CYL
TRANSMISSION	4-SPEED MANUAL, REAR-WHEEL DRIVE
POWER	70KW (95BHP)
TORQUE	149NM (110LB FT)
TOP SPEED	177KM/H (110MPH)
0–96KM/H (0–60MPH)	N/A

LOTUS ELITE

Colin Chapman's first attempt at a reasonably practical road car, the Elite was also the world's first glassfibre monocoque. This meant the car's weight was kept to a minimum, and while refinement was poor, the handling was a revelation. Nearly 1000 examples were produced – with Lotus losing money on each one.

COUNTRY OF ORIGIN	UK
YEARS OF PRODUCTION	1958–63
DISPLACEMENT	1216CC (74CI)
CONFIGURATION	FRONT-MOUNTED 4-CYL
TRANSMISSION	4-SPEED MANUAL, REAR-WHEEL DRIVE
POWER	52KW (71BHP)
TORQUE	104NM (77LB FT)
TOP SPEED	180KM/H (112MPH)
0–96KM/H (0–60MPH)	11.4SEC

PEERLESS GT

The Peerless could have been an all-time great British GT, but it never fulfilled the promise it delivered. Based on Triumph TR3 mechanicals, this sporting coupé featured a glassfibre bodyshell over a spaceframe chassis, but cashflow problems led to the firm's bankruptcy – although the project was revived as the Warwick in 1961.

COUNTRY OF ORIGIN	UK
YEARS OF PRODUCTION	1958–62
DISPLACEMENT	1991CC (121CI)
CONFIGURATION	FRONT-MOUNTED 4-CYL
TRANSMISSION	4-SPEED MANUAL, REAR-WHEEL DRIVE
POWER	74KW (100BHP)
TORQUE	160NM (118LB FT)
TOP SPEED	166KM/H (103MPH)
0–96KM/H (0–60MPH)	12.8SEC

trailing-arm rear suspension. Buyers could specify the engine, typically a Coventry-Climax overhead-cam four-cylinder unit. With 61kW (83bhp) and weighing 660kg (1452lb), the car gave a sprightly performance. Other popular engine options were the 1.5-litre MGA, the side-valve Ford 100E or the new 105E 'Kent' engine, as used in the Anglia.

COUNTRY OF ORIGIN	UK
YEARS OF PRODUCTION	1958–67
DISPLACEMENT	1216CC (74CI)
CONFIGURATION	FRONT-MOUNTED 4-CYL
TRANSMISSION	4-SPEED MANUAL, REAR-WHEEL DRIVE
POWER	61KW (83BHP)
TORQUE	102NM (75LB FT)
TOP SPEED	163KM/H (101MPH)
0–96KM/H (0–60MPH)	10.8SEC

AC GREYHOUND

If it hadn't been for the Aceca (a fixed-head Ace), a lot more Greyhounds would have been sold. But this more costly, less agile car didn't make sense for a lot of buyers when compared to its smaller brother. Just 83 examples were sold, thanks to a price tag nearly double that of the Jaguar XK150.

COUNTRY OF ORIGIN	UK
YEARS OF PRODUCTION	1959–63
DISPLACEMENT	1971CC (120CI)
CONFIGURATION	FRONT-MOUNTED 6-CYL
TRANSMISSION	4-SPEED MANUAL, REAR-WHEEL DRIVE
POWER	77KW (105BHP)
TORQUE	175NM (129LB FT)
TOP SPEED	167KM/H (104MPH)
0–96KM/H (0–60MPH)	11.4SEC

AUSTIN HEALEY 3000

At the 1952 Earls Court motor show, Donald Healey showed his Hundred sportscar; a tie-up with Austin swiftly followed, and when the car went into production in 1953 it was badged as an Austin Healey. Initially the vehicles featured four-cylinder engines, then there was the six-cylinder 2.6-litre 100-Six, before the more powerful 3000 arrived in 1959.

COUNTRY OF ORIGIN	UK
YEARS OF PRODUCTION	1959–69
DISPLACEMENT	2912CC (178CI)
CONFIGURATION	FRONT-MOUNTED 6-CYL
TRANSMISSION	4-SPEED MANUAL O/D, REAR-WHEEL DRIVE
POWER	97KW (132BHP)
TORQUE	226NM (167LB FT)
TOP SPEED	180KM/H (112MPH)
0–96KM/H (0–60MPH)	11.5SEC

DAIMLER SP250

The SP250 was a big departure for Daimler, which was used to building saloons and limousines. Here was a two-seater sportscar with a 2.5-litre V8 in the front and suspension heavily influenced by Triumph's TR3A. With disc brakes and that powerful all-new engine, it should have been a winner, but the styling was too controversial.

COUNTRY OF ORIGIN	UK
YEARS OF PRODUCTION	1959–64
DISPLACEMENT	2548CC (155CI)
CONFIGURATION	FRONT-MOUNTED V8
TRANSMISSION	4-SPEED MANUAL, REAR-WHEEL DRIVE
POWER	103KW (140BHP)
TORQUE	203NM (150LB FT)
TOP SPEED	194KM/H (121MPH)
0–96KM/H (0–60MPH)	10.2SEC

DATSUN FAIRLADY
While most of the world was still struggling to take Japanese cars seriously, Datsun was trying to enter the sportscar market with its Fairlady. A lightweight bodyshell (with separate chassis) was developed throughout the 1960s to the point where it could give many European sportscars a run for their money.

COUNTRY OF ORIGIN	JAPAN
YEARS OF PRODUCTION	1959–70
DISPLACEMENT	1982CC (121CI)
CONFIGURATION	FRONT-MOUNTED 4-CYL
TRANSMISSION	5-SPEED MANUAL, REAR-WHEEL DRIVE
POWER	99KW (135BHP)
TORQUE	197NM (145LB FT)
TOP SPEED	183KM/H (114MPH)
0–96KM/H (0–60MPH)	10.2SEC

FACEL VEGA FACELLIA
Whereas Facel Vega had previously focused on large-engined exclusive cars, the Facellia was an attempt at reaching a wider audience. Consequently it was fitted with a 1.6-litre four-cylinder engine, which was to prove Facel Vega's undoing – it was unreliable and lost the company its hard-won reputation for quality.

COUNTRY OF ORIGIN	FRANCE
YEARS OF PRODUCTION	1960–64
DISPLACEMENT	1647CC (101CI)
CONFIGURATION	FRONT-MOUNTED 4-CYL
TRANSMISSION	4-SPEED MANUAL, REAR-WHEEL DRIVE
POWER	85KW (115BHP)
TORQUE	144NM (106LB FT)
TOP SPEED	171KM/H (106MPH)
0–96KM/H (0–60MPH)	11.9SEC

BONNET DJET
The first ever mid-engined road car, the Djet was the brainchild of Frenchman René Bonnet, who had previously made sports and racing cars under the banner of CD. The Djet used Renault running gear, with independent suspension and disc brakes all round. Matra built the car; from 1964 it owned the project outright.

COUNTRY OF ORIGIN	FRANCE
YEARS OF PRODUCTION	1961–64
DISPLACEMENT	1108CC (68CI)
CONFIGURATION	REAR-MOUNTED 4-CYL
TRANSMISSION	4-SPEED MANUAL, REAR-WHEEL DRIVE
POWER	48KW (65BHP)
TORQUE	91NM (67LB FT)
TOP SPEED	164KM/H (102MPH)
0–96KM/H (0–60MPH)	N/A

GINETTA G4
Although there was a G2 before it, the G4 was the first car from Ginetta to be sold in any quantity. It could be bought ready-built, or in kit form for those on a budget, as it meant avoiding purchase tax. Underneath the sporty glassfibre bodywork there was Ford Anglia 105E power, later upgraded to a Cortina 1500 powerplant.

COUNTRY OF ORIGIN	UK
YEARS OF PRODUCTION	1961–69
DISPLACEMENT	997CC (61CI)
CONFIGURATION	FRONT-MOUNTED 4-CYL
TRANSMISSION	4-SPEED MANUAL, REAR-WHEEL DRIVE
POWER	29KW (40BHP)
TORQUE	72NM (53LB FT)
TOP SPEED	137KM/H (85MPH)
0–96KM/H (0–60MPH)	N/A

MG MIDGET

Just like the original Midget that had brought sportscars to the masses, the 1961 edition was effectively a rebadged Austin Healey Sprite – or was it the other way round? The first cars featured 948cc (58ci) engines; 1098cc (67ci) units were fitted from 1962 while 1966 saw the 1275cc (78ci) powerplant fitted.

COUNTRY OF ORIGIN	UK
YEARS OF PRODUCTION	1961–79
DISPLACEMENT	1275CC (78CI)
CONFIGURATION	FRONT-MOUNTED 4-CYL
TRANSMISSION	4-SPEED MANUAL, REAR-WHEEL DRIVE
POWER	48KW (65BHP)
TORQUE	98NM (72LB FT)
TOP SPEED	151KM/H (94MPH)
0–96KM/H (0–60MPH)	14.1SEC

RELIANT SABRE

Reliant had long been associated with odd three-wheeled vehicles, so its decision to build a 'proper' sportscar seemed an odd one. The car's development, however, was already paid for, as it had been funded by and produced for the Israelis, who called it the Sabra. There were four- or six-cylinder versions available.

COUNTRY OF ORIGIN	UK
YEARS OF PRODUCTION	1961–66
DISPLACEMENT	2553CC (156CI)
CONFIGURATION	FRONT-MOUNTED 6-CYL
TRANSMISSION	4-SPEED MANUAL O/D, REAR-WHEEL DRIVE
POWER	80KW (109BHP)
TORQUE	186NM (137LB FT)
TOP SPEED	175KM/H (109MPH)
0–96KM/H (0–60MPH)	9.9SEC

TRIUMPH TR4 AND 4A

Leaving behind the antiquated side-screen TR2 and TR3 for good, the TR4 was a much more modern sportscar that took Triumph through the 1960s. Many of the mechanicals were carried over, although the engine was enlarged. The big advance was in 1965, when the TR4A arrived, with all-independent suspension.

COUNTRY OF ORIGIN	UK
YEARS OF PRODUCTION	1961–67
DISPLACEMENT	2138CC (130CI)
CONFIGURATION	FRONT-MOUNTED 4-CYL
TRANSMISSION	4-SPEED MANUAL O/D, REAR-WHEEL DRIVE
POWER	76KW (104BHP)
TORQUE	179NM (132LB FT)
TOP SPEED	175KM/H (109MPH)
0–96KM/H (0–60MPH)	11.4SEC

VOLKSWAGEN KARMANN-GHIA TYPE 34

Otherwise known as the Type 34, the Karmann Ghia 1500 and 1600 were part of the Type 3 family, following on from the saloon, convertible and estate that had already been introduced. The car was designed by Ghia but built by Karmann and sold by VW alongside its other cars, including the now-coveted Karmann-Ghia 1200.

COUNTRY OF ORIGIN	GERMANY
YEARS OF PRODUCTION	1961–69
DISPLACEMENT	1493CC (91CI)
CONFIGURATION	REAR-MOUNTED FLAT-FOUR
TRANSMISSION	4-SPEED MANUAL, REAR-WHEEL DRIVE
POWER	33KW (45BHP)
TORQUE	113NM (83LB FT)
TOP SPEED	145KM/H (90MPH)
0–96KM/H (0–60MPH)	21.7SEC

VOLVO 1800

Immortalized as the car driven by The Saint, the first 1800s were two-door coupés, with a 1.8-litre four-cylinder engine, although later cars featured a 2-litre unit. However, from 1969 the coupé was canned and a two-door sporting estate was offered instead – the 1800ES, using the same formula as Reliant's Scimitar GTE.

COUNTRY OF ORIGIN	SWEDEN
YEARS OF PRODUCTION	1961–69
DISPLACEMENT	1778CC (109CI)
CONFIGURATION	FRONT-MOUNTED 4-CYL
TRANSMISSION	4-SPEED MANUAL, REAR-WHEEL DRIVE
POWER	85KW (115BHP)
TORQUE	152NM (112LB FT)
TOP SPEED	180KM/H (112MPH)
0–96KM/H (0–60MPH)	12.2SEC

ASA 1000GT

Enzo Ferrari wanted to build a small sportscar, so he got Giotto Bizzarini to design the running gear, Giugiaro to design the car and Bertone to build it. But after the car debuted at the 1961 Turin Motor Show, Ferrari lost interest, so the project was sold to ASA, which built it instead.

COUNTRY OF ORIGIN	ITALY
YEARS OF PRODUCTION	1962–68
DISPLACEMENT	1032CC (63CI)
CONFIGURATION	FRONT-MOUNTED 4-CYL
TRANSMISSION	4-SPEED MANUAL, REAR-WHEEL DRIVE
POWER	62KW (84BHP)
TORQUE	N/A
TOP SPEED	185KM/H (115MPH)
0–96KM/H (0–60MPH)	12.5SEC

MG MGB

When it came to affordable sportscars, the MGB was unbeatable. With production lasting nearly two decades, there were open and closed versions offered, virtually all of them powered by the same B-Series 1.8-litre engine. Easy to find and simple to restore, the MGB has one of the biggest followings of any classic car.

COUNTRY OF ORIGIN	UK
YEARS OF PRODUCTION	1962–80
DISPLACEMENT	1798CC (110CI)
CONFIGURATION	FRONT-MOUNTED 4-CYL
TRANSMISSION	4-SPEED MANUAL, REAR-WHEEL DRIVE
POWER	70KW (95BHP)
TORQUE	149NM (110LB FT)
TOP SPEED	166KM/H (103MPH)
0–96KM/H (0–60MPH)	12.2SEC

TRIUMPH VITESSE

A sportier version of the ultra-practical Herald made a lot of sense, so Triumph decided to slot its 1.6-litre straight-six into the car and tweak the styling a bit. The brakes were upgraded too, while overdrive was now available. From 1966 there was a 2-litre powerplant fitted.

COUNTRY OF ORIGIN	UK
YEARS OF PRODUCTION	1962–71
DISPLACEMENT	1998CC (122CI)
CONFIGURATION	FRONT-MOUNTED 6-CYL
TRANSMISSION	4-SPEED MANUAL O/D, REAR-WHEEL DRIVE
POWER	76kW (104BHP)
TORQUE	159NM (117LB FT)
TOP SPEED	163KM/H (101MPH)
0–96KM/H (0–60MPH)	11.3SEC

ALPINE A110

With its steel backbone chassis and glassfibre bodywork, the A110 was strong and light – and fast too. There was a variety of engines fitted during its lifetime, all made by Renault and ranging from a 956cc (58ci) unit to a 1605cc (98ci) version. Renault gearboxes were used initially, then Alpine made its own five-speed unit.

COUNTRY OF ORIGIN	FRANCE
YEARS OF PRODUCTION	1963–74
DISPLACEMENT	1605CC (98CI)
CONFIGURATION	REAR-MOUNTED 4-CYL
TRANSMISSION	5-SPEED MANUAL, REAR-WHEEL DRIVE
POWER	101kW (138BHP)
TORQUE	144NM (106LB FT)
TOP SPEED	204KM/H (127MPH)
0–96KM/H (0–60MPH)	6.3SEC

CHEVROLET CORVETTE STING RAY

Chevrolet's second take on the Corvette theme was daring, with a split rear window on the coupé and fake vents on the bonnet – both of which would disappear within a year of launch. All-round disc brakes arrived in 1965, along with side-exit exhaust pipes and the option of a 6.5-litre V8.

COUNTRY OF ORIGIN	USA
YEARS OF PRODUCTION	1963–67
DISPLACEMENT	5359CC (327CI)
CONFIGURATION	FRONT-MOUNTED V8
TRANSMISSION	4-SPEED MANUAL, REAR-WHEEL DRIVE
POWER	221kW (300BHP)
TORQUE	488NM (360LB FT)
TOP SPEED	225KM/H (140MPH)
0–96KM/H (0–60MPH)	6.5SEC

FORD LOTUS CORTINA MK 1

When Ford's Walter Hayes suggested a Lotus-engined Cortina back in the early 1960s, nobody realized just what an icon the car would become. The standard Cortina 1500 bottom end was retained, but there was a Lotus twin-cam head and a pair of Weber carburettors, to guarantee electrifying performance.

COUNTRY OF ORIGIN	UK
YEARS OF PRODUCTION	1963–66
DISPLACEMENT	1558CC (95CI)
CONFIGURATION	FRONT-MOUNTED 4-CYL
TRANSMISSION	4-SPEED MANUAL, REAR-WHEEL DRIVE
POWER	77kW (105BHP)
TORQUE	146NM (108LB FT)
TOP SPEED	171KM/H (106MPH)
0–96KM/H (0–60MPH)	9.9SEC

LANCIA FULVIA

Replacing the Appia in 1963 was the Fulvia, with a new V4 engine but sharing the front-wheel drive layout of the Flavia, along with the suspension and braking systems. At first there was just a saloon offered, but from 1962 there was a coupé and in 1967 Zagato launched its own coupé.

COUNTRY OF ORIGIN	ITALY
YEARS OF PRODUCTION	1963–73
DISPLACEMENT	1298CC (79CI)
CONFIGURATION	FRONT-MOUNTED V4
TRANSMISSION	4-SPEED MANUAL, FRONT-WHEEL DRIVE
POWER	64KW (87BHP)
TORQUE	114NM (84LB FT)
TOP SPEED	164KM/H (102MPH)
0–96KM/H (0–60MPH)	15.6SEC

MERCEDES SL PAGODA

Replacing the outlandish and costly Gullwing and Roadster models of the 300SL, the SL 'Pagoda' was far more affordable and almost as stylish. Styled by Paul Bracq, the Pagoda was so-called because of its roofline. During its eight-year production run, there was a choice of 230, 250 and 280SL derivatives.

COUNTRY OF ORIGIN	GERMANY
YEARS OF PRODUCTION	1963–71
DISPLACEMENT	2778CC (170CI)
CONFIGURATION	FRONT-MOUNTED 6-CYL
TRANSMISSION	4-SPEED MANUAL, REAR-WHEEL DRIVE
POWER	125KW (170BHP)
TORQUE	240NM (177LB FT)
TOP SPEED	195KM/H (121MPH)
0–96KM/H (0–60MPH)	9.3SEC

PORSCHE 901

It was to become the definitive supercar, but when the 911 made its debut in 1963, it was fitted with a mere 1991cc flat-six, developing just 97kW (130bhp). Initially known as the 901, Peugeot objected to the name, so Porsche renamed its baby the 911 – and it would go on to redefine the supercar as it was developed over subsequent decades.

COUNTRY OF ORIGIN	GERMANY
YEARS OF PRODUCTION	1963–
DISPLACEMENT	1991CC (121CI)
CONFIGURATION	REAR-MOUNTED FLAT-6
TRANSMISSION	4-SPEED MANUAL, REAR-WHEEL DRIVE
POWER	97KW (130BHP)
TORQUE	173NM (128LB FT)
TOP SPEED	209KM/H (130MPH)
0–96KM/H (0–60MPH)	9.0SEC

MARCOS 1800

The first Marcos was an ungainly affair called the GT. The 1800 turned the corner for this British company and went on to become an all-time classic. At first there was Volvo 1800 power, but later on there would be Ford Cortina engines fitted instead, from a 1500cc (92ci) unit to a tuned 1650cc (101ci) version.

COUNTRY OF ORIGIN	UK
YEARS OF PRODUCTION	1964–65
DISPLACEMENT	1778CC (109CI)
CONFIGURATION	FRONT-MOUNTED 4-CYL
TRANSMISSION	4-SPEED MANUAL, REAR-WHEEL DRIVE
POWER	84KW (114BHP)
TORQUE	149NM (110LB FT)
TOP SPEED	185KM/H (115MPH)
0–96KM/H (0–60MPH)	9.1SEC

Ultimate Dream Car 12:
Chevrolet Corvette ZR-1

The Corvette had already been in production for well over three decades before the first cutting-edge derivative was produced – the ZR-1. The new model featured a high-tech engine and six-speed manual gearbox, the first time anywhere in the world that such a transmission had been offered. And it wasn't just any six-speed gearbox; under certain conditions, to save fuel, a solenoid intervened to prevent second and third gears from being used under acceleration.

The Corvette had become lacklustre, so General Motors enlisted the help of Lotus to save the day. Lotus was asked to design and develop a V8 engine that would allow the Corvette to take on any supercar, and beat it. The results of Lotus' labours was an all-alloy 5.7-litre powerplant that featured four valves per cylinder and a pair of camshafts for each bank of cylinders. Chevrolet's initial plan had been to retain the existing Corvette engine, but fit four-valve heads to it. That way, the engine bay wouldn't need to be significantly re-engineered. But in the event, the ZR-1 was developed as a wider version of the standard car, so the powerplant could fit between the wheelarches. The engine was known as the LT5 unit, and it was created because the existing engine wouldn't have met noise and emission regulations in force at the time.

Despite the impressive performance on offer, the ZR-1 was no stripped-out race-track special. It was fitted with all the luxury equipment demanded by America's drivers. The standard specification sheet included items such as air conditioning, a solar glass roof panel, electric windows and central locking. All this conspired to push the car's kerb weight up to nearly 1.63 tonnes (1.6 tons), which didn't help the car's agility, although it couldn't be denied that the car was impressively fast.

COUNTRY OF ORIGIN	USA
YEARS OF PRODUCTION	1989–95
DISPLACEMENT	5727CC (349CI)
CONFIGURATION	FRONT-MOUNTED V8
TRANSMISSION	6-SPEED MANUAL, REAR-WHEEL DRIVE
POWER	276KW (375BHP)
TORQUE	502NM (370LB FT)
TOP SPEED	275KM/H (171MPH)
0–96KM/H (0–60MPH)	5.6SEC

MATRA JET

Matra didn't plan to get into car manufacturing as such, but when René Bonnet couldn't afford to pay for work on his Djet sportscar, the best solution was to take the project on. The Renault 8 engine initially gave 51kW (70bhp), but from 1966 a 1255cc (77ci) unit was fitted, with 76kW (103bhp).

COUNTRY OF ORIGIN	FRANCE
YEARS OF PRODUCTION	1964–68
DISPLACEMENT	1108CC (68CI)
CONFIGURATION	MID-MOUNTED 4-CYL
TRANSMISSION	4-SPEED MANUAL, REAR-WHEEL DRIVE
POWER	51kW (70BHP)
TORQUE	117NM (86LB FT)
TOP SPEED	175KM/H (109MPH)
0–96KM/H (0–60MPH)	9.8SEC

MINI COOPER S

As soon as John Cooper worked his magic on the Mini, the car was destined to become an icon. At first there were just Cooper models, but it didn't take long to come up with something faster and better equipped – the S, with a larger, more powerful engine than the standard car.

COUNTRY OF ORIGIN	UK
YEARS OF PRODUCTION	1964–71
DISPLACEMENT	1275CC (78CI)
CONFIGURATION	FRONT-MOUNTED 4-CYL
TRANSMISSION	4-SPEED MANUAL, FRONT-WHEEL DRIVE
POWER	56kW (76BHP)
TORQUE	107NM (79LB FT)
TOP SPEED	156KM/H (97MPH)
0–96KM/H (0–60MPH)	10.9SEC

AC 428

AC knew the popularity of the Cobra couldn't last, so it set out to build a grand tourer that was civilized enough to cross continents in one hit. There were fixed-head and convertible bodystyles available, with the designs being undertaken by Frua. But the resulting 428 was too expensive; it cost more than an Aston Martin DB6.

COUNTRY OF ORIGIN	UK
YEARS OF PRODUCTION	1965–73
DISPLACEMENT	7014CC (428CI)
CONFIGURATION	FRONT-MOUNTED V8
TRANSMISSION	3-SPEED AUTO, REAR-WHEEL DRIVE
POWER	254kW (345BHP)
TORQUE	626NM (462LB FT)
TOP SPEED	224KM/H (139MPH)
0–96KM/H (0–60MPH)	5.9SEC

ABARTH 695SS

Britain had the Mini Cooper; Italy had a whole raft of Fiat 500-based Abarths. Both were breathed-on city cars that could give much bigger, more powerful cars a run for their money. In the case of the 695SS, the cars were amazingly fast for their size, with agility to match.

COUNTRY OF ORIGIN	ITALY
YEARS OF PRODUCTION	1965
DISPLACEMENT	690CC (42CI)
CONFIGURATION	REAR-MOUNTED 2-CYL
TRANSMISSION	5-SPEED MANUAL, REAR-WHEEL DRIVE
POWER	59kW (80BHP)
TORQUE	N/A
TOP SPEED	142KM/H (88MPH)
0–96KM/H (0–60MPH)	N/A

DE TOMASO VALLELUNGA

This was the first car to come from Alejandro De Tomaso's fledgling car-making outfit, and while later cars from his company featured V8 power, the Vallelunga was fitted with a 1.5-litre powerplant from the Ford Cortina. There was a pressed-steel backbone chassis and independent suspension, but the car flexed badly when driven hard.

COUNTRY OF ORIGIN	ITALY
YEARS OF PRODUCTION	1965–67
DISPLACEMENT	1498CC (91CI)
CONFIGURATION	MID-MOUNTED 4-CYL
TRANSMISSION	5-SPEED MANUAL, REAR-WHEEL DRIVE
POWER	74KW (100BHP)
TORQUE	N/A
TOP SPEED	193KM/H (120MPH)
0–96KM/H (0–60MPH)	10.0SEC

INTERMECCANICA ITALIA

The Italia grew from the remains of the aborted TVR-based Griffith Omega project; 150 body/chassis units had already been produced when the project was cancelled. Frank Reisner saw an opportunity and fitted the cars with Ford Mustang V8 power, and despite the cars being poorly finished, around 1000 were sold.

COUNTRY OF ORIGIN	USA
YEARS OF PRODUCTION	1965–71
DISPLACEMENT	4949CC (302CI)
CONFIGURATION	FRONT-MOUNTED V8
TRANSMISSION	4-SPEED MANUAL, REAR-WHEEL DRIVE
POWER	184KW (250BHP)
TORQUE	431NM (318LB FT)
TOP SPEED	201KM/H (125MPH)
0–96KM/H (0–60MPH)	8.8SEC

SOVAM

After years of building specialist coachwork for light commercial vehicles, Sovam launched its own sportscar. Even with glassfibre bodywork the car was slow, thanks to its Renault 4 running gear. Consequently, 1.1- and 1.3-litre editions were released, but they made no money, so Sovam went back to the commercials.

COUNTRY OF ORIGIN	FRANCE
YEARS OF PRODUCTION	1965–69
DISPLACEMENT	1255CC (77CI)
CONFIGURATION	FRONT-MOUNTED 4-CYL
TRANSMISSION	4-SPEED MANUAL, FRONT-WHEEL DRIVE
POWER	76KW (103BHP)
TORQUE	117NM (86LB FT)
TOP SPEED	194KM/H (121MPH)
0–96KM/H (0–60MPH)	N/A

ALFA ROMEO SPIDER

Forever linked with Dustin Hoffman and his role in the film *The Graduate*, Alfa's Spider was originally built with a rounded-off 'boat tail', otherwise known as the Duetto. This didn't last long, though; from 1969 the cars featured a Kamm tail, which was much more squared off, more practical, but rather less pretty.

COUNTRY OF ORIGIN	ITALY
YEARS OF PRODUCTION	1966–93
DISPLACEMENT	1570CC (96CI)
CONFIGURATION	FRONT-MOUNTED 4-CYL
TRANSMISSION	5-SPEED MANUAL, REAR-WHEEL DRIVE
POWER	80KW (109BHP)
TORQUE	140NM (103LB FT)
TOP SPEED	179KM/H (111MPH)
0–96KM/H (0–60MPH)	11.2SEC

FIAT 124 SPIDER

Fiat always had the American market in mind when it produced the 124 Spider, which is why the car was only ever available with left-hand drive. It was sold in mainland Europe, though, with 1.6-litre power initially, before graduating to fuel-injected 2-litre power towards the end of production.

COUNTRY OF ORIGIN	ITALY
YEARS OF PRODUCTION	1966–82
DISPLACEMENT	1608CC (98CI)
CONFIGURATION	FRONT-MOUNTED 4-CYL
TRANSMISSION	5-SPEED MANUAL, REAR-WHEEL DRIVE
POWER	81kW (110BHP)
TORQUE	137NM (101LB FT)
TOP SPEED	180KM/H (112MPH)
0–96KM/H (0–60MPH)	12.2SEC

FIAT DINO

Although there were convertible (Spider) and coupé versions of the Dino, they didn't look related. Equipped with the same 2.4-litre V6 as Ferrari's Dino, the Fiat of the same name handled fabulously but looked awkward in open-topped form. The coupé was much more elegant, despite the fact that it was 30.5cm (12in) longer.

COUNTRY OF ORIGIN	ITALY
YEARS OF PRODUCTION	1966–73
DISPLACEMENT	2418CC (148CI)
CONFIGURATION	FRONT-MOUNTED V6
TRANSMISSION	5-SPEED MANUAL, REAR-WHEEL DRIVE
POWER	132kW (180BHP)
TORQUE	216NM (159LB FT)
TOP SPEED	209KM/H (130MPH)
0–96KM/H (0–60MPH)	7.7SEC

GILBERN INVADER

An updated version of the Genie, the Invader addressed the problems of the earlier car by adopting bigger brakes and more suitable suspension settings. Still fitted was Ford's Essex V6 in 3-litre form, while a four-speed manual gearbox with overdrive was standard – although an automatic transmission was available.

COUNTRY OF ORIGIN	UK
YEARS OF PRODUCTION	1966–74
DISPLACEMENT	2994CC (183CI)
CONFIGURATION	FRONT-MOUNTED V6
TRANSMISSION	4-SPEED MANUAL O/D, REAR-WHEEL DRIVE
POWER	104kW (141BHP)
TORQUE	245NM (181LB FT)
TOP SPEED	185KM/H (115MPH)
0–96KM/H (0–60MPH)	10.7SEC

HONDA S800

Honda's first attempt at a two-seater sportscar was the S500 of 1963, with chain drive and a separate chassis – which was dated even for then. Honda decided to update the design with a bigger engine, a conventional transmission and a choice of either convertible or coupé bodystyles, with much-improved handling.

COUNTRY OF ORIGIN	JAPAN
YEARS OF PRODUCTION	1966–71
DISPLACEMENT	791CC (48CI)
CONFIGURATION	FRONT-MOUNTED 4-CYL
TRANSMISSION	4-SPEED MANUAL, REAR-WHEEL DRIVE
POWER	51kW (70BHP)
TORQUE	66NM (49LB FT)
TOP SPEED	151KM/H (94MPH)
0–96KM/H (0–60MPH)	13.4SEC

LOTUS EUROPA

Intended to be a car for Europe (hence the name), the Europa was radical for Lotus, with its mid-engined layout and Renault 16 powerplant. It was initially criticized for its cramped cabin, poor rear visibility and fixed side windows – at least the latter were dispensed with in a 1968 facelift.

COUNTRY OF ORIGIN	UK
YEARS OF PRODUCTION	1966–75
DISPLACEMENT	1558CC (95CI)
CONFIGURATION	MID-MOUNTED 4-CYL
TRANSMISSION	4-SPEED MANUAL, REAR-WHEEL DRIVE
POWER	77KW (105BHP)
TORQUE	140NM (103LB FT)
TOP SPEED	188KM/H (117MPH)
0–96KM/H (0–60MPH)	7.0SEC

SAAB SONETT II

There were three variations on the Sonett theme – Saab's attempt at building a practical sportscar for the masses. Just six copies of the first version were built, with the second-generation (Sonett II) car arriving in 1966. At first there was a two-stroke engine fitted, but from 1967 the Saab 96's V4 unit was transplanted.

COUNTRY OF ORIGIN	SWEDEN
YEARS OF PRODUCTION	1966–70
DISPLACEMENT	1498CC (91CI)
CONFIGURATION	FRONT-MOUNTED V4
TRANSMISSION	4-SPEED MANUAL, FRONT-WHEEL DRIVE
POWER	54KW (73BHP)
TORQUE	94NM (69LB FT)
TOP SPEED	164KM/H (102MPH)
0–96KM/H (0–60MPH)	12.5SEC

TRIUMPH GT6

The GT6 was known as the poor man's E-Type, and it blended the six-cylinder engine from the Vitesse with an enclosed Spitfire bodyshell. The silhouette was taken from the Spitfires that had competed at Le Mans in the early 1960s, while the mechanicals were virtually identical to those of the Vitesse.

COUNTRY OF ORIGIN	UK
YEARS OF PRODUCTION	1966–73
DISPLACEMENT	1998CC (122CI)
CONFIGURATION	FRONT-MOUNTED 6-CYL
TRANSMISSION	4-SPEED MANUAL O/D, REAR-WHEEL DRIVE
POWER	76KW (104BHP)
TORQUE	159NM (117LB FT)
TOP SPEED	180KM/H (112MPH)
0–96KM/H (0–60MPH)	10.1SEC

UNIPOWER GT

Inspired by Carlo Abarth's tiny GTs, Ford engineer Ernie Unger sketched designs for a Mini 850-powered sports car of his own during the mid-1960s. A mid-engined prototype was built and tested, and when the money ran out forklift builder Universal Power Drives stepped in, to bolster its image with a GT car.

COUNTRY OF ORIGIN	UK
YEARS OF PRODUCTION	1966–70
DISPLACEMENT	998CC (61CI)
CONFIGURATION	MID-MOUNTED 4-CYL
TRANSMISSION	4-SPEED MANUAL, REAR-WHEEL DRIVE
POWER	40KW (55BHP)
TORQUE	77NM (57LB FT)
TOP SPEED	154KM/H (96MPH)
0–96KM/H (0–60MPH)	12.6SEC

ALFA ROMEO 1750 GTV

The GTV (Gran Turismo Veloce) was one of designer Giorgetto Giugaro's finer moments – and he's not renowned for turning out sloppy work. Making its debut in 1963, the 1750 GTV handled superbly, thanks to its double-wishbone suspension at the front along with a live rear axle suspended by trailing arms.

COUNTRY OF ORIGIN	ITALY
YEARS OF PRODUCTION	1967–77
DISPLACEMENT	1779CC (109CI)
CONFIGURATION	FRONT-MOUNTED 4-CYL
TRANSMISSION	5-SPEED MANUAL, REAR-WHEEL DRIVE
POWER	97KW (132BHP)
TORQUE	186NM (137LB FT)
TOP SPEED	187KM/H (116MPH)
0–96KM/H (0–60MPH)	9.3SEC

FORD LOTUS CORTINA MK 2

The second-generation Lotus Cortina never had the cachet of the original – perhaps it was because the cars were built by Ford rather than Lotus. More usable than its predecessors, the Mk 2 was still fitted with the Lotus twin-cam engine of its forebear, although performance stayed much the same.

COUNTRY OF ORIGIN	UK
YEARS OF PRODUCTION	1967–70
DISPLACEMENT	1558CC (95CI)
CONFIGURATION	FRONT-MOUNTED 4-CYL
TRANSMISSION	4-SPEED MANUAL, REAR-WHEEL DRIVE
POWER	80KW (109BHP)
TORQUE	144NM (106LB FT)
TOP SPEED	169KM/H (105MPH)
0–96KM/H (0–60MPH)	9.9SEC

MAZDA COSMO

The world's first mass-produced rotary car, the Cosmo 110S was also the first sportscar to come from Mazda. It was certainly innovative, with its front-wheel drive, front disc brakes and wishbone front suspension, but the rotary engine was to prove unreliable, although Mazda stuck with it and developed it to be far more durable.

COUNTRY OF ORIGIN	JAPAN
YEARS OF PRODUCTION	1967–72
DISPLACEMENT	1964CC (120CI)
CONFIGURATION	FRONT-MOUNTED ROTARY
TRANSMISSION	4-SPEED MANUAL, REAR-WHEEL DRIVE
POWER	81KW (110BHP)
TORQUE	130NM (96LB FT)
TOP SPEED	185KM/H (115MPH)
0–96KM/H (0–60MPH)	10.2SEC

TRIDENT CLIPPER

The first Clippers used a 287kW (390bhp) 4.7-litre Ford V8 mounted in an Austin-Healey 3000 chassis, later swapped for a Triumph TR6 frame. But at £1923 ($5288) in kit form, the Clipper cost nearly as much as an Aston Martin DB5, so Trident did well to reach a high of 25 cars in its best year.

COUNTRY OF ORIGIN	UK
YEARS OF PRODUCTION	1967–78
DISPLACEMENT	5562CC (339CI)
CONFIGURATION	FRONT-MOUNTED V8
TRANSMISSION	AUTOMATIC, REAR-WHEEL DRIVE
POWER	179KW (243BHP)
TORQUE	393NM (290LB FT)
TOP SPEED	220KM/H (137MPH)
0–96KM/H (0–60MPH)	N/A

TRIUMPH TR5

Looking the same as the car it replaced, the TR5 was a big improvement over the TR4a, as it used an ultra-smooth straight-six, complete with Lucas mechanical fuel injection. Cars bound for the USA were known as the TR250, and were equipped with twin carburettors instead.

COUNTRY OF ORIGIN	UK
YEARS OF PRODUCTION	1967–68
DISPLACEMENT	2498CC (152CI)
CONFIGURATION	FRONT-MOUNTED 6-CYL
TRANSMISSION	4-SPEED MANUAL O/D, REAR-WHEEL DRIVE
POWER	110KW (150BHP)
TORQUE	222NM (164LB FT)
TOP SPEED	193KM/H (120MPH)
0–96KM/H (0–60MPH)	8.8SEC

TVR VIXEN

The Vixen was closely related to the Grantura, and changes over its predecessor weren't that far-reaching. A larger rear window, a bonnet scoop and different rear styling with new rear light clusters were the most obvious differences, and there was a change to a Ford-built 1599cc (98ci) engine. The four-speed gearbox was also sourced from Ford.

COUNTRY OF ORIGIN	UK
YEARS OF PRODUCTION	1967–73
DISPLACEMENT	1599CC (98CI)
CONFIGURATION	FRONT-MOUNTED 4-CYL
TRANSMISSION	4-SPEED MANUAL, REAR-WHEEL DRIVE
POWER	65KW (88BHP)
TORQUE	130NM (96LB FT)
TOP SPEED	171KM/H (106MPH)
0–96KM/H (0–60MPH)	11SEC

MORGAN PLUS 8

When it comes to alarming drives, the Plus 8 ranks up there with the AC Cobra. With its crude chassis and massive torque, the car was unfeasibly easy to get out of shape. To cut weight, there was the option of alloy body panels from 1977, while in 1990 engine capacity rose to 3.9 litres.

COUNTRY OF ORIGIN	UK
YEARS OF PRODUCTION	1968–2003
DISPLACEMENT	3946CC (241CI)
CONFIGURATION	FRONT-MOUNTED V8
TRANSMISSION	5-SPEED MANUAL, REAR-WHEEL DRIVE
POWER	140KW (190BHP)
TORQUE	319NM (235LB FT)
TOP SPEED	195KM/H (121MPH)
0–96KM/H (0–60MPH)	6.1SEC

OPEL GT

The Opel GT was like a scaled-down Chevrolet Corvette, which is perhaps no surprise, as both cars were the product of General Motors. Buyers on a budget could choose a 1.1-litre engine, but by far the most popular was a 1.9-litre unit that gave lively performance to go with the agile handling.

COUNTRY OF ORIGIN	GERMANY
YEARS OF PRODUCTION	1968–73
DISPLACEMENT	1897CC (116CI)
CONFIGURATION	FRONT-MOUNTED 4-CYL
TRANSMISSION	4-SPEED MANUAL, REAR-WHEEL DRIVE
POWER	66KW (90BHP)
TORQUE	146NM (108LB FT)
TOP SPEED	185KM/H (115MPH)
0–96KM/H (0–60MPH)	12.0SEC

PIPER GTT

It looked like a kit car, but the Piper was always built by the factory – then finished off at home by the customer to escape the dreaded purchase tax. Using a glassfibre bodyshell on a multi-tube chassis, the Piper was just 99cm (39in) high – and ultimately more costly than a Jaguar E-Type.

COUNTRY OF ORIGIN	UK
YEARS OF PRODUCTION	1968–74
DISPLACEMENT	1599CC (98CI)
CONFIGURATION	FRONT-MOUNTED 4-CYL
TRANSMISSION	4-SPEED MANUAL, REAR-WHEEL DRIVE
POWER	65KW (88BHP)
TORQUE	N/A
TOP SPEED	193KM/H (120MPH)
0–96KM/H (0–60MPH)	N/A

RELIANT SCIMITAR GTE

It wasn't the original sporting estate, but the Scimitar was the first one that most people noticed. With its non-rusting glassfibre bodyshell and Ford V6 engine, there was plenty of power but not much weight, so the car was suitably quick – while also able to lug all sorts of loads, thanks to fold-down seats.

COUNTRY OF ORIGIN	UK
YEARS OF PRODUCTION	1968–86
DISPLACEMENT	2994CC (183CI)
CONFIGURATION	FRONT-MOUNTED V6
TRANSMISSION	4-SPEED MANUAL O/D, REAR-WHEEL DRIVE
POWER	101KW (138BHP)
TORQUE	233NM (172LB FT)
TOP SPEED	188KM/H (117MPH)
0–96KM/H (0–60MPH)	10.7SEC

ALFA ROMEO JUNIOR Z

The first 1.3-litre Junior Zs were produced in 1969 by renowned Italian coachbuilder Zagato; it was this Alfa Romeo collaboration that gave the car its name. Zagato had also designed the Junior Z, and with its hatchback layout the car was eminently practical, very good looking and modern.

COUNTRY OF ORIGIN	ITALY
YEARS OF PRODUCTION	1969–75
DISPLACEMENT	1290CC (79CI)
CONFIGURATION	FRONT-MOUNTED 4-CYL
TRANSMISSION	5-SPEED MANUAL, REAR-WHEEL DRIVE
POWER	65KW (89BHP)
TORQUE	137NM (101LB FT)
TOP SPEED	169KM/H (105MPH)
0–96KM/H (0–60MPH)	11SEC

DATSUN 240Z

Aimed directly at the American market, the 240Z had the looks, the handling and a powerful free-revving engine that were pretty much unbeatable for the money – especially as the car was priced below many of its key rivals. It was no wonder the 240Z became an icon, just like its successors.

COUNTRY OF ORIGIN	JAPAN
YEARS OF PRODUCTION	1969–74
DISPLACEMENT	2393CC (146CI)
CONFIGURATION	FRONT-MOUNTED 6-CYL
TRANSMISSION	5-SPEED MANUAL, REAR-WHEEL DRIVE
POWER	111KW (151BHP)
TORQUE	198NM (146LB FT)
TOP SPEED	201KM/H (125MPH)
0–96KM/H (0–60MPH)	8.0SEC

FERRARI 246GT

In 1968 Ferrari launched its 2-litre 206 junior supercar; it lasted just a season. It was quickly replaced by the 246GT and GTS (targa), which offered a genuine 241km/h (150mph) from a 2.4-litre cast-iron V6. As well as being one of the most beautiful cars ever made, the 246 was also Ferrari's first mid-engined production car.

COUNTRY OF ORIGIN	ITALY
YEARS OF PRODUCTION	1969–74
DISPLACEMENT	2419CC (148CI)
CONFIGURATION	MID-MOUNTED V6
TRANSMISSION	5-SPEED MANUAL, REAR-WHEEL DRIVE
POWER	143KW (195BHP)
TORQUE	225NM (166LB FT)
TOP SPEED	238KM/H (148MPH)
0–96KM/H (0–60MPH)	7.1SEC

FORD ESCORT MK I RS1600

This was a car for those who wanted plenty of performance but didn't want to shout about it. Even though it looked little different from basic Escorts, this one featured the Escort Twin Cam's stiffer bodyshell along with tuned suspension and an alloy cylinder head complete with twin camshafts and 16 valves.

COUNTRY OF ORIGIN	GERMANY/UK
YEARS OF PRODUCTION	1970–74
DISPLACEMENT	1599CC (98CI)
CONFIGURATION	FRONT-MOUNTED 4-CYL
TRANSMISSION	4-SPEED MANUAL, REAR-WHEEL DRIVE
POWER	88KW (120BHP)
TORQUE	152NM (112LB FT)
TOP SPEED	182KM/H (113MPH)
0–96KM/H (0–60MPH)	8.9SEC

LIGIER JS2

The JS2 carried the initials of Jo Schlesser, a friend of the car's maker Guy Ligier. It featured a pressed-steel platform clothed in a glassfibre bodyshell. Sat in the middle was a transversely mounted V6 from the Citroen SM, while there was independent suspension all round along with servo-assisted disc brakes.

COUNTRY OF ORIGIN	FRANCE
YEARS OF PRODUCTION	1970–77
DISPLACEMENT	2965CC (181CI)
CONFIGURATION	MID-MOUNTED V6
TRANSMISSION	5-SPEED MANUAL, REAR-WHEEL DRIVE
POWER	140KW (190BHP)
TORQUE	255NM (188LB FT)
TOP SPEED	246KM/H (153MPH)
0–96KM/H (0–60MPH)	N/A

OPEL MANTA A-SERIES

With Ford's Capri flying out of the showrooms, Opel wanted a slice of the budget two-seater coupé market. It introduced the Ascona-based Manta in 1970, with a wide choice of trim levels and engine configurations. The Manta didn't catch on like the Capri, but half a million found buyers.

COUNTRY OF ORIGIN	GERMANY
YEARS OF PRODUCTION	1970–75
DISPLACEMENT	1897CC (116CI)
CONFIGURATION	FRONT-MOUNTED 4-CYL
TRANSMISSION	4-SPEED MANUAL, REAR-WHEEL DRIVE
POWER	66KW (90BHP)
TORQUE	146NM (108LB FT)
TOP SPEED	169KM/H (105MPH)
0–96KM/H (0–60MPH)	12.2SEC

Ultimate Dream Car 13:
Honda NSX

Until the point when the NSX first went into production, there was an assumption that a true supercar had to be temperamental, and a bit of a beast to drive if you really wanted to get the best out of it. In typical Japanese fashion, however, the engineers at Honda created a car that was exhilarating to drive but didn't compromise when it came to usability and reliability.

During the development of the NSX, Honda was a key player in Formula One, in terms of engine supply. While it would have been easy to have fitted a V10, a 3-litre V6 was soon settled upon, for reasons of low weight. To allow the V6 to breathe as freely as possible, there were four valves for each cylinder. There was also variable valve timing (or VTEC in Honda parlance), which was the key to low-end torque while also offering plenty of top-end power.

One of the benefits of opting for a V6 in place of the V8s and V12s often seen elsewhere was that the NSX's engine could be installed transversely. This enabled the car to have a shorter wheelbase than usual, which Honda claimed made it more nimble than its rivals. There was just one model available when the NSX was launched, but in time the family expanded. Honda produced a very limited number of NSX Type Rs in 1992 for the Japanese market only and by 1995 the NSX-T had arrived, with T-bar targa top. At the same time there was also the option of an automatic gearbox, with that model dubbed the F-Matic. Two years later the 3-litre V6 was superseded by a 3.2-litre unit to give a bit more power as well as a useful increase in torque. The biggest change for the NSX came in 2002 though, when it received a face-lift with fixed headlights. In the same year, a second iteration of the Type-R, dubbed NSX-R, was released in 2002, again exclusively for Japan.

COUNTRY OF ORIGIN	JAPAN
YEARS OF PRODUCTION	1990–2005
DISPLACEMENT	2977CC (182CI)
CONFIGURATION	MID-ENGINED V6
TRANSMISSION	5-SPEED MANUAL, REAR-WHEEL DRIVE
POWER	202KW (274BHP)
TORQUE	485NM (210LB FT)
TOP SPEED	261KM/H (162MPH)
0–96KM/H (0–60MPH)	5.2SEC

SAAB SONETT III

Saab made its final attempt at building a sportscar with the launch of the Sonett III in 1970. Although the car was redesigned by Italian styling house Coggiola, buyers continued to shun the model, and in 1974 Saab finally got the message that its core business was building safe family cars.

COUNTRY OF ORIGIN	SWEDEN
YEARS OF PRODUCTION	1970–74
DISPLACEMENT	1699CC (104CI)
CONFIGURATION	FRONT-MOUNTED V4
TRANSMISSION	4-SPEED MANUAL, FRONT-WHEEL DRIVE
POWER	54KW (73BHP)
TORQUE	115NM (85LB FT)
TOP SPEED	171KM/H (106MPH)
0–96KM/H (0–60MPH)	12.0SEC

TOYOTA CELICA

Toyota's first Celica was unveiled in 1970. It used the floorpan and mechanicals of the Carina, and there was a choice of engines. A new five-speed gearbox was developed for the car and although the Celica had the lines of a sportscar, it wasn't built for ultimate speed or handling – smoothness, reliability and comfort were the priorities.

COUNTRY OF ORIGIN	JAPAN
YEARS OF PRODUCTION	1970–77
DISPLACEMENT	1588CC (97CI)
CONFIGURATION	FRONT-MOUNTED 4-CYL
TRANSMISSION	5-SPEED MANUAL, REAR-WHEEL DRIVE
POWER	77KW (105BHP)
TORQUE	137NM (101LB FT)
TOP SPEED	169KM/H (105MPH)
0–96KM/H (0–60MPH)	11.5SEC

TRIUMPH STAG

This was another Triumph that should have been a world beater, but poor engineering let the car down. Overheating engines were par for the course, and while the Stag makes a superbly reliable grand tourer now, back in the 1970s the car became untouchable due to its build-quality issues.

COUNTRY OF ORIGIN	UK
YEARS OF PRODUCTION	1970–77
DISPLACEMENT	2997CC (183CI)
CONFIGURATION	FRONT-MOUNTED V8
TRANSMISSION	4-SPEED MANUAL O/D, REAR-WHEEL DRIVE
POWER	107KW (145BHP)
TORQUE	230NM (170LB FT)
TOP SPEED	188KM/H (117MPH)
0–96KM/H (0–60MPH)	9.7SEC

ALPINE A310

Although the A310 looked a lot more modern than its A110 predecessor, it was basically the same car under the skin. At first there was a 1.6-litre Renault unit fitted, but this didn't give the car enough performance, so the 2.6-litre 'Douvrin' V6 unit was substituted instead – which was much more torquey, too.

COUNTRY OF ORIGIN	FRANCE
YEARS OF PRODUCTION	1971–84
DISPLACEMENT	2664CC (163CI)
CONFIGURATION	REAR-MOUNTED V6
TRANSMISSION	5-SPEED MANUAL, REAR-WHEEL DRIVE
POWER	103KW (140BHP)
TORQUE	148NM (109LB FT)
TOP SPEED	220KM/H (137MPH)
0–96KM/H (0–60MPH)	8.6SEC

BMW 3.0 CSL

If you had plenty of money in the early 1970s and wanted an understated grand tourer, you bought a BMW 3.0 CS. But BMW turned up the heat considerably when it created 1000 examples of a road-ready European touring car – the 3.0 CSL. Most of its panels were alloy to save weight.

COUNTRY OF ORIGIN	GERMANY
YEARS OF PRODUCTION	1971
DISPLACEMENT	3003CC (183CI)
CONFIGURATION	FRONT-MOUNTED 6-CYL
TRANSMISSION	4-SPEED MANUAL, REAR-WHEEL DRIVE
POWER	147KW (200BHP)
TORQUE	270NM (199LB FT)
TOP SPEED	214KM/H (133MPH)
0–96KM/H (0–60MPH)	7.6SEC

LOTUS ELAN SPRINT

Perhaps the purest sportscar ever made, the Elan was practical while also being unfeasibly nimble. The latter trait was down to its light weight, courtesy of a glassfibre bodyshell with a steel backbone chassis. Because it weighed so little, only small, economical engines were needed, so the Elan was amazingly cheap to run.

COUNTRY OF ORIGIN	UK
YEARS OF PRODUCTION	1971–73
DISPLACEMENT	1558CC (95CI)
CONFIGURATION	FRONT-MOUNTED 4-CYL
TRANSMISSION	4-SPEED MANUAL, REAR-WHEEL DRIVE
POWER	93KW (126BHP)
TORQUE	153NM (113LB FT)
TOP SPEED	195KM/H (121MPH)
0–96KM/H (0–60MPH)	6.7SEC

MERCEDES R107 SL

Replacing the Pagoda SL was never going to be easy, but Mercedes pulled it off with the R107. The series lasted nearly two decades. Initially there was a choice of 3.5- or 4.5-litre V8s, but in time there were six-cylinder units offered, along with 5- and 5.6-litre V8 units.

COUNTRY OF ORIGIN	GERMANY
YEARS OF PRODUCTION	1971–89
DISPLACEMENT	4973CC (303CI)
CONFIGURATION	FRONT-MOUNTED V8
TRANSMISSION	AUTOMATIC, REAR-WHEEL DRIVE
POWER	177KW (240BHP)
TORQUE	404NM (298LB FT)
TOP SPEED	229KM/H (142MPH)
0–96KM/H (0–60MPH)	7.2SEC

Mid-engined cars usually carried huge price tags, so when Fiat launched its eminently affordable X1/9 in 1972, it really put a cat among the pigeons. At first there was a 1290cc (79ci) engine fitted, and there were disc brakes all round, a removable targa top and pop-up headlights. From 1978 a 1.5-litre engine was fitted.

COUNTRY OF ORIGIN	ITALY
YEARS OF PRODUCTION	1972–89
DISPLACEMENT	1498CC (91CI)
CONFIGURATION	MID-MOUNTED 4-CYL
TRANSMISSION	5-SPEED MANUAL, REAR-WHEEL DRIVE
POWER	63KW (85BHP)
TORQUE	118NM (87LB FT)
TOP SPEED	177KM/H (110MPH)
0–96KM/H (0–60MPH)	10.8SEC

BITTER CD

First shown as an Opel concept at the 1969 Frankfurt Motor Show, Erich Bitter took over the project after the decision was taken not to proceed any further. Bitter outsourced the construction to Baur, while Frua updated the design. Motive power came from a Chevrolet 5.4-litre V8, while the Diplomat's platform was used.

COUNTRY OF ORIGIN	GERMANY
YEARS OF PRODUCTION	1973–79
DISPLACEMENT	5354CC (327CI)
CONFIGURATION	FRONT-MOUNTED V8
TRANSMISSION	3-SPEED AUTO, REAR-WHEEL DRIVE
POWER	169KW (230BHP)
TORQUE	427NM (315LB FT)
TOP SPEED	208KM/H (129MPH)
0–96KM/H (0–60MPH)	9.4SEC

CATERHAM SEVEN

Carrying on where the Lotus Seven left off, the Caterham has evolved over the years to offer ever more modern engines, longer cockpits and a much-developed chassis. In CSR form the car shared little with its forebears, save for the classic lines; there was more power and agility than ever before.

COUNTRY OF ORIGIN	UK
YEARS OF PRODUCTION	1973–
DISPLACEMENT	2296CC (140CI)
CONFIGURATION	FRONT-MOUNTED 4-CYL
TRANSMISSION	6-SPEED MANUAL, REAR-WHEEL DRIVE
POWER	191KW (260BHP)
TORQUE	271NM (200LB FT)
TOP SPEED	249KM/H (155MPH)
0–96KM/H (0–60MPH)	3.1SEC

ILINGA AF2

Australia isn't noted for its home-grown supercars – perhaps it's because cars such as the Ilinga never really took off. With its Rover-sourced V8 up front and Borg-Warner manual gearbox, the car was well specified, but the economies of scale simply weren't there; buyers stuck with their Holdens instead.

COUNTRY OF ORIGIN	AUSTRALIA
YEARS OF PRODUCTION	1973–75
DISPLACEMENT	4400CC (268CI)
CONFIGURATION	FRONT-MOUNTED V8
TRANSMISSION	4-SPEED MANUAL, REAR-WHEEL DRIVE
POWER	162KW (220BHP)
TORQUE	400NM (295LB FT)
TOP SPEED	N/A
0–96KM/H (0–60MPH)	N/A

MATRA BAGHEERA

In 1969, Matra switched its allegiances from Renault to rival French car maker Simca, to develop the Bagheera. In typical French fashion, the car featured a unique selling point – three-abreast seating. There was also a glass frameless hatchback, while the car was constructed featuring a plastic bodyshell over a spaceframe chassis.

COUNTRY OF ORIGIN	FRANCE
YEARS OF PRODUCTION	1973–80
DISPLACEMENT	1442CC (88CI)
CONFIGURATION	FRONT-MOUNTED 4-CYL
TRANSMISSION	4-SPEED MANUAL, REAR-WHEEL DRIVE
POWER	66KW (90BHP)
TORQUE	119NM (88LB FT)
TOP SPEED	177KM/H (110MPH)
0–96KM/H (0–60MPH)	11.6SEC

MGB GT V8

Various aftermarket tuners had tried fitting the Rover V8 into the MGB bodyshell, most notably Costello. MG took the hint and offered a V8-powered B – but only in closed GT form. The V8 weighed much the same as the cast-iron four-cylinder unit usually fitted, so this B was fast but still nicely balanced.

COUNTRY OF ORIGIN	UK
YEARS OF PRODUCTION	1973–76
DISPLACEMENT	3528CC (215CI)
CONFIGURATION	FRONT-MOUNTED V8
TRANSMISSION	4-SPEED MANUAL O/D, REAR-WHEEL DRIVE
POWER	101KW (137BHP)
TORQUE	262NM (193LB FT)
TOP SPEED	200KM/H (124MPH)
0–96KM/H (0–60MPH)	8.6SEC

PORSCHE 914

Developed in conjunction with Volkswagen, the 914 is overlooked by most Porsche fans because of its humble origins. Yet the car is great to drive in 2.0-litre form, with strong performance and superb handling. It also looks different, with that targa panel and the pop-up headlamps.

COUNTRY OF ORIGIN	GERMANY
YEARS OF PRODUCTION	1973–76
DISPLACEMENT	1971CC (120CI)
CONFIGURATION	MID-MOUNTED FLAT-4
TRANSMISSION	5-SPEED MANUAL, REAR-WHEEL DRIVE
POWER	74KW (100BHP)
TORQUE	157NM (116LB FT)
TOP SPEED	190KM/H (118MPH)
0–96KM/H (0–60MPH)	10.5SEC

VAUXHALL FIRENZA DROOP SNOOT

In the early 1970s Vauxhall was trying to capture the youth market. The result was a Firenza coupé with a tweaked Magnum 2.3-litre engine, beefed-up transmission and a wind-cheating glassfibre nosecone to cut drag by 30 per cent. The plan was to produce at least 1000 examples each year, but just 204 were built.

COUNTRY OF ORIGIN	UK
YEARS OF PRODUCTION	1973–75
DISPLACEMENT	2279CC (139CI)
CONFIGURATION	FRONT-MOUNTED 4-CYL
TRANSMISSION	4-SPEED MANUAL, REAR-WHEEL DRIVE
POWER	96KW (131BHP)
TORQUE	195NM (144LB FT)
TOP SPEED	193KM/H (120MPH)
0–96KM/H (0–60MPH)	9.4SEC

BRICKLIN SV-1

In many ways the SV-1 project was like the De Lorean that would follow a few years later. Malcolm Bricklin persuaded the Canadian government to fund a new gull-winged sportscar, with V8 power. The car looked good, but unfortunately the build quality was poor and the project quickly failed.

COUNTRY OF ORIGIN	CANADA
YEARS OF PRODUCTION	1974–75
DISPLACEMENT	5896CC (360CI)
CONFIGURATION	FRONT-MOUNTED V8
TRANSMISSION	3-SPEED AUTO, REAR-WHEEL DRIVE
POWER	162KW (220BHP)
TORQUE	427NM (315LB FT)
TOP SPEED	196KM/H (122MPH)
0–96KM/H (0–60MPH)	9.9SEC

LANCIA MONTECARLO

Originally conceived as a Fiat, the Montecarlo should have carried a 3-litre V6. The 1970s fuel crisis led to a change of heart and the Montecarlo appeared with Lancia Beta power instead. Handling and braking problems led to the car being withdrawn in 1978, but a revised version of the car appeared in 1980.

COUNTRY OF ORIGIN	ITALY
YEARS OF PRODUCTION	1975–84
DISPLACEMENT	1995CC (122CI)
CONFIGURATION	MID-MOUNTED 4-CYL
TRANSMISSION	5-SPEED MANUAL, REAR-WHEEL DRIVE
POWER	88KW (120BHP)
TORQUE	164NM (121LB FT)
TOP SPEED	192KM/H (119MPH)
0–96KM/H (0–60MPH)	9.8SEC

VOLKSWAGEN SCIROCCO

Designed by Giugiaro and engineered by Karmann, the Scirocco was based on Volkswagen's Golf, so all the mechanical parts were carried over largely unchanged. Volkswagen had to outsource the development because it was too busy trying to engineer the Golf – its most important car since the Beetle was launched.

COUNTRY OF ORIGIN	GERMANY
YEARS OF PRODUCTION	1974–81
DISPLACEMENT	1588CC (97CI)
CONFIGURATION	FRONT-MOUNTED 4-CYL
TRANSMISSION	4-SPEED MANUAL, FRONT-WHEEL DRIVE
POWER	81KW (110BHP)
TORQUE	132NM (97LB FT)
TOP SPEED	185KM/H (115MPH)
0–96KM/H (0–60MPH)	8.8SEC

FERRARI 308GTB/GTS

The 308GTB and GTS (targa version) represented quite a departure for Ferrari; here were its first mid-engined production cars with V8 engines. Designed to supersede the V6-powered 246 'Dino', the GTB and GTS were born on the back of the success of the four-seater 308 GT4, which had been introduced in 1973.

COUNTRY OF ORIGIN	ITALY
YEARS OF PRODUCTION	1975
DISPLACEMENT	2927CC (179CI)
CONFIGURATION	MID-MOUNTED V8
TRANSMISSION	5-SPEED MANUAL, REAR-WHEEL DRIVE
POWER	188KW (255BHP)
TORQUE	245NM (181LB FT)
TOP SPEED	249KM/H (155MPH)
0–96KM/H (0–60MPH)	7.3SEC

VOLKSWAGEN GOLF GTI

Few cars have had an impact like the first Golf GTi – the car that launched a thousand copies. Volkswagen initially kept the car solely for the home market, but word got out that the car was rather good to drive while also being practical. Exports began and the company never looked back.

COUNTRY OF ORIGIN	GERMANY
YEARS OF PRODUCTION	1975–83
DISPLACEMENT	1781CC (109CI)
CONFIGURATION	FRONT-MOUNTED 4-CYL
TRANSMISSION	5-SPEED MANUAL, FRONT-WHEEL DRIVE
POWER	82kW (112BHP)
TORQUE	148NM (109LB FT)
TOP SPEED	182KM/H (113MPH)
0–96KM/H (0–60MPH)	8.3SEC

VAUXHALL CHEVETTE HS

Its rear-wheel drive chassis meant that even in standard form the Chevette (known as the Kadett in Europe) was good fun to drive. Once Vauxhall had bolted in a 2.3-litre engine with an alloy twin-cam head and 16 valves, however, the car just came alive. With just 400 examples constructed, they're now highly prized.

COUNTRY OF ORIGIN	UK
YEARS OF PRODUCTION	1976–80
DISPLACEMENT	2279CC (139CI)
CONFIGURATION	FRONT-MOUNTED 4-CYL
TRANSMISSION	5-SPEED MANUAL, REAR-WHEEL DRIVE
POWER	99kW (135BHP)
TORQUE	182NM (134LB FT)
TOP SPEED	185KM/H (115MPH)
0–96KM/H (0–60MPH)	8.5SEC

FORD ESCORT MK 2 RS2000

Launched on the back of Ford's rallying success throughout the 1970s, the RS2000 looked like no other Mk 2 Escort, even though many of the mechanicals were largely unchanged. There was, however, a 2-litre Pinto engine installed, tuned to give 81kW (110bhp), thanks to a free-flowing exhaust system and raised compression ratio.

COUNTRY OF ORIGIN	UK
YEARS OF PRODUCTION	1976–80
DISPLACEMENT	1993CC (122CI)
CONFIGURATION	FRONT-MOUNTED 4-CYL
TRANSMISSION	4-SPEED MANUAL, REAR-WHEEL DRIVE
POWER	81kW (110BHP)
TORQUE	161NM (119LB FT)
TOP SPEED	175KM/H (109MPH)
0–96KM/H (0–60MPH)	8.6SEC

LAMBORGHINI SILHOUETTE

Carrying on from where the Urraco left off, the Silhouette took over the earlier car's engine and bodyshell, but with a twist – there was now a targa configuration. The 2+2 seating was also ditched, because it compromised the car's sporting credentials; this redesign also ensured that there was somewhere to stow the roof.

COUNTRY OF ORIGIN	ITALY
YEARS OF PRODUCTION	1976–79
DISPLACEMENT	2996CC (183CI)
CONFIGURATION	MID-MOUNTED V8
TRANSMISSION	5-SPEED MANUAL, REAR-WHEEL DRIVE
POWER	195kW (265BHP)
TORQUE	164NM (195LB FT)
TOP SPEED	259KM/H (161MPH)
0–96KM/H (0–60MPH)	N/A

SAAB 99 TURBO

It may have looked dull, but the 99 Turbo was a cult car – there were very few turbocharged cars available when it was launched. Saab took its Triumph-derived engine and bolted a Garrett T3 turbo to it, dropping the compression ratio while adding electronic fuel injection at the same time.

COUNTRY OF ORIGIN	SWEDEN
YEARS OF PRODUCTION	1977–80
DISPLACEMENT	1985CC (121CI)
CONFIGURATION	FRONT-MOUNTED 4-CYL
TRANSMISSION	4-SPEED MANUAL, FRONT-WHEEL DRIVE
POWER	107kW (145BHP)
TORQUE	236NM (174LB FT)
TOP SPEED	196KM/H (122MPH)
0–96KM/H (0–60MPH)	8.9SEC

CHEVROLET CORVETTE PACE CAR

To celebrate 25 years of Corvette production in 1978, the car was chosen as pace car for the 62nd Indianapolis – so Chevrolet produced more than 6000 replicas for sale as street cars. The brakes were beefed up and so was the suspension, while power was also increased thanks to engine and exhaust modifications.

COUNTRY OF ORIGIN	USA
YEARS OF PRODUCTION	1978
DISPLACEMENT	5735CC (350CI)
CONFIGURATION	FRONT-MOUNTED V8
TRANSMISSION	3-SPEED AUTO, REAR-WHEEL DRIVE
POWER	162kW (220BHP)
TORQUE	353NM (260LB FT)
TOP SPEED	210KM/H (125MPH)
0–96KM/H (0–60MPH)	8.2SEC

MAZDA RX-7

By the time the first-generation RX-7 appeared in 1978, everybody else had given up on the idea of developing a rotary-engined car. But Mazda persisted, and this car worked brilliantly. Fuel consumption was high, but the RX-7 handled superbly, even though its mechanical specification was otherwise rather ordinary.

COUNTRY OF ORIGIN	JAPAN
YEARS OF PRODUCTION	1978–85
DISPLACEMENT	2292CC (140CI)
CONFIGURATION	FRONT-MOUNTED ROTARY
TRANSMISSION	5-SPEED MANUAL, REAR-WHEEL DRIVE
POWER	77kW (105BHP)
TORQUE	144NM (106LB FT)
TOP SPEED	188KM/H (117MPH)
0–96KM/H (0–60MPH)	9.9SEC

TVR 3000S

Sold officially as the Convertible, the car has only retrospectively become known as the 3000S. Based closely on the 3000M, the S was the car that formed the basis of the S-Series, which became the entry-level TVR from 1986 and culminated in the monster V8-S.

COUNTRY OF ORIGIN	UK
YEARS OF PRODUCTION	1978–79
DISPLACEMENT	2994CC (183CI)
CONFIGURATION	FRONT-MOUNTED 6-CYL
TRANSMISSION	4-SPEED MANUAL, REAR-WHEEL DRIVE
POWER	101KW (138BHP)
TORQUE	236NM (174LB FT)
TOP SPEED	195KM/H (121MPH)
0–96KM/H (0–60MPH)	7.7SEC

AC 3000ME

It was in 1973 that the 3000ME made its debut, but it would be another six years before any cars were delivered to customers. Initially there was Maxi power, but production cars featured Ford's Essex V6, although it was re-engineered to take Alfa Romeo V6 power when the project was sold on in 1984.

COUNTRY OF ORIGIN	UK
YEARS OF PRODUCTION	1979–84
DISPLACEMENT	2994CC (183CI)
CONFIGURATION	MID-MOUNTED V6
TRANSMISSION	5-SPEED MANUAL, REAR-WHEEL DRIVE
POWER	101KW (138BHP)
TORQUE	236NM (174LB FT)
TOP SPEED	193KM/H (120MPH)
0–96KM/H (0–60MPH)	8.5SEC

TALBOT SUNBEAM LOTUS

You wouldn't think that this unassuming car was capable of it, but the Talbot Sunbeam Lotus won the 1981 World Rally Championship. It was all down to the spiced-up mechanicals, which included a twin-cam Lotus engine, with twin Weber carburettors, along with uprated and lowered suspension plus a five-speed gearbox.

COUNTRY OF ORIGIN	UK
YEARS OF PRODUCTION	1979–81
DISPLACEMENT	2174CC (133CI)
CONFIGURATION	FRONT-MOUNTED 4-CYL
TRANSMISSION	5-SPEED MANUAL, REAR-WHEEL DRIVE
POWER	110KW (150BHP)
TORQUE	203NM (150LB FT)
TOP SPEED	195KM/H (121MPH)
0–96KM/H (0–60MPH)	7.4SEC

TRIUMPH TR8

It took four years for a V8-engined version of the TR7 to become available, and even then it was offered to US buyers only. A tiny number of right-hand drive cars were made, but the bulk of production consisted of left-hand drive convertibles, although a few coupés were also completed.

COUNTRY OF ORIGIN	UK
YEARS OF PRODUCTION	1979–81
DISPLACEMENT	3528CC (215CI)
CONFIGURATION	FRONT-MOUNTED V8
TRANSMISSION	5-SPEED MANUAL, REAR-WHEEL DRIVE
POWER	101KW (137BHP)
TORQUE	224NM (165LB FT)
TOP SPEED	193KM/H (120MPH)
0–96KM/H (0–60MPH)	8.4SEC

Ultimate Dream Car 14:
Cizeta V16T

The outrageous Cizeta came about thanks to the supercar boom of the late 1980s. It was the brain-child of Claudio Zampolli, a wealthy businessman who sold and serviced Italian exotica in Los Angeles. He got talking to wealthy car enthusiast Giorgio Moroder; it was through this partnership that the car took its title, for its full name was Cizeta-Moroder V16T. Cizeta, pronounced chee-zeta, is the Italian way of saying the initials CZ, for Claudio Zampolli. The V16T was short for a V16-engined car with a T-drive, which is how the drive was taken from the powerplant.

A capacity of 5995cc (366ci) meant that the claimed power output was 412kW (560bhp) at a dizzying 8000rpm – although its red-line was set at 9000rpm. At full chat the noise was awe-inspiring, with two overhead camshafts per bank and 64 valves. The engine was no less than 1.5m (5ft) wide, which is why there was no alternative to taking the drive from its middle. In effect, the powerplant was effectively a pair of V8s mated to each other, with the power taken from the middle via a T-shaped transmission. This offered five manually selected gears, which then transitted the power to the rear wheels.

The V16T was yet another creation of Marcello Gandini, the man who must have designed more supercars than anyone else. Despite the prototype having first been shown in 1989, it was another three years before the first cars were delivered. In the meantime Moroder had lost interest and walked away, taking his money with him. With funding a serious issue, and the Lamborghini Diablo having been launched at half the price, it was only a matter of time before the company called it a day, although it lingered on until 1995. However, that's not the end of the story. In 2005 Zampolli unveiled a roadster version of the V16T, with the promise of up to another four to follow.

COUNTRY OF ORIGIN	ITALY
YEARS OF PRODUCTION	1991–94
DISPLACEMENT	5995CC (366CI)
CONFIGURATION	MID-MOUNTED V16
TRANSMISSION	5-SPEED MANUAL, REAR-WHEEL DRIVE
POWER	412KW (560BHP)
TORQUE	636NM (469LB FT)
TOP SPEED	328KM/H (204MPH) (CLAIMED)
0–96KM/H (0–60MPH)	4.4SEC (CLAIMED)

MITSUBISHI STARION

While turbocharged Japanese cars are now ten-a-penny, in the early 1980s they were quite a novelty. The Starion was one of the first of the breed. Initially it suffered from terrible turbo lag, but in time the engine capacity grew and the lag was banished to turn the car into a real flier.

COUNTRY OF ORIGIN	JAPAN
YEARS OF PRODUCTION	1982–89
DISPLACEMENT	1997CC (122CI)
CONFIGURATION	FRONT-MOUNTED 4-CYL
TRANSMISSION	5-SPEED MANUAL, REAR-WHEEL DRIVE
POWER	130KW (177BHP)
TORQUE	290NM (214LB FT)
TOP SPEED	214KM/H (133MPH)
0–96KM/H (0–60MPH)	6.9SEC

HONDA CIVIC CRX

One of the greatest ever hot hatches, the CRX has been around in several guises. It started out as a 1.5-litre car, but was quickly transformed into a 1.6-litre screamer that possessed almost unreal agility, thanks to its lightweight and double-wishbone suspension (complete with anti-roll bars) all round.

COUNTRY OF ORIGIN	JAPAN
YEARS OF PRODUCTION	1983–92
DISPLACEMENT	1595CC (97CI)
CONFIGURATION	FRONT-MOUNTED 4-CYL
TRANSMISSION	5-SPEED MANUAL, FRONT-WHEEL DRIVE
POWER	109KW (148BHP)
TORQUE	145NM (107LB FT)
TOP SPEED	225KM/H (140MPH)
0–96KM/H (0–60MPH)	7.2SEC

MERCEDES 190E 2.3–16

Making its debut at the 1983 Frankfurt Motor Show, the 190E 2.3–16 was designed to take Mercedes into the German touring cars series. The engine was tuned by Cosworth and based on the 2.3-litre unit already available in the E-Class; from 1988 this was changed for a 2.5-litre unit.

COUNTRY OF ORIGIN	GERMANY
YEARS OF PRODUCTION	1983–92
DISPLACEMENT	2299CC (140CI)
CONFIGURATION	FRONT-MOUNTED 4-CYL
TRANSMISSION	5-SPEED MANUAL, REAR-WHEEL DRIVE
POWER	136KW (185BHP)
TORQUE	235NM (173LB FT)
TOP SPEED	230KM/H (143MPH)
0–96KM/H (0–60MPH)	8.0SEC

PONTIAC FIERO

Conceived as a competitor to the Toyota MR2, the Fiero offered many of the same ingredients, including a relatively small engine mounted in the middle and driving the rear wheels. The car was designed for the American market only, though; despite this, there was the option of a 2.5-litre four-cylinder engine as well as a V6.

COUNTRY OF ORIGIN	USA
YEARS OF PRODUCTION	1983–1989
DISPLACEMENT	2834CC (173CI)
CONFIGURATION	MID-MOUNTED V6
TRANSMISSION	5-SPEED MANUAL, REAR-WHEEL DRIVE
POWER	99KW (135BHP)
TORQUE	230NM (170LB FT)
TOP SPEED	193KM/H (120MPH)
0–96KM/H (0–60MPH)	7.4SEC

TVR 350I

Starting out as the range-topping Tasmin, the 350i later became a model in its right, leaving its six-cylinder 280i sibling behind. Powered by Rover's 3.5-litre V8 with up to 145kW (197bhp), and with a glassfibre bodyshell keeping weight down, the car was fast. There was nothing else like it for the money.

COUNTRY OF ORIGIN	UK
YEARS OF PRODUCTION	1983–90
DISPLACEMENT	3528CC (215CI)
CONFIGURATION	FRONT-MOUNTED V8
TRANSMISSION	5-SPEED MANUAL, REAR-WHEEL DRIVE
POWER	145KW (197BHP)
TORQUE	298NM (220LB FT)
TOP SPEED	216KM/H (134MPH)
0–96KM/H (0–60MPH)	6.5SEC

VAUXHALL ASTRA GTE

With Volkswagen's Golf selling so well, all the mainstream car makers wanted a hot hatch of their own in the early 1980s. This was Vauxhall's contribution to the party, sold elsewhere as the Opel Kadett. In fuel-injected form the car was quick, but all too often overlooked in favour of Ford's XR3i.

COUNTRY OF ORIGIN	GERMANY/UK
YEARS OF PRODUCTION	1983–84
DISPLACEMENT	1796CC (110CI)
CONFIGURATION	FRONT-MOUNTED 4-CYL
TRANSMISSION	5-SPEED MANUAL, FRONT-WHEEL DRIVE
POWER	85KW (115BHP)
TORQUE	150NM (111LB FT)
TOP SPEED	187KM/H (116MPH)
0–96KM/H (0–60MPH)	9.2SEC

FIAT STRADA ABARTH 130TC

The ultimate derivative of the otherwise rather dull Fiat Strada, the 130TC was a true performance car with its free-revving engine, sports interior and superb chassis. There was also a fair turn of speed available too, thanks to a double overhead-cam 2-litre engine that was fed by a pair of Weber carburettors.

COUNTRY OF ORIGIN	ITALY
YEARS OF PRODUCTION	1984–87
DISPLACEMENT	1995CC (122CI)
CONFIGURATION	FRONT-MOUNTED 4-CYL
TRANSMISSION	5-SPEED MANUAL, FRONT-WHEEL DRIVE
POWER	96KW (130BHP)
TORQUE	176NM (130LB FT)
TOP SPEED	196KM/H (122MPH)
0–96KM/H (0–60MPH)	8.1SEC

MARCOS MANTULA

After a long gap in production, Jem Marsh bought back the rights to produce the Marcos, and once again the cars continued to be built. This time, however, it was the classic Rover V8 that provided motive power, at first in 3.5-litre form but from 1989 there was a 3.9-litre version of the unit fitted.

COUNTRY OF ORIGIN	UK
YEARS OF PRODUCTION	1984–2000
DISPLACEMENT	3528CC (215CI)
CONFIGURATION	FRONT-MOUNTED V8
TRANSMISSION	5-SPEED MANUAL, REAR-WHEEL DRIVE
POWER	140KW (190BHP)
TORQUE	298NM (220LB FT)
TOP SPEED	214KM/H (133MPH)
0–96KM/H (0–60MPH)	5.4SEC

SAAB 900 TURBO 16S

Also known as the Aero, the 16S was the first car in the world to feature a turbocharged 16-valve powerplant. With an intercooler also fitted, the engine was capable of developing a healthy 129kW (175bhp), although trying to push all this through the front wheels meant it could be a handful in the wet.

COUNTRY OF ORIGIN	SWEDEN
YEARS OF PRODUCTION	1984–93
DISPLACEMENT	1985CC (121CI)
CONFIGURATION	FRONT-MOUNTED 4-CYL
TRANSMISSION	5-SPEED MANUAL, FRONT-WHEEL DRIVE
POWER	129kW (175BHP)
TORQUE	273NM (201LB FT)
TOP SPEED	209KM/H (130MPH)
0–96KM/H (0–60MPH)	8.9SEC

TOYOTA MR2 MK I

Having shown its SV-3 concept at the 1983 Tokyo Motor Show, there was an overwhelmingly positive response to Toyota's proposal for a budget mid-engined sportscar. Within a year the production version of the Midship Runabout two-seater (MR2) was born, and it went on to revolutionize the affordable sportscar market.

COUNTRY OF ORIGIN	JAPAN
YEARS OF PRODUCTION	1984–89
DISPLACEMENT	1588CC (97CI)
CONFIGURATION	MID-MOUNTED 4-CYL
TRANSMISSION	5-SPEED MANUAL, REAR-WHEEL DRIVE
POWER	90kW (122BHP)
TORQUE	142NM (105LB FT)
TOP SPEED	195KM/H (121MPH)
0–96KM/H (0–60MPH)	7.7SEC

FERRARI 328GTB/GTS

A decade after its introduction, the 308GTB and GTS were ready for a refresh – step forward, the 328. With an enlarged version of the mid-mounted V8 and some minor tweaks to the nose, the car was just the shot in the arm that Ferrari needed, as the car was as successful as its predecessor.

COUNTRY OF ORIGIN	ITALY
YEARS OF PRODUCTION	1985–89
DISPLACEMENT	3185CC (194CI)
CONFIGURATION	MID-MOUNTED V8
TRANSMISSION	5-SPEED MANUAL, REAR-WHEEL DRIVE
POWER	199kW (270BHP)
TORQUE	302NM (223LB FT)
TOP SPEED	257KM/H (160MPH)
0–96KM/H (0–60MPH)	6.4SEC

PORSCHE 944 TURBO

The 944 was the car that the 924 should really have been, but when Porsche turned up the heat in 1985 to create the 944 Turbo, it was really quite a car. However, things got even better in 1988, when the Turbo S was unleashed, with 201kW (247bhp) in place of the standard car's 162kW (220bhp).

COUNTRY OF ORIGIN	GERMANY
YEARS OF PRODUCTION	1985–88
DISPLACEMENT	2479CC (151CI)
CONFIGURATION	FRONT-MOUNTED 4-CYL
TRANSMISSION	5-SPEED MANUAL, REAR-WHEEL DRIVE
POWER	162kW (220BHP)
TORQUE	329NM (243LB FT)
TOP SPEED	245KM/H (152MPH)
0–96KM/H (0–60MPH)	6.3SEC

EVANTE 140TC

The original Lotus Elan is one of the best driver's cars ever made, so it made a lot of sense to offer an updated version in the 1980s. That's just what Evante did for five years, with the 140TC, which could match the Lotus for balance, handling and performance – and beat it comprehensively on build quality.

COUNTRY OF ORIGIN	UK
YEARS OF PRODUCTION	1986–91
DISPLACEMENT	1699CC (104CI)
CONFIGURATION	FRONT-MOUNTED 4-CYL
TRANSMISSION	5-SPEED MANUAL, REAR-WHEEL DRIVE
POWER	103KW (140BHP)
TORQUE	175NM (129LB FT)
TOP SPEED	212KM/H (132MPH)
0–96KM/H (0–60MPH)	6.4SEC

RENAULT 5 GT TURBO

Following Peugeot's hugely successful 205GTi, Renault mustered a riposte. It used a heavily modified four-cylinder 1397cc (85ci) engine from the Renault 8 Gordini – a pushrod unit dating back to the 1950s, turbocharged with an air-cooled Garrett T2 turbocharger.

COUNTRY OF ORIGIN	FRANCE
YEARS OF PRODUCTION	1986–91
DISPLACEMENT	1397CC (85CI)
CONFIGURATION	FRONT-MOUNTED 4-CYL
TRANSMISSION	5-SPEED MANUAL, FRONT-WHEEL DRIVE
POWER	85KW (115BHP)
TORQUE	164NM (121LB FT)
TOP SPEED	201KM/H (125MPH)
0–96KM/H (0–60MPH)	7.1SEC

JAGUAR XJR-S

Jaguar's XJS was first seen in 1975, so by the late 1980s it was getting pretty long in the tooth. Tom Walkinshaw was called in to bring the car up to date – he chose to tighten up the suspension, increase the V12's capacity to six litres and fit larger wheels and tyres.

COUNTRY OF ORIGIN	UK
YEARS OF PRODUCTION	1988–94
DISPLACEMENT	5993CC (366CI)
CONFIGURATION	FRONT-MOUNTED V12
TRANSMISSION	AUTOMATIC, REAR-WHEEL DRIVE
POWER	234KW (318BHP)
TORQUE	491NM (362LB FT)
TOP SPEED	253KM/H (157MPH)
0–96KM/H (0–60MPH)	7.0SEC

PEUGEOT 205GTI 1.9

When it comes to the all-time great cars in terms of driving enjoyment, the 205GTi is up there towards the top. An astonishingly agile car, the 205GTi started out as a 1.6-litre car that wasn't all that quick – but the 1.9-litre car was a total revelation as an all-round driver's car.

COUNTRY OF ORIGIN	FRANCE
YEARS OF PRODUCTION	1988–91
DISPLACEMENT	1905CC (116CI)
CONFIGURATION	FRONT-MOUNTED 4-CYL
TRANSMISSION	5-SPEED MANUAL, FRONT-WHEEL DRIVE
POWER	96KW (130BHP)
TORQUE	161NM (119LB FT)
TOP SPEED	200KM/H (124MPH)
0–96KM/H (0–60MPH)	7.9SEC

VOLKSWAGEN CORRADO

The Corrado was a modern-day Scirocco, as it was a sporting hatch based on the then-current Golf. That meant the Mk II Golf provided the mechanics, which in turn meant the Corrado handled superbly but was practical with it. With VW's VR6 engine installed, the Corrado was turned into a giant killer.

COUNTRY OF ORIGIN	GERMANY
YEARS OF PRODUCTION	1988–95
DISPLACEMENT	2792CC (170CI)
CONFIGURATION	FRONT-MOUNTED V6
TRANSMISSION	5-SPEED MANUAL, FRONT-WHEEL DRIVE
POWER	131KW (178BHP)
TORQUE	240NM (177LB FT)
TOP SPEED	225KM/H (140MPH)
0–96KM/H (0–60MPH)	6.8SEC

LOTUS ELAN SE

The golden rule with any proper sportscar is that it must have rear-wheel drive – at least until this car arrived. Despite its turbocharged engine feeding power to the front, there was no torque steer. Performance was strong, thanks to the lightweight plastic bodyshell, while the wishbone suspension reduced roll in corners.

COUNTRY OF ORIGIN	UK
YEARS OF PRODUCTION	1989–94
DISPLACEMENT	1588CC (97CI)
CONFIGURATION	FRONT-MOUNTED 4-CYL
TRANSMISSION	5-SPEED MANUAL, FRONT-WHEEL DRIVE
POWER	121KW (165BHP)
TORQUE	201NM (148LB FT)
TOP SPEED	219KM/H (136MPH)
0–96KM/H (0–60MPH)	6.5SEC

MAZDA MX-5

While everyone else had given up on affordable open-topped sportscars, Mazda set the world alight with its MX-5 in 1989. Using the original Lotus Elan for inspiration, the MX-5 featured a small four-cylinder engine at the front, driving the rear wheels. With double-wishbone suspension all round, the handling was a revelation.

COUNTRY OF ORIGIN	JAPAN
YEARS OF PRODUCTION	1989–97
DISPLACEMENT	1839CC (112CI)
CONFIGURATION	FRONT-MOUNTED 4-CYL
TRANSMISSION	5-SPEED MANUAL, REAR-WHEEL DRIVE
POWER	96KW (130BHP)
TORQUE	152NM (112LB FT)
TOP SPEED	196KM/H (122MPH)
0–96KM/H (0–60MPH)	8.2SEC

MG MAESTRO TURBO

A Maestro featuring in a chapter about dream cars? Surely not! Well, actually, this was a car that was let down by its badge because the boosted Maestro was quick and handled well – and it was practical too. With its uprated brakes and suspension, the car was a blast, but just 505 were made.

COUNTRY OF ORIGIN	UK
YEARS OF PRODUCTION	1989–91
DISPLACEMENT	1994CC (122CI)
CONFIGURATION	FRONT-MOUNTED 4-CYL
TRANSMISSION	5-SPEED MANUAL, FRONT-WHEEL DRIVE
POWER	112KW (152BHP)
TORQUE	229NM (169LB FT)
TOP SPEED	208KM/H (129MPH)
0–96KM/H (0–60MPH)	6.9SEC

PANTHER SOLO

If it hadn't been for the Toyota MR2, the Solo might have succeeded. It was initially intended to be a cheap sportscar, but the MR2 cleaned up, so Panther took the car upmarket, spending a fortune in the process. The car was fast but poorly made and too costly; just a dozen were built.

COUNTRY OF ORIGIN	UK
YEARS OF PRODUCTION	1989–1990
DISPLACEMENT	1993CC (122CI)
CONFIGURATION	MID-MOUNTED IN-LINE FOUR, TURBOCHARGED
TRANSMISSION	5-SPEED MANUAL, FOUR-WHEEL DRIVE
POWER	150KW (204BHP)
TORQUE	268NM (198LB FT)
TOP SPEED	229KM/H (142MPH)
0–96KM/H (0–60MPH)	7.0SEC

PONTIAC TURBO TRANS AM

The Trans Am was 20 years old in 1989, so Pontiac built this version to celebrate the occasion. Offering power with economy, the interior was loaded with gadgetry to make the driver's life easier. There was stiffer suspension, which was also tweaked to ensure the car's cornering limits were higher than previously.

COUNTRY OF ORIGIN	USA
YEARS OF PRODUCTION	1989
DISPLACEMENT	3785CC (231CI)
CONFIGURATION	FRONT-MOUNTED V6
TRANSMISSION	4-SPEED AUTO, REAR-WHEEL DRIVE
POWER	188KW (255BHP)
TORQUE	461NM (340LB FT)
TOP SPEED	253KM/H (157MPH)
0–96KM/H (0–60MPH)	5.1SEC

VAUXHALL CALIBRA

One of the best-looking cars of the 1990s, this svelte coupé was nothing more than an Opel Vectra in a party dress. That meant the mechanicals were generally unadventurous, but there was a turbocharged 2-litre offered, complete with a four-wheel drive system to tame the 201 horses on offer.

COUNTRY OF ORIGIN	GERMANY/UK
YEARS OF PRODUCTION	1989–97
DISPLACEMENT	1998CC (122CI)
CONFIGURATION	FRONT-MOUNTED 4-CYL
TRANSMISSION	6-SPEED MANUAL, FOUR-WHEEL DRIVE
POWER	148KW (201BHP)
TORQUE	281NM (207LB FT)
TOP SPEED	241KM/H (150MPH)
0–96KM/H (0–60MPH)	6.3SEC

NISSAN SUNNY GTI-R

The GTi-R was an amazing car, as it was based on a rather dull shopping trolley yet was packed with technology such as a turbocharged 2-litre engine and a remarkably sophisticated four-wheel drive system complete with viscous couplings and limited-slip differentials. Those in the know could tell, but this was one understated car.

COUNTRY OF ORIGIN	JAPAN
YEARS OF PRODUCTION	1990–94
DISPLACEMENT	1998CC (122CI)
CONFIGURATION	FRONT-MOUNTED 4-CYL
TRANSMISSION	5-SPEED MANUAL, FOUR-WHEEL DRIVE
POWER	162KW (220BHP)
TORQUE	267NM (197LB FT)
TOP SPEED	216KM/H (134MPH)
0–96KM/H (0–60MPH)	6.1SEC

Ultimate Dream Car 15:
Dodge Viper RT/10

When the Dodge Viper RT/10 was first shown at the 1989 Detroit Motor Show, everyone went wild. There was no way the Chrysler Corporation was going to build anything as outrageous as this 8-litre V10 monster. With 294kW (400bhp) and 610Nm (450lb ft) of torque on offer, it was just too mad to ever go into production. Except it did, because by 1992 the car was available to buy; by 1996 a closed coupé version had been launched; and more than a decade after the original concept was shown, a new Viper was in the showrooms.

Although the Viper RT/10 used modern equipment such as disc brakes at the front and rear along with independent rear suspension, there wasn't much else to keep the driver out of trouble. Four-wheel drive, traction control and anti-lock brakes were all rejected because they diluted the driving experience too much. The truck-based engine was mechanically very simple, with overhead valves and a complete reliance on size rather than technology to provide massive power and torque. Comfort also wasn't important; anything that added weight unnecessarily was omitted. There was no roof, although a simple, tensioned piece of fabric to offer basic protection from the elements wouldn't take much to engineer.

All this weight loss and power overload would have been in vain if the car's looks hadn't been anything other than jaw-droppingly dramatic – and the Viper RT/10 was more than happy to rise to the challenge. In true hot-rod style there were side-exit exhausts, while there was also a massive bonnet to hide the V10 engine. Huge scallops ahead of the doors allowed hot air to exit from the engine bay, and the enormous wheels and tyres showed that the Viper RT/10 meant business. There wasn't a straight line on the whole car – every surface was curved in at least one plane – and there was also the minimum of decoration both inside and out.

COUNTRY OF ORIGIN	USA
YEARS OF PRODUCTION	1992–2003
DISPLACEMENT	7997CC (488CI)
CONFIGURATION	FRONT-MOUNTED V10
TRANSMISSION	6-SPEED MANUAL, REAR-WHEEL DRIVE
POWER	294KW (400BHP)
TORQUE	610NM (450LB FT)
TOP SPEED	256KM/H (159MPH)
0–96KM/H (0–60MPH)	4.6SEC

TOYOTA CELICA GT4

Toyota introduced the first Celica GT4 in 1987 with just one aim – to win the World Rally Championship. The company was successful in its quest, but Toyota's customers won as well, because they could buy a road-going version of this four-wheel drive hot-shot.

COUNTRY OF ORIGIN	JAPAN
YEARS OF PRODUCTION	1990–93
DISPLACEMENT	1998CC (122CI)
CONFIGURATION	FRONT-MOUNTED 4-CYL
TRANSMISSION	5-SPEED MANUAL, FOUR-WHEEL DRIVE
POWER	150KW (204BHP)
TORQUE	275NM (203LB FT)
TOP SPEED	229KM/H (142MPH)
0–96KM/H (0–60MPH)	7.9SEC

AUDI S2

There had never been any problem spotting one of the original turbocharged Quattros on the road, but the S2 was a real Q-car. Despite massive power and huge performance, the car looked as innocuous as its much tamer siblings. Incredibly capable, the S2 never captured the imagination like the Quattro had done.

COUNTRY OF ORIGIN	GERMANY
YEARS OF PRODUCTION	1991–95
DISPLACEMENT	2226CC (136CI)
CONFIGURATION	FRONT-MOUNTED V6
TRANSMISSION	5-SPEED MANUAL, FOUR-WHEEL DRIVE
POWER	169KW (230BHP)
TORQUE	373NM (275LB FT)
TOP SPEED	237KM/H (147MPH)
0–96KM/H (0–60MPH)	5.7SEC

GINETTA G33

Take a look at the G33, and it could only be a low-volume British sportscar. You might be inclined to think it was a kit car, but the G33 was available only in fully built form direct from the factory. Powered by a 3.9-litre Rover V8, the G33 was blisteringly quick, but just 100 or so were made.

COUNTRY OF ORIGIN	UK
YEARS OF PRODUCTION	1991–93
DISPLACEMENT	3946CC (241CI)
CONFIGURATION	FRONT-MOUNTED V8
TRANSMISSION	5-SPEED MANUAL, FRONT-WHEEL DRIVE
POWER	146KW (198BHP)
TORQUE	298NM (220LB FT)
TOP SPEED	220KM/H (137MPH)
0–96KM/H (0–60MPH)	5.3SEC

HONDA BEAT

One of the many K-Cars that proliferated in the 1990s, Honda's Beat was like most of them in that it packed as much technology as possible into one tiny package. However, while most rivals were turbocharged, the Beat was normally aspirated – yet it still produced nearly 74kW (100bhp) per litre.

COUNTRY OF ORIGIN	JAPAN
YEARS OF PRODUCTION	1991–96
DISPLACEMENT	656CC (40CI)
CONFIGURATION	MID-MOUNTED 3-CYL
TRANSMISSION	5-SPEED MANUAL, REAR-WHEEL DRIVE
POWER	47KW (64BHP)
TORQUE	60NM (44LB FT)
TOP SPEED	140KM/H (87MPH)
0–96KM/H (0–60MPH)	9.8SEC

SUBARU SVX

Usually associated with agricultural pick-up trucks, Subaru caught everyone unawares with the introduction of its SVX in 1991. With its flat-six engine up front and four-wheel drive, there was no shortage of either power or traction – but it was costly and its looks were an acquired taste, so the car was doomed to fail.

COUNTRY OF ORIGIN	JAPAN
YEARS OF PRODUCTION	1991–96
DISPLACEMENT	3318CC (203CI)
CONFIGURATION	FRONT-MOUNTED FLAT-6
TRANSMISSION	5-SPEED MANUAL, FOUR-WHEEL DRIVE
POWER	169KW (230BHP)
TORQUE	309NM (228LB FT)
TOP SPEED	232KM/H (144MPH)
0–96KM/H (0–60MPH)	8.7SEC

SUZUKI CAPPUCCINO

This pint-sized sportscar from Suzuki came about because of Japan's tax-break laws; by restricting the car to a 657cc (40ci) engine, it was cheaper to run than a full-sized car. The tiny capacity made little difference, though; there was still 47kW (64bhp) available, thanks to a turbocharger and a 9000rpm redline.

COUNTRY OF ORIGIN	JAPAN
YEARS OF PRODUCTION	1991–97
DISPLACEMENT	657CC (40CI)
CONFIGURATION	FRONT-MOUNTED 3-CYL
TRANSMISSION	5-SPEED MANUAL, REAR-WHEEL DRIVE
POWER	47KW (64BHP)
TORQUE	85NM (63LB FT)
TOP SPEED	137KM/H (85MPH)
0–96KM/H (0–60MPH)	8.0SEC

LIGHT CAR COMPANY ROCKET

The brainchild of Gordon Murray and Chris Craft, the Rocket was the ultimate in lightweight sportscars that put performance above all else – while remaining relatively affordable. There was a multi-tube spaceframe chassis and Yamaha FZR1000 power, complete with five valves per cylinder, four carburettors and an 11,000rpm redline.

COUNTRY OF ORIGIN	UK
YEARS OF PRODUCTION	1992–98
DISPLACEMENT	1002CC (61CI)
CONFIGURATION	MID-MOUNTED 4-CYL
TRANSMISSION	5-SPEED MANUAL, REAR-WHEEL DRIVE
POWER	105KW (143BHP)
TORQUE	104NM (77LB FT)
TOP SPEED	211KM/H (131MPH)
0–96KM/H (0–60MPH)	5.0SEC

MG RV8

Even now there are many who say the MGB should never have been revived; it was already 30 years old when the RV8 burst onto the scene. However, with V8 power, a traditional British interior and those classic lines, the car worked well – and with a few sympathetic tweaks it's even better.

COUNTRY OF ORIGIN	UK
YEARS OF PRODUCTION	1992–95
DISPLACEMENT	3946CC (241CI)
CONFIGURATION	FRONT-MOUNTED V8
TRANSMISSION	5-SPEED MANUAL, REAR-WHEEL DRIVE
POWER	140KW (190BHP)
TORQUE	317NM (234LB FT)
TOP SPEED	219KM/H (136MPH)
0–96KM/H (0–60MPH)	6.9SEC

LANCIA/ZAGATO HYENA

The Lancia Integrale isn't a bad starting point for any car; when Zagato was commissioned to design and build 75 examples of an Integrale-based supercar, the Hyena was the result. With ultra-clean lines and a bespoke carbon fibre interior, the cars looked every bit as good as they performed.

COUNTRY OF ORIGIN	ITALY
YEARS OF PRODUCTION	1993–94
DISPLACEMENT	1995CC (122CI)
CONFIGURATION	FRONT-MOUNTED 4-CYL
TRANSMISSION	5-SPEED MANUAL, FOUR-WHEEL DRIVE
POWER	154KW (210BHP)
TORQUE	298NM (220LB FT)
TOP SPEED	230KM/H (143MPH)
0–96KM/H (0–60MPH)	5.4SEC

RENAULT CLIO WILLIAMS

While the Renault 5 GT Turbo had relied on a boosted engine to offer thrills, the Clio Williams focused on 16-valve technology for better breathing and greater efficiency. With 2 litres and 110kW (150bhp), the car proved an instant hit – so much so that Renault released another two generations of Clio Williams.

COUNTRY OF ORIGIN	FRANCE
YEARS OF PRODUCTION	1993–96
DISPLACEMENT	1988CC (122CI)
CONFIGURATION	FRONT-MOUNTED 4-CYL
TRANSMISSION	5-SPEED MANUAL, FRONT-WHEEL DRIVE
POWER	110KW (150BHP)
TORQUE	168NM (124LB FT)
TOP SPEED	195KM/H (121MPH)
0–96KM/H (0–60MPH)	7.6SEC

WIESMANN ROADSTER

With a bit of Alfa in there along with some Jaguar and some Austin Healey, the Wiesmann's design was a real hotch-potch of design themes. First built in 1993, the Roadster featured BMW straight-six power, in 3-litre guise for the MF30; or the MF3 could be ordered with a 3.3-litre engine.

COUNTRY OF ORIGIN	GERMANY
YEARS OF PRODUCTION	1993–
DISPLACEMENT	2979CC (182CI)
CONFIGURATION	FRONT-MOUNTED 6-CYL
TRANSMISSION	5-SPEED MANUAL, REAR-WHEEL DRIVE
POWER	170KW (231BHP)
TORQUE	300NM (221LB FT)
TOP SPEED	232KM/H (144MPH)
0–96KM/H (0–60MPH)	5.9SEC

MERCEDES C36 AMG

Keen to offer an AMG performance derivative of all its key cars, Mercedes let its tuning arm loose on the C-Class, with this as the result. Looking remarkably restrained, the C36 featured a stretched straight-six plus bigger wheels and brakes and lower, stiffer suspension. The giveaway, though, was a pair of square exhaust pipes.

COUNTRY OF ORIGIN	GERMANY
YEARS OF PRODUCTION	1994–97
DISPLACEMENT	3606CC (220CI)
CONFIGURATION	FRONT-MOUNTED 6-CYL
TRANSMISSION	4-SPEED AUTO, REAR-WHEEL DRIVE
POWER	197KW (268BHP)
TORQUE	380NM (280LB FT)
TOP SPEED	245KM/H (152MPH)
0–96KM/H (0–60MPH)	6.0SEC

MITSUBISHI FTO

At first the FTO was intended to be offered in Japan
only, but the car proved too popular elsewhere and it was
exported to all sorts of countries. With front-wheel drive
and a jewel of a 2-litre V6 engine, the FTO handled
superbly. It also looked great, while the cabin was
luxurious too.

COUNTRY OF ORIGIN	JAPAN
YEARS OF PRODUCTION	1994–2000
DISPLACEMENT	1999CC (122CI)
CONFIGURATION	FRONT-MOUNTED V6
TRANSMISSION	5-SPEED MANUAL, FRONT-WHEEL DRIVE
POWER	147KW (200BHP)
TORQUE	199NM (147LB FT)
TOP SPEED	229KM/H (142MPH)
0–96KM/H (0–60MPH)	7.0SEC

FIAT BARCHETTA

The chassis of the first-generation Punto may not seem like
the ideal starting point for a two-seater sportscar, but it
worked well for the Barchetta. Available in left-hand drive
only, this lightweight sportscar offered a fun driving
experience with its 1.8-litre twin-cam petrol engine.

COUNTRY OF ORIGIN	ITALY
YEARS OF PRODUCTION	1995-
DISPLACEMENT	1747CC (107CI)
CONFIGURATION	FRONT-MOUNTED 4-CYL
TRANSMISSION	6-SPEED MANUAL, FRONT-WHEEL DRIVE
POWER	96KW (130BHP)
TORQUE	159NM (117LB FT)
TOP SPEED	200KM/H (124MPH)
0–96KM/H (0–60MPH)	8.7SEC

NISSAN 200SX

The 200SX was already something of an institution by
the time Nissan created an all-new car in 1994. With
its turbocharged engine and rear-wheel drive, this was a
real driver's car, especially with its multi-link rear
suspension. It wasn't just about go, however – the car was
a real looker too.

COUNTRY OF ORIGIN	JAPAN
YEARS OF PRODUCTION	1994–2001
DISPLACEMENT	1998CC (122CI)
CONFIGURATION	FRONT-MOUNTED 4-CYL
TRANSMISSION	5-SPEED MANUAL, REAR-WHEEL DRIVE
POWER	145KW (197BHP)
TORQUE	264NM (195LB FT)
TOP SPEED	229KM/H (142MPH)
0–96KM/H (0–60MPH)	6.5SEC

PANOZ ROADSTER

Conceived as a modern-day Cobra, the Roadster
featured a lightweight bodyshell, double-wishbone
supension all round and massive power to give an
undiluted driving experience. By 1996 there was
an alloy-bodied option, with the 32-valve Ford V8
and a chassis also made of alloy to reduce weight
to a minimum.

COUNTRY OF ORIGIN	USA
YEARS OF PRODUCTION	1994–
DISPLACEMENT	4601CC (281CI)
CONFIGURATION	FRONT-MOUNTED V8
TRANSMISSION	5-SPEED AUTOMATIC, REAR-WHEEL DRIVE
POWER	224KW (305BHP)
TORQUE	407NM (300LB FT)
TOP SPEED	209KM/H (130MPH)
0–96KM/H (0–60MPH)	4.5SEC

LOTUS ELISE

With the original Elan being one of the most revered sportscars ever made, Lotus was keen to repeat the trick with its Elise. It did too, but this time the engine was in the middle while the bodyshell was built around a high-tech extruded aluminium chassis, for maximum rigidity and minimum weight.

COUNTRY OF ORIGIN	UK
YEARS OF PRODUCTION	1996–2000
DISPLACEMENT	1796CC (110CI)
CONFIGURATION	MID-MOUNTED 4-CYL
TRANSMISSION	5-SPEED MANUAL, REAR-WHEEL DRIVE
POWER	87kW (118BHP)
TORQUE	165NM (122LB FT)
TOP SPEED	203KM/H (126MPH)
0–96KM/H (0–60MPH)	6.1SEC

MITSUBISHI EVO IV

Initially intended to be available on the Japanese domestic market only, the Lancer Evos were seized upon by overseas customers because they offered so much performance for so little money. With turbocharged engines driving all four wheels, the cars held the road like virtually nothing else.

COUNTRY OF ORIGIN	JAPAN
YEARS OF PRODUCTION	1996–98
DISPLACEMENT	1997CC (122CI)
CONFIGURATION	FRONT-MOUNTED 4-CYL
TRANSMISSION	5-SPEED MANUAL, FOUR-WHEEL DRIVE
POWER	206kW (280BHP)
TORQUE	353NM (260LB FT)
TOP SPEED	233KM/H (145MPH)
0–96KM/H (0–60MPH)	4.8SEC

MITSUBISHI GALANT VR4

There were three generations of Galant VR4 offered, with this one being the last. They all featured four-wheel drive, but this version had a larger engine than its predecessors, with a 2.5-litre V6 unit fitted. For the first time, it was available as an estate as well as a saloon.

COUNTRY OF ORIGIN	JAPAN
YEARS OF PRODUCTION	1996–2002
DISPLACEMENT	2498CC (152CI)
CONFIGURATION	FRONT-MOUNTED V6
TRANSMISSION	5-SPEED MANUAL, FOUR-WHEEL DRIVE
POWER	206kW (280BHP)
TORQUE	362NM (267LB FT)
TOP SPEED	245KM/H (152MPH)
0–96KM/H (0–60MPH)	5.9SEC

MERCEDES C43 AMG

Just in case the C36 didn't offer enough performance, Mercedes decided to drop a bigger engine into its C-Class for 1997. To make sure there was enough power on offer, a V8 was chosen, which was lighter than the previous straight-six thanks to its alloy construction. The result was a much better balanced car.

COUNTRY OF ORIGIN	GERMANY
YEARS OF PRODUCTION	1997–2000
DISPLACEMENT	4266CC (260CI)
CONFIGURATION	FRONT-MOUNTED V8
TRANSMISSION	5-SPEED AUTO, REAR-WHEEL DRIVE
POWER	222kW (302BHP)
TORQUE	409NM (302LB FT)
TOP SPEED	249KM/H (155MPH)
0–96KM/H (0–60MPH)	5.9SEC

PLYMOUTH PROWLER

First shown as a concept, Plymouth would have been mad not to put the Prowler into production, such was the demand. Looking utterly authentic, the Prowler was light and handled well thanks to fully independent suspension – but it was fitted with a V6 rather than the V8 it should have had.

COUNTRY OF ORIGIN	USA
YEARS OF PRODUCTION	1997–2002
DISPLACEMENT	3523CC (215CI)
CONFIGURATION	FRONT-MOUNTED V6
TRANSMISSION	4-SPEED AUTO, REAR-WHEEL DRIVE
POWER	157KW (214BHP)
TORQUE	300NM (221LB FT)
TOP SPEED	225KM/H (140MPH)
0–96KM/H (0–60MPH)	7.0SEC

AUDI TT COUPÉ

From the moment the wraps were pulled off the original Coupé, the car had to go into production. Looking like nothing else around, the car may have been a Volkswagen Golf underneath, but that didn't stop it becoming the hottest property around when it went on sale in 1998.

COUNTRY OF ORIGIN	GERMANY
YEARS OF PRODUCTION	1998–2006
DISPLACEMENT	1781CC (109CI)
CONFIGURATION	FRONT-MOUNTED 4-CYL
TRANSMISSION	6-SPEED MANUAL, FOUR-WHEEL DRIVE
POWER	165KW (225BHP)
TORQUE	279NM (206LB FT)
TOP SPEED	225KM/H (140MPH)
0–96KM/H (0–60MPH)	6.4SEC

BMW M COUPÉ

While there were lesser versions of the Z3 Coupé for some markets, others received only the full-fat M version. That meant the fabulous 3.2-litre straight-six usually seen in the M3, and while the car's lines were challenging, it was a far better drive than the M Roadster thanks to the extra torsional rigidity.

COUNTRY OF ORIGIN	GERMANY
YEARS OF PRODUCTION	1998–2003
DISPLACEMENT	3246CC (198CI)
CONFIGURATION	FRONT-MOUNTED 6-CYL
TRANSMISSION	6-SPEED SEMI-AUTO, REAR-WHEEL DRIVE
POWER	239KW (325BHP)
TORQUE	350NM (258LB FT)
TOP SPEED	249KM/H (155MPH)
0–96KM/H (0–60MPH)	4.3SEC

BMW M ROADSTER

The M Roadster was far more than a Z3 with the M3's powerplant shoehorned in. The most important change was the adoption of a far better rear suspension layout along with front suspension from the M3. While the US edition offered just 176kW (240bhp), European cars had around a third more power.

COUNTRY OF ORIGIN	GERMANY
YEARS OF PRODUCTION	1998–2002
DISPLACEMENT	3246CC (198CI)
CONFIGURATION	FRONT-MOUNTED 6-CYL
TRANSMISSION	6-SPEED SEMI-AUTO, REAR-WHEEL DRIVE
POWER	239KW (325BHP)
TORQUE	350NM (258LB FT)
TOP SPEED	249KM/H (155MPH)
0–96KM/H (0–60MPH)	5.3SEC

Ultimate Dream Car 16:
McLaren F1

During the supercar glut of the 1980s and 1990s, the McLaren was the most outrageous, most powerful and also most intelligently designed supercar of the lot. It was also one of the lightest and most practical; from the outset it had the best possible packaging while also being incredibly fast and stable. Although the F1's bodyshell looks relatively free of extraneous details, there's a lot going on to keep the centre of pressure as constant as possible. This pressure is what gives the car stability at high speeds, and it was aided by devices such as the adjustable aerofoil at the rear of the car (which deployed under braking), the fixed headlamps and the small aerofoil just below the windscreen.

The body itself was made entirely of carbon composites, in keeping with its 'most advanced road car ever' tag. The monocoque incorporated the rear wings and front bulkheads; built up from 94 separate sections of carbon fibre, it also incorporated various aluminium and nomex honeycomb structures. The mid-mounted engine was bought in from BMW Motorsport; the 6064cc (370ci) all-alloy V12 weighed just 260kg (572lb). Following Formula One practice, there was a small carbon clutch and aluminium flywheel for an ultra-fast engine response. A five-speed gearbox offered ratios spaced for the fastest possible acceleration to 257km/h (160mph), with the top gear set for comfortable cruising at speeds of 322km/h (200mph) or more.

There was no power assistance for the steering or servo assistance for the brakes – the F1 was to offer driving in its purest form. Suspension was by unequal-length double wishbones all round and there was no four-wheel drive or traction control – that just added weight and complexity. But while McLaren had intended to make 300 examples before finishing production, barely a third of that number were built before the car went out of production in 1996.

COUNTRY OF ORIGIN	UK
YEARS OF PRODUCTION	1993–96
DISPLACEMENT	6064CC (370CI)
CONFIGURATION	MID-MOUNTED V12
TRANSMISSION	6-SPEED MANUAL, REAR-WHEEL DRIVE
POWER	461KW (627BHP)
TORQUE	649NM (479LB FT)
TOP SPEED	386KM/H (240MPH)
0–96KM/H (0–60MPH)	3.6SEC

MAZDA RX-8

First seen as the RX Evolv concept, the RX-8 was a breath of fresh air when it arrived in 2003. Although its twin-rotor Wankel engine didn't really offer enough torque and was hopelessly thirsty, the car was great to drive and innovatively packaged, with its unusual door system.

COUNTRY OF ORIGIN	JAPAN
YEARS OF PRODUCTION	2003–
DISPLACEMENT	2616CC (160CI)
CONFIGURATION	FRONT-MOUNTED ROTARY
TRANSMISSION	6-SPEED MANUAL, REAR-WHEEL DRIVE
POWER	170kW (231BHP)
TORQUE	210NM (155LB FT)
TOP SPEED	235KM/H (146MPH)
0–96KM/H (0–60MPH)	6.2SEC

PORSCHE BOXSTER S

Porsche desperately needed a cheaper car if it was to expand, and the Boxster proved to be just the ticket. With its mid-mounted flat-six and superlative handling, the car proved a massive hit. The various engine options included 2.5-, 2.7- and 3.2-litre versions of the water-cooled six-cylinder unit.

COUNTRY OF ORIGIN	GERMANY
YEARS OF PRODUCTION	2003–05
DISPLACEMENT	3179CC (194CI)
CONFIGURATION	MID-MOUNTED FLAT-6
TRANSMISSION	6-SPEED MANUAL, REAR-WHEEL DRIVE
POWER	196kW (266BHP)
TORQUE	310NM (229LB FT)
TOP SPEED	266KM/H (165MPH)
0–96KM/H (0–60MPH)	5.7SEC

SMART ROADSTER

The Smart Roadster deserved to succeed, it really did. It was great to drive, engineered beautifully and looked as individual as Smart's other cars. Its lack of practicality could be a problem, but the real killer was its cost – Smart couldn't make any money on the car, so it had to die after just three years.

COUNTRY OF ORIGIN	GERMANY
YEARS OF PRODUCTION	2003–06
DISPLACEMENT	698CC (43CI)
CONFIGURATION	MID-MOUNTED 4-CYL
TRANSMISSION	SEQUENTIAL 6-SPEED, REAR-WHEEL DRIVE
POWER	59kW (80BHP)
TORQUE	110NM (81LB FT)
TOP SPEED	175KM/H (109MPH)
0–96KM/H (0–60MPH)	10.9SEC

ALPINA ROADSTER S

Although BMW would make its Z4M Roadster available later on, when Alpina launched its Roadster S in 2004 there was nothing from BMW that could touch it. With its 3.4-litre engine, the car was good for 272km/h (169mph) – bolt the optional hard top in place, and the top speed climbed by another 5km/h (3mph).

COUNTRY OF ORIGIN	GERMANY
YEARS OF PRODUCTION	2004–
DISPLACEMENT	3346CC (204CI)
CONFIGURATION	FRONT-MOUNTED 6-CYL
TRANSMISSION	6-SPEED MANUAL, REAR-WHEEL DRIVE
POWER	221kW (300BHP)
TORQUE	361NM (266LB FT)
TOP SPEED	277KM/H (172MPH)
0–96KM/H (0–60MPH)	5.1SEC

CHRYSLER CROSSFIRE SRT-6

It may have looked distinctive, but there were few takers for the blisteringly quick Chrysler Crossfire SRT-6 because it was based on the ancient first-generation Mercedes SLK platform. That ensured it was never dynamically as good as it looked, which in Roadster form was very good indeed.

COUNTRY OF ORIGIN	USA
YEARS OF PRODUCTION	2004–
DISPLACEMENT	3199CC (195CI)
CONFIGURATION	FRONT-MOUNTED V6
TRANSMISSION	5-SPEED AUTO, REAR-WHEEL DRIVE
POWER	243KW (330BHP)
TORQUE	420NM (310LB FT)
TOP SPEED	249KM/H (155MPH)
0–96KM/H (0–60MPH)	5.0SEC

MERCEDES SLK55 AMG

While the first-generation SLK had steering that felt completely detached from the car, this new edition was a far better drive. Even better, in 5.5-litre AMG-tuned form, it was an absolute blast. At last it was capable of taking on the BMW Z4 and Porsche Boxster, even if it rarely won the battle.

COUNTRY OF ORIGIN	GERMANY
YEARS OF PRODUCTION	2004–
DISPLACEMENT	5439CC (332CI)
CONFIGURATION	FRONT-MOUNTED V8
TRANSMISSION	6-SPEED SEMI-AUTO, REAR-WHEEL DRIVE
POWER	261KW (355BHP)
TORQUE	510NM (376LB FT)
TOP SPEED	249KM/H (155MPH)
0–96KM/H (0–60MPH)	4.8SEC

VOLKSWAGEN GOLF R32

When Volkswagen shoehorned a 3.2-litre V6 into the fourth-generation Golf, it created a superb range-topper. So the company repeated the trick with the fifth-generation edition, this time with even more power thanks to a reworked inlet manifold. VW's DSG sequential clutchless manual transmission was also available.

COUNTRY OF ORIGIN	GERMANY
YEARS OF PRODUCTION	2005–
DISPLACEMENT	3189CC (195CI)
CONFIGURATION	FRONT-MOUNTED V6
TRANSMISSION	6-SPEED MANUAL, FOUR-WHEEL DRIVE
POWER	184KW (250BHP)
TORQUE	320NM (236LB FT)
TOP SPEED	249KM/H (155MPH)
0–96KM/H (0–60MPH)	6.5SEC

ALFA ROMEO BRERA V6 Q4

Alfa Romeo's replacement for the GTV looked sensational, so it was only fitting that it was available with a state-of-the-art four-wheel drive transmission when the 3.2-litre V6 powerplant was specified. Based on the 159 saloon, the Q4 transmission could send the power to whichever end of the car could best put it down.

COUNTRY OF ORIGIN	ITALY
YEARS OF PRODUCTION	2006–
DISPLACEMENT	3195CC (195CI)
CONFIGURATION	FRONT-MOUNTED V6
TRANSMISSION	6-SPEED MANUAL, FOUR-WHEEL DRIVE
POWER	188KW (256BHP)
TORQUE	323NM (238LB FT)
TOP SPEED	240KM/H (149MPH)
0–96KM/H (0–60MPH)	6.9SEC

AUDI TT COUPÉ

With the original TT having caused such a sensation, Audi was keen to maintain the momentum by updating the car without losing its identity. The company did a brilliant job, creating much more of a driver's car thanks to a Golf GTi platform, while also sharpening up the looks.

COUNTRY OF ORIGIN	GERMANY
YEARS OF PRODUCTION	2006–
DISPLACEMENT	1984CC (121CI)
CONFIGURATION	FRONT-MOUNTED 4-CYL
TRANSMISSION	6-SPEED SEMI-AUTO, FRONT-WHEEL DRIVE
POWER	145KW (197BHP)
TORQUE	281NM (207LB FT)
TOP SPEED	240KM/H (149MPH)
0–96KM/H (0–60MPH)	6.5SEC

BMW 650CI

With its challenging looks you'd think that BMW would have had a problem shifting the 6-Series, but anything with that hallowed spinning propeller will sell, and the 650Ci was no exception. Another Chris Bangle creation, the 650Ci was available as a coupé or a convertible.

COUNTRY OF ORIGIN	GERMANY
YEARS OF PRODUCTION	2006–
DISPLACEMENT	4800CC (293CI)
CONFIGURATION	FRONT-MOUNTED V8
TRANSMISSION	6-SPEED MANUAL, REAR-WHEEL DRIVE
POWER	270KW (367BHP)
TORQUE	491NM (362LB FT)
TOP SPEED	249KM/H (155MPH)
0–96KM/H (0–60MPH)	5.4SEC

BROOKE ME190

Looking like the Light Car Company Rocket, but with two-abreast seating, the ME190 was meant to evoke memories of 1950s Grand Prix racers. The looks certainly did that, but the ME190 was rather more usable thanks to a choice of modern Ford or Vauxhall powerplants.

COUNTRY OF ORIGIN	UK
YEARS OF PRODUCTION	2006–
DISPLACEMENT	1998CC (122CI)
CONFIGURATION	MID-MOUNTED 4-CYL
TRANSMISSION	6-SPEED MANUAL/4-SPEED AUTO, REAR-WHEEL DRIVE
POWER	132KW (179BHP)
TORQUE	217NM (160LB FT)
TOP SPEED	N/A
0–96KM/H (0–60MPH)	4.9SEC

LOTUS EUROPA S

With the Elise having sold well thanks to its great driving experience, Lotus decided to offer a bigger, better-trimmed version of the car. The Europa S also used a name from Lotus' past, but while the Elise had proved a hit from day one, the Europa never caught the imagination in the same way.

COUNTRY OF ORIGIN	UK
YEARS OF PRODUCTION	2006–
DISPLACEMENT	1998CC (122CI)
CONFIGURATION	MID-MOUNTED 4-CYL
TRANSMISSION	6-SPEED MANUAL, REAR-WHEEL DRIVE
POWER	145KW (197BHP)
TORQUE	271NM (200LB FT)
TOP SPEED	230KM/H (143MPH)
0–96KM/H (0–60MPH)	5.5SEC

OPEL GT

Reviving a great badge from Opel's past, the GT was based on the Saturn Sky usually reserved for American buyers. After years of languishing in the doldrums, this was Opel's chance to show that it could still build cars which were great to drive and to look at, with this Mazda MX-5 rival.

COUNTRY OF ORIGIN	GERMANY
YEARS OF PRODUCTION	2006–
DISPLACEMENT	1998CC (121CI)
CONFIGURATION	FRONT-MOUNTED 4-CYL
TRANSMISSION	5-SPEED MANUAL, REAR-WHEEL DRIVE
POWER	191KW (260BHP)
TORQUE	349NM (258LB FT)
TOP SPEED	233KM/H (145MPH)
0–96KM/H (0–60MPH)	6.0SEC

VOLVO C70

The original C70, with a folding cloth roof, had been a terrible thing to drive, with a bodyshell that was so weak it was untrue. Its successor was much more tasty, though, with its folding hardtop and sharp lines – and in true Volvo fashion it was safer than many fixed-head cars.

COUNTRY OF ORIGIN	SWEDEN
YEARS OF PRODUCTION	2006–
DISPLACEMENT	2521CC (154CI)
CONFIGURATION	FRONT-MOUNTED 5-CYL
TRANSMISSION	6-SPEED MANUAL, FRONT-WHEEL DRIVE
POWER	162KW (220BHP)
TORQUE	320NM (236LB FT)
TOP SPEED	241KM/H (150MPH)
0–96KM/H (0–60MPH)	7.4SEC

ARTEGA GT

Blending the looks of a Porsche Cayman with those of a Lotus Elise, the Artega GT was designed by Henrik Fisker, the man also responsible for Aston Martin's DB9. The Artega, which was about the size of a Mazda MX-5, was powered by a tuned version of Volkswagen's 3.6-litre FSi V6.

COUNTRY OF ORIGIN	USA
YEARS OF PRODUCTION	2007–
DISPLACEMENT	3597CC (219CI)
CONFIGURATION	MID-MOUNTED V6
TRANSMISSION	6-SPEED MANUAL, REAR-WHEEL DRIVE
POWER	220KW (300BHP)
TORQUE	349 NM (258LB FT)
TOP SPEED	270KM/H (168MPH)
0–96KM/H (0–60MPH)	5.0SEC

HONDA CIVIC TYPE R

With its first-generation Type R having been such a success, Honda had to create a new edition for its eighth-generation Civic. The car already looked incredibly distinctive in standard form, so Honda had to pull out all the stops to give the Type R even more aggressive looks.

COUNTRY OF ORIGIN	JAPAN
YEARS OF PRODUCTION	2007–
DISPLACEMENT	1998CC (122CI)
CONFIGURATION	FRONT-MOUNTED 4-CYL
TRANSMISSION	6-SPEED MANUAL, FRONT-WHEEL DRIVE
POWER	146KW (198BHP)
TORQUE	193NM (142LB FT)
TOP SPEED	255KM/H (140MPH)
0–96KM/H (0–60MPH)	7.4SEC

Muscle Cars

Use the phrase 'muscle car' and everyone instantly thinks of wide-arched Mustangs and Pontiacs covered in loud graphics. While those are some of the most iconic muscle cars ever made, there have been plenty more subtle models built along the way – and not all of them in America. Indeed, the first car listed in this chapter is a British car: it may have been fitted with a good old American flathead V8, but it was devised and constructed in England. That was the Allard J2, a real hot-rod of a car, but undeniably something with serious muscle.

Around the time the Allard was going out of production, Buick was busy getting ready to introduce its Century. Sure, a 6-litre V8 wasn't exactly original – what was newsworthy was GM's motivation for building the Century. The company's big rivals were starting to get interested in shoehorning massively powerful engines into their cars – often unassuming vehicles that gave no clue as to their potency. The Century signalled the start of the power battle fought between America's big three car makers, Chrysler, Ford and General Motors.

Just a year after the arrival of the Century, Chrysler unveiled one of its all-time great models; the 300. Offering as much power as the Buick, there was an even higher top speed on offer, along with even greater acceleration. This was Chrysler's signal that the gauntlet had been well and truly thrown down, and over the coming two decades or so there would be ever greater power offered to give ferociously quick acceleration, if not necessarily particularly great top speeds. That was what this was all about; it was the drag strips that created these cars, where acceleration ruled and terminal speeds were of relatively little importance. Cars were geared to get away from the line as quickly as possible, with little or no attention paid to how well corners could be handled – or how quickly the car would be able to stop.

This was the era of there being no substitute for cubic inches; efficiency mattered little with both fuel and power being cheap. Car makers thought nothing of shoehorning a 7-litre V8 into the nose of a car that frankly didn't have the chassis to cope with an engine half as big. With torque figures frequently exceeding 500lb ft, some of the cars were an utter nightmare to drive, as they simply couldn't handle the grunt. However, many of these beasts were made in small numbers, guaranteeing their future collectability.

The American car manufacturers may have dominated the muscle car market, but they didn't have it exclusively to themselves. Over in Europe, TVR was busy creating a muscle car of its own in the form of the 4.7-litre Tuscan V8. Sure, the powerplant was American, but the rest of the car was British – although, sadly, the car was as tricky to tame as many of its US contemporaries. It was exactly the same story with the Sunbeam Tiger, which was little more than an Alpine with the same 4.7-litre V8 stuffed under the bonnet.

Rather easier to tame was the Mercedes 300SEL 6.3, engineered the way only a German car can be. There were no shortcuts for this beast of a hot-rod, the spirit of which lives on in a whole range of Mercedes models. While American muscle cars are now rather rarer than they once were, the breed is thankfully alive and well in Europe.

Aplina's B10 is one of their most impressive offerings.

243

ALLARD J2

Perhaps the best-known of all the Allards, the J2 and J2X were stripped-out racing specials for the road. That's why there was so little bodywork – weight had to be minimized to give the best performance. Under the bonnet was usually a Cadillac V8, although some cars featured a Mercury unit.

COUNTRY OF ORIGIN	UK
YEARS OF PRODUCTION	1950–54
DISPLACEMENT	5420CC (331CI)
CONFIGURATION	FRONT-MOUNTED V8
TRANSMISSION	3-SPEED MANUAL, REAR-WHEEL DRIVE
POWER	118kW (160BHP)
TORQUE	N/A
TOP SPEED	177KM/H (110MPH)
0–96KM/H (0–60MPH)	10.0SEC

BUICK CENTURY

There was a horsepower war taking place in Detroit in the 1950s, and this was Buick's weapon of choice. The Century was Buick's fastest ever car and one of the quickest cars to come out of the USA at the time. Even in entry-level form it could hit 177km/h (110mph).

COUNTRY OF ORIGIN	USA
YEARS OF PRODUCTION	1954–58
DISPLACEMENT	5962CC (364CI)
CONFIGURATION	FRONT-MOUNTED V8
TRANSMISSION	3-SPEED MANUAL, REAR-WHEEL DRIVE
POWER	221kW (300BHP)
TORQUE	N/A
TOP SPEED	185KM/H (115MPH)
0–96KM/H (0–60MPH)	9.0SEC

CHRYSLER C300

Anybody who bought a C300 is what we would now call an early adopter; this was one of the world's first muscle cars. With fine handling and power aplenty from its Hemi V8 engine, the 300 was based on the Windsor two-door coupé, but with parts carried over from the New Yorker and Imperial.

COUNTRY OF ORIGIN	USA
YEARS OF PRODUCTION	1955
DISPLACEMENT	5424CC (331CI)
CONFIGURATION	FRONT-MOUNTED V8
TRANSMISSION	2-SPEED AUTO, REAR-WHEEL DRIVE
POWER	2231kW (300BHP)
TORQUE	4683NM (345LB FT)
TOP SPEED	209KM/H (130MPH)
0–96KM/H (0–60MPH)	8.9SEC

DE SOTO PACESETTER

Their cars may have looked as though they were built for comfort rather than speed, but De Soto produced some of the most powerful cars of the era, thanks to the availability of Chrysler's Hemi powerplant. As a result, De Sotos were typically much more powerful than their rivals – and more luxurious inside as well.

COUNTRY OF ORIGIN	USA
YEARS OF PRODUCTION	1956
DISPLACEMENT	5587CC (341CI)
CONFIGURATION	FRONT-MOUNTED V8
TRANSMISSION	2-SPEED AUTO, REAR-WHEEL DRIVE
POWER	235kW (320BHP)
TORQUE	495NM (365LB FT)
TOP SPEED	185KM/H (115MPH)
0–96KM/H (0–60MPH)	10.2SEC

PLYMOUTH FURY

Immortalized as Christine in the book and film of the same name, the Fury was an understated muscle car, but nobody had thought of the term back then. Always fitted with Chrysler's biggest V8s, the Fury also handled brilliantly, thanks to its 'Torsion Air Ride' suspension and its low centre of gravity.

COUNTRY OF ORIGIN	USA
YEARS OF PRODUCTION	1956–58
DISPLACEMENT	5735CC (350CI)
CONFIGURATION	FRONT-MOUNTED V8
TRANSMISSION	3-SPEED AUTO, REAR-WHEEL DRIVE
POWER	224KW (305BHP)
TORQUE	502NM (370LB FT)
TOP SPEED	196KM/H (122MPH)
0–96KM/H (0–60MPH)	8.0SEC

CHEVROLET IMPALA

Many claim that the Impala was the world's first true muscle car, with the model spawning Chevrolet's Super Sport (SS) performance brand. There were saloons, estates, convertibles and coupés on offer, each powered by a 5.4-litre V8 for swift progress with peerless refinement. SS models featured a 6.7-litre V8.

COUNTRY OF ORIGIN	USA
YEARS OF PRODUCTION	1960–65
DISPLACEMENT	5359CC (327CI)
CONFIGURATION	FRONT-MOUNTED V8
TRANSMISSION	3-SPEED AUTO, REAR-WHEEL DRIVE
POWER	184KW (250BHP)
TORQUE	475NM (350LB FT)
TOP SPEED	172KM/H (107MPH)
0–96KM/H (0–60MPH)	10.0SEC

OLDSMOBILE SUPER 88

The Super 88 was Oldsmobile's factory hot-rod, and more than 16,000 were sold in 1960 alone. With its independent front suspension, the car handled well for such a huge beast, although things weren't helped by the live axle at the rear. It was fast, though, with the V8 powerplant easy to tune up even further.

COUNTRY OF ORIGIN	USA
YEARS OF PRODUCTION	1960
DISPLACEMENT	6077CC (371CI)
CONFIGURATION	FRONT-MOUNTED V8
TRANSMISSION	3-SPEED AUTO, REAR-WHEEL DRIVE
POWER	224KW (305BHP)
TORQUE	556NM (410LB FT)
TOP SPEED	185KM/H (115MPH)
0–96KM/H (0–60MPH)	10.2SEC

PONTIAC VENTURA

Pontiac was at the forefront when it came to muscle cars – its Ventura is one of the earliest examples of the breed. Featuring what was known as a 'bubble top', the Ventura featured ultra-thin pillars that gave the car a far more elegant look than was normal for the time.

COUNTRY OF ORIGIN	USA
YEARS OF PRODUCTION	1960–61
DISPLACEMENT	6372CC (383CI)
CONFIGURATION	FRONT-MOUNTED V8
TRANSMISSION	3-SPEED AUTO, REAR-WHEEL DRIVE
POWER	256KW (348BHP)
TORQUE	583NM (430LB FT)
TOP SPEED	N/A
0–96KM/H (0–60MPH)	8.2SEC

CHEVROLET IMPALA SS

With a shape that dated back to the 'seagull wing' design of 1959, the 1961 Impala was related to the Biscayne and Bel Air models, but it was a very different car. Presenting a slimmer profile with a larger glass area, the SS was a dealer-fit option package with more upmarket interior trim.

COUNTRY OF ORIGIN	USA
YEARS OF PRODUCTION	1961–64
DISPLACEMENT	6704CC (409CI)
CONFIGURATION	FRONT-MOUNTED V8
TRANSMISSION	4-SPEED MANUAL, REAR-WHEEL DRIVE
POWER	265KW (360BHP)
TORQUE	570NM (420LB FT)
TOP SPEED	217KM/H (135MPH)
0–96KM/H (0–60MPH)	7.8SEC

FORD FALCON

While high-performance Falcons were generally used for drag racing in the USA, European-spec cars had more powerful engines and were successfully campaigned as road racers in the 1960s. There was ample power from the 4734cc (289ci) in V8, while weight was reduced by some panels being made of glassfibre.

COUNTRY OF ORIGIN	USA
YEARS OF PRODUCTION	1962–64
DISPLACEMENT	4734CC (289CI)
CONFIGURATION	FRONT-MOUNTED V8
TRANSMISSION	4-SPEED MANUAL, REAR-WHEEL DRIVE
POWER	199KW (271BHP)
TORQUE	423NM (312LB FT)
TOP SPEED	217KM/H (135MPH)
0–96KM/H (0–60MPH)	6.4SEC

PONTIAC GRAND PRIX

Thanks to the GTO, Pontiac's image was on a high in the 1960s, and the Grand Prix was a total hit for the company. One of the high points of this model's career was the 1967 model year, unique in that it was the only season in which there were both coupé and convertible derivatives offered.

COUNTRY OF ORIGIN	USA
YEARS OF PRODUCTION	1962–68
DISPLACEMENT	6552CC (400CI)
CONFIGURATION	FRONT-MOUNTED V8
TRANSMISSION	4-SPEED MANUAL, REAR-WHEEL DRIVE
POWER	257KW (350BHP)
TORQUE	597NM (440LB FT)
TOP SPEED	177KM/H (110MPH)
0–96KM/H (0–60MPH)	9.4SEC

FORD GALAXIE 500XL

When Ford launched its 'Total Performance' campaign in the 1960s, it got into motorsport in a big way. The idea was that it would lead to greater sales if customers knew just how capable Ford's muscle cars were. This was one of the most focused of the breed, built specially for the drag strip.

COUNTRY OF ORIGIN	USA
YEARS OF PRODUCTION	1963
DISPLACEMENT	6994CC (427CI)
CONFIGURATION	FRONT-MOUNTED V8
TRANSMISSION	4-SPEED MANUAL, REAR-WHEEL DRIVE
POWER	313KW (425BHP)
TORQUE	651NM (480LB FT)
TOP SPEED	185KM/H (115MPH)
0–96KM/H (0–60MPH)	4.7SEC

PLYMOUTH SAVOY 426

With America's Big Three doing battle on the drag strip as well as the race track in the early 1960s, Chrysler chose to unleash the Savoy 426. The engine was the company's most powerful: a 7-litre V8 a 13.5:1 compression ratio, free-flow exhaust system and dual four-barrel carburettors.

COUNTRY OF ORIGIN	USA
YEARS OF PRODUCTION	1963
DISPLACEMENT	6980CC (426CI)
CONFIGURATION	FRONT-MOUNTED V8
TRANSMISSION	3-SPEED AUTO, REAR-WHEEL DRIVE
POWER	313KW (425BHP)
TORQUE	637NM (470LB FT)
TOP SPEED	201KM/H (125MPH)
0–96KM/H (0–60MPH)	5.0SEC

PONTIAC GTO

When it comes to American legends, the Pontiac GTO is right up there at the top. Although the first GTOs had arrived many years earlier, this completely restyled series is one of the most sought-after now that the cars have attained classic status. One of the tamer options was a 6519cc (389ci) in V8.

COUNTRY OF ORIGIN	USA
YEARS OF PRODUCTION	1963–70
DISPLACEMENT	6554CC (400CI)
CONFIGURATION	FRONT-MOUNTED V8
TRANSMISSION	4-SPEED MANUAL, REAR-WHEEL DRIVE
POWER	265KW (360BHP)
TORQUE	603NM (445LB FT)
TOP SPEED	193KM/H (120MPH)
0–96KM/H (0–60MPH)	6.4SEC

CHEVROLET CHEVELLE SS

The year 1964 was a landmark one for Chevrolet, which started to offer a range of engines for its mid-sized Chevelle. There were various V8s offered, but the tastiest of the lot was the L76 unit usually seen in the Corvette; it complemented this luxury cruiser superbly.

COUNTRY OF ORIGIN	USA
YEARS OF PRODUCTION	1964
DISPLACEMENT	5359CC (321CI)
CONFIGURATION	FRONT-MOUNTED V8
TRANSMISSION	4-SPEED MANUAL, REAR-WHEEL DRIVE
POWER	221KW (300BHP)
TORQUE	N/A
TOP SPEED	185KM/H (115MPH)
0–96KM/H (0–60MPH)	N/A

MERCURY COMET CYCLONE

It may have sounded fast, but in standard form the Comet wasn't much of a road racer – which is why Mercury decided to change all that with the Cyclone option. With a 4.7-litre V8 up front, there was suddenly plenty of power, especially with high-lift camshaft, raised compression ratio and four-barrel carburettor.

COUNTRY OF ORIGIN	USA
YEARS OF PRODUCTION	1964–65
DISPLACEMENT	4735CC (289CI)
CONFIGURATION	FRONT-MOUNTED V8
TRANSMISSION	4-SPEED MANUAL, REAR-WHEEL DRIVE
POWER	199KW (271BHP)
TORQUE	423NM (312LB FT)
TOP SPEED	200KM/H (124MPH)
0–96KM/H (0–60MPH)	7.4SEC

PLYMOUTH BARRACUDA

One of the best-looking and most revered muscle cars ever made was Plymouth's Barracuda – especially the later cars which were known as 'Cudas. Intended to take on the Ford Mustang, the Barracuda was based on the Valiant saloon, and was offered with a choice of six- or eight-cylinder powerplants.

COUNTRY OF ORIGIN	USA
YEARS OF PRODUCTION	1964–74
DISPLACEMENT	4474CC (273CI)
CONFIGURATION	FRONT-MOUNTED V8
TRANSMISSION	3-SPEED AUTO, REAR-WHEEL DRIVE
POWER	173KW (235BHP)
TORQUE	380NM (280LB FT)
TOP SPEED	187KM/H (116MPH)
0–96KM/H (0–60MPH)	9.2SEC

PONTIAC GTO

Many saw this as the first true muscle car, although there had been earlier cars that had a better claim to the title. The car was created by dropping a big-block V8 into the bodyshell of a Pontiac Tempest, with the name shamelessly stolen from Ferrari's 250GTO.

COUNTRY OF ORIGIN	USA
YEARS OF PRODUCTION	1964–67
DISPLACEMENT	6362CC (388CI)
CONFIGURATION	FRONT-MOUNTED V8
TRANSMISSION	4-SPEED MANUAL, REAR-WHEEL DRIVE
POWER	268KW (365BHP)
TORQUE	575NM (424LB FT)
TOP SPEED	193KM/H (120MPH)
0–96KM/H (0–60MPH)	6.5SEC

SUNBEAM TIGER

To create the Sunbeam Tiger, a Ford V8 was planted in the engine bay of an Alpine Series IV and the structure was barely altered. Rack-and-pinion steering was fitted and the rear suspension was modified with the addition of a Panhard rod to help put the power down – which it struggled to do.

COUNTRY OF ORIGIN	UK
YEARS OF PRODUCTION	1964–67
DISPLACEMENT	4261CC (260CI)
CONFIGURATION	FRONT-MOUNTED V8
TRANSMISSION	4-SPEED MANUAL, REAR-WHEEL DRIVE
POWER	121KW (164BHP)
TORQUE	350NM (258LB FT)
TOP SPEED	188KM/H (117MPH)
0–96KM/H (0–60MPH)	9.5SEC

PONTIAC CATALINA

Often overshadowed by the GTO, the Catalina was a mid-sized car that had all the essentials of a great muscle car – including superb tunability. One of the highlights of the range was the 2+2 option, which featured uprated suspension, limited-slip differential and an uprated 6.9-litre V8 in a choice of three states of tune.

COUNTRY OF ORIGIN	USA
YEARS OF PRODUCTION	1965
DISPLACEMENT	6898CC (421CI)
CONFIGURATION	FRONT-MOUNTED V8
TRANSMISSION	4-SPEED MANUAL, REAR-WHEEL DRIVE
POWER	277KW (376BHP)
TORQUE	625NM (461LB FT)
TOP SPEED	201KM/H (125MPH)
0–96KM/H (0–60MPH)	7.0SEC

CHEVROLET CHEVELLE SS396

With Pontiac selling lots of GTOs and Oldsmobile doing well with its 4-4-2, Chevrolet wanted a piece of the action. GM had previously agreed to cap its cars at 6554cc (400ci), hence the 6489cc (396ci) in the Chevelle, with its L78 big-block Corvette powerplant giving 276kW (375bhp) and a 209km/h (130mph) top speed.

COUNTRY OF ORIGIN	USA
YEARS OF PRODUCTION	1966
DISPLACEMENT	6489CC (396CI)
CONFIGURATION	FRONT-MOUNTED V8
TRANSMISSION	4-SPEED MANUAL, REAR-WHEEL DRIVE
POWER	276KW (375BHP)
TORQUE	563NM (415LB FT)
TOP SPEED	209KM/H (130MPH)
0–96KM/H (0–60MPH)	6.0SEC

CHEVROLET II SS

You couldn't buy many cars in 1966 that looked more understated than this one, but with Corvette L79 V8 power under the bonnet the SS was an amazingly quick car. However, while it was quick it was also frightening to drive thanks to leaf-spring suspension and drum brakes all round.

COUNTRY OF ORIGIN	USA
YEARS OF PRODUCTION	1966
DISPLACEMENT	5358CC (327CI)
CONFIGURATION	FRONT-MOUNTED V8
TRANSMISSION	4-SPEED MANUAL, REAR-WHEEL DRIVE
POWER	257KW (350BHP)
TORQUE	488NM (360LB FT)
TOP SPEED	198KM/H (123MPH)
0–96KM/H (0–60MPH)	6.5SEC

Ultimate Dream Car 17:
Pagani Zonda

Horacio Pagani set up a company specializing in carbon composites and engineering; he launched his first car in 1999. Pagani's initial idea was that the car would be named after Fangio, but when the great racing driver died before the project was completed, the new car was called the Zonda, after a wind from the Andes.

Powering the car was a mid-mounted Mercedes V12, while the basis for the Zonda was a series of chrome moly steel space frames, which were attached to a carbon fibre centre section. A chrome moly steel and carbon fibre roll bar was then bolted and heat-bound to the chassis – the whole structure offered incredible stiffness while also being remarkably light.

There was independent suspension all round, which consisted of aluminium wishbones, coil springs over dampers and anti-roll bars at each end, with the whole lot incorporating anti-dive and anti-squat geometry. As you'd expect, the braking department was pretty special. The system was engineered by Brembo, with servo-assisted 355mm (14in) ventilated discs at front and rear. Initially there was no anti-lock option, though, as this robbed the system of feel. Although the Zonda was an incredibly modern car in its engineering and design, the interior wasn't quite as cutting-edge. There was alloy detailing and Alcantara upholstery, and the toggle switches and swathes of leather were very traditional – but also extremely comfortable.

By 2002 a 7.3-litre version of the Zonda had been launched. Called the C12S, it offered 408kW (555bhp) and a top speed of some 322km/h (200mph). Even more spectacular was the Roadster, which arrived in 2003. Mechanically the same as the C12S, and with a kerb weight of just 1280kg (2816lb), it still gave a top speed of around 322km/h (200mph). Compare that weight with Lamborghini's Murcielago Roadster (1715kg/3773lb), and you can see how effective the carbon fibre bodyshell was.

COUNTRY OF ORIGIN	ITALY
YEARS OF PRODUCTION	1999–
DISPLACEMENT	7291CC (445CI)
CONFIGURATION	MID-MOUNTED V12
TRANSMISSION	6-SPEED MANUAL, REAR-WHEEL DRIVE
POWER	408KW (555BHP)
TORQUE	750NM (553LB FT)
TOP SPEED	322KM/H (200MPH) APPROX
0–96KM/H (0–60MPH)	3.7SEC

CHEVROLET IMPALA SS427

Chevrolet marketed the Impala SS427 as the car 'for the man who'd buy a sportscar if it had this much room'. By transplanting the Corvette's torquey 6994cc (427ci) V8 into the Impala's five-seater pillarless coupé bodyshell, it created a stylish sporting car without the compromise of an out-and-out sportscar.

COUNTRY OF ORIGIN	USA
YEARS OF PRODUCTION	1967–68
DISPLACEMENT	6994CC (427CI)
CONFIGURATION	FRONT-MOUNTED V8
TRANSMISSION	4-SPEED MANUAL, REAR-WHEEL DRIVE
POWER	283KW (385BHP)
TORQUE	624NM (460LB FT)
TOP SPEED	212KM/H (132MPH)
0–96KM/H (0–60MPH)	7.1SEC

DODGE CHARGER

One of the most iconic muscle cars of its era, the Charger was launched in 1965 with a range of engine choices from 5209cc (318ci) right up to the legendary 6980cc (426ci) in Hemi. With torsion bar front suspension and leaf springs at the back, the car could be a handful – but few cared.

COUNTRY OF ORIGIN	USA
YEARS OF PRODUCTION	1967–70
DISPLACEMENT	6980CC (426CI)
CONFIGURATION	FRONT-MOUNTED V8
TRANSMISSION	4-SPEED MANUAL, REAR-WHEEL DRIVE
POWER	313KW (425BHP)
TORQUE	664NM (490LB FT)
TOP SPEED	216KM/H (134MPH)
0–96KM/H (0–60MPH)	5.3SEC

OLDSMOBILE 4-4-2

A muscle car through and through, the 4-4-2 looked superb with its fastback bodyshell, and while it was fast, it was very conventionally engineered. The car's name was derived from its 6551cc (400ci) engine, four-barrel carburettor and two exhausts, while there were both coupé and convertible options offered.

COUNTRY OF ORIGIN	USA
YEARS OF PRODUCTION	1967–71
DISPLACEMENT	6551CC (400CI)
CONFIGURATION	FRONT-MOUNTED V8
TRANSMISSION	3-SPEED AUTO, REAR-WHEEL DRIVE
POWER	213KW (290BHP)
TORQUE	597NM (440LB FT)
TOP SPEED	193KM/H (120MPH)
0–96KM/H (0–60MPH)	10.3SEC

PLYMOUTH GTX 426 HEMI

A direct response to Pontiac's GTO, the GTX was more of a fearsomely quick luxury car than an out-and-out road racer. There was power aplenty with its 7-litre V8, but braking was still by drums all round, and an automatic gearbox was standard fare – although discs and a manual were options.

COUNTRY OF ORIGIN	USA
YEARS OF PRODUCTION	1967–69
DISPLACEMENT	6980CC (426CI)
CONFIGURATION	FRONT-MOUNTED V8
TRANSMISSION	3-SPEED AUTO, REAR-WHEEL DRIVE
POWER	313KW (425BHP)
TORQUE	664NM (490LB FT)
TOP SPEED	204KM/H (127MPH)
0–96KM/H (0–60MPH)	4.8SEC

SHELBY MUSTANG GT500

Carroll Shelby had already worked his magic on the Mustang, creating the GT350 in 1965. However, for those who wanted more power there was a 7-litre Mustang available from 1967. The GT500 offered a big-block V8, heavy-duty suspension and a fresh grille to distance it from lesser models.

COUNTRY OF ORIGIN	USA
YEARS OF PRODUCTION	1967–69
DISPLACEMENT	7013CC (428CI)
CONFIGURATION	FRONT-MOUNTED V8
TRANSMISSION	4-SPEED MANUAL, REAR-WHEEL DRIVE
POWER	261KW (355BHP)
TORQUE	569NM (420LB FT)
TOP SPEED	225KM/H (140MPH)
0–96KM/H (0–60MPH)	7.2SEC

TVR TUSCAN V8

The original TVR Griffith hadn't been that well built and could be a beast to drive quickly. The Tuscan attempted to address those issues by being far better built and having a much more civilized chassis, but everyone remembered the Griffith's shortcomings, so buyers stayed away.

COUNTRY OF ORIGIN	UK
YEARS OF PRODUCTION	1967–70
DISPLACEMENT	4727CC (288CI)
CONFIGURATION	FRONT-MOUNTED V8
TRANSMISSION	4-SPEED MANUAL, REAR-WHEEL DRIVE
POWER	199KW (271BHP)
TORQUE	426NM (314LB FT)
TOP SPEED	249KM/H (155MPH)
0–96KM/H (0–60MPH)	7.5SEC

AMC AMX

This was AMC's attempt at building its image to take on Chevrolet's Corvette and Ford's Mustang. But while those rivals already enjoyed iconic status by this point – and great styling – the AMX just looked odd. A 4752cc (290ci) V8 was standard fare for the AMX, but a 6.4-litre unit could be specified.

COUNTRY OF ORIGIN	USA
YEARS OF PRODUCTION	1968–70
DISPLACEMENT	6391CC (390CI)
CONFIGURATION	FRONT-MOUNTED V8
TRANSMISSION	4-SPEED MANUAL, REAR-WHEEL DRIVE
POWER	232KW (315BHP)
TORQUE	576NM (425LB FT)
TOP SPEED	193KM/H (120MPH)
0–96KM/H (0–60MPH)	6.6SEC

CHEVROLET CAMARO RS/SS

If you wanted luxury on your 1968 Camaro, you ordered it with the RS pack; if it was power you were after, you had to tick the SS option box. Go for the latter, and you'd get heavy-duty suspension along with a 5.7-litre engine – but if that wasn't enough it was possible to specify a 6.4-litre unit.

COUNTRY OF ORIGIN	USA
YEARS OF PRODUCTION	1968
DISPLACEMENT	6489CC (396CI)
CONFIGURATION	FRONT-MOUNTED V8
TRANSMISSION	3-SPEED AUTO, REAR-WHEEL DRIVE
POWER	239KW (325BHP)
TORQUE	556NM (410LB FT)
TOP SPEED	209KM/H (130MPH)
0–96KM/H (0–60MPH)	6.6SEC

CHEVROLET NOVA SS

If you were on a restricted budget but wanted large amounts of power, the Nova SS was the car for you in the 1960s. Usually equipped with six-cylinder engines, the Novas were transformed by the fitment of V8 powerplants, with various options available between 180 and 277kW (245 and 375bhp).

COUNTRY OF ORIGIN	USA
YEARS OF PRODUCTION	1968–72
DISPLACEMENT	5735CC (350CI)
CONFIGURATION	FRONT-MOUNTED V8
TRANSMISSION	3-SPEED AUTO, REAR-WHEEL DRIVE
POWER	221kW (300BHP)
TORQUE	515NM (380LB FT)
TOP SPEED	201KM/H (125MPH)
0–96KM/H (0–60MPH)	8.0SEC

MERCEDES 300SEL 6.3

The Mercedes 300SEL 6.3 started out as a private venture in 1966 by company engineer Erich Waxenberger, who wanted to create the ultimate super-saloon. He transplanted the 6.3-litre V8 from the Mercedes 600 limousine into the W109 S-Class bodyshell, creating the ultimate Q car in the process.

COUNTRY OF ORIGIN	GERMANY
YEARS OF PRODUCTION	1968–72
DISPLACEMENT	6332CC (386CI)
CONFIGURATION	FRONT-MOUNTED V8
TRANSMISSION	AUTOMATIC, REAR-WHEEL DRIVE
POWER	184kW (250BHP)
TORQUE	500NM (369LB FT)
TOP SPEED	216KM/H (134MPH)
0–96KM/H (0–60MPH)	7.1SEC

MERCURY COUGAR GT-E

Introduced as a 1967 model, the Cougar was more of a refined boulevard cruiser than an all-out muscle car. For its second season, however, it turned into a real fire-breather when it was equipped with a 6994cc (427ci) V8 that pumped out nearly 287kW (390bhp) and a completely mad 624Nm (460lb ft) of torque.

COUNTRY OF ORIGIN	USA
YEARS OF PRODUCTION	1968
DISPLACEMENT	6994CC (427CI)
CONFIGURATION	FRONT-MOUNTED V8
TRANSMISSION	3-SPEED AUTO, REAR-WHEEL DRIVE
POWER	287kW (390BHP)
TORQUE	624NM (460LB FT)
TOP SPEED	206KM/H (128MPH)
0–96KM/H (0–60MPH)	7.0SEC

OLDSMOBILE HURST

In a bid to get round GM's policy of fitting engines no bigger than 6552cc (400ci), Oldsmobile teamed up with Hurst to offer this monster Cutlass with a 7456cc (455ci) powerplant. To help get the power down, the car also featured the 4-4-2 suspension package.

COUNTRY OF ORIGIN	USA
YEARS OF PRODUCTION	1968–69
DISPLACEMENT	7456CC (455CI)
CONFIGURATION	FRONT-MOUNTED V8
TRANSMISSION	3-SPEED AUTO, REAR-WHEEL DRIVE
POWER	221KW (300BHP)
TORQUE	556NM (410LB FT)
TOP SPEED	212KM/H (132MPH)
0–96KM/H (0–60MPH)	6.8SEC

PLYMOUTH ROAD RUNNER

As a no-frills, budget-priced muscle car, the Road Runner was very successful, combining cartoon-character personality with powerful engines. Although Plymouth expected to sell just 2500 in its first year, nearly 45,000 Road Runners were sold across just two seasons, and the name lived on in the next generation of 'Satellite' cars.

COUNTRY OF ORIGIN	USA
YEARS OF PRODUCTION	1968–70
DISPLACEMENT	7207CC (440CI)
CONFIGURATION	FRONT-MOUNTED V8
TRANSMISSION	3-SPEED AUTO, REAR-WHEEL DRIVE
POWER	324KW (440BHP)
TORQUE	678NM (500LB FT)
TOP SPEED	220KM/H (137MPH)
0–96KM/H (0–60MPH)	5.0SEC

AMC HURST SC/RAMBLER 'A'

Based on the popular Rambler Rogue, the Hurst SC/Rambler A was one of the most original and unconventional of the muscle cars. AMC stuffed its biggest engine into its boxiest car, stuck a scoop on the bonnet and that was it – but the car was a serious contender on the drag strip.

COUNTRY OF ORIGIN	USA
YEARS OF PRODUCTION	1969
DISPLACEMENT	6392CC (390CI)
CONFIGURATION	FRONT-MOUNTED V8
TRANSMISSION	4-SPEED MANUAL, REAR-WHEEL DRIVE
POWER	232KW (315BHP)
TORQUE	N/A
TOP SPEED	183KM/H (114MPH)
0–96KM/H (0–60MPH)	N/A

BUICK GS400

The GS400 wasn't really much of a supercar; in a straight line it was amazingly fast, but everything went bad when the car reached a corner. It was fabulously comfortable, though, and hardly short of power, thanks to a four-barrel carb, raised compression ratio and cold-air hood induction system.

COUNTRY OF ORIGIN	USA
YEARS OF PRODUCTION	1969
DISPLACEMENT	6552CC (400CI)
CONFIGURATION	FRONT-MOUNTED V8
TRANSMISSION	3-SPEED AUTO, REAR-WHEEL DRIVE
POWER	254KW (345BHP)
TORQUE	597NM (440LB FT)
TOP SPEED	201KM/H (125MPH)
0–96KM/H (0–60MPH)	5.8SEC

CHEVROLET CAMARO ZL-1

Amid concern that some muscle cars were getting too muscular, the Automotive Manufacturers' Association banned engines over 6552cc (400ci) in anything other than full-sized cars and Corvettes. GM found a way around the ban, though, and shoehorned its 6994cc (427ci) V8 into the ZL-1, to create the ultimate Camaro.

COUNTRY OF ORIGIN	USA
YEARS OF PRODUCTION	1969
DISPLACEMENT	6994CC (427CI)
CONFIGURATION	FRONT-MOUNTED V8
TRANSMISSION	4-SPEED MANUAL, REAR-WHEEL DRIVE
POWER	316KW (430BHP)
TORQUE	610NM (450LB FT)
TOP SPEED	201KM/H (125MPH)
0–96KM/H (0–60MPH)	5.3SEC

CHEVROLET CHEVELLE YENKO

The Camaro was the car most famously linked with Don Yenko, but in 1969 he also tried his hand at tuning the Chevelle. A bigger engine was the obvious first step, but there was also a disc brake conversion, the option of a manual transmission and heavy-duty suspension to get the power down.

COUNTRY OF ORIGIN	USA
YEARS OF PRODUCTION	1969
DISPLACEMENT	6997CC (427CI)
CONFIGURATION	FRONT-MOUNTED V8
TRANSMISSION	3-SPEED AUTO, REAR-WHEEL DRIVE
POWER	331KW (450BHP)
TORQUE	624NM (460LB FT)
TOP SPEED	177KM/H (110MPH)
0–96KM/H (0–60MPH)	5.7SEC

DODGE CHARGER 500

Dodge had a habit of producing ferociously powerful cars that looked rather innocuous – and nowhere was this more true than with the Charger 500. There were two engines available, with the smaller of the pair being the 6978cc (426ci) Hemi unit. Sitting alongside was the 7210cc (440ci) Magnum powerplant.

COUNTRY OF ORIGIN	USA
YEARS OF PRODUCTION	1969
DISPLACEMENT	6978CC (426CI)
CONFIGURATION	FRONT-MOUNTED V8
TRANSMISSION	4-SPEED MANUAL, REAR-WHEEL DRIVE
POWER	313KW (425BHP)
TORQUE	664NM (490LB FT)
TOP SPEED	222KM/H (138MPH)
0–96KM/H (0–60MPH)	6.1SEC

DODGE DART GTS

When the Dart debuted back in 1963, its performance was lukewarm, to say the least. But Dodge developed it, fitting ever-larger engines until the 5.6-litre GTS surfaced in 1969. This was the performance option, with tuned suspension and wider tyres – which didn't help much once the limit had been breached.

COUNTRY OF ORIGIN	USA
YEARS OF PRODUCTION	1969
DISPLACEMENT	5571CC (340CI)
CONFIGURATION	FRONT-MOUNTED V8
TRANSMISSION	4-SPEED MANUAL, REAR-WHEEL DRIVE
POWER	213KW (290BHP)
TORQUE	488NM (360LB FT)
TOP SPEED	190KM/H (118MPH)
0–96KM/H (0–60MPH)	6.8SEC

DODGE SUPER BEE

In a bid to lead the muscle-car pack, Dodge took a basic Coronet and stuffed a 7.2-litre engine in the nose. A free-flow exhaust and Six Pack carburettor system ensured plenty of horses, and to rein it all in there was heavy-duty torsion-bar suspension at the front.

COUNTRY OF ORIGIN	USA
YEARS OF PRODUCTION	1969
DISPLACEMENT	7210CC (440CI)
CONFIGURATION	FRONT-MOUNTED V8
TRANSMISSION	4-SPEED MANUAL, REAR-WHEEL DRIVE
POWER	287KW (390BHP)
TORQUE	664NM (490LB FT)
TOP SPEED	209KM/H (130MPH)
0–96KM/H (0–60MPH)	6.0SEC

FORD MUSTANG BOSS 302

Released as a limited production special in 1969, the Mustang Boss 302 proved highly successful on both road and track. Although the car was highly potent in standard form, that didn't stop many who bought them from shoehorning bigger, more powerful engines into them, as well as tuning the suspension for better handling.

COUNTRY OF ORIGIN	USA
YEARS OF PRODUCTION	1969
DISPLACEMENT	4947CC (302CI)
CONFIGURATION	FRONT-MOUNTED V8
TRANSMISSION	4-SPEED MANUAL, REAR-WHEEL DRIVE
POWER	294KW (400BHP)
TORQUE	465NM (343LB FT)
TOP SPEED	240KM/H (149MPH)
0–96KM/H (0–60MPH)	4.8SEC

FORD MUSTANG BOSS 429

When Ford wanted to use a new engine in NASCAR, it had to build 500 production cars using the powerplant to qualify. So, instead of installing its 7-litre V8 into the Torino, it shoehorned it into the Mustang to produce the costliest non-Shelby Mustang ever. The engine was so big, the front suspension had to be re-engineered to accommodate it.

COUNTRY OF ORIGIN	USA
YEARS OF PRODUCTION	1969–70
DISPLACEMENT	7030CC (429CI)
CONFIGURATION	FRONT-MOUNTED V8
TRANSMISSION	4-SPEED MANUAL, REAR-WHEEL DRIVE
POWER	276KW (375BHP)
TORQUE	610NM (450LB FT)
TOP SPEED	190KM/H (118MPH)
0–96KM/H (0–60MPH)	6.8SEC

FORD MUSTANG MACH 1

Sitting between the Boss 429 and the 302, the Mach 1 featured a 7-litre V8 that was available in three states of tune – although that didn't stop some from tuning it further. With tuned suspension, the Mach 1 could put its power down more effectively than other Mustangs, but it was still a handful.

COUNTRY OF ORIGIN	USA
YEARS OF PRODUCTION	1969–73
DISPLACEMENT	7013CC (428CI)
CONFIGURATION	FRONT-MOUNTED V8
TRANSMISSION	3-SPEED AUTO, REAR-WHEEL DRIVE
POWER	246KW (335BHP)
TORQUE	597NM (440LB FT)
TOP SPEED	195KM/H (121MPH)
0–96KM/H (0–60MPH)	5.3SEC

FORD TORINO TALLADEGA

In the late 1960s, Ford and Chrysler were battling it out in NASCAR. In 1969, Ford revealed its aero-styled Torinos, which cleaned up in the year's stock-car racing by collecting 30 victories. To satisfy homologation rules, at least 500 road-going versions had to be built, and this was the result.

COUNTRY OF ORIGIN	USA
YEARS OF PRODUCTION	1969
DISPLACEMENT	7011CC (428CI)
CONFIGURATION	FRONT-MOUNTED V8
TRANSMISSION	3-SPEED AUTO, REAR-WHEEL DRIVE
POWER	246KW (335BHP)
TORQUE	597NM (440LB FT)
TOP SPEED	209KM/H (130MPH)
0–96KM/H (0–60MPH)	5.8SEC

PONTIAC GTO JUDGE

Although the GTO was seen as a highly desirable muscle car, Pontiac wanted to give its range a shot in the arm by creating a halo edition. That was the Judge, launched in 1969 with 6552cc (400ci) in a Ram Air III V8. With a hydraulic camshaft, Rochester four-barrel carburettor and free-flowing exhaust manifolds, there was 269kW (366bhp) on tap.

COUNTRY OF ORIGIN	USA
YEARS OF PRODUCTION	1969–71
DISPLACEMENT	6552CC (400CI)
CONFIGURATION	FRONT-MOUNTED V8
TRANSMISSION	3-SPEED AUTO, REAR-WHEEL DRIVE
POWER	269KW (366BHP)
TORQUE	603NM (445LB FT)
TOP SPEED	198KM/H (123MPH)
0–96KM/H (0–60MPH)	6.2SEC

PONTIAC TRANS AM

While Pontiac introduced its Firebird in 1967, it would be another two years before the ultra-desirable Trans Am derivative was offered. In this form it lasted just one season, because in 1970 a heavily revised bodyshell was introduced for the series. The 5733cc (350ci) V8 was one of Chevrolet's all-time great engines.

COUNTRY OF ORIGIN	USA
YEARS OF PRODUCTION	1969
DISPLACEMENT	5733CC (350CI)
CONFIGURATION	FRONT-MOUNTED V8
TRANSMISSION	3-SPEED AUTO, REAR-WHEEL DRIVE
POWER	184KW (250BHP)
TORQUE	400NM (295LB FT)
TOP SPEED	225KM/H (140MPH)
0–96KM/H (0–60MPH)	6.8SEC

AMC REBEL MACHINE

Following hot on the heels of the SC/Rambler from the previous year, AMC claimed that the Rebel Machine wasn't especially fast, but it could still give its rivals a run for their money. The car was offered for just one season, though, with a mere 2326 examples being sold.

COUNTRY OF ORIGIN	USA
YEARS OF PRODUCTION	1970
DISPLACEMENT	6391CC (390CI)
CONFIGURATION	FRONT-MOUNTED V8
TRANSMISSION	4-SPEED MANUAL, REAR-WHEEL DRIVE
POWER	250KW (340BHP)
TORQUE	583NM (430LB FT)
TOP SPEED	185KM/H (115MPH)
0–96KM/H (0–60MPH)	6.4SEC

BUICK GSX

For those who felt the standard GS455 wasn't enough, Buick unleashed a monster in 1970 in the shape of the GSX. Everything was uprated – as, indeed, it needed to be – thanks to the 7.5-litre powerhouse in the nose that was officially rated at 265kW (360bhp), but which was even more powerful than that in reality.

COUNTRY OF ORIGIN	USA
YEARS OF PRODUCTION	1970
DISPLACEMENT	7456CC (455CI)
CONFIGURATION	FRONT-MOUNTED V8
TRANSMISSION	4-SPEED MANUAL, REAR-WHEEL DRIVE
POWER	265KW (360BHP)
TORQUE	691NM (510LB FT)
TOP SPEED	198KM/H (123MPH)
0–96KM/H (0–60MPH)	5.5SEC

CHEVROLET CHEVELLE SS454

One of the most outrageous muscle cars ever built, the Chevelle SS454 featured a 7437cc (454ci) V8 and an even more outrageous 678Nm (500lb ft) of torque. The V8 was GM's fearsome LS-6 unit, complete with high-compression forged pistons, forged steel crankshaft and high-lift camshaft – it was a complete monster.

COUNTRY OF ORIGIN	USA
YEARS OF PRODUCTION	1970
DISPLACEMENT	7437CC (454CI)
CONFIGURATION	FRONT-MOUNTED V8
TRANSMISSION	4-SPEED MANUAL, REAR-WHEEL DRIVE
POWER	331KW (450BHP)
TORQUE	678NM (500LB FT)
TOP SPEED	201KM/H (125MPH)
0–96KM/H (0–60MPH)	6.1SEC

CHEVROLET EL CAMINO SS454

Although the El Camino SS454 was available from 1970 until 1977, it was offered with the thunderous LS6 for only the first season. Later cars featured an LS5 powerplant, with lower compression and hence less power – and consequently less performance. To help put the power down, there was the option of a Positraction limited-slip differential.

COUNTRY OF ORIGIN	USA
YEARS OF PRODUCTION	1970–77
DISPLACEMENT	7437CC (454CI)
CONFIGURATION	FRONT-MOUNTED V8
TRANSMISSION	4-SPEED MANUAL, REAR-WHEEL DRIVE
POWER	265kW (360BHP)
TORQUE	678Nm (500LB FT)
TOP SPEED	209KM/H (130MPH)
0–96KM/H (0–60MPH)	7.0SEC

CHEVROLET CAMARO SS396

Chevrolet's Camaro redesign for 1970 proved an instant hit – especially when the SS396 version was offered. Available in 257kW (350bhp – L-34) or 216kW (375bhp – L-78) guises, the SS396 actually displaced 6587cc (402ci). Standard features were heavy-duty suspension, stronger rear axle and 356mm (14in) wheels, while the L-84 featured a four-barrel carburettor.

COUNTRY OF ORIGIN	USA
YEARS OF PRODUCTION	1970
DISPLACEMENT	6587CC (402CI)
CONFIGURATION	FRONT-MOUNTED V8
TRANSMISSION	4-SPEED MANUAL, REAR-WHEEL DRIVE
POWER	216kW (375BHP)
TORQUE	563Nm (415LB FT)
TOP SPEED	206KM/H (128MPH)
0–96KM/H (0–60MPH)	6.2SEC

CHEVROLET MONTE CARLO SS454

Underneath that rather dull exterior, there was a real powerhouse in the form of Chevrolet's LS-5 and LS-6 V8s. If the latter was ordered in its highest state of tune, there was 330kW (450bhp) on tap, yet the car was utterly tractable and easily capable of transporting five in comfort.

COUNTRY OF ORIGIN	USA
YEARS OF PRODUCTION	1970–71
DISPLACEMENT	7437CC (454CI)
CONFIGURATION	FRONT-MOUNTED V8
TRANSMISSION	4-SPEED MANUAL, REAR-WHEEL DRIVE
POWER	265kW (360BHP)
TORQUE	678Nm (500LB FT)
TOP SPEED	212KM/H (132MPH)
0–96KM/H (0–60MPH)	7.1SEC

DODGE CHALLENGER

With Ford Mustangs, Chevrolet Camaros and Pontiac Firebirds flying out of the showrooms, Dodge needed a rival (its Charger had proved to be too big). The Challenger and its sibling the Plymouth Barracuda had to change that with a choice of coupés and convertibles, but the cars were thirsty and poorly built.

COUNTRY OF ORIGIN	USA
YEARS OF PRODUCTION	1970–74
DISPLACEMENT	7202CC (439CI)
CONFIGURATION	FRONT-MOUNTED V8
TRANSMISSION	4-SPEED MANUAL, REAR-WHEEL DRIVE
POWER	276KW (375BHP)
TORQUE	644NM (475LB FT)
TOP SPEED	209KM/H (130MPH)
0–96KM/H (0–60MPH)	6.0SEC

DODGE CHALLENGER R/T SE

The Challenger is such an icon that it's been revived for the twenty-first century. This twentieth-century version was the ultimate; the R/T stood for Road and Track, and the SE meant there were luxuries such as leather trim and a vinyl roof fitted. Just 3979 were built, however.

COUNTRY OF ORIGIN	USA
YEARS OF PRODUCTION	1970–71
DISPLACEMENT	7207CC (440CI)
CONFIGURATION	FRONT-MOUNTED V8
TRANSMISSION	4-SPEED MANUAL, REAR-WHEEL DRIVE
POWER	287KW (390BHP)
TORQUE	664NM (490LB FT)
TOP SPEED	206KM/H (128MPH)
0–96KM/H (0–60MPH)	7.2SEC

DODGE CHALLENGER T/A

This version of the Challenger wasn't as powerful as its R/T SE stablemate, yet it looked a lot more showy, thanks to those stripes and all the decals. To get the greatest amount of power possible from the 5569cc (340ci) small-block V8, there were three Holley two-barrel carburettors plumbed in.

COUNTRY OF ORIGIN	USA
YEARS OF PRODUCTION	1970
DISPLACEMENT	5569CC (340CI)
CONFIGURATION	FRONT-MOUNTED V8
TRANSMISSION	4-SPEED MANUAL, REAR-WHEEL DRIVE
POWER	213KW (290BHP)
TORQUE	468NM (345LB FT)
TOP SPEED	201KM/H (125MPH)
0–96KM/H (0–60MPH)	5.8SEC

DODGE CORONET R/T

The Coronet R/T was the first mid-sized Dodge muscle car to offer both performance and luxury in one package. There were two engines available; a 7207cc (440ci) Magnum unit or the 6978cc (426ci) Hemi, the latter unit being by far the rarer of the two – of 2615 R/Ts built, just 13 featured Hemi power.

COUNTRY OF ORIGIN	USA
YEARS OF PRODUCTION	1970
DISPLACEMENT	7207CC (440CI)
CONFIGURATION	FRONT-MOUNTED V8
TRANSMISSION	3-SPEED AUTO, REAR-WHEEL DRIVE
POWER	276KW (375BHP)
TORQUE	651NM (480LB FT)
TOP SPEED	198KM/H (123MPH)
0–96KM/H (0–60MPH)	6.6SEC

FORD TORINO COBRA

While the Torino GT was a great muscle car, the Cobra version was for those who felt that there could never be enough power. With its 7-litre big-block powerplant, the car had forged pistons, an oil cooler, a high-flow Holley carburettor and the option of a Traction Lok limited-slip differential.

COUNTRY OF ORIGIN	USA
YEARS OF PRODUCTION	1970
DISPLACEMENT	7030CC (429CI)
CONFIGURATION	FRONT-MOUNTED V8
TRANSMISSION	3-SPEED MANUAL, REAR-WHEEL DRIVE
POWER	272KW (370BHP)
TORQUE	610NM (450LB FT)
TOP SPEED	190KM/H (118MPH)
0–96KM/H (0–60MPH)	5.9SEC

MERCURY COUGAR ELIMINATOR

Since the Eliminator was longer and heavier than the Mustang, it was able to harness its power better through improved grip levels. It needed to – while the 7011cc (428ci) V8 was officially rated at 246kW (335bhp), it actually put out more than 294kW (400bhp). The lower figure was quoted to fool the insurance companies.

COUNTRY OF ORIGIN	USA
YEARS OF PRODUCTION	1970
DISPLACEMENT	7011CC (428CI)
CONFIGURATION	FRONT-MOUNTED V8
TRANSMISSION	3-SPEED AUTO, REAR-WHEEL DRIVE
POWER	246KW (335BHP)
TORQUE	597NM (440LB FT)
TOP SPEED	171KM/H (106MPH)
0–96KM/H (0–60MPH)	5.6SEC

MERCURY CYCLONE SPOILER

Based on the Mercury Montego platform, the Cyclone Spoiler was a complete beast with its 7-litre, big-block V8. Offering massive torque with acceleration to match, this was a car that was much happier on the drag strip than on twisty roads, thanks to its leaf-spring rear suspension and coil springs at the front.

COUNTRY OF ORIGIN	USA
YEARS OF PRODUCTION	1970–71
DISPLACEMENT	7030CC (429CI)
CONFIGURATION	FRONT-MOUNTED V8
TRANSMISSION	4-SPEED MANUAL, REAR-WHEEL DRIVE
POWER	272KW (370BHP)
TORQUE	610NM (450LB FT)
TOP SPEED	203KM/H (126MPH)
0–96KM/H (0–60MPH)	6.2SEC

OLDSMOBILE 4-4-2 W-30

The W-30 option was offered from 1966, but until 1970 Oldsmobile wouldn't fit any engine bigger than 6552cc (400ci) to its cars. This ban was lifted in 1970, paving the way for this 7456cc (455ci) monster. The W-30 came with glassfibre bonnet, rear spoiler and 357mm (14in) alloy wheels.

COUNTRY OF ORIGIN	USA
YEARS OF PRODUCTION	1970–72
DISPLACEMENT	7456CC (455CI)
CONFIGURATION	FRONT-MOUNTED V8
TRANSMISSION	4-SPEED MANUAL, REAR-WHEEL DRIVE
POWER	221KW (300BHP)
TORQUE	556NM (410LB FT)
TOP SPEED	208KM/H (129MPH)
0–96KM/H (0–60MPH)	7.1SEC

OLDSMOBILE CUTLASS RALLYE 350

Muscle cars were offering so much power by the end of the 1960s that car manufacturers had to reduce the power output a bit. The Rallye 350 was such a car, with its small-block V8 – although there was still 228kW (310bhp) on tap. All Rallyes were painted yellow, while the suspension was upgraded over the standard Cutlass.

COUNTRY OF ORIGIN	USA
YEARS OF PRODUCTION	1970
DISPLACEMENT	5735CC (350CI)
CONFIGURATION	FRONT-MOUNTED V8
TRANSMISSION	3-SPEED AUTO, REAR-WHEEL DRIVE
POWER	228KW (310BHP)
TORQUE	529NM (390LB FT)
TOP SPEED	196KM/H (122MPH)
0–96KM/H (0–60MPH)	7.0SEC

PLYMOUTH DUSTER 340

To kick off the 1970s, the Chrysler Corporation attempted to create a new entry-level muscle car. This was achieved by combining its powerful 5569cc (340ci) V8 with a light, two-door version of the Plymouth Valiant bodyshell to create the high-performance Duster 340. From 1974, the 340 was replaced by the Duster 360.

COUNTRY OF ORIGIN	USA
YEARS OF PRODUCTION	1970–74
DISPLACEMENT	5569CC (340CI)
CONFIGURATION	FRONT-MOUNTED V8
TRANSMISSION	3-SPEED AUTO, REAR-WHEEL DRIVE
POWER	202KW (275BHP)
TORQUE	461NM (340LB FT)
TOP SPEED	193KM/H (120MPH)
0–96KM/H (0–60MPH)	6.0SEC

PLYMOUTH HEMI CUDA

This is one of the most sought-after muscle cars ever built, thanks to its combination of understated looks and massive power. For 1970 there was an all-new car, now called simply the Cuda; it could cover the quarter mile faster than just about anything else on the market, but did just 10km (6 miles) to every gallon in the process.

COUNTRY OF ORIGIN	USA
YEARS OF PRODUCTION	1970
DISPLACEMENT	6981CC (426CI)
CONFIGURATION	FRONT-MOUNTED V8
TRANSMISSION	4-SPEED MANUAL, REAR-WHEEL DRIVE
POWER	313KW (425BHP)
TORQUE	664NM (490LB FT)
TOP SPEED	217KM/H (135MPH)
0–96KM/H (0–60MPH)	5.8SEC

Ultimate Dream Car 18:
Koenigsegg CC8S

The rationale behind the Koenigsegg CC was that it should be the car to beat the McLaren F1. However, while the rationale might have been straightforward, producing something that could take on the McLaren and win was no easy task – but it was a challenge that the Swedish company was quite happy to meet. The goals of the project were a top speed of 389km/h (242mph), delivered by a power output of 482kW (655bhp), a drag co-efficient of 0.28–0.32 and a kerb weight of just 1100kg (2420lb).

At the end of 1995, Koenigsegg built its first prototype, with most of 1996 taken up testing it. It had a mere 368kW (500bhp), but the chassis was honed to perfection so that when the power was boosted there would be no problem taming it. By the end of 1998, the first big breakthrough took place, when a carbon semi-monocoque was adopted, along with fully adjustable all-wishbone suspension. By summer 2000, the first production-ready car was finished; and in autumn of the same year the car made its world debut at the Paris Motor Show.

The paddle-shift transmission was something rarely seen at this point in time, while there was a control system that allowed the driver to adjust the chassis, aerodynamics and braking parameters from the cockpit. And the braking system was a work of art – just like the 457mm (18in) magnesium wheels wrapped in ultra-low profile rubber.

The massive power, superb attention to detail and great design were a pretty impressive mix for a first attempt. And that was the point – this was just the start. The Koenigsegg was developed even further to become the CCR, complete with 592kW (806bhp) V8 power. Suffice to say, neither the CC8S or the CCR were cars for the fearless.

COUNTRY OF ORIGIN	SWEDEN
YEARS OF PRODUCTION	2001–
DISPLACEMENT	4600CC (281CI)
CONFIGURATION	MID-MOUNTED V8, SUPERCHARGED
TRANSMISSION	6-SPEED SEMI-AUTO, REAR-WHEEL DRIVE
POWER	482KW (655BHP)
TORQUE	750NM (553LB FT)
TOP SPEED	389KM/H (242MPH) (CLAIMED)
0–96KM/H (0–60MPH)	3.2SEC

PLYMOUTH SUPERBIRD

Developed from the Road Runner, the Superbird was designed to defeat Ford's Talladegas in the NASCAR superspeedway series. Shortly after Plymouth's road rocket appeared, NASCAR changed the rules, so Superbirds were allowed to race in the 1970 season only. All cars featured a vinyl roof to hide the questionable bodywork above the flush-fitted rear window.

COUNTRY OF ORIGIN	USA
YEARS OF PRODUCTION	1970
DISPLACEMENT	6978CC (426CI)
CONFIGURATION	FRONT-MOUNTED V8
TRANSMISSION	4-SPEED MANUAL, REAR-WHEEL DRIVE
POWER	313KW (425BHP)
TORQUE	664NM (490LB FT)
TOP SPEED	225KM/H (140MPH)
0–96KM/H (0–60MPH)	6.1SEC

PONTIAC FIREBIRD

The second-generation Firebird is one of Pontiac's greatest ever success stories. When launched in 1970, there were four variants: Firebird, Esprit, Formula and Trans Am, the last two being the performance versions. The fruitiest derivatives were fitted with 7457cc (455ci) V8s producing up to 254kW (345bhp) offered from 1973.

COUNTRY OF ORIGIN	USA
YEARS OF PRODUCTION	1970–1980
DISPLACEMENT	7457CC (455CI)
CONFIGURATION	FRONT-MOUNTED V8
TRANSMISSION	4-SPEED MANUAL, REAR-WHEEL DRIVE
POWER	254KW (345BHP)
TORQUE	N/A
TOP SPEED	209KM/H (130MPH)
0–96KM/H (0–60MPH)	5.5SEC

CHRYSLER VALIANT CHARGER VH R/T

The Charger was a short-wheelbase coupé based on the Australian-market Valiant. It was introduced in 1971, and there was a choice of V8 powerplants, which gave the car a very tempting power-to-weight ratio. These engines also allowed drivers to make the most of the car's agility.

COUNTRY OF ORIGIN	AUSTRALIA
YEARS OF PRODUCTION	1971–76
DISPLACEMENT	5897CC (360CI)
CONFIGURATION	FRONT-MOUNTED V8
TRANSMISSION	3-SPEED AUTO, REAR-WHEEL DRIVE
POWER	206KW (280BHP)
TORQUE	N/A
TOP SPEED	200KM/H (124MPH)
0–96KM/H (0–60MPH)	N/A

FORD FALCON XY GT-HO

The Ford Falcon was based on the XR four-door saloon, but in place of the original straight-six there was a much more potent 4.7-litre V8. Even more tempting, however, was the GT-HO, the latter part standing for 'Handling Option'; with its 5.8-litre V8, the car was an absolute beast.

COUNTRY OF ORIGIN	USA
YEARS OF PRODUCTION	1971
DISPLACEMENT	5751CC (351CI)
CONFIGURATION	FRONT-MOUNTED V8
TRANSMISSION	4-SPEED MANUAL, REAR-WHEEL DRIVE
POWER	221KW (300BHP)
TORQUE	515NM (380LB FT)
TOP SPEED	232KM/H (144MPH)
0–96KM/H (0–60MPH)	5.7SEC

PLYMOUTH CUDA 383

Another great looker from the Chrysler stable, the Cuda 383 wasn't as extreme as many of the muscle cars that had gone before – it had just 221kW (300bhp) from its 6.3-litre V8. The chassis was conventional Chrysler, with torsion bar front suspension that was lowered over standard to improve the handling.

COUNTRY OF ORIGIN	USA
YEARS OF PRODUCTION	1971–72
DISPLACEMENT	6276CC (383CI)
CONFIGURATION	FRONT-MOUNTED V8
TRANSMISSION	3-SPEED AUTO, REAR-WHEEL DRIVE
POWER	221kW (300BHP)
TORQUE	556NM (410LB FT)
TOP SPEED	193KM/H (120MPH)
0–96KM/H (0–60MPH)	7.8SEC

PLYMOUTH ROAD RUNNER

The original Road Runner had been a runaway success for Chrysler, so the company offered a substantially redesigned car for 1971. Underneath there was little different, but the interior was more modern, while the track was wider and the wheelbase shorter. Most cars received a 6.2-litre V8, but some featured a 7-litre unit.

COUNTRY OF ORIGIN	USA
YEARS OF PRODUCTION	1971
DISPLACEMENT	6980CC (426CI)
CONFIGURATION	FRONT-MOUNTED V8
TRANSMISSION	4-SPEED MANUAL, REAR-WHEEL DRIVE
POWER	313kW (425BHP)
TORQUE	664NM (490LB FT)
TOP SPEED	201KM/H (125MPH)
0–96KM/H (0–60MPH)	5.7SEC

FORD GRAND TORINO SPORT

The redesigned Torino became a single model series in 1972, split into just two options: the base and Grand Torino. While not as sharp-looking as their previous incarnations, they had the trademark muscle car swept-back roofline and the classic formula of a V8 engine mounted up front and driving the rear wheels.

COUNTRY OF ORIGIN	USA
YEARS OF PRODUCTION	1972–76
DISPLACEMENT	5749CC (351CI)
CONFIGURATION	FRONT-MOUNTED V8
TRANSMISSION	4-SPEED MANUAL, REAR-WHEEL DRIVE
POWER	182kW (248BHP)
TORQUE	405NM (299LB FT)
TOP SPEED	N/A
0–96KM/H (0–60MPH)	6.8SEC

PONTIAC FIREBIRD FORMULA 400

Many manufacturers had given up on muscle cars by the early 1970s because of the strict emissions laws. Pontiac persevered, however, by reducing the fuelling – but this didn't have too much of an effect on the available torque. Hence the cars still accelerated smartly, but weren't as thirsty.

COUNTRY OF ORIGIN	USA
YEARS OF PRODUCTION	1974
DISPLACEMENT	6554CC (400CI)
CONFIGURATION	FRONT-MOUNTED V8
TRANSMISSION	3-SPEED AUTO, REAR-WHEEL DRIVE
POWER	169KW (230BHP)
TORQUE	308NM (277LB FT)
TOP SPEED	190KM/H (118MPH)
0–96KM/H (0–60MPH)	9.4SEC

PONTIAC TRANS AM SD

With the world going through a fuel crisis, it was virtually impossible to find customers for gas-guzzling muscle cars. That didn't stop Pontiac developing the Super Duty 455 edition of its Trans Am, though – a car that lasted until 1976 before General Motors pulled the plug, thanks to its ultra-thirsty 7453cc (455ci) V8.

COUNTRY OF ORIGIN	USA
YEARS OF PRODUCTION	1974–76
DISPLACEMENT	7453CC (455CI)
CONFIGURATION	FRONT-MOUNTED V8
TRANSMISSION	3-SPEED AUTO, REAR-WHEEL DRIVE
POWER	228KW (310BHP)
TORQUE	529NM (390LB FT)
TOP SPEED	212KM/H (132MPH)
0–96KM/H (0–60MPH)	5.4SEC

CHEVROLET COSWORTH VEGA 75

Muscle cars should feature a massive V8 in the nose – at least, that's what the typical American performance car buyer thought in the 1970s. So a relatively small car with a hi-tech four-cylinder engine was never going to be taken seriously, which is too bad because the Vega 75 was more capable than it looked.

COUNTRY OF ORIGIN	USA
YEARS OF PRODUCTION	1975–76
DISPLACEMENT	1998CC (122CI)
CONFIGURATION	FRONT-MOUNTED 4-CYL
TRANSMISSION	4-SPEED MANUAL, REAR-WHEEL DRIVE
POWER	81KW (110BHP)
TORQUE	145NM (107LB FT)
TOP SPEED	180KM/H (112MPH)
0–96KM/H (0–60MPH)	12.3SEC

MERCEDES 450SEL 6.9

In case the 300SEL 6.3 wasn't enough, Mercedes outdid itself by offering an even bigger V8 engine in the newer S-Class. This time based on the W116 S-Class introduced in 1972, the 450SEL 6.9 was the world's first car to be offered with electronic anti-lock braking.

COUNTRY OF ORIGIN	GERMANY
YEARS OF PRODUCTION	1975–80
DISPLACEMENT	6834CC (417CI)
CONFIGURATION	FRONT-MOUNTED V8
TRANSMISSION	AUTOMATIC, REAR-WHEEL DRIVE
POWER	210KW (286BHP)
TORQUE	549NM (405LB FT)
TOP SPEED	225KM/H (140MPH)
0–96KM/H (0–60MPH)	7.3SEC

PONTIAC CAN AM

Although muscle cars were one of the defining motoring moments of the 1960s, there were one or two in the 1970s that stood out from the anaemic designs that proliferated. The Can Am was one example, created when Pontiac dropped a 6552cc (400ci) V8 into the nose of its Le Mans coupé.

COUNTRY OF ORIGIN	USA
YEARS OF PRODUCTION	1977
DISPLACEMENT	6552CC (400CI)
CONFIGURATION	FRONT-MOUNTED V8
TRANSMISSION	3-SPEED AUTO, REAR-WHEEL DRIVE
POWER	147KW (200BHP)
TORQUE	441NM (325LB FT)
TOP SPEED	193KM/H (120MPH)
0–96KM/H (0–60MPH)	8.6SEC

DODGE L'IL RED EXPRESS

Using the Adventurer 150 as its base, this was Dodge's attempt at creating a factory custom pick-up. With its 5.9-litre V8 in the front, the L'il Red Express was one of the fastest vehicles on the road in 1979, and it proved a real hit. The engine was effectively a police-spec unit, with high-lift cam and four-barrel carburettor.

COUNTRY OF ORIGIN	USA
YEARS OF PRODUCTION	1978–79
DISPLACEMENT	5899CC (360CI)
CONFIGURATION	FRONT-MOUNTED V8
TRANSMISSION	3-SPEED AUTO, REAR-WHEEL DRIVE
POWER	165KW (225BHP)
TORQUE	400NM (295LB FT)
TOP SPEED	190KM/H (118MPH)
0–96KM/H (0–60MPH)	6.6SEC

SHELBY CHARGER GLH-S

With lines like those, this could only be a child of the 1980s. Horribly dated now, the Charger was incredibly potent for the time, and now very collectable, as just 1000 copies were produced. Someone had a sense of humour – GLH-S was short for 'Goes Like Hell-Some more'. It was successor to the GLH.

COUNTRY OF ORIGIN	USA
YEARS OF PRODUCTION	1986–87
DISPLACEMENT	2200CC (134CI)
CONFIGURATION	FRONT-MOUNTED 4-CYL
TRANSMISSION	5-SPEED MANUAL, FRONT-WHEEL DRIVE
POWER	213KW (289BHP)
TORQUE	371NM (274LB FT)
TOP SPEED	201KM/H (125MPH)
0–96KM/H (0–60MPH)	5.4SEC

SHELBY DAKOTA

Dodge introduced its Dakota pick-up in 1987, and it would take another two years for Carroll Shelby to work his magic on it, ditching the original 3.9-litre V6 for a 5.2-litre V8. At the same time, he fitted Goodyear Eagle tyres, a limited-slip differential and stiffer suspension – transforming the car in the process.

COUNTRY OF ORIGIN	USA
YEARS OF PRODUCTION	1989
DISPLACEMENT	5211CC (318CI)
CONFIGURATION	FRONT-MOUNTED V8
TRANSMISSION	4-SPEED AUTO, REAR-WHEEL DRIVE
POWER	129KW (175BHP)
TORQUE	366NM (270LB FT)
TOP SPEED	192KM/H (119MPH)
0–96KM/H (0–60MPH)	8.5SEC

CHEVROLET 454 SS PICK UP

As fuel concerns died out in the early 1980s, Chevrolet decided to offer a full-on performance pick-up once more – the 7.4-litre SS454. With its long-stroke V8 powerplant ,there was plenty of low-down torque, and with its lowered back axle ratio (to just 4.10:1), acceleration was suitably swift.

COUNTRY OF ORIGIN	USA
YEARS OF PRODUCTION	1990–93
DISPLACEMENT	7440CC (454CI)
CONFIGURATION	FRONT-MOUNTED V8
TRANSMISSION	4-SPEED AUTO, REAR-WHEEL DRIVE
POWER	188KW (255BHP)
TORQUE	549NM (405LB FT)
TOP SPEED	193KM/H (120MPH)
0–96KM/H (0–60MPH)	4.2SEC

MERCEDES 500E

Based on the Mercedes W124 saloon, the 500E (known as the E500 from 1994) was built with the close cooperation of Porsche. Indeed, it was Porsche that built the cars, known internally as the Velvet Hammer and each one equipped with every conceivable piece of equipment as standard.

COUNTRY OF ORIGIN	GERMANY
YEARS OF PRODUCTION	1990–95
DISPLACEMENT	4973CC (303CI)
CONFIGURATION	FRONT-MOUNTED V8
TRANSMISSION	AUTOMATIC, REAR-WHEEL DRIVE
POWER	240KW (326BHP)
TORQUE	480NM (354LB FT)
TOP SPEED	251KM/H (156MPH)
0–96KM/H (0–60MPH)	6.3SEC

GMC SYCLONE

Built for just one season, the Syclone was the precursor to the more practical Typhoon. Matching the carrying capacity of a pick-up with the performance (if not necessarily the handling) of supercars such as the Corvette ZR-1, the Syclone could go round corners too thanks to its four-wheel drive transmission.

COUNTRY OF ORIGIN	USA
YEARS OF PRODUCTION	1991
DISPLACEMENT	4293CC (262CI)
CONFIGURATION	FRONT-MOUNTED V8
TRANSMISSION	4-SPEED AUTO, FOUR-WHEEL DRIVE
POWER	206KW (280BHP)
TORQUE	475NM (350LB FT)
TOP SPEED	201KM/H (125MPH)
0–96KM/H (0–60MPH)	5.2SEC

GMC TYPHOON

Having created the barking-mad Syclone the previous year, GMC continued on its quest to turn its image into one of building performance cars. To that end, it built a five-seater SUV with a turbocharged and intercooled GMC Jimmy powerplant, mated to a four-wheel drive system to help get the power down.

COUNTRY OF ORIGIN	USA
YEARS OF PRODUCTION	1991–92
DISPLACEMENT	4293CC (262CI)
CONFIGURATION	FRONT-MOUNTED V8
TRANSMISSION	4-SPEED AUTO, FOUR-WHEEL DRIVE
POWER	206KW (280BHP)
TORQUE	475NM (350LB FT)
TOP SPEED	200KM/H (124MPH)
0–96KM/H (0–60MPH)	5.4SEC

FORD F-150 LIGHTNING

With pick-up trucks among the most popular vehicles on US roads, it made sense for Ford to beef up its best-selling F-150 into something special. Through the Windsor small-block V8 up front and shorter, stiffer springs at each corner, the Lightning was astonishingly fast and had the handling to match.

COUNTRY OF ORIGIN	USA
YEARS OF PRODUCTION	1993–96
DISPLACEMENT	5751CC (351CI)
CONFIGURATION	FRONT-MOUNTED V8
TRANSMISSION	4-SPEED MANUAL, REAR-WHEEL DRIVE
POWER	177KW (240BHP)
TORQUE	461NM (340LB FT)
TOP SPEED	193KM/H (120MPH)
0–96KM/H (0–60MPH)	7.5SEC

FORD MUSTANG COBRA R

When the Cobra R was unveiled, it was the fastest Mustang ever to come from Ford. It was the work of Ford's Special Vehicle Team, and offered more power than normal, and less weight for maximum agility. As well as losing the sound deadening, the air-con and power windows were ditched.

COUNTRY OF ORIGIN	USA
YEARS OF PRODUCTION	1995
DISPLACEMENT	5751CC (351CI)
CONFIGURATION	FRONT-MOUNTED V8
TRANSMISSION	5-SPEED MANUAL, REAR-WHEEL DRIVE
POWER	221KW (300BHP)
TORQUE	495NM (365LB FT)
TOP SPEED	241KM/H (150MPH)
0–96KM/H (0–60MPH)	5.5SEC

ALPINA B10

Famous for its understated tuned BMWs, Alpina excelled itself with the B10. BMW had barely launched a fresh generation of 5-Series when Alpina announced it was offering an upgraded 535i, with its trademark finned wheels, front and rear spoilers and the option of two turbos, giving up to 265kW (360bhp).

COUNTRY OF ORIGIN	GERMANY
YEARS OF PRODUCTION	1998–2005
DISPLACEMENT	3430CC (209CI)
CONFIGURATION	FRONT-MOUNTED 6-CYL
TRANSMISSION	5-SPEED MANUAL, REAR-WHEEL DRIVE
POWER	187kW (254BHP)
TORQUE	325NM (240LB FT)
TOP SPEED	253KM/H (157MPH)
0–96KM/H (0–60MPH)	7.0SEC

FORD F350 SUPER DUTY

When it comes to metal for your money, the F350 Super Duty was pretty hard to beat. With it 6.8-litre V10 engine, and 2.74-tonne (2.7-ton) kerb weight, this was one huge truck, capable of towing nearly 5.08 tonnes (5 tons), yet it was able to sprint from a standing start to 96km/h (60mph) in barely more than 10 seconds.

COUNTRY OF ORIGIN	USA
YEARS OF PRODUCTION	1999–
DISPLACEMENT	6800CC (415CI)
CONFIGURATION	FRONT-MOUNTED V10
TRANSMISSION	4-SPEED AUTO, FOUR-WHEEL DRIVE
POWER	202kW (275BHP)
TORQUE	556NM (410LB FT)
TOP SPEED	154KM/H (96MPH)
0–96KM/H (0–60MPH)	10.2SEC

HOLDEN MONARO

The Monaro was first sold by Holden in 1968, lasting right through to 1979. Holden showed a performance coupé concept in 1998 and was urged to build it; the car was swiftly nicknamed the Monaro. Offered with six- or eight-cylinder engines, the car was later exported to Europe.

COUNTRY OF ORIGIN	AUSTRALIA
YEARS OF PRODUCTION	2001–05
DISPLACEMENT	5665CC (346CI)
CONFIGURATION	FRONT-MOUNTED V8
TRANSMISSION	6-SPEED MANUAL, REAR-WHEEL DRIVE
POWER	260kW (353BHP)
TORQUE	500NM (369LB FT)
TOP SPEED	249KM/H (155MPH)
0–96KM/H (0–60MPH)	5.9SEC

DODGE RAM V10

A pick-up truck the size of a house needs something decent under the bonnet – like a Dodge Viper V10. That's just what the Ram offered, although the engine was detuned and the top speed was restricted to 182km/h (113mph). It was big and brutal – this was no agile sportscar.

COUNTRY OF ORIGIN	USA
YEARS OF PRODUCTION	2002–
DISPLACEMENT	7997CC (488CI)
CONFIGURATION	FRONT-MOUNTED V10
TRANSMISSION	3-SPEED AUTO, REAR-WHEEL DRIVE
POWER	221kW (300BHP)
TORQUE	610NM (450LB FT)
TOP SPEED	182KM/H (113MPH)
0–96KM/H (0–60MPH)	8.5SEC

CHEVROLET SSR

There have been some weird crossover vehicles, but few have matched the SSR, or Super Sport Roadster. Combining a pick-up with a coupé-cabriolet, the SSR was based on the Chevrolet Trailblazer but with retro styling and a folding hardtop that retracted into the load bay.

COUNTRY OF ORIGIN	USA
YEARS OF PRODUCTION	2003–06
DISPLACEMENT	6000CC (366CI)
CONFIGURATION	FRONT-MOUNTED V8
TRANSMISSION	6-SPEED MANUAL, REAR-WHEEL DRIVE
POWER	294kW (400BHP)
TORQUE	542NM (400LB FT)
TOP SPEED	211KM/H (131MPH)
0–96KM/H (0–60MPH)	5.3SEC

VAUXHALL MONARO VXR

When it came to affordable muscle, the Vauxhall Monaro was pretty hard to beat in the UK. However, there was a run-out edition in 2006, which offered even more power for astonishingly small amounts of money. With a supercharged 5.7-litre V8, the VXR500 offered a monstrous 368kW (500bhp).

COUNTRY OF ORIGIN	UK/AUSTRALIA
YEARS OF PRODUCTION	2005
DISPLACEMENT	5665CC (346CI)
CONFIGURATION	FRONT-MOUNTED V8
TRANSMISSION	6-SPEED MANUAL, REAR-WHEEL DRIVE
POWER	368kW (500BHP)
TORQUE	677NM (499LB FT)
TOP SPEED	298KM/H (185MPH)
0–96KM/H (0–60MPH)	4.8SEC

AUDI S5

Built to directly compete with BMW's M3 coupé, the S5 was a typically understated powerhouse from Audi. Based on the less powerful A5 coupé, the S5 was fitted with the same naturally aspirated V8 as the equally reserved S4, with Audi's famous quattro four-wheel drive system to get the power down.

COUNTRY OF ORIGIN	GERMANY
YEARS OF PRODUCTION	2007–
DISPLACEMENT	4163CC
CONFIGURATION	FRONT-MOUNTED V8
TRANSMISSION	6-SPEED MANUAL, FOUR-WHEEL DRIVE
POWER	354BHP
TORQUE	325LB FT
TOP SPEED	155MPH
0–96KM/H (0–60MPH)	5.1SEC

Ultra Exclusive

Many would argue that the cars in this chapter are the very essence of what a dream car is all about; available in tiny numbers, very expensive and invariably hugely powerful and luxurious too. It's a sound argument; there's a school of thought which says that dreams shouldn't be too attainable, and that's definitely the case for the cars included here. Some of the vehicles in this group are so rare that the entry in this book is the only time you're ever likely to see one. Let's face it, when was the last time you saw a Duesenberg of any kind, or a Cord 812?

When new, none of these cars were especially affordable, and the passing of time has only sent most of them even further out of reach. If you want to buy an Auburn Speedster or Aston Martin Le Mans now, you're going to need a huge amount of cash to pay for it. However, not every single entry is outrageously costly; sometimes the cars were merely produced in limited numbers. That's why the BMW M3 CSL and Mitsubishi Shogun Evolution are here. While neither was a car for paupers when new, they weren't so expensive that nobody could afford them. The reason they're here is because of their very limited availability. Indeed, the M3 CSL could have sold out several times over, but BMW deliberately restricted supplies to ensure the car remained exclusive. You won't find many cars like that in this chapter, though; this is the place to look if you really want to do some dreaming.

The first part of the chapter focuses on the coachbuilt grand tourers of a bygone era; prewar cars that were for the seriously wealthy only. Cars from Rolls-Royce, Bentley and Hispano-Suiza were amazingly costly in ex-factory chassis form – then there was a bespoke body to be paid for to clothe it. It was no wonder that so few were made; there simply weren't enough people who could afford them.

The post-war era brought with it a new way of building cars, but that didn't necessarily make them affordable. You still needed access to a lot of money if you wanted to buy a Pegaso, Salmson or Dual-Ghia, but the cars were bought as a finished item rather than having to go through the separate stages of buying a chassis then having to get a bodyshell made for it.

Most of the cars here are ultra-luxurious tourers, but there are a few exceptions such as the Jaguar XKSS and Ferrari 250GTO, as well as the Aston Martin DB4 GT Zagato. All racers for the road, these cars put performance before comfort, and while they weren't necessarily a success in sales terms or even on the track, they're all now some of the most sought after cars on the planet.

Although the ultra-exclusive cars of more recent years will always be hugely desirable, they'll never have the glamour of their ancestors. Still, that's unlikely to worry the owners of cars such as the Rolls-Royce Phantom or Maybach 62S, who buy their cars for everyday use, valuing comfort and exclusivity above all else. After all, the person who buys either of these cars is likely to have plenty of cash left over to also buy something rather more collectible for occasional use only – the typical Rolls-Royce owner has another half-dozen cars at their disposal…

Just 208 examples of the Bentley R-Type Continental were produced.

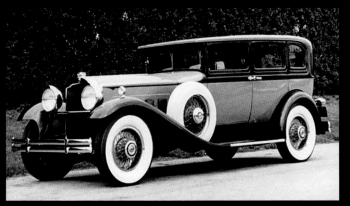

PACKARD EIGHT

Replacing the original Twin Six, the Eight featured a straight-eight powerplant, a unit that would be the backbone of Packard's production throughout the 1930s. However, an all-new engine with the same configuration would be launched in 1939, by which time servo-assisted brakes had also appeared.

COUNTRY OF ORIGIN	USA
YEARS OF PRODUCTION	1923–42
DISPLACEMENT	6306CC (385CI)
CONFIGURATION	FRONT-MOUNTED 8-CYL
TRANSMISSION	3-SPEED MANUAL, REAR-WHEEL DRIVE
POWER	107kW (145BHP)
TORQUE	N/A
TOP SPEED	N/A
0–96KM/H (0–60MPH)	N/A

ROLLS-ROYCE PHANTOM I

Also known as the 40/50 New Phantom, this was yet another superlative car from Rolls-Royce, available with a choice of saloon, open tourer or coupé bodystyles. With gas-filled shock absorbers and servo-assisted brakes, the car was advanced – but there was still no synchromesh for the gearbox.

COUNTRY OF ORIGIN	UK
YEARS OF PRODUCTION	1925–29
DISPLACEMENT	7668CC (468CI)
CONFIGURATION	FRONT-MOUNTED 6-CYL
TRANSMISSION	4-SPEED MANUAL, REAR-WHEEL DRIVE
POWER	N/A
TORQUE	N/A
TOP SPEED	129KM/H (80MPH)
0–96KM/H (0–60MPH)	24.0SEC

DAIMLER DOUBLE SIX

The Daimler Double Six was equipped with Britain's first ever V12 engine, cast in four blocks of three with detachable cylinder heads. The car was created because the wealthy required ultra-refined cars that were powerful, and few cars met these criteria. Production, however, was necessarily limited because of the car's high price.

COUNTRY OF ORIGIN	UK
YEARS OF PRODUCTION	1926–37
DISPLACEMENT	7136CC (435CI)
CONFIGURATION	FRONT-MOUNTED V12
TRANSMISSION	4-SPEED MANUAL, REAR-WHEEL DRIVE
POWER	110kW (150BHP)
TORQUE	N/A
TOP SPEED	129KM/H (80MPH)
0–96KM/H (0–60MPH)	N/A

STUTZ VERTICAL EIGHT

Stutz had done well with its Bearcat, but by the 1920s the company's popularity was fading. To pull itself out of the mire, the Vertical Eight was conceived, a car that was as fast as the Bentleys at Le Mans in 1928. The range was renamed SV16 in 1931, to fit in with the newly introduced DV32.

COUNTRY OF ORIGIN	USA
YEARS OF PRODUCTION	1926–35
DISPLACEMENT	4894CC (299CI)
CONFIGURATION	FRONT-MOUNTED 8-CYL
TRANSMISSION	3-SPEED MANUAL, REAR-WHEEL DRIVE
POWER	85kW (115BHP)
TORQUE	323NM (238LB FT)
TOP SPEED	N/A
0–96KM/H (0–60MPH)	N/A

VOISIN C11

Gabriel Voisin was a man of vision; he engineered his cars to be as refined and comfortable as possible. The C11 was a case in point. The passengers were moved forward to sit between the axles, while the engines used sleeve valves, which were much quieter than the poppet-valve alternative.

COUNTRY OF ORIGIN	FRANCE
YEARS OF PRODUCTION	1926–28
DISPLACEMENT	2330CC (142CI)
CONFIGURATION	FRONT-MOUNTED 6-CYL
TRANSMISSION	3-SPEED MANUAL, REAR-WHEEL DRIVE
POWER	49KW (66BHP)
TORQUE	N/A
TOP SPEED	116KM/H (72MPH)
0–96KM/H (0–60MPH)	N/A

MINERVA AK

You'd probably struggle to name many cars that have been made in Belgium, but the Minerva was just such a beast – and a truly luxurious one at that. This was one of the finest cars Europe had to offer, with most of the vehicles being snapped up by Hollywood film stars, thanks to its grandeur.

COUNTRY OF ORIGIN	BELGIUM
YEARS OF PRODUCTION	1927–37
DISPLACEMENT	5954CC (363CI)
CONFIGURATION	FRONT-MOUNTED 6-CYL
TRANSMISSION	4-SPEED MANUAL, REAR-WHEEL DRIVE
POWER	110KW (150BHP)
TORQUE	N/A
TOP SPEED	145KM/H (90MPH)
0–96KM/H (0–60MPH)	N/A

BENTLEY SPEED SIX

Based on the 6.5-Litre, the Speed Six was an ultra-exclusive Bentley featuring a 6.6-litre overhead-cam engine that was fitted with four valves for each cylinder, something that wouldn't become commonplace for decades. It was of little use, though – by 1931, Bentley had been acquired by Rolls-Royce.

COUNTRY OF ORIGIN	UK
YEARS OF PRODUCTION	1928–30
DISPLACEMENT	6597CC (403CI)
CONFIGURATION	FRONT-MOUNTED 6-CYL
TRANSMISSION	4-SPEED MANUAL, REAR-WHEEL DRIVE
POWER	132KW (180BHP)
TORQUE	N/A
TOP SPEED	138KM/H (86MPH)
0–96KM/H (0–60MPH)	N/A

PIERCE-ARROW STRAIGHT-EIGHT

Pierce-Arrow couldn't have seen the Depression coming, which was a shame because it developed a new range of luxury cars at just the wrong time. The car was very well received, but suddenly there weren't enough people who could afford such a prestigious motor, although the company lingered on until 1938.

COUNTRY OF ORIGIN	USA
YEARS OF PRODUCTION	1928–38
DISPLACEMENT	5587CC (341CI)
CONFIGURATION	FRONT-MOUNTED 8-CYL
TRANSMISSION	4-SPEED MANUAL, REAR-WHEEL DRIVE
POWER	85KW (115BHP)
TORQUE	N/A
TOP SPEED	138KM/H (85MPH)
0–96KM/H (0–60MPH)	N/A

Ultimate Dream Car 19:
Ferrari Enzo

Just like its forebears, the Ferrari Enzo would be the closest thing to a Formula One car for the road, packing the very best technology into the most advanced bodyshell possible. Money would be no object, and production would be limited to just 349 examples. Yet while the Enzo has earned a reputation for being fearsomely quick and massively expensive, it's also one of the safest and cleanest supercars ever made.

The starting point for the Enzo was its predecessor, the F50. Ferrari took that car and worked out where its weak points were, addressing them in turn so that the Enzo wouldn't suffer from any of them. Ferrari's main objectives with the Enzo were refinement and good performance at low engine speeds. As usual, Pininfarina came up with the styling, having been briefed that the new car would be available as a coupé only. Of course, the car had to be dramatic, but it also had to be aerodynamically efficient, aggressive, and hopefully even beautiful too. Whether the latter was achieved is open to debate, but it certainly scores on all the other points – it would be hard to imagine how a car could pack any more visual drama.

Because it was felt that the F50 hadn't offered sufficient torque because of its relatively small capacity of 4.7 litres, the Enzo's completely new V12 had a displacement of 6 litres. Redlined at 8200rpm, the 65° unit featured four belt-driven camshafts, with variable inlet and exhaust valve timing along with a continuously variable inlet manifold to increase torque. Brembo came up with a carbon-ceramic braking system that didn't suffer poor performance when cold, but which also didn't fade when the car was driven mercilessly. With the discs measuring 380mm (15in) in diameter, there were six-pot calipers at the front and four-pot at the rear.

COUNTRY OF ORIGIN	ITALY
YEARS OF PRODUCTION	2002–04
DISPLACEMENT	5998CC (366CI)
CONFIGURATION	MID-MOUNTED V12
TRANSMISSION	6-SPEED MANUAL, REAR-WHEEL DRIVE
POWER	478KW (650BHP)
TORQUE	658NM (485LB FT)
TOP SPEED	349KM/H (217MPH)
0–100KM/H (0–62MPH)	3.6SEC

VOISIN 32-140

Gabriel Voisin produced some of the most lavish and innovative cars ever created. With ostentatious lines, his creations were generally big and heavy while always being very expensive. The 32-140 was available as a saloon, two- or four-door coupé or convertible, but few of any type were made.

COUNTRY OF ORIGIN	FRANCE
YEARS OF PRODUCTION	1930–34
DISPLACEMENT	5830CC (356CI)
CONFIGURATION	FRONT-MOUNTED 6-CYL
TRANSMISSION	4-SPEED MANUAL, REAR-WHEEL DRIVE
POWER	96KW (130BHP)
TORQUE	N/A
TOP SPEED	N/A
0–96KM/H (0–60MPH)	N/A

BUGATTI ROYALE

Although the Royale was hailed as the car of kings – hence the nickname – Bugatti never actually managed to sell any of these cars to royalty. The most lavish car of its day, the Bugatti Type 41 was over 6m (20ft) long, but even the super-rich couldn't afford it. Just six cars were built over two years.

COUNTRY OF ORIGIN	FRANCE
YEARS OF PRODUCTION	1931–1933
DISPLACEMENT	12,763CC (779CI)
CONFIGURATION	FRONT-MOUNTED 8-CYL
TRANSMISSION	3-SPEED MANUAL, REAR-WHEEL DRIVE
POWER	202KW (275BHP)
TORQUE	N/A
TOP SPEED	188KM/H (117MPH)
0–96KM/H (0–60MPH)	N/A

MAYBACH ZEPPELIN

At the turn of the 19th century, Wilhelm Maybach was associated with prestigious engineers and products. When he died of pneumonia in 1929, his son Karl took over the business and decided to move into car production. The Zeppelin of 1931 was his second car, after the W5 of 1927.

COUNTRY OF ORIGIN	GERMANY
YEARS OF PRODUCTION	1931–40
DISPLACEMENT	7995CC (488CI)
CONFIGURATION	FRONT-MOUNTED V12
TRANSMISSION	5-SPEED MANUAL, REAR-WHEEL DRIVE
POWER	147KW (200BHP)
TORQUE	N/A
TOP SPEED	171KM/H (106MPH)
0–96KM/H (0–60MPH)	N/A

STUTZ DV32

Things were getting very tough for America's luxury car makers in the early 1930s, and while some had the resources to develop new models, Stutz didn't. What it did do was create a twin-cam version of its straight-eight engine, complete with four valves for each cylinder.

COUNTRY OF ORIGIN	USA
YEARS OF PRODUCTION	1931–35
DISPLACEMENT	5271CC (322CI)
CONFIGURATION	FRONT-MOUNTED 8-CYL
TRANSMISSION	4-SPEED MANUAL, REAR-WHEEL DRIVE
POWER	115KW (156BHP)
TORQUE	407NM (300LB FT)
TOP SPEED	145KM/H (90MPH)
0–96KM/H (0–60MPH)	N/A

ASTON MARTIN LE MANS

An evolution of the International, the Le Mans is the finest of the prewar Aston Martins, with its much sportier lines, lower-slung chassis, side-exit exhaust and Moss gearbox. There were three bodies available: a two-seater sports and a choice of long- or short-wheelbase four-seater sports models.

COUNTRY OF ORIGIN	UK
YEARS OF PRODUCTION	1932–34
DISPLACEMENT	1495CC (91CI)
CONFIGURATION	FRONT-MOUNTED 4-CYL
TRANSMISSION	4-SPEED MANUAL, REAR-WHEEL DRIVE
POWER	55KW (75BHP)
TORQUE	N/A
TOP SPEED	129KM/H (80MPH)
0–96KM/H (0–60MPH)	24.6SEC

DUESENBERG SJ

The standard Duesenberg wasn't enough for some. Hence the option of a supercharged model, the SJ (some cars even featured two superchargers). The most powerful car in the world when it went on sale in 1932, the SJ was equipped with four-wheel braking and alloy panels, to keep weight down.

COUNTRY OF ORIGIN	USA
YEARS OF PRODUCTION	1932–37
DISPLACEMENT	6882CC (420CI)
CONFIGURATION	FRONT-MOUNTED 8-CYL
TRANSMISSION	3-SPEED MANUAL, REAR-WHEEL DRIVE
POWER	235KW (320BHP)
TORQUE	576NM (425LB FT)
TOP SPEED	209KM/H (130MPH)
0–96KM/H (0–60MPH)	8.5SEC

FRAZER NASH TT REPLICA

One of the most popular of the Frazer Nashes, the TT replica was so called because of its success during the TT races of the early 1930s. With its set-back radiator, cycle wings and squared-off fuel tank, the TT certainly looked the part – and it went just as well too, especially in super-charged form with 110kW (150bhp).

COUNTRY OF ORIGIN	UK
YEARS OF PRODUCTION	1932–38
DISPLACEMENT	1496CC (91CI)
CONFIGURATION	FRONT-MOUNTED 4-CYL
TRANSMISSION	4-SPEED MANUAL, REAR-WHEEL DRIVE
POWER	46KW (62BHP)
TORQUE	N/A
TOP SPEED	129KM/H (80MPH)
0–96KM/H (0–60MPH)	8.8SEC

HISPANO SUIZA J12

The seriously wealthy were spoiled for choice when it came to buying cars in the 1930s, with the J12 being one of the most exclusive vehicles available anywhere thanks to its 9.4-litre V12 engine. Capable of 161km/h (100mph), the J12 was massive yet usually offered space for just two people, such was the size of its engine and gearbox.

COUNTRY OF ORIGIN	SPAIN
YEARS OF PRODUCTION	1932–38
DISPLACEMENT	9424CC (575CI)
CONFIGURATION	FRONT-MOUNTED 12-CYL
TRANSMISSION	3-SPEED MANUAL, REAR-WHEEL DRIVE
POWER	140KW (190BHP)
TORQUE	N/A
TOP SPEED	161KM/H (100MPH)
0–96KM/H (0–60MPH)	12.0SEC

BUGATTI TYPE 57

The Type 57 was an attempt at building an exotic, luxurious and fast grand tourer, and it was the last great car to come from the original Bugatti. Power was supplied by a 3257cc (199ci) double overhead cam straight-eight, and there were touring, saloon, coach, coupé and cabriolet bodies all available.

COUNTRY OF ORIGIN	FRANCE
YEARS OF PRODUCTION	1933–40
DISPLACEMENT	3257CC (199CI)
CONFIGURATION	FRONT-MOUNTED 8-CYL
TRANSMISSION	4-SPEED MANUAL, REAR-WHEEL DRIVE
POWER	99KW (135BHP)
TORQUE	N/A
TOP SPEED	153KM/H (95MPH)
0–96KM/H (0–60MPH)	N/A

HISPANO SUIZA K6

The K6 was launched just as a global recession was starting to bite. Instead of downsizing its cars, Hispano Suiza continued as before – despite the fact that virtually nobody could afford such luxury. It was only a matter of time before the company was forced to close it doors for the last time.

COUNTRY OF ORIGIN	SPAIN
YEARS OF PRODUCTION	1934–38
DISPLACEMENT	5184CC (97CI)
CONFIGURATION	FRONT-MOUNTED 6-CYL
TRANSMISSION	3-SPEED MANUAL, REAR-WHEEL DRIVE
POWER	92KW (125BHP)
TORQUE	N/A
TOP SPEED	N/A
0–96KM/H (0–60MPH)	N/A

TRIUMPH DOLOMITE STRAIGHT EIGHT

Built to take on the best that Europe could offer, the Dolomite Straight-Eight was a copy of Alfa Romeo's 2300. The car was masterminded by Donald Healey, but it was unfortunate that Triumph wasn't in a position to indulge in such luxuries, and the car went out of production after just three examples had been made.

COUNTRY OF ORIGIN	UK
YEARS OF PRODUCTION	1934–35
DISPLACEMENT	1990CC (121CI)
CONFIGURATION	FRONT-MOUNTED 8-CYL
TRANSMISSION	MANUAL REAR-WHEEL DRIVE
POWER	88KW (120BHP)
TORQUE	N/A
TOP SPEED	177KM/H (110MPH)
0–96KM/H (0–60MPH)	N/A

AUBURN SPEEDSTER

One of the most romantic cars of the 1930s, the Speedster was obligatory transport for Hollywood stars of the day, as they were the only ones who could afford them. Everything was built by hand to the most exacting standards – this was a car of both luxury and power.

COUNTRY OF ORIGIN	USA
YEARS OF PRODUCTION	1935–37
DISPLACEMENT	4589CC (280CI)
CONFIGURATION	FRONT-MOUNTED 8-CYL
TRANSMISSION	3-SPEED MANUAL, REAR-WHEEL DRIVE
POWER	110KW (150BHP)
TORQUE	312NM (230LB FT)
TOP SPEED	174KM/H (108MPH)
0–96KM/H (0–60MPH)	10.0SEC

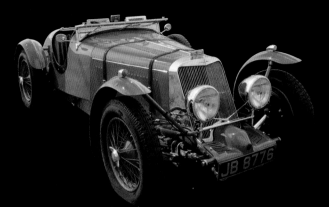

SQUIRE
When it came to exotic cars in the 1930s, few were more desirable than the Squire. This racer for the road featured performance and handling on a par with the best racers of the day, while also being able to outbrake many of them. Unsurprisingly, the cars were very expensive, and just seven were built.

COUNTRY OF ORIGIN	UK
YEARS OF PRODUCTION	1935–36
DISPLACEMENT	1496CC (91CI)
CONFIGURATION	FRONT-MOUNTED 4-CYL
TRANSMISSION	3-SPEED MANUAL REAR-WHEEL DRIVE
POWER	74kW (100BHP)
TORQUE	N/A
TOP SPEED	161KM/H (100MPH)
0–96KM/H (0–60MPH)	10.5SEC

BMW 328
Just eight years after it started building the Dixi, BMW introduced the 328, one of the most revered sportscars ever created. With a completely redesigned version of the 2-litre straight-six usually seen in the 303, the 328 was capable of 150km/h (93mph), thanks to the three Solex carburettors that gave a healthy 59kW (80bhp).

COUNTRY OF ORIGIN	GERMANY
YEARS OF PRODUCTION	1936–39
DISPLACEMENT	1971CC (120CI)
CONFIGURATION	FRONT-MOUNTED 6-CYL
TRANSMISSION	4-SPEED MANUAL, REAR-WHEEL DRIVE
POWER	59kW (80BHP)
TORQUE	126NM (93LB FT)
TOP SPEED	150KM/H (93MPH)
0–96KM/H (0–60MPH)	8.0SEC

CORD 812
With its V8 power and front-wheel drive, the Cord 812 was quite a beast. It was horrifically costly to build too, thanks to its monocoque construction. It looked amazing, though, with its pop-up headlamps and coffin-shaped bonnet, and there was electro-vacuum operation for the transmission. Great, but too costly to make sense.

COUNTRY OF ORIGIN	USA
YEARS OF PRODUCTION	1936–37
DISPLACEMENT	4729CC (289CI)
CONFIGURATION	FRONT-MOUNTED V8
TRANSMISSION	4-SPEED SEMI-AUTO, FRONT-WHEEL DRIVE
POWER	140kW (190BHP)
TORQUE	353NM (260LB FT)
TOP SPEED	177KM/H (110MPH)
0–96KM/H (0–60MPH)	13.5SEC

DELAHAYE 135
Delahaye was just another small manufacturer of nicely built touring cars when it stumbled on the idea of fitting an engine from one of its trucks. Performance was transformed, and the 135 was created in the process. Offered officially were a two-door saloon and cabriolet, but numerous specials were also created.

COUNTRY OF ORIGIN	FRANCE
YEARS OF PRODUCTION	1936–52
DISPLACEMENT	3227CC (197CI)
CONFIGURATION	FRONT-MOUNTED 6-CYL
TRANSMISSION	4-SPEED MANUAL, REAR-WHEEL DRIVE
POWER	88kW (120BHP)
TORQUE	N/A
TOP SPEED	161KM/H (100MPH)
0–96KM/H (0–60MPH)	14.0SEC

CUNNINGHAM C-3

Briggs Cunningham was a rich playboy who acquired a race car company and set about creating his own exclusive cars. They would be suitable for both road and racing, with the C-3 being his third model. The cars were too costly, though, and just 18 coupés plus nine cabriolets were created.

COUNTRY OF ORIGIN	USA
YEARS OF PRODUCTION	1952–55
DISPLACEMENT	5422CC (331CI)
CONFIGURATION	FRONT -MOUNTED V8
TRANSMISSION	3-SPEED MANUAL, REAR-WHEEL DRIVE
POWER	228KW (310BHP)
TORQUE	N/A
TOP SPEED	193KM/H (120MPH)
0–96KM/H (0–60MPH)	6.9SEC

FIAT 8V

Deciding to broaden its range in the early 1950s, Fiat created a V8-engined luxury car. The car was poorly received, and so, having already developed the 2-litre V8, Fiat decided to create a sportscar that could use it. The 8V was an instant success, but its hand-built nature meant it would always be exclusive.

COUNTRY OF ORIGIN	ITALY
YEARS OF PRODUCTION	1952–55
DISPLACEMENT	1996CC (122CI)
CONFIGURATION	FRONT-MOUNTED V8
TRANSMISSION	5-SPEED MANUAL, REAR-WHEEL DRIVE
POWER	77KW (105BHP)
TORQUE	145NM (107LB FT)
TOP SPEED	193KM/H (120MPH)
0–96KM/H (0–60MPH)	12.6SEC

CADILLAC ELDORADO

Cadillac reckoned there was the opportunity to get some of its more wealthy customers to spend more cash, so the Eldorado was launched in 1953 as an extension of the Series 62 range. But it was too costly, with just 532 being sold – so the price was dropped and the car started to sell.

COUNTRY OF ORIGIN	USA
YEARS OF PRODUCTION	1953
DISPLACEMENT	5424CC (331CI)
CONFIGURATION	FRONT-MOUNTED V8
TRANSMISSION	3-SPEED AUTO, REAR-WHEEL DRIVE
POWER	154KW (210BHP)
TORQUE	447NM (330LB FT)
TOP SPEED	187KM/H (116MPH)
0–96KM/H (0–60MPH)	12.6SEC

BRISTOL 404

An evolution of the 403, the Bristol 404 was the first car from the company to incorporate spare wheel and battery housings within the front wheelarches – features that would characterize Bristols in later years. There was also a shorter chassis, which made the car more agile, while a four-door version was also offered, the 405.

COUNTRY OF ORIGIN	UK
YEARS OF PRODUCTION	1953–55
DISPLACEMENT	1971CC (120CI)
CONFIGURATION	FRONT-MOUNTED 6-CYL
TRANSMISSION	4-SPEED MANUAL, REAR-WHEEL DRIVE
POWER	77KW (105BHP)
TORQUE	167NM (123LB FT)
TOP SPEED	185KM/H (115MPH)
0–96KM/H (0–60MPH)	N/A

EDWARDS AMERICA

Sterling Edwards had a dream; he wanted to build an exclusive luxury car, having already created a special in 1949. He built another in 1951, while in 1953 the America emerged. Initially the car featured Oldsmobile Rocket V8 power, but later cars had Lincoln or Cadillac power (although only six cars were built).

COUNTRY OF ORIGIN	USA
YEARS OF PRODUCTION	1953–55
DISPLACEMENT	5422CC (331CI)
CONFIGURATION	FRONT-MOUNTED V8
TRANSMISSION	4-SPEED AUTO, REAR-WHEEL DRIVE
POWER	154KW (210BHP)
TORQUE	N/A
TOP SPEED	185KM/H (115MPH)
0–96KM/H (0–60MPH)	10.0SEC

SALMSON 2300 SPORT

Probably the best car ever to come out of Salmson's Billancourt factory was also its last. An all-steel coachbuilt body made no sense, adding to production costs. Incredibly, there were no fewer than seven versions available before production settled down in 1954. But within two years the car was dead, along with the company.

COUNTRY OF ORIGIN	FRANCE
YEARS OF PRODUCTION	1953–56
DISPLACEMENT	2312CC (141CI)
CONFIGURATION	FRONT-MOUNTED 4-CYL
TRANSMISSION	4-SPEED MANUAL, REAR-WHEEL DRIVE
POWER	77KW (105BHP)
TORQUE	N/A
TOP SPEED	169KM/H (105MPH)
0–96KM/H (0–60MPH)	N/A

BRISTOL 405

The only four-door car ever offered by Bristol, the 405 was based on the 404, which meant it came with a 1971cc (120ci) six-cylinder engine. However, unlike the 404 there was the option of overdrive; automatic transmissions would be standardized from the introduction of the 406 in 1958.

COUNTRY OF ORIGIN	UK
YEARS OF PRODUCTION	1954–58
DISPLACEMENT	1971CC (120CI)
CONFIGURATION	FRONT-MOUNTED 6-CYL
TRANSMISSION	4-SPEED MANUAL, REAR-WHEEL DRIVE
POWER	77KW (105BHP)
TORQUE	167NM (123LB FT)
TOP SPEED	166KM/H (103MPH)
0–96KM/H (0–60MPH)	N/A

FACEL VEGA FV

The FV was the first car to come from the Facel Vega works, which had previously produced bodies for Panhard and Simca. Setting a template for future models from the company, there was a 4.5-litre De Soto V8 engine, in a tubular chassis with a live rear axle. Later there would be a 5.8-litre Chrysler V8 offered.

COUNTRY OF ORIGIN	FRANCE
YEARS OF PRODUCTION	1954–58
DISPLACEMENT	5801CC (354CI)
CONFIGURATION	FRONT-MOUNTED V8
TRANSMISSION	3-SPEED AUTO, REAR-WHEEL DRIVE
POWER	239KW (325BHP)
TORQUE	583NM (430LB FT)
TOP SPEED	209KM/H (130MPH)
0–96KM/H (0–60MPH)	8.5SEC

FACEL VEGA HK500

An updated version of the FVS, the HK500 featured redesigned bodywork along with a 265kW (360bhp), 6.3-litre Chrysler V8. Superbly built and always very costly, the HK500 didn't handle especially well but was a superb grand tourer once equipment such as power steering and disc brakes had been standardized.

COUNTRY OF ORIGIN	FRANCE
YEARS OF PRODUCTION	1958–61
DISPLACEMENT	6286CC (384CI)
CONFIGURATION	FRONT-MOUNTED V8
TRANSMISSION	4-SPEED MANUAL, REAR-WHEEL DRIVE
POWER	265KW (360BHP)
TORQUE	542NM (400LB FT)
TOP SPEED	209KM/H (130MPH)
0–96KM/H (0–60MPH)	8.5SEC

LINCOLN CONTINENTAL MK IV

This wasn't a car for those on a budget – everything about the Mk IV was huge, from the engine to the price tag. Using the biggest V8 available from Detroit, the Continental featured surprisingly restrained styling, while the mechanicals were hardly cutting edge – there was leaf-spring suspension all round.

COUNTRY OF ORIGIN	USA
YEARS OF PRODUCTION	1958–60
DISPLACEMENT	7046CC (430CI)
CONFIGURATION	FRONT-MOUNTED V8
TRANSMISSION	3-SPEED AUTO, REAR-WHEEL DRIVE
POWER	257KW (350BHP)
TORQUE	664NM (490LB FT)
TOP SPEED	190KM/H (118MPH)
0–96KM/H (0–60MPH)	10.4SEC

CADILLAC ELDORADO BIARRITZ

Some of the most outrageous cars ever built, the 1959 Cadillacs featured the largest fins ever fitted to any car, scaling a massive 1067mm (42in) in height. Offered as a coupé, saloon, convertible or limousine, the cars weighed more than 2.03 tonnes (2 tons) and were more than 6m (20ft) long.

COUNTRY OF ORIGIN	USA
YEARS OF PRODUCTION	1959
DISPLACEMENT	6384CC (390CI)
CONFIGURATION	FRONT-MOUNTED V8
TRANSMISSION	3-SPEED AUTO, REAR-WHEEL DRIVE
POWER	254KW (345BHP)
TORQUE	590NM (435LB FT)
TOP SPEED	185KM/H (115MPH)
0–96KM/H (0–60MPH)	12.0SEC

DESOTO ADVENTURER

Restyled for 1959, the DeSoto began to look more like the up-market Chrysler. There weren't many colour schemes to choose from, but the Adventurer came with the most standard features of any DeSoto model. Power was still provided by a V8, now tuned to 257kW (350bhp). Just 687 Adventurers were produced, all in 1959.

COUNTRY OF ORIGIN	USA
YEARS OF PRODUCTION	1959
DISPLACEMENT	6273CC (383CI)
CONFIGURATION	FRONT-MOUNTED V8
TRANSMISSION	3-SPEED AUTO, REAR-WHEEL DRIVE
POWER	257KW (350BHP)
TORQUE	N/A
TOP SPEED	238KM/H (148MPH)
0–96KM/H (0–60MPH)	9.5SEC

FERRARI 250GT SWB

If you could afford it (which few could), the grand tourer to have in the 1950s was Ferrari's 250GT SWB , or short wheelbase. With its lightweight all-alloy body and 3-litre V12 engine, the SWB offered sublime handling and fabulous agility, with a turn of speed that was quite astonishing for the time.

COUNTRY OF ORIGIN	ITALY
YEARS OF PRODUCTION	1959–1962
DISPLACEMENT	2953CC (180CI)
CONFIGURATION	FRONT-MOUNTED V12
TRANSMISSION	4-SPEED MANUAL, REAR-WHEEL DRIVE
POWER	206KW (280BHP)
TORQUE	275NM (203LB FT)
TOP SPEED	225KM/H (140MPH)
0–96KM/H (0–60MPH)	6.5SEC

MASERATI 5000GT

Forced to abandon motorsport in 1957, Maserati was left with a load of 450S racing engines that needed homes. They were fitted to the 3500GT, which was restyled and renamed the 5000GT. Just 32 were built, bodied by a variety of coachbuilders such as Frua, Bertone and Vignale.

COUNTRY OF ORIGIN	ITALY
YEARS OF PRODUCTION	1959–64
DISPLACEMENT	4941CC (302CI)
CONFIGURATION	FRONT-MOUNTED V8
TRANSMISSION	4-SPEED MANUAL, REAR-WHEEL DRIVE
POWER	250KW (340BHP)
TORQUE	442NM (326LB FT)
TOP SPEED	282KM/H (175MPH)
0–96KM/H (0–60MPH)	6.5SEC

ROLLS-ROYCE PHANTOM V/VI

One of the biggest cars ever made by Rolls-Royce, the Phantom V was superseded by the Phantom VI in 1968. Both cars were much the same, with huge rear cabins – these were cars for those who preferred to be chauffeured. The Phantom VI was the last Rolls-Royce to feature a separate chassis.

COUNTRY OF ORIGIN	UK
YEARS OF PRODUCTION	1959–92
DISPLACEMENT	6750CC (412CI)
CONFIGURATION	FRONT-MOUNTED V8
TRANSMISSION	4-SPEED AUTO, REAR-WHEEL DRIVE
POWER	N/A
TORQUE	N/A
TOP SPEED	169KM/H (105MPH)
0–96KM/H (0–60MPH)	13.8SEC

CITROEN DS DECAPOTABLE

Created by coachbuilder Henri Chapron and based on the chassis of the DS Safari (estate), the DS Decapotable (convertible) was produced for 11 years, during which time only 1365 examples were built.. The mechanicals were carried over unchanged, which meant a magic carpet ride and power assistance for everything was standard.

COUNTRY OF ORIGIN	FRANCE
YEARS OF PRODUCTION	1960–71
DISPLACEMENT	2175CC (133CI)
CONFIGURATION	FRONT -MOUNTED 4-CYL
TRANSMISSION	4-SPEED MANUAL, FRONT-WHEEL DRIVE
POWER	80KW (109BHP)
TORQUE	169NM (125LB FT)
TOP SPEED	187KM/H (116MPH)
0–96KM/H (0–60MPH)	11.2SEC

CHRYSLER GHIA L6.4

Starting out as a one-off design study inspired by the Ghia Dart, which had been designed by Virgil Exner, the L6.4 went into production for just two years. During that time, a mere 26 examples were built – because the cars were so fantastically expensive that virtually nobody could afford them.

COUNTRY OF ORIGIN	USA
YEARS OF PRODUCTION	1960–62
DISPLACEMENT	6279CC (383CI)
CONFIGURATION	FRONT-MOUNTED V8
TRANSMISSION	3-SPEED AUTO, REAR-WHEEL DRIVE
POWER	246kW (335BHP)
TORQUE	N/A
TOP SPEED	225KM/H (140MPH)
0–96KM/H (0–60MPH)	N/A

ASTON MARTIN DB4 GT ZAGATO

The ultimate derivative of the DB4 family came along in 1960, designed by Italian coachbuilder Zagato. Combining the short-wheelbase chassis of the DB4 GT with the ultra-powerful 231kW (314bhp) version of the 3.7-litre straight-six, this was Aston's fastest-ever six-cylinder car. The car was also very fast because of its ultra-lightweight alloy bodyshell.

COUNTRY OF ORIGIN	UK
YEARS OF PRODUCTION	1961–63
DISPLACEMENT	3670CC (224CI)
CONFIGURATION	FRONT-MOUNTED 6-CYL
TRANSMISSION	4-SPEED MANUAL, REAR-WHEEL DRIVE
POWER	231kW (314BHP)
TORQUE	377NM (278LB FT)
TOP SPEED	246KM/H (153MPH)
0–96KM/H (0–60MPH)	6.1SEC

FACEL VEGA II

Once again, Facel Vega put one of its models under the scalpel, updating the lines of the HK500 while also boosting the V8's power to 287kW (390bhp). With a greater glass area than before, the car was even better looking, while Dunlop disc brakes were now standard on all cars.

COUNTRY OF ORIGIN	FRANCE
YEARS OF PRODUCTION	1961–64
DISPLACEMENT	6286CC (384CI)
CONFIGURATION	FRONT-MOUNTED V8
TRANSMISSION	4-SPEED MANUAL, REAR-WHEEL DRIVE
POWER	287kW (390BHP)
TORQUE	N/A
TOP SPEED	240KM/H (149MPH)
0–96KM/H (0–60MPH)	8.3SEC

LINCOLN CONTINENTAL

When it came to weight or cost-saving measures, there weren't even any token gestures from Lincoln where the Continental was concerned. Everything about this car was super-sized, from the engine to the bodyshell. With power activation for everything from the windows to the seats, the Continental was incredibly advanced for its time.

COUNTRY OF ORIGIN	USA
YEARS OF PRODUCTION	1961–69
DISPLACEMENT	7046CC (430CI)
CONFIGURATION	FRONT-MOUNTED V8
TRANSMISSION	3-SPEED AUTO, REAR-WHEEL DRIVE
POWER	221kW (300BHP)
TORQUE	630NM (465LB FT)
TOP SPEED	188KM/H (117MPH)
0–96KM/H (0–60MPH)	11.2SEC

FERRARI 250GTO

Now one of the most valuable cars in the world, the 250GTO was a low-volume racing special. Indeed, its name is short for Gran Turismo Homologato, or homologation special for motorsport. Under the guidance of Giotto Bizzarini, the GTO was developed in a matter of weeks – and was still winning races in 1964.

COUNTRY OF ORIGIN	ITALY
YEARS OF PRODUCTION	1962
DISPLACEMENT	2953CC (180CI)
CONFIGURATION	FRONT-MOUNTED V12
TRANSMISSION	5-SPEED MANUAL, REAR-WHEEL DRIVE
POWER	265KW (360BHP)
TORQUE	N/A
TOP SPEED	274KM/H (170MPH)
0–96KM/H (0–60MPH)	6.0SEC

MASERATI SEBRING

Yet another Maserati that could trace its roots back to the 3500GT, the Sebring was designed by Vignale and built on the short-wheelbase chassis of the 3500GTi convertible. At first it was called the 3500GTi, but the Sebring tag was quickly adopted. It was also marketed as a 2+2, but in reality was just a two-seater.

COUNTRY OF ORIGIN	ITALY
YEARS OF PRODUCTION	1962–66
DISPLACEMENT	3485CC (213CI)
CONFIGURATION	FRONT-MOUNTED 6-CYL
TRANSMISSION	5-SPEED MANUAL, REAR-WHEEL DRIVE
POWER	173KW (235BHP)
TORQUE	315NM (232LB FT)
TOP SPEED	220KM/H (137MPH)
0–96KM/H (0–60MPH)	8.4SEC

SUNBEAM VENEZIA

Although the Sunbeam Venezia has an exotic name, it's nothing more than a dressed-up Hillman Super Minx. Charging near Jaguar money for a car with a 1592cc (97ci) four-cylinder engine meant sales would be hard to find. Such was the case with the Venezia, which was launched in September 1963 and which lasted less than two seasons.

COUNTRY OF ORIGIN	UK/ITALY
YEARS OF PRODUCTION	1963–65
DISPLACEMENT	1592CC (97CI)
CONFIGURATION	FRONT-MOUNTED 4-CYL
TRANSMISSION	4-SPEED MANUAL, REAR-WHEEL DRIVE
POWER	65KW (88BHP)
TORQUE	127NM (94LB FT)
TOP SPEED	161KM/H (100MPH)
0–96KM/H (0–60MPH)	N/A

MASERATI QUATTROPORTE

Supercars were meant to be utterly impractical, seating only two, but Maserati had other ideas when it launched its four-door, four-seater Quattroporte in 1963. The world's fastest four-door car was styled by Frua and built by Vignale. The chassis was new, but the engine was based on one of Maserati's racing units.

COUNTRY OF ORIGIN	ITALY
YEARS OF PRODUCTION	1963–70
DISPLACEMENT	4136CC (252CI)
CONFIGURATION	FRONT-MOUNTED V8
TRANSMISSION	5-SPEED MANUAL, REAR-WHEEL DRIVE
POWER	191KW (260BHP)
TORQUE	262NM (193LB FT)
TOP SPEED	209KM/H (130MPH)
0–96KM/H (0–60MPH)	8.3SEC

Ultimate Dream Car 20:
Bugatti Veyron

The Veyron was first shown to the world in spring 2001, at the Geneva Motor Show. Within months, at the Frankfurt Motor Show of the same year, there was a redesigned car. As it was unveiled, the word was that by 2003 the EB16.4 Veyron would be on sale. That became 2004, which in turn became 2005 – and then 2006.

At the heart of the Veyron was an 8-litre W16 engine, although the initial plan had been to use a 6.3-litre W18 unit – this pushed out 408kW (555bhp), which clearly wasn't anything like enough. The answer, at first, seemed to be to bore the unit out, but this produced some major reliability issues, which is why a more compact W16 powerplant was developed.

The W16 that was developed was essentially a pair of narrow-angle V8s mated together with a common crankshaft, with the whole unit being mounted longitudinally ahead of the rear axle on a separate aluminium subframe. With a displacement of 7993cc (488ci), the engine was amazingly compact at just 710mm (28in) in length and 767mm (30in) in width, but by the time a quartet of turbochargers were bolted in place, the engine bay started to get rather crowded. To help boost power even further, there were two water-to-air intercoolers, while direct fuel injection, variable valve timing and dry-sump lubrication were all on the menu as well.

Haldex four-wheel drive helped put the power down, while the gearbox was a seven-speed sequential manual unit. The underside of the car was as finely engineered as the top, with diffusers at the back to suck the car onto the ground at high speeds. As speeds rose, a spoiler at the rear automatically rose to increase downforce levels. Suspension was by double wishbones all round, with electronic damping as well as variable ride height. Brakes were ceramic discs while the tyres featured run-flat technology.

COUNTRY OF ORIGIN	GERMANY
YEARS OF PRODUCTION	2005–
DISPLACEMENT	7993CC (488CI)
CONFIGURATION	MID-MOUNTED W16, QUAD-TURBO
TRANSMISSION	7-SPEED SEQUENTIAL MANUAL
POWER	726KW (987BHP)
TORQUE	1250NM (922LB FT)
TOP SPEED	406KM/H (252MPH)
0–100KM/H (0–62MPH)	3.0SEC

MONTEVERDI 375

Peter Monteverdi set out to build a series of cars that were fast and luxurious, to take on established marques such as Ferrari and Rolls-Royce. His 375 was typical of the breed – a big car with Chrysler 7.2-litre V8 power. There were coupés and limousines available – but very few were made.

COUNTRY OF ORIGIN	SWITZERLAND
YEARS OF PRODUCTION	1967–77
DISPLACEMENT	7206CC (440CI)
CONFIGURATION	FRONT-MOUNTED V8
TRANSMISSION	5-SPEED MANUAL, REAR-WHEEL DRIVE
POWER	279kW (380BHP)
TORQUE	651NM (480LB FT)
TOP SPEED	245KM/H (152MPH)
0–96KM/H (0–60MPH)	6.3SEC

DAIMLER DS420

If you were a dignitary of any kind in the UK during the 1970s, it was a DS420 that swished you from one meeting to another. Based on a Jaguar 420G platform, it stayed in production until 1992. Most remaining examples have now passed to funeral directors and wedding car hire companies.

COUNTRY OF ORIGIN	UK
YEARS OF PRODUCTION	1968–92
DISPLACEMENT	4235CC (259CI)
CONFIGURATION	FRONT-MOUNTED 6-CYL
TRANSMISSION	3-SPEED AUTO, REAR-WHEEL DRIVE
POWER	180kW (245BHP)
TORQUE	382NM (282LB FT)
TOP SPEED	169KM/H (105MPH)
0–96KM/H (0–60MPH)	N/A

LINCOLN CONTINENTAL III

With a bonnet that was over 1.8m (6ft) long, the Continental II wasn't a car for shrinking violets, but while this car was absolutely enormous, it was available as a two-door coupé only. Inside there was wood and leather, while the 7.5-litre engine had a four-barrel carburettor to give plenty of performance.

COUNTRY OF ORIGIN	USA
YEARS OF PRODUCTION	1968–71
DISPLACEMENT	7538CC (460CI)
CONFIGURATION	FRONT-MOUNTED V8
TRANSMISSION	3-SPEED AUTO, REAR-WHEEL DRIVE
POWER	268kW (365BHP)
TORQUE	678NM (500LB FT)
TOP SPEED	198KM/H (123MPH)
0–96KM/H (0–60MPH)	10.3SEC

ROLLS-ROYCE CORNICHE

When Rolls-Royce launched its Silver Shadow in 1965, there were two-door coupé and convertible versions available. However, it wasn't until 1971 that the Corniche became a model in its own right, with all of the mechanicals being the same as those fitted to the Silver Shadow.

COUNTRY OF ORIGIN	UK
YEARS OF PRODUCTION	1971–94
DISPLACEMENT	6750CC (412CI)
CONFIGURATION	FRONT-MOUNTED V8
TRANSMISSION	3-SPEED AUTO, REAR-WHEEL DRIVE
POWER	N/A
TORQUE	N/A
TOP SPEED	193KM/H (120MPH)
0–96KM/H (0–60MPH)	9.6SEC

PANTHER J72

Robert Jankel set up Panther Cars, and his first project was the J72. Intended to look like a Jaguar SS100, the J72 featured Jaguar engines in straight-six or V12 guises, both of which gave dramatic acceleration. The ride was hard and the handling poor, yet around 300 examples were produced.

COUNTRY OF ORIGIN	UK
YEARS OF PRODUCTION	1972–81
DISPLACEMENT	4235CC (258CI)
CONFIGURATION	FRONT-MOUNTED 6-CYL
TRANSMISSION	4-SPEED MANUAL O/D, REAR-WHEEL DRIVE
POWER	140KW (190BHP)
TORQUE	271NM (200LB FT)
TOP SPEED	183KM/H (114MPH)
0–96KM/H (0–60MPH)	6.4SEC

LANCIA STRATOS

Although the Stratos was shown in concept form at the 1970 Turin Motor Show, it would be another three years before 500 examples were produced for rally homologation. Powered by Ferrari's V6 'Dino' engine, the Stratos proved to be a real force in rallying, as it won three world rally championships.

COUNTRY OF ORIGIN	ITALY
YEARS OF PRODUCTION	1973–75
DISPLACEMENT	2418CC (148CI)
CONFIGURATION	MID-MOUNTED V6
TRANSMISSION	5-SPEED MANUAL, REAR-WHEEL DRIVE
POWER	140KW (190BHP)
TORQUE	225NM (166LB FT)
TOP SPEED	225KM/H (140MPH)
0–96KM/H (0–60MPH)	6.8 SEC

MONICA GT

When French railway tycoon Jean Tastevin couldn't find the grand tourer he wanted, he set about building his own. With its spaceframe chassis and bodywork made of hand-milled steel, the GT featured all-round disc brakes and a modified Chrysler-sourced 5.6-litre V8. Panther bought the project after 35 cars had been made.

COUNTRY OF ORIGIN	FRANCE
YEARS OF PRODUCTION	1974–75
DISPLACEMENT	5560CC (339CI)
CONFIGURATION	FRONT-MOUNTED V8
TRANSMISSION	5-SPEED MANUAL, REAR-WHEEL DRIVE
POWER	224KW (305BHP)
TORQUE	447NM (330LB FT)
TOP SPEED	233KM/H (145MPH)
0–96KM/H (0–60MPH)	N/A

PANTHER DE VILLE

Based loosely on the Bugatti Royale, the De Ville was one of the most costly cars in the world when it went on sale in 1974. With power from a choice of Jaguar straight-six or V12 engines, buyers could opt for a saloon or an even more costly convertible. Just 60 were built.

COUNTRY OF ORIGIN	UK
YEARS OF PRODUCTION	1974–85
DISPLACEMENT	5343CC (326CI)
CONFIGURATION	FRONT-MOUNTED V12
TRANSMISSION	AUTOMATIC, REAR-WHEEL DRIVE
POWER	196KW (266BHP)
TORQUE	412NM (304LB FT)
TOP SPEED	220KM/H (137MPH)
0–96KM/H (0–60MPH)	N/A

ASTON MARTIN VANTAGE ZAGATO

At first there was a coupé only, but when that was
an instant sell-out it was clear an encore was needed.
Step forward, the convertible. With those awkward lines
typical of a Zagato, the V8 may have been challenging to
look at, but nobody could deny it was a success – thanks
to speculators out to make a quick buck.

COUNTRY OF ORIGIN	UK
YEARS OF PRODUCTION	1986–89
DISPLACEMENT	5340CC (326CI)
CONFIGURATION	FRONT-MOUNTED V8
TRANSMISSION	5-SPEED AUTO, REAR-WHEEL DRIVE
POWER	318KW (432BHP)
TORQUE	536NM (395LB FT)
TOP SPEED	295KM/H (183MPH)
0–96KM/H (0–60MPH)	4.8SEC

BMW M3

To homologate its M3 for Group A racing, BMW had to
build 5000 road-going versions. While the suspension was
essentially a carry-over from the standard car, the engine
was new, there was a limited-slip diff and the brakes were
uprated. From the moment it went on sale, the original M3
became an icon.

COUNTRY OF ORIGIN	GERMANY
YEARS OF PRODUCTION	1986–90
DISPLACEMENT	2302CC (140CI)
CONFIGURATION	FRONT-MOUNTED 4-CYL
TRANSMISSION	5-SPEED MANUAL, REAR-WHEEL DRIVE
POWER	162KW (220BHP)
TORQUE	244NM (180LB FT)
TOP SPEED	232KM/H (144MPH)
0–96KM/H (0–60MPH)	6.7SEC

BMW Z1

The Z1 came about by accident. It was originally just a test
mule for a new type of suspension for the 3-Series, but
BMW hit on the idea of creating a sharp-looking bodyshell
for the car. They showed it to the public and everybody
wanted one. It was fitted with a 2.5-litre straight-six, and
more than 8000 were built in total.

COUNTRY OF ORIGIN	GERMANY
YEARS OF PRODUCTION	1986–90
DISPLACEMENT	2494CC (152CI)
CONFIGURATION	FRONT-MOUNTED 6-CYL
TRANSMISSION	5-SPEED MANUAL, REAR-WHEEL DRIVE
POWER	125KW (170BHP)
TORQUE	222NM (164LB FT)
TOP SPEED	219KM/H (136MPH)
0–96KM/H (0–60MPH)	7.9SEC

PORSCHE 959

The world's fastest car when it was launched, the
959 was also the world's most technically advanced
car of any kind. With its sophisticated electronically
controlled four-wheel drive transmission, the 959
was phenomenally fast, thanks to a twin-turbo flat-six
in the rear and an ultra-light bodyshell.

COUNTRY OF ORIGIN	GERMANY
YEARS OF PRODUCTION	1987–88
DISPLACEMENT	2851CC (174CI)
CONFIGURATION	REAR-ENGINED FLAT-6
TRANSMISSION	6-SPEED MANUAL, FOUR-WHEEL DRIVE
POWER	331KW (450BHP)
TORQUE	502NM (370LB FT)
TOP SPEED	317KM/H (197MPH)
0–96KM/H (0–60MPH)	3.6 SEC

MERCEDES 190 EVO II

When Mercedes needed to homologate a car for Group A racing, it decided to focus on the Cosworth-engined 190E. In 1988 came the Evo I, but the following year there was the completely mad Evo II, with massively flared wheelarches and comedic rear wing – which was adjustable, just like the front spoiler.

COUNTRY OF ORIGIN	GERMANY
YEARS OF PRODUCTION	1989
DISPLACEMENT	2463CC (150CI)
CONFIGURATION	FRONT-MOUNTED 4-CYL
TRANSMISSION	5-SPEED MANUAL, REAR-WHEEL DRIVE
POWER	171KW (232BHP)
TORQUE	245NM (181LB FT)
TOP SPEED	251KM/H (156MPH)
0–96KM/H (0–60MPH)	6.8SEC

PORSCHE 911 SPEEDSTER

The Speedster name is one of the most evocative in motoring – Porsche was keen to capitalize on it with the 930 series 911. As it was coming to the end of its life, Porsche offered a Speedster derivative, with a cut-down windscreen and fairing behind the cockpit.

COUNTRY OF ORIGIN	GERMANY
YEARS OF PRODUCTION	1989
DISPLACEMENT	3164CC (193CI)
CONFIGURATION	REAR-MOUNTED FLAT-6
TRANSMISSION	5-SPEED MANUAL, REAR-WHEEL DRIVE
POWER	170KW (231BHP)
TORQUE	283NM (209LB FT)
TOP SPEED	245KM/H (152MPH)
0–96KM/H (0–60MPH)	6.3SEC

JANKEL TEMPEST

Based on the Corvette L98 chassis, the Tempest featured a kevlar bodyshell and a supercharged 6.7-litre V8 engine to offer ultimate power with minimum weight. With a choice of four-speed auto or six-speed manual gearboxes, this handbuilt car broke the 0–96km/h (0–60mph) speed record in 1992, at 3.89 seconds.

COUNTRY OF ORIGIN	UK
YEARS OF PRODUCTION	1990–92
DISPLACEMENT	6700CC (409CI)
CONFIGURATION	FRONT-MOUNTED V8
TRANSMISSION	4-SPEED AUTO, REAR-WHEEL DRIVE
POWER	393KW (535BHP)
TORQUE	824NM (608LB FT)
TOP SPEED	322KM/H (200MPH)
0–96KM/H (0–60MPH)	3.9SEC

BENTLEY CONTINENTAL R

For many years, Bentleys had been little more than badge-engineered stablemates of an equivalent Rolls-Royce, but the Continental R was a fresh approach for the company. Based on the same floorpan as the Turbo R (so closely related to the Silver Spirit), the Continental R featured Bentley's classic 6.75-litre V8.

COUNTRY OF ORIGIN	UK
YEARS OF PRODUCTION	1991–2002
DISPLACEMENT	6750CC (412CI)
CONFIGURATION	FRONT-MOUNTED V8
TRANSMISSION	AUTOMATIC, REAR-WHEEL DRIVE
POWER	283KW (385BHP)
TORQUE	750NM (553LB FT)
TOP SPEED	243KM/H (151MPH)
0–96KM/H (0–60MPH)	6.1SEC

JANKEL GOLD LABEL

When it came to ultra-expensive, hyper-exclusive cars, nobody could compete with the Jankel Gold Label. Using a Bentley 6.75-litre V8 and a hand-built alloy bodyshell, the Gold Label was fitted with every possible piece of luxury equipment while also being able to top 249km/h (155mph).

COUNTRY OF ORIGIN	UK
YEARS OF PRODUCTION	1991–95
DISPLACEMENT	6750CC (412CI)
CONFIGURATION	FRONT-MOUNTED V8
TRANSMISSION	4-SPEED AUTO, REAR-WHEEL DRIVE
POWER	N/A
TORQUE	N/A
TOP SPEED	249KM/H (155MPH)
0–96KM/H (0–60MPH)	4.9SEC

BENTLEY AZURE

Just about the costliest and largest car available when it first went on sale, Bentley's Azure is an occasion on wheels. Beautifully styled by Pininfarina, this Bentley featured adaptive dampers and self-levelling suspensions for the perfect ride/handling balance. With masses of space, comfort, refinement and performance, the Azure owner wanted for nothing.

COUNTRY OF ORIGIN	UK
YEARS OF PRODUCTION	1995–2003
DISPLACEMENT	6750CC (412CI)
CONFIGURATION	FRONT-MOUNTED V8
TRANSMISSION	AUTOMATIC, REAR-WHEEL DRIVE
POWER	283KW (385BHP)
TORQUE	750NM (553LB FT)
TOP SPEED	241KM/H (150MPH)
0–96KM/H (0–60MPH)	6.3SEC

PORSCHE 911 TURBO (993)

This would be the last of the air-cooled 911s; there could be no further development of the powerplant, so it was replaced by an all-new water-cooled unit. Using twin turbos for less lag, the car also had four-wheel drive, although in normal driving conditions just the rear wheels were powered.

COUNTRY OF ORIGIN	GERMANY
YEARS OF PRODUCTION	1995–98
DISPLACEMENT	3600CC (220CI)
CONFIGURATION	REAR-MOUNTED FLAT-6
TRANSMISSION	6-SPEED MANUAL, FOUR-WHEEL DRIVE
POWER	300KW (408BHP)
TORQUE	540NM (398LB FT)
TOP SPEED	290KM/H (180MPH)
0–96KM/H (0–60MPH)	4.5SEC

MITSUBISHI SHOGUN EVOLUTION

Mitsubishi was one of the key players in the Paris–Dakar Rally in the 1990s, so the company capitalized on its successes by offering a road-going version of the race car. With massively flared wheelarches, the car wasn't all show – there was also 206kW (280bhp) on tap from the 3.5-litre V6.

COUNTRY OF ORIGIN	JAPAN
YEARS OF PRODUCTION	1997–98
DISPLACEMENT	3497CC (213CI)
CONFIGURATION	FRONT-MOUNTED V6
TRANSMISSION	5-SPEED SEMI-AUTO, FOUR-WHEEL DRIVE
POWER	206KW (280BHP)
TORQUE	347NM (256LB FT)
TOP SPEED	201KM/H (125MPH)
0–96KM/H (0–60MPH)	8.0SEC

MERCEDES CLK GTR

With a mere 25 cars built – all sold before the car was even announced – the CLK GTR was extremely special. It was created to allow Mercedes to take part in endurance racing at Le Mans, yet the road cars would have to be as clean and safe as any regular production CLK.

COUNTRY OF ORIGIN	GERMANY
YEARS OF PRODUCTION	1998–99
DISPLACEMENT	6898CC (421CI)
CONFIGURATION	MID-MOUNTED V12
TRANSMISSION	6-SPEED MANUAL, REAR-WHEEL DRIVE
POWER	450KW (612BHP)
TORQUE	776NM (572LB FT)
TOP SPEED	320KM/H (199MPH)
0–100KM/H (0–62MPH)	3.8SEC

NISSAN R390

The R390 came about because Nissan was desperate to win the Le Mans 24 Hours. When the project started, just one Japanese car had ever won the race (a Mazda); to qualify, Nissan would have to build a single road car. The cars never won Le Mans, but at least one road-going R390 was produced.

COUNTRY OF ORIGIN	JAPAN
YEARS OF PRODUCTION	1998
DISPLACEMENT	3500CC (214CI)
CONFIGURATION	MID-MOUNTED V8, TWIN-TURBO
TRANSMISSION	6-SPEED SEQUENTIAL MANUAL, REAR-WHEEL DRIVE
POWER	396KW (539BHP)
TORQUE	637NM (470LB FT)
TOP SPEED	282KM/H (175MPH)
0–96KM/H (0–60MPH)	3.9SEC

PORSCHE 911 TURBO

Known as the 996, this was the first generation of 911 to be fitted with a water-cooled engine, although it was still of flat-six configuration. Derived from the 911 GT1 powerplant, this edition of the Turbo was available only with four-wheel drive; it needed it when the engine was optionally boosted to 331kW (450bhp).

COUNTRY OF ORIGIN	GERMANY
YEARS OF PRODUCTION	2000–05
DISPLACEMENT	3600CC (220CI)
CONFIGURATION	REAR-MOUNTED FLAT-6
TRANSMISSION	6-SPEED MANUAL, FOUR-WHEEL DRIVE
POWER	309KW (420BHP)
TORQUE	560NM (413LB FT)
TOP SPEED	306KM/H (190MPH)
0–96KM/H (0–60MPH)	4.2SEC

ROLLS-ROYCE CORNICHE

The original Corniche had bitten the dust in 1994, but Rolls-Royce decided to dust the badges down and offer a new Corniche before it focused solely on the Phantom limousine. Fitted with the classic 6.75-litre pushrod V8 in lightly turbocharged form, the car was typically silent and swift.

COUNTRY OF ORIGIN	UK
YEARS OF PRODUCTION	2000–02
DISPLACEMENT	6750CC (412CI)
CONFIGURATION	FRONT-MOUNTED V8
TRANSMISSION	3-SPEED AUTO, REAR-WHEEL DRIVE
POWER	239KW (325BHP)
TORQUE	610NM (450LB FT)
TOP SPEED	217KM/H (135MPH)
0–96KM/H (0–60MPH)	7.6SEC

MERCEDES S600 PULLMAN

The original Mercedes 600 had become a legend in its own lifetime, but the second edition arrived and left without anyone noticing. This third generation left little impression too, despite its huge price tag and stretched S-Class bodyshell. Those on a budget could select a V8 engine in place of the standard V12.

COUNTRY OF ORIGIN	GERMANY
YEARS OF PRODUCTION	2001–05
DISPLACEMENT	5786CC (353CI)
CONFIGURATION	FRONT-MOUNTED V12
TRANSMISSION	6-SPEED AUTO, REAR-WHEEL DRIVE
POWER	270KW (367BHP)
TORQUE	530NM (391LB FT)
TOP SPEED	249KM/H (155MPH)
0–96KM/H (0–60MPH)	7.1SEC

BMW M3 CSL

Never one to miss an opportunity, BMW spotted that an even more focused M3 might just sell, so it unveiled the CSL edition in 2003. Greater use of plastic composites allowed the car's weight to be reduced, while the straight-six was tuned further to coax an astonishing 261kW (355bhp) from it.

COUNTRY OF ORIGIN	GERMANY
YEARS OF PRODUCTION	2003
DISPLACEMENT	3246CC (198CI)
CONFIGURATION	FRONT-MOUNTED 6-CYL
TRANSMISSION	5-SPEED MANUAL, REAR-WHEEL DRIVE
POWER	261KW (355BHP)
TORQUE	370NM (273LB FT)
TOP SPEED	249KM/H (155MPH)
0–96KM/H (0–60MPH)	5.3SEC

ROLLS-ROYCE PHANTOM

Under BMW ownership, it was clear that Rolls-Royce could produce a worthy successor for the unloved Silver Seraph – but could it command the title of the best car in the world? That was debatable, but it certainly gave its rivals a run for their money, especially in long-wheelbase form.

COUNTRY OF ORIGIN	UK
YEARS OF PRODUCTION	2003–
DISPLACEMENT	6749CC (412CI)
CONFIGURATION	FRONT-MOUNTED V12
TRANSMISSION	6-SPEED AUTO, REAR-WHEEL DRIVE
POWER	333KW (453BHP)
TORQUE	720NM (531LB FT)
TOP SPEED	240KM/H (149MPH)
0–96KM/H (0–60MPH)	5.9SEC

FERRARI 575 SUPERAMERICA

The Superamerica was much more than just a drop-top 575. Not only was the engine more powerful than the standard car's, but there was also a paddle-shift transmission available. More importantly, though, the innovative revolving roof mechanism had never been seen on a production car before.

COUNTRY OF ORIGIN	ITALY
YEARS OF PRODUCTION	2005
DISPLACEMENT	5748CC (351CI)
CONFIGURATION	FRONT-MOUNTED V12
TRANSMISSION	6-SPEED SEMI-AUTO, REAR-WHEEL DRIVE
POWER	397KW (540BHP)
TORQUE	588NM (434LB FT)
TOP SPEED	320KM/H (199MPH)
0–96KM/H (0–60MPH)	4.6SEC

FISKER LATIGO

Many people reckoned BMW's 6-Series had rather challenging looks. One solution was to shop elsewhere, while another was to get it rebodied. That's where Fisker came in with the Latigo, which could be based on the 650Ci, or even the M6 for those who were addicted to power.

COUNTRY OF ORIGIN	GERMANY
YEARS OF PRODUCTION	2006–
DISPLACEMENT	4999CC (305CI)
CONFIGURATION	FRONT-MOUNTED V10
TRANSMISSION	6-SPEED SEMI-AUTO, REAR-WHEEL DRIVE
POWER	373KW (507BHP)
TORQUE	519NM (383LB FT)
TOP SPEED	249KM/H (155MPH)
0–96KM/H (0–60MPH)	4.6SEC

FISKER TRAMONTO

This was another rebodied German supercar – in this case, the Mercedes SL55 AMG. The car could be kept mechanically standard, or it was possible to specify a supercharger installation, in conjunction with Kleeman – this gave 448kW (610bhp) and 881kW (650lb ft) of torque to drop the 0–96km/h (0–62mph) time to just 3.6 seconds.

COUNTRY OF ORIGIN	GERMANY
YEARS OF PRODUCTION	2006–
DISPLACEMENT	5439CC (332CI)
CONFIGURATION	FRONT-MOUNTED V8
TRANSMISSION	6-SPEED SEMI-AUTO, REAR-WHEEL DRIVE
POWER	380KW (517BHP)
TORQUE	720NM (531LB FT)
TOP SPEED	249KM/H (155MPH)
0–96KM/H (0–60MPH)	4.5SEC

MAYBACH 62S

DaimlerChrysler showed its Maybach revival as a concept at the 1997 Tokyo Motor Show, and the car became one of the most eagerly awaited vehicles until it appeared in production form in 2002. In 2006, the 62S was introduced, with an even more powerful version of the V12 engine.

COUNTRY OF ORIGIN	GERMANY
YEARS OF PRODUCTION	2006
DISPLACEMENT	5980CC (365CI)
CONFIGURATION	FRONT-MOUNTED V12
TRANSMISSION	5-SPEED AUTO, REAR-WHEEL DRIVE
POWER	450KW (612BHP)
TORQUE	999NM (737LB FT)
TOP SPEED	249KM/H (155MPH)
0–96KM/H (0–60MPH)	5.2SEC

MERCEDES S65 AMG

When it comes to stupidly fast luxury cars, nobody does it quite like Mercedes. Following in the footsteps of the 300SEL 6.3 and 450SEL 6.9, the AMG-tuned S65 offered enough torque to pull a jumbo jet, and enough equipment and refinement to put its rivals to shame.

COUNTRY OF ORIGIN	GERMANY
YEARS OF PRODUCTION	2006–
DISPLACEMENT	5981CC (365CI)
CONFIGURATION	FRONT-MOUNTED V12
TRANSMISSION	6-SPEED SEMI-AUTO, REAR-WHEEL DRIVE
POWER	450KW (612BHP)
TORQUE	999NM (737LB FT)
TOP SPEED	249KM/H (155MPH)
0–96KM/H (0–60MPH)	4.4SEC

PORSCHE 911 TURBO

Once the 997 edition of the 911 had been unveiled, it was assumed there would be a turbocharged version – Porsche wasn't going to miss an opportunity. Sure enough, the 3.6-litre flat-six was fitted with a pair of turbochargers, with variable vane geometry to produce a whopping 353kW (480bhp).

COUNTRY OF ORIGIN	GERMANY
YEARS OF PRODUCTION	2006–
DISPLACEMENT	3600CC (220CI)
CONFIGURATION	REAR-MOUNTED FLAT-6
TRANSMISSION	6-SPEED MANUAL, FOUR-WHEEL DRIVE
POWER	353kW (480BHP)
TORQUE	620NM (457LB FT)
TOP SPEED	309KM/H (192MPH)
0–96KM/H (0–60MPH)	3.9SEC

SPYKER D12 PEKING TO PARIS

With SUVs all the rage in 2006, it was hard to find one that your neighbour wouldn't have. However, for a massive sum, Spyker would create one of its ultra-rare D12s for you. This was made almost entirely of alloy, and the attention to detail was phenomenal; even the exhaust pipes were engraved!

COUNTRY OF ORIGIN	HOLLAND
YEARS OF PRODUCTION	2006–
DISPLACEMENT	5998CC (388CI)
CONFIGURATION	FRONT-MOUNTED W12
TRANSMISSION	6-SPEED SEMI-AUTO, FOUR-WHEEL DRIVE
POWER	367kW (500BHP)
TORQUE	610NM (450LB FT)
TOP SPEED	300KM/H (187MPH)
0–96KM/H (0–60MPH)	N/A

BENTLEY BROOKLANDS

This model, based on the Azure, was the most powerful car made by Bentley. With even niche manufacturers ramping up production to generate much-needed cash, Bentley didn't fall into that trap with the Brooklands; production was limited to just 550 units during the lifetime of the car.

COUNTRY OF ORIGIN	UK
YEARS OF PRODUCTION	2007
DISPLACEMENT	6751CC (411CI)
CONFIGURATION	FRONT-MOUNTED V8
TRANSMISSION	6-SPEED SEMI-AUTO, REAR-WHEEL DRIVE
POWER	389kW (530BHP)
TORQUE	1049NM (774LB FT)
TOP SPEED	296KM/H (184MPH)
0–96KM/H (0–60MPH)	5.3SEC

ROLLS-ROYCE PHANTOM DROPHEAD

The Drophead Coupé was much more than an open-topped Phantom, as it featured a shorter bodyshell with a completely new set of panels. Based around an all-alloy spaceframe, the Drophead Coupé featured the same mechanicals as the Phantom, which meant there was plenty of power from the 6.75-litre V12.

COUNTRY OF ORIGIN	UK
YEARS OF PRODUCTION	2007–
DISPLACEMENT	6749CC (411CI)
CONFIGURATION	FRONT-MOUNTED V12
TRANSMISSION	6-SPEED AUTO, REAR-WHEEL DRIVE
POWER	333kW (453BHP)
TORQUE	719NM (531LB FT)
TOP SPEED	239KM/H (149MPH)
0–96KM/H (0–60MPH)	5.9SEC

Index